THE BIG BOOK OF MOUNTAINEERING

Edited by
Bruno Moravetz

With a Foreword by
Reinhold Messner

Translated by
Diana Stone Peters
and Frederick G. Peters;

Article on "Matterhorn,
Eiger, Grandes Jorasses,"
translated by
Rita and Robert Kimber.

Woodbury, New York
Barron's
London

First U.S. Edition 1980, Barron's Educational Series, Inc.
solely with respect to the English language edition

©Copyright 1978, Hoffmann und Campe Verlag with respect to the German language edition

All inquiries should be addressed to:
Barron's Educational Series, Inc.
113 Crossways Park Drive
Woodbury, New York 11797

Library of Congress Catalog Card No. 80-9

International Standard Book No. 0-8120-5332-X

Library of Congress Cataloging in Publication Data
Main entry under title:

The Big book of mountaineering.

   Translation of Das Grosse Buch der Berge.
   Includes index.
   1. Mountaineering—Addresses, essays, lectures.
I. Moravetz, Bruno, 1921-
GV200.G7613   796.5′22   80-9
ISBN 0-8120-5332-X

PRINTED IN HONG KONG

THE
BIG BOOK
OF
MOUNTAINEERING

Contents

Reinhold Messner

Letter from Nanga Parbat

Diamir Valley
July 10. 1978

Dear Ilona,

I have been under way for the past several days and am now once again in the Diamir Valley below Nanga Parbat. I am happy to be here and away from Europe, where my life is so hectic. Gradually, I hope to be able to find myself again. The need to break loose, to reach these valleys, and to climb these mountains is getting stronger every year. I feel myself connected in some way to Europe, and yet I do not know what will happen if my life there continues to be as spasmodic and harried as it is at present. I remember well our trip to Dhaulagiri last year. It took me a long time to achieve the inner peace that in the past characterized the end of all my great climbs. This time I am glad to say that I have already found peace before starting the ascent. I can now truly comprehend why many religions had their origin in the mountains. Here in the peace and solitude of the mountain peaks, here where meditation leads me into a state of inner balance as I climb, I too am overcome with feelings of self-understanding, of belonging to the world, and of being alone with the cosmos.

There are still completely unspoiled valleys in the world. This is the third time I have been in the Diamir Valley and nothing has changed. If mountain climbers can refrain from interfering with the ecology of these valleys, above all by scrupulously restraining themselves from leaving behind on the mountaintops all the tokens of our so-called civilization, these mountains will remain interesting, challenging, and mysteriously pure for centuries to come. The Schlagintweit brothers were the first to enter this territory. They were followed by Sven Hedin and Humboldt. What they saw, I see today. Nothing has changed. Naturally, I no longer come here to explore or conquer as they did. The great question mark for me is not the mountain or the unknown valley—it is myself. I take comfort in knowing that these wild, untouched regions of the earth can provide me with access to myself. I feel I am also responsible for the continued existence of

6

mountaineering. But my contributions to the sport, like those of others, also depend in part on my bringing down from the mountain whatever I have carried up.

I was horrified when I reached the south saddle of Mount Everest. During my first ascent a fearful storm was howling, which had swept the snow off all the rocks. The summit—I must admit it frankly though it bring disgrace upon our whole profession—is the world's highest garbage heap. Masses of empty oxygen tanks, tent poles, scraps of tent material, even cookers and gas cylinders—everything lay strewn about at this imposing height of nearly 8,000 meters (26,246 feet). The second time I reached the summit, two meters of snow lay on the ground. Everything was clean—at least on the surface. In my opinion, not only mountain climbers and Alpine Clubs should feel a duty in regard to ecological matters; the media too should become involved. I have always spoken out against the use of technological aids in climbing. While my initial views were based solely on concepts of sportsmanship and ethics, they are now confirmed by ecological necessity. Furthermore, I am convinced that mountain climbing can only preserve its fascination if nothing remains behind on the mountain: no hooks, no sleeping bags, no plastic bags, and no shattered glass. The wild places of the earth must remain unspoiled, be they deserts, mountain plateaus, perpendicular walls of rock and ice, walls in the Alps, in South America, or in the Himalayas.

When I recall your book, many images come vividly to mind, but especially the picture of the summit of Nanga Parbat as it cast its shadow across the entire landscape. How I now delight in climbing when the summit of Nanga Parbat casts its shadow over me. As I climb, I often have your picture in my mind and hope that I too will experience this image from the top, thereby realizing my last and ultimate Alpine dream: climbing to the summit of Nanga Parbat alone, tracing a route up the most difficult face of this 8,000-meter peak—one of the highest mountains in the world—in solitude, thus reaching for the absolute limits of Alpinism, an ideal that for me represents the ultimate dialogue between man and mountain.

By the way, Paul Preuss was the first person, the first mountaineer, not only to have expressed this fundamental concept but also to have experienced its implications to the limit. His first ascent of the Guglia di Brenta, which he made in 1911 without hooks, rope, or companions, simply climbing—or should I say dancing?—up the east face alone and then returning, is the model that inspires me as I make my solo climb of Nanga Parbat. The only difference between his climb and my present enterprise, which will probably be my last great Alpine feat, is that the Guglia is 5,000 meters (16,404 feet) lower, whereas both the dimensions and the risks involved on Nanga Parbat are significantly greater.

Paul Preuss is one of the few models I have had in my climbing career, and I am glad that you wrote about him in your book, as well as about Walter Bonatti. Paul Preuss not only approached the mountain with integrity, he also attempted to engage with mountains and mountaineering in an intellectual and spiritual level. I had the feeling as I paged through your book that you too are concerned with a broad spectrum of opinion regarding the meaning of mountaineering, that you too want to make certain that mountaineers will not be regarded as mere monkeys on a cliff, and that mountaineering, far from being a competitive sport, will come to be recognized for what it should be—one of man's truly great opportunities for self-discovery.

A few days ago I learned that Chris Bonington and his team experienced a disaster on K2. This affected me a great deal. I regard Chris Bonington as the most capable expedition leader of recent decades and was extremely depressed when I heard that Nick Estcourt perished on the climb. Doug Scott escaped once again—as on the Ogre and elsewhere. Scott is probably the most remarkable climber in the English-speaking world.

You know, Mora, that I have obtained an official permit to climb K2 next year, but I don't know whether I will do it. For the present I am completely preoccupied with the idea of climbing Nanga Parbat alone and have pushed everything else aside—or, shall we say, postponed thinking about other things until some future date. Only because I have no strong ties to any other human being at the moment, am I able to consider advancing into the ultimate solitude. I do not yet know whether I will be able to bear such isolation, such solitude at the very borders of existence, such loneliness in the zone of death at the top of the world.

By now I have often experienced the rarefied air of an 8,000-meter peak and have certainly gone through enough at such altitudes. And yet I still do not really know why I must climb to these heights, or even who I am. It's not that I have come to Nanga Parbat now in search of a final answer. Nor did I really begin my career as a climber in order to plumb the meaning of my existence. I began because my father took me with him when he climbed and because these early childhood experiences filled me with enthusiasm. But why do I go on? I still do not know.

Your book contains a wealth of opinions, pictures, and

impressions. Do you feel you have succeeded in offering the world at last a complete mosaic of mountain climbing? I hope so. In any event, you will have achieved a great deal if every climber who reads the book comes away with greater knowledge than he had before, having experienced to the full your words, the pictures, the impressions, the experiences recorded. I know it is impossible to translate our feelings and moods into words. We can only intimate, suggest—we can do no more. To experience the mountains fully, to make them part of oneself, to understand this phenomenon of nature—naively, intuitively—one must climb them oneself. One must experience the Sherpas of Nepal personally; one must get to know the porters who drag one's loads to the top, as I am now getting to know my porters in the Diamir. To really grasp the dimensions of an 8,000-meter peak, one must fight the resistance of one's own body as it struggles for survival in the oxygen-thin air. One need only climb through the gorges for a few days to realize how colossal the forces must have been to have pushed giants like these up out of the earth.

If I recall correctly, a chapter of your book is entitled "Mountain Climbers Are Children of Their Times." you are so right! One can only understand a man like Eugen Guido Lammer in the perspective of his times. The same holds true for Edward Whymper and for Chris Bonington. I, myself, an intellectual manqué, tired of the bureaucracy and industrialization of Europe, find in climbing a small way to express myself, to realize my nature. I am neither farmer, nor collector, nor hunter; nor am I a researcher or adventurer in the classical sense. I am merely a human being who has chosen to search for his human dimensions in the mountains. I do not believe that the act of climbing or even the mountains themselves provide us with a key to the meaning of existence. And yet, standing on the highest peaks, how often was I not plunged into the thick of life, hurled into the center of living without time to ask "why" or "what does life mean?"

You should be here now, Mora. The access route to the mountain is nowhere near as difficult as the ascent to the foot of Dhaulagiri, and I know how long you have been dreaming of Nanga Parbat. But this time I have resolved to climb by myself. Of course, a doctor and an official escort will accompany me to the base camp, as is required by the Mountaineering Rules of Pakistan. But I will climb Nanga Parbat alone, utterly alone—perhaps this time to answer one of the most fundamental questions of human existence: how can man cope with isolation? When I return in four or five weeks, I hope to be able to read your book thoroughly. I am greatly looking forward to it, even though I have already seen the pictures and am familiar with so much of its content. My eagerness to read your book is matched only by my impatience for tomorrow, which will bring me one step closer to the mountain, one step higher in the familiar, yet unfamiliar, Diamir Valley. I am not looking forward to returning to Europe. For now, my heart and soul are here. Nor do I want to see Nanga Parbat as one among many others on my list of climbs. I want to experience it one last time—deeply, fully. But I am looking forward to seeing you again, my dear Yeti.

Reinhold Messner

1

Conqueror of the highest mountains on every continent: Reinhold Messner from Villnöss in the South Tyrol. He has stood on the summits of Mount Everest in Asia, the Carstensz Top (Sukarno Peak) in New Guinea, the Aconcagua in South America, Mount McKinley in Alaska, Mont Blanc in Europe, and the Kibo in the Kilimanjaro massif, highest elevation in Africa. Under a broiling equatorial sun, Messner climbs a steep ice flank to the top.

2

Grossglockner: highest peak in Austria. Ten thousand people a year drive up the Glockner-strasse to the Franz-Joseph-Heights, continuing by foot along the Pasterzen Kees, a glacial stream. The north face of the Grossglockner lies straight ahead.

The Prince-Bishop, Count Salm-Reifferschied of Klagen-furt, authorized the first ascent. Although a hut was built, the first assault in August 1799 ended on the Kleinglockner. A year later the proud mountain was again attacked, this time by a "large and hand-picked group" invited by the Prince-Bishop himself. The team consisted of clergymen, scientists, and carpenters who provided large wooden beams for a summit cross; mountain peasants acted as porters. His Eminence the Pastor Horasch from Döllach, found it too taxing to inch up the mountain. He left the safety of the rope, traversed the mountain flank, and on July 28, 1800, was the first man to stand on the summit of the Gross-glockner.

The historic climb of 1800 proceeded up the east flank (to the left of the summit). More difficult tours follow routes up the north face, the Glockner Wall, or through ice crevasses. The Pallavicini Crevasse, for example, offers a steep route leading directly to the summit. One of the most beautiful routes crosses the northwest ridge (from right to left) and includes the Hoffmannspitze, the Glocknerwand-Krone, and the Teufelshorn.

3a

3b

3a/3b
The Matterhorn: one of the most famous and beautiful mountains in the world. This 360° panoramic view
was photographed in September by means of a camera fixed to a helicopter which hovered above the summit
at an altitude of 4,000 meters (13,123 feet) above sea level.

Machapuchare (Machapucharé), one of the many romantic and beautiful mountains in the world which have been compared with the Matterhorn. Rising to the north of Pokhara, its twin-peaked summit, the so-called "fish tail," falls short of reaching 7,000 meters (22,965 feet) by a bare 12 feet. Rich in legend, gods and demons are said to dwell here.

In 1957, a team of British climbers made the first assault. After surmounting enormous difficulties, David Cox and Wilfrid Noyce finally had to give up on a steep icy ridge within fifty meters (164 feet) of the summit. Machapuchare—one of the most photographed mountains in the world—is still unconquered. With the failure of the British expedition, the mountain truly came to be regarded as the inviolate home of the gods.

5

6

Mount Everest: first discovered in 1852 by surveyors. Called Chomo Longma (Chomolungma) even in ancient Tibet, it is called Sagarmatha in modern Nepal. The world's highest mountain owes the name by which it is generally known to Sir George Everest, who was the head of the Surveyor-General's Office in India from 1823 to 1843. Ironically, Sir George never saw the mountain named for him. Its official height was established in 1955: 8,848 meters (29,028 feet).

British mountaineers were already preparing to climb Mount Everest at the turn of the century. At that time, however, the borders of Tibet and Nepal were closed to the West and the initial assaults could not begin until 1921. On May 29th, 1953 the New Zealander Edmund Hillary and the Sherpa Tenzing reached the top, the first human beings to stand upon the highest point on earth.

6

Lake Titicaca: the world's highest navigable lake. The boundary line separating Bolivia from Peru runs right through this body of water situated on the Altiplanicie Plateau (Altiplano), 3,800 meters (12,467 feet) above sea level. Approximately 190 kilometers (118 miles) long and 50 kilometers (31 miles) wide, the lake is surrounded by such giants of the Andes as Ancohuma, Illampu, and Huayna Potosi, all over 6,000 meters (19,700 feet) high. La Paz, the capital of Bolivia, is not far away.

The Aymara who once cultivated the shores of Lake Titicaca used to worship this body of water as the cradle of their god Viracocha. The lake is now a great tourist attraction. In 1872 donkeys carried the first steamship in small pieces up the mountain trails. Temple ruins on Sun Island still guard secrets from the Inca civilization. Indians descended from tribes once ruled by Incas even today sail across the water to this long island on the lake where they offer sacrifices to the Sun God. In accordance with ancient ritual, sacrifices (which can include a llama) are made as the last rays of the setting sun fall.

9

Citlaltepetl: Mexico's highest snow-covered volcano. Lying to the east of Ixtaccihuatl and Popocatepetl near the city of Orizaba, this peak is usually called Pico de Orizaba (9).

An ancient legend recounted by the first inhabitants of that part of Central America which today is Mexico tells of how a youth was once forbidden to marry the princess he adored. This youth, the snow-covered volcano Popocatepetl, still gazes toward the beloved maiden, the volcano Ixtaccihuatl, not far away. Both lie in eternal sleep. Popocatepetl rises up just beyond the capital city of Mexico, once the center of the Aztec civilization. Gases still escape from its crater. Many tourists climb its lava slopes and gentle snow fields, following the same routes taken by Spanish mercenaries who came with Hernando Cortez to conquer the Aztec realm for the Spanish crown.

Fujiyama: Japan's sacred mountain. Also called Fuji-San, Fuji, or Mount Fuji, this extinct volcano, 3,776 meters (12,388 feet) high, is regarded as the dwelling place of the goddess of flowering trees. More than 300,000 people a year make summer pilgrimages to the top, passing holy Shinto shrines as they ascend. The tenth shrine is located at the top in a desolate landscape strewn with the debris of modern civilization. A radar and weather station lies not far beyond. Wretched barrack-like hotels now stand where once Zen Buddhist monks were housed.

1

Machu Picchu: Inca ruins in south-central Peru. The ruins of this Inca border settlement, built around 1450 high above the Urubamba River, were not discovered until 1911. The well-preserved exterior walls show a clear separation between the temples and the people's living quarters. Machu Picchu may also have been one of the military colonies established by the great Inca conqueror Pachacutec Inca Yupanqui (1438–71) for use by those who were conscripted into *mita* service.

12

Sinai: a mountain desert between continents and peoples. The mountains of the Sinai have been fought over from time immemorial. One of these desolate mountain peaks was ascended by Moses, though the exact peak cannot be identified. Here in the Sinai Moses is said to have received the ten commandments. Exhausted, hungry, weakened by the heat of the sun, plagued by the cold of the mountain night, he perceived the word of God as spirit, idea, and will. His body was now nothing more than a vessel for thought and reflection.

Martin Hörrmann

Laws Come from the Mountains

According to tradition, legend, and myth, gods have always inhabited barren mountainous landscapes. It may well be that the remoteness of the mountains, as well as the lofty heights of their summits, caused men to regard the peaks as the thrones of gods. The Sinai Peninsula is a wild and rugged mountain terrain. In the north, massifs reach heights of over 1,600 meters (5,249 feet) and, in the south, they soar up yet a 1,000 meters (3,281 feet) higher. Was it Gabal Al Igma or some other mountain peak that the Israelites passed on their journey to the Promised Land? Or did the journey take them further south to the mountainous landscape known today as Gabal Katrina, the Catherine Mountain, at whose foot a convent has been standing since the sixth century? Where was the burning bush located? Where did Moses receive the Law? Science cannot locate these places.

In almost all cultures, there are sacred mountains where gods dwell in inaccessible heights far above mankind. The ancient Greeks had their Mount Olympus, which tourists can still visit today. The Indians have Meru, the Persians the Elburz Mountains, and the Romans their Capitoline Hill.

The massiveness of mountains, their literally towering appearance, the forces of nature, the clouds, storms, rains, snows, rock falls, glaciers, avalanches—all these phenomena whose immeasurable power frightened man in ancient times also caused him to designate the peaks as the dwelling place of gods. Men knew and still know that gods who rule the heights have no form. Nevertheless, men honor them. In the Christian world, men place crosses upon mountaintops. In the Sinai, believers make pilgrimages to the Catherine Mountain and hold religious services there. This or that person climbs boldly up its steep rocky walls, seeking direct contact with God. Having reached the summit after an arduous climb, many a mountain climber, however enlightened he may consider himself to be, has been overcome by the profound feeling that life and being merely run their course according to predetermined laws.

Mount Sinai, also called *Horeb*, has played a significant role in our culture for the past three thousand years. Surprisingly, the mountain has not entered our cultural imagination merely as a mountain. And yet, Mount Sinai represents a wonderful combination of just those archaic and primeval powers associated with mountains in general, which have always shaped men's lives and continue to do so today.

The archetypal image of "the mountain," which has played so formative a role in the collective psyche of man, finds its most impressive physical correlative in Mount Sinai, for this mountain, which is associated with the Ten Commandments, has ultimately shaped the lives of Western man. All of us know what the Ten Commandments mean—even those of us who reject them. Whether or not we like it, our cultural, religious, and ethical heritage has been molded by this archetype, by Mount Sinai. The laws of life have been brought down from the mountain, and we still abide by them today.

The geographical location of this mountain, which possesses such profound archetypal significance for man, cannot be firmly established. Tradition has assigned the mountain to a place on the southern part of the peninsula in the Near East that is also named Sinai. Considerable skill is needed to reach its summit. If this was the mountain Moses climbed, he was certainly no mean climber! However, it is uncertain whether the mountain designated as Sinai on our modern maps is really the one that Moses climbed. But whether or not Moses climbed this Mount Sinai or some other peak is not important. The mountain's true significance lies in its archetypal meaning for Western man today.

Let us pause to recall the Biblical story of the Exodus, which is to some degree imbued with political significance. An ethnic minority, a peripheral group in Egyptian society, kept in subservience to and imprisoned by a dictatorial pharaoh—this little group of oppressed Israelites sets out upon its way under the leadership of Moses. The journey is to lead to freedom, to an independent life, to the formation of a self-determined state. A mountain appears. It will play a determinative role in this people's quest for emancipation. The little group believes it needs rules to regulate its social intercourse. This insight dawns—so the story goes—in the presence of a mountain. These rules—so the leader says—are to be discovered on a mountaintop. He believes that, if he can find his way to the summit, the rules will be revealed and the climber, the seeker, will know them!

Moses sets out upon his quest. But he doesn't take everyone along. At most, only one other person accompanies him. A variation of the story tells us that Moses took Aaron with him on his first ascent of Mount Sinai. This variation does not grip the imagination. What rivets us is the image of the lonely climber, Moses, who strictly forbids his people to follow him. One need only think of today's mass mountain climbs to realize how wise Moses' orders were. And so, Moses climbs by himself to the summit spur. Up to this point, the climb was apparently not too difficult. But the summons he perceived, intuitively recognized, and followed commands him to continue on to the very top. For it is only there that he can find what he had hoped he would receive from the mountain, what he had waited so long for.

Moses continues on. He makes his discoveries, receives his information, takes it down on two stone tablets. Both he and the tablets are safe and sound. An archetype. It is a primal image, but not only an image. It is a real, actual experience. And who among us, who has chosen to experience a mountain, has not returned to earth to transform the experience into a resolution, a rule, a precept!

What really happened here? This is what happened: According to the traditional religious history of the ancient people of Israel, the Ten Commandments came into being on a mountaintop and were given into the keeping of a man named Moses. These are the same commandments that we still learn and that are supposed to govern our behavior. They exist as norms and regulations even for those who do not practice them too literally in their daily lives. This episode is recounted in an ancient language of images: on a mountain, laws are discovered that will regulate human social intercourse and determine the ethics of our entire cultural horizon. There are treasures that must be protected if life is to continue in a meaningful way. The mountain teaches this, but only he who can face the mountain, by being true to himself, can hear the lesson. Thus, the mountain comes to be the source of knowledge, of wisdom—assuming, of course, that one has climbed the right mountain. To express this in the language of religious images, one has to take possession of the mountain with the right god. The mountain itself does not yield truths. It is the god enthroned upon its heights who reveals everything to man. This fundamental idea was presented long ago in a language of images: a primeval, archetypal language whose images were capable of manifold interpretation. One thing is clear, however, mountains themselves are not gods. Religious veneration of mountains is false. To be sure, mountains can facilitate experiences that are priceless and cannot be compressed into material form, nor can they be fathomed by reason alone. This is why such experiences take on binding religious significance. Of course, they need not occur on mountains, but they can and often do. The archetypal mountain can communicate with man at any time and in any age. But it can also remain silent.

The laws that were once brought down from the mountain were regulations to protect things necessary to life: they governed truth, one's good reputation, love, the marriage bond, ritual, play, goods and chattels—life itself. They do not restrict life. On the contrary, they promote and expand it. The mountain teaches about life. On the mountain one learns of life itself because it is there that life is most endangered, that life can be dangerous. And, as noted before, the mountain's teaching is revealed in a language of images. Archetypal. Let us again pause, this time to meditate upon a fundamental hypothesis: It is perhaps not given to man to speak of that which has shaped him most profoundly except in the form of images.

The mountain becomes an image. It becomes an archetype that can influence us at our profoundest level of being. It is precisely because the experiences we undergo on mountains are so concentrated that they can retain significance when applied to life in general. Regarding the Sinai story as a prototypical experience, I believe a general rule can be formulated: Laws that make life possible for man are experienced on the mountain. Revelation is made manifest, palpably real.

The picture is clear: mankind receives its rules, regulations, and laws from the mountains. Many people acknowledge how right it seems that they have discovered their own rules of conduct or have had their modes of life confirmed upon a mountain. Man's experiences on the mountain, his experiences of the mountain itself, point beyond anything he can verify through the powers of logic and reason alone.

Viewed from the perspective of the religious impulse, one can say that mountains exercise a transcendent power. What does this mean? It means first of all that mountains make one feel very small. One is reduced in size, no matter how tall one may be. It is for this reason that so many people instinctively feel that "the human animal," however "great" he feels himself to be, can profit from climbing a mountain, from becoming a little worm again—in solitude, unwitnessed, without television.

Let me go further! When I said previously that the mountain possesses archetypal significance, I meant that the image of a mountain can be, in many cases, often is, endowed with unique, undeniable meaning, meaning for which there is no substitute. As a human being, I have felt the mountain impress its image on the very origins of my existence. It has shaped my life. It was the original temple—the temple that appeared on the First Day of the Creation.

The ancients knew the word *model*. A model is a fundamental form that can be used to impress patterns on fabrics and shapes on pastry dough. A model is pressed down on amorphous material. It gives shape. The mountain is a model that impresses its shape on man when he looks to it for experience.

What kind of experience? One kind has already been mentioned—the experience of feeling how small, how pitiful, how impotent man is, how dependent on others for better or for worse. "The wind blows over the mountain," only the wind. Man is left behind to face his inevitable death. In the mountains, one necessarily experiences the transient nature of life, the feeling of exposure, of total danger, and—for this very reason—one hangs on to life. "Be careful!" is the motto, and it is a good one, for something can always go wrong, no matter how cautious one has been. One also feels happiness, joy, gaiety, the delight in knowing that one has made it, one has succeeded. How stupid it is to become frivolous as soon as one is safe. But how equally stupid it is to cling to safety and remain below just because a climb happens not to go well. It is folly to tell others what to think and how to feel. Yet this, too, is part of the experience of the mountains. When people become serious, they talk differently to each other. The more serious they become, the more polite they are. As if one's personal experiences could consolidate and also guide future generations like the Ten Commandments that Moses brought back!

It is striking that mountains have played a central role in the development of many religions. In earlier times, almost all advanced cultures regarded a mountain as a particularly sacred place. In each case, it was regarded as the dwelling place of gods, godheads, a group of deities, or a single god, depending on the religion involved. The fact that religions vary in this respect is not important. The significant fact is that peoples of all ages have undergone experiences on the mountain that pointed beyond individual human existence. As a result of such experience or, at least, while it is happening, man ceases to be imprisoned within his body.

He transcends himself. Moreover, returning to the world, he is better equipped to give order and value to the social framework within which he lives. The mountain is fascinating, almost seductive—even as a religious model. One can get lost upon a mountain, take the wrong paths, plunge into the depths. But the mountain can also lead to a heightening, can help man to advance through life.

In countless traditions, stories exist that tell of a holy mountain at the center of the world, whose summit touches heaven and whose roots reach down to the underworld. In many variations, which have appeared over thousands of years, the sacred mountain is regarded as the axis of the world—axis mundi—for it is said to connect heaven, earth, and the underworld. The notion of a mountain as the axis of the world connecting everything in the cosmos, joining together all things conceivable to the mind of man, is a primal religious idea that is not limited to the so-called advanced religions, but is also found among primitive peoples. (In this regard, of course, the question remains open as to who is primitive and who is not!) One encounters this idea in prehistoric monuments. Mountain symbols are also particularly evident in stories concerning the origin of the world. The most striking examples come from India and China. The symbol of a holy mountain as the world's axis spread from these ancient centers of culture into central Asia and Siberia, as well as to Indonesia and Oceania. The name of the mountain Meru, which appears in the Indian cosmology, also exists in the religions of the Mongolian and Siberian peoples, and its mythical image serves as a model for the Barabudur Temple of Java. Ancient Mesopotamian beliefs tell us that all lands group themselves around a mountain called "the mountain of all lands" and that this mountain connects heaven and earth. A "sacred" mountain on earth is basically a visible manifestation of an archetypal image and is, therefore, also understood as existing at the center of the world. Peoples at various times have also attempted to give tangible form to the archetype of the cosmic mountain in their religious structures. The towers of the famous temples of Babylon are typical examples. In Judaism, too, one can find traces of the ancient notion that a sacred mountain exists at the center of the world. Here, the generalized concept of a holy mountain connecting heaven and earth has found specific formulation in the so-called "sacred cliffs of Jerusalem." In the Christian religion, the idea has found expression in a single peak, Golgotha, the place where Jesus Christ was crucified. It is clear that the significance mountains have always possessed for man cannot be comprehended by the results of scientific investigation.

It may be that science cannot grasp the significance mountains have for man. Nevertheless, that we can speak at all of a scientific approach to mountains is the result of a process of intellectual enlightenment that has influenced all of us to a greater or lesser degree. During the Age of Enlightenment, man unlearned his superstitious fear of gods, dark powers, and other religious nonsense. Thus, man no longer had to avoid the mountains out of fear that the gods who dwelled there would destroy him if he came too close. In a sense, to climb a mountain meant to be enlightened. The more enlightened one was, the more one climbed; the more one climbed, the more enlightened one was.

Why do mountains remain so fascinating? We have asked this question often enough. We have sought an answer in ourselves, from our friends. We have combed the sources, seeking answers, testing answers. We have published our opinions, criticized them—and have never been content to let the matter rest. Thank God!

Even now no satisfying answer is possible. The single essential truth is this: When I reflect upon those experiences that have made me happy, as well as upon those that have made me feel inexpressibly and pitifully small, I realize that each and every one of them had its source in the mountains. And for me, this is all that matters.   □

Hoimar von Ditfurth

How the Earth Got Its Mountains

Whenever the earth quakes anywhere, the world is immediately informed of the horrors of collapsed houses, destroyed villages, and human casualties. Whenever the surfaces of the earth open up, whenever tidal waves caused by submarine terrors flood islands and coasts—it is then that one becomes fully aware of the fact that the earth is still very much in motion. Long before man evolved into man in his present form (about three million years ago), mountains had already been evolving for a hundred million years, an almost inconceivable period of time. Faced with a span of so many millions of years, scientists have made only a modest beginning in the investigation of the geological evolution of mountains. As in all disciplines in which results are derived from hypothetical assumptions, so, too, in the study of the origin of mountains, geologists have been unable to agree on a theory. Apart from the difficulty of establishing a unified theory regarding the most fundamental questions of origin, the scientist is also faced with the fact that each particular mountain undergoes change from year to year, as is observed even by attentive laymen on their hikes. Rain and snow, wind and sun contribute to the deformation process. Though the resultant changes are minute compared with the massive size of a mountain, they are constant and arise from the unceasing alternation of heat and cold as the seasons change. Man is a more important cause of change. In no time at all he can destroy what it took aeons to create.

The eruptions of active volcanos, which spew forth their molten masses, reveal just how tremendous are the powers that still reside at the core of the earth. In the following discussion, a geological survey of the possible origin of mountains will be undertaken. Geology is a complex and comprehensive science of the earth, in which theories are offered not only for the origin but also for the development and change of the earth as well as its living creatures, whose remains still exist in fossilized form.

At the beginning of the nineteenth century, when geologists began to rack their brains over the question of how mountains evolved, they found themselves confronted by a host of problems. Before this, the Plutonists, an early group of geologists, believed that all elevations of the earth's surface were a result of volcanic activity. Their theories soon proved to be inadequate. Volcanic activity, of course, did play a part in the development of mountains. In 1538, which is quite recent in geological terms, a new mountain erupted in Pozzuoli near Vesuvius before the eyes of the astonished natives. It was called Monte Nuovo. But this mountain, as well as a few other examples, proved to be an exception. No traces of volcanic activity could be found either in the Alps or in the Apennines. Rather, evidence existed that not only contradicted the Plutonists' theory but also pointed to a totally different and inexplicable mechanism for mountain formation: the Alps as well as all the other mountains in the world showed visible folds. They seemed to consist of layers that had been pushed and folded in upon themselves by powerful lateral forces.

The theory of sedimentation, which explained the layered characteristic of mountains, could not be reconciled with the otherwise illuminating "baked apple hypothesis." According to this theory, the globe shrank as the earth cooled off. Mountains arose as a result of the corrugation of the earth's crust, which had become too large for the shrinking interior.

The unresolved questions were exacerbated by the fact that one can find in most mountains an abundance of fossils, for example, the petrified remains of mussels, water snails, and other sea creatures. How could such organisms have found their way into the mountain? How could they have reached a height thousands of meters above sea level?

For centuries pious writers had been able to answer this question by interpreting the fossils as admonishing remnants of the biblical deluge. But critical and scientific minds had again and again pondered quite different possibilities. One of the most brilliant of these thinkers was Leonardo da Vinci. In the fifteenth century, he put forward the extravagant idea that schools of fish once swam over those same Italian mountain peaks now crossed by migrating birds.

When in the course of the nineteenth century a complete geological survey of the globe had been completed, a further and no less difficult question appeared. How could one explain the fact that most of the earth's mountains form two gigantic ridges, which basically connect most of our planet? One range spans the entire Pacific. The other stretches from the Atlas Mountains and the Pyrenees across the Alps and the Caucasus to the Himalayas. What is the significance of this pattern that seemed to embrace the whole earth?

It is only in the last fifteen years that a convincing answer has been found for all the questions. Even if certain points remain unresolved, we now believe we know why all the large mountains are formed in layers and why they appear wrinkled even to the casual observer. Today we also know that da Vinci was correct and that fish did swim over the tops of our mountain ranges. Moreover, the fact that mountains form two great chains has lost its mystery. Even though the Plutonists' explanation of volcanic activity proved to be too simple and (quite literally) too superficial, it is certain today that mountains arose as a result of forces stemming from the earth's interior.

The well-known theory of continental drift led toward the ultimate solution of the problem. It was advanced and established in the 1920s by the famous German geologist Alfred Wegener. The point of departure for this theory was the fact that the Atlantic contours of the South American continent perfectly matched those of the African continent. Wegener was also able to prove that particular structures on both continents corresponded to each other. From these observations he concluded that the two continents originally formed one unit, which then broke apart into two pieces and drifted away from each other like two floes of ice.

This theory received a great deal of attention when it first appeared. For years geologists throughout the world debated its merits. Therefore, it is simply not true that Wegener was initially ridiculed for his hypothesis, as was later believed. What is true, however, is that the theory of continental drift was eventually rejected in scientific circles. A fundamental question arose that no one could answer: from where did all the energy come that would be necessary to move whole continents across the surface of the earth? Even Wegener could not answer this question. For this reason, the scientific world passed him by. In 1930, at the age of fifty, he perished while on an expedition to Greenland. Wegener died an embittered man, having failed to convince the world that his theory was correct.

Today we know that Alfred Wegener's theory was right. For a long time, there has existed an abundance of evidence supporting continental drift. The following is an amusing example of one of these proofs. A related species of miniature crayfish was discovered in two different places and at great distances from each other: in a river estuary in South America and in another estuary lying directly opposite in Africa. These crayfish are found only in these two places. As freshwater organisms, it is not possible for them to have crossed the Atlantic Ocean and survived. Conclusion: these crayfish must be descendants of a single population whose members were carried off in two directions when the land masses moved apart and drifted away from each other. Since that time, they have continued to develop separately.

Today we know where the energy came from that permitted continental land masses to drift across the globe. The driving force comes from the center of the earth. Powerful convection currents from the hot core of the earth reach the cooled crust of the globe and provide the propulsion for which Wegener looked in vain all his life. For our purposes, the single most important fact is that nearly every question concerning the origin and structure of mountains, which troubled geologists in the past, has now been satisfactorily answered.

Less than twenty years ago, several quite unexpected discoveries led to a renewed interest in the theory of continental drift. By now, means were also available for a thorough investigation of this theory. The history of these discoveries begins with an absolutely unexpected finding, one that may with justification be regarded as sensational. The data collected some twenty years ago during various oceanographic research trips began to point in one direction: all rock samples brought up from the ocean floor were found to be ridiculously young in comparison with the age of continental rock.

Rock billions of years old exists in many places on the earth's surface (as has been determined by radiocarbon analysis). On the other hand, no matter where one bored in the floors of the Atlantic or Pacific Oceans, there was no rock to be found more than a hundred million years old. But why should the ocean floor be so much younger than the continental parts of the earth's crust? This posed a problem worthy of intensive investigation. In the course of several years of study, a strange picture began to emerge out of the mass of data. In the middle of the two great oceans there existed a kind of undersea mountain ridge that ran north to south and consisted of volcanic material. Here the ocean floor was youngest, only a few million years old. The further that one moved east or west from the ridge, the older were the samples taken from the ocean floor. Remarkably, the age of the samples taken from both sides of the undersea ridge appeared to rise symmetrically: if a sample of a particular age was found a few hundred kilometers to the east of the ridge, it could be predicted that a sample of the same age would be found at the same distance to the west of the ridge.

There was only one explanation for these facts: in some way or other, a new ocean floor came into being on top of the ridge. It almost immediately shifted to the right and to the left, and drifted toward the continents on both sides of the ocean. Precise investigations, which have been carried out since 1969 by the famous research ship *Glomar Challenger*, revealed the presence of an eruption zone on the underwater ridge as well as evidence of comparatively high temperature in this region. What has been occurring thousands of meters under the surface of the ocean is now fully understood. Along the whole ridge, volcanic material erupted from the mantle of the earth and formed a new and youthful ocean floor, which was immediately pushed to both sides of the eruption zone by the force of material constantly pouring out from the earth's interior. In this way, volcanic material slowly moved symmetrically east and west.

The oldest rock samples nearest the coast permit a count-back to that period of the earth's history when this process must have begun. One hundred million years ago the Atlantic Ocean did not yet exist. At that time the American and Euro-African continents formed one coherent mass. These continents have been moving apart since then at the rate of a few centimeters (1 to 3 inches) per year.

Alfred Wegener's theory was proved to be correct forty years after the death of its proponent. The continental crust, which split into blocks, swims upon the viscous material of the outer part of the earth's mantle. The mantle transports the material as if by conveyor belt in the direction of the convection current that rises up from the earth's core.

In order to understand the energy involved in this movement, a problem that Wegener could not solve, we need only consider the dimensions of the layers involved in the drift. The continental blocks have an average thickness of 30 kilometers (18.6 miles) and, in exceptional cases, 80 kilometers (49.7 miles). The ocean floor is only 5 to 10 kilometers (3 to 6 miles) thick. Thus, it is not surprising that the viscous masses of the earth's interior break through the ocean floor and split the earth's crust, driving the blocks apart. The earth's mantle, on the other hand, has a thickness of almost 3,000 kilometers (1,864 miles). The convection currents produced in the mantle by the rising of hot material to the top and the simultaneous sinking of cool masses to the bottom occur in large areas of this portion of the earth.

If we transfer these dimensions to a globe with a diameter of 120 centimeters (47.24 inches), the crust's thickness would be 3 millimeters (1.1181 inches) deep, given a mantle of 30 centimeters (11.81 inches). The ground under our feet is in reality not as firm as people imagine. In fact, the earth, which is covered by a thin, cool crust, is really a drop of fiery liquid matter floating freely in space. This drop is only stable because it floats freely. If the earth were to be placed upon a solid foundation, it would immediately break down into a glowing puddle. Thus, it is no surprise that individual scraps of the cool crust can be set into motion by the fire that lies below.

This explanation has only been worked out within the past ten years. It has largely resolved the major problems that confronted geologists for a long time in their investigation of the origin of mountains. There can no longer be any doubt about how mountains are formed: most of the mountains on earth arose through the casting up and compression of the earth's crust at those places where two continental masses collided during the drift.

If our life span encompassed millions of years instead of merely several decades, we would observe that the earth's surface is in constant motion and that a multitude of independent blocks or crust plates are moving about at various speeds and in different directions. These crust plates collide with each other. They become deformed and compressed at their edges. Our situation resembles that of a hypothetical microorganism whose life expectancy is a thousandth of a second. As it perches on the crest of a fiery wave, it regards its world as being rigid and motionless, just as we regard the earth. Were this hypothetical creature to obtain a wider perspective, it would doubtless have difficulty in understanding why its world should appear to others as a wave!

"Plate tectonics" are the magical words that many geologists employ in order to explain the problems involved in the formation of mountains. With regard to many places on the earth, geologists have indeed succeeded in formulating detailed answers on the basis of this theory. A particularly striking result of the application of plate tectonics was the discovery of so-called subduction zones. The search for these zones began immediately after the discovery of the conveyor-belt movement of the ocean floor. With the discovery of this movement, the existence of such zones was theoretically established.

The idea of subduction zones rests upon a principle of equilibrium: if in one place the ocean floor is undergoing a constant process of renewed formation, then it is certain that somewhere else it is undergoing a simultaneous and equal process of destruction, because the surface of the earth does not expand. The first region where such changes were occurring was quickly and easily found. Evidently, the entire east coast of the Pacific Ocean, from Alaska to the southernmost tip of the North American continent, formed a subduction zone. Here, a young ocean floor approaching from the west is pressed under the blocks that form the North American continent and disappears slowly into the interior of the earth.

This is the reason why the whole Pacific belt is one of the most active earthquake areas of the world. The friction of the crust plates, which is produced when the ocean floor is pushed underneath the continental blocks, must lead to violent shock. Moreover, it is now quite clear why there are so many active volcanoes in the path of this same eruption zone.

A process of melting occurs along the margins of the continental plates, whereby the sinking oceanic floor, carrying along fragments of the continental crust, becomes fused with the upper surfaces of the earth's mantle. The processes of magmatic differentiation and gas emission lead in many places to the eruption of molten material through the earth's surface.

The main uplifts even here are not primarily the result of direct volcanic origin. The Cordillera range, stretching more than 15,000 kilometers (9,321 miles) from north to south, was not thrust up to the height of over 6,000 meters (19,685 feet) because of the earth's heat, but rather because of the collision of the Pacific and Atlantic plates. According to the theory of plate tectonics, the same explanation applies to the formation of the other great mountain chains of the world.

The Pyrenees were formed as a result of a collision of the Iberian and West European plates. The Alps arose when a Mediterranean plate moved slowly north and pushed up a central European plate. The Himalayas owe their origin to the collision of the Indian continent with a gigantic Asian continental plate.

How does the sedimentation of nearly all nonvolcanic mountains and mountain chains fit into this picture? For this, too, a ready explanation now exists. The great age of many continental rocks proves that the continents themselves are very stable and that, in contrast to the much thinner ocean plates, they did not undergo processes of melting and reformation. Most geologists consider continents to be relatively rigid. They also believe that continents have retained their fundamental shape, by and large, unchanged by the passage of many aeons of the earth's history. This is basically true despite the

Movements of the Earth's Crust (arrows) in the Alps-Apennine Region

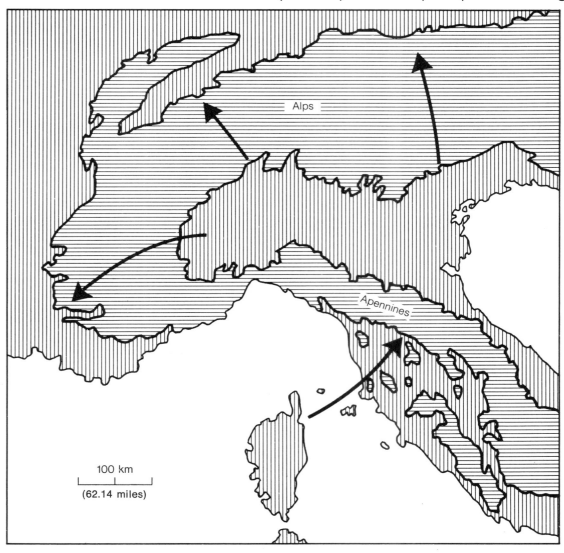

Alps

Apennines

100 km
(62.14 miles)

Basic Outline of Plate Tectonics

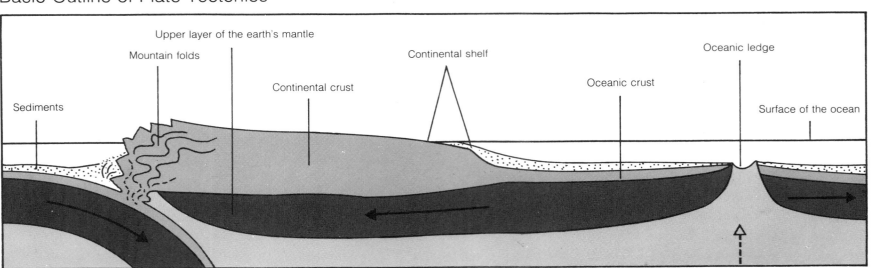

Upper layer of the earth's mantle

Mountain folds

Continental shelf

Oceanic ledge

Sediments

Continental crust

Oceanic crust

Surface of the ocean

appearance of new contours as a result of local fragmentization due to faulting. (This, by the way, is merely a modification of Alfred Wegener's original assumption that continental blocks are relatively flexible, an assumption that was the starting point of his attempt to reconstruct a single, coherent supercontinent believed to have existed in primeval times.)

However stable the earth's crust may be on the continental masses, it is not without elasticity even there. Powerful forces from the earth's interior tug at the lower strata. As a result, a vertical movement constantly occurs throughout the continental mass. Because of this movement, there is practically no region on earth that has not at some point in geological history existed under water for greater or lesser periods of time. During these periods, sediments were deposited that characterize every ocean floor. In the course of millions of years, this sediment became rock. Later, this rock was thrust upward and formed mountains as a result of processes described by plate tectonics. This, then, explains the stratified appearance of mountains, as pointed out before, a phenomenon that had once seemed so incomprehensible. Before the uplift, schools of fish did swim over what was later to form a chain of mountains. At the same time, the remains of the most varied forms of sea life collected in the sediments of the ocean floor.

The geological theory of plate tectonics is ready to provide an answer for any question that arises concerning the formation of mountains, even for the most peculiar phenomena. Over the past twenty years, observations have coalesced step by step and piece by piece to form a convincing and unified picture. However, this picture is not quite perfect after all. On closer inspection, it reveals a few flaws. No one denies that plate-tectonic analysis of the earth's crust has ushered in a new epoch in geological research. This approach has provided a multitude of the most interesting and illuminating insights, ones that cannot be ignored. As is usual in science, however, this fruitful new theory not only solved many old problems but also gave rise to new ones.

Today, many geologists believe that in the theory of plate tectonics they possess a patent for the understanding of every process that occurs in the earth's crust. But there are also other voices that remind us that science does not recognize permanent recipes, does not accept pat answers for all questions. The Soviet geologist Vladimir Belussov first raised some objections in 1970.

Since Belussov first uttered his "no," a debate has been going on at the periphery of the mainstream of geological research. On the one side are the advocates of plate tectonics; on the other are a small but increasing number of critics. The debate has been quite passionate. Rumor has it that at many universities and institutes one can easily distinguish the advocates from their opponents by observing who greets whom.

The critics do not deny the great advance made possible by the theory. They merely point out that their colleagues have been carried away by the progress made over the past few years and have, therefore, overestimated the universal applicability of this approach. They agree that this theory can explain why the most important mountains on the earth are concentrated in two vast ranges encompassing the whole globe. They also admit that the contours of these ranges may well be the result of gigantic and coherent cracks in the earth's crust.

But they have also pointed out certain contradictions. Belussov has called attention to particular places on earth that don't appear to have been explained by plate tectonics. The African continent is one example. According to the theorists, this continent consists of a single rigid crust plate except for the East African rift valley running into the extension of the Red Sea. Regarded from the mid-Atlantic ocean floor rise, the plate would have to have drifted east. Regarded from the central Indian rise, it would, on the other hand, have had to have drifted west. Finally, in order to explain the formation of the Atlas Mountains and the Alps, the plate would have had to have drifted north. Even for an exotic continent, this is a bit too much!

Many geologists resolve this problem by asserting that the earth's crust is really divided into numerous, ever-smaller crusts that drift independently of their neighbors. Thus the scientists are able to account for any drift direction that their theory requires. By proceeding in such a fashion, however, these theorists approach a method forbidden in science: the so-called method of *petitio principii* whereby the hypothesis sought is assumed to be beyond question. Therefore, the evidence gathered is interpreted in such a way as to support the desired result.

In light of the above contradictions, Belussov is not the only geologist to have expressed the belief that other, as yet undiscovered, mechanisms exist that will eventually explain the origin of mountains.

The most interesting attempt to find a new explanation was one made by Hans Georg Wunderlich, a geologist from Tübingen. For several years, Wunderlich worked in the northern Apennines and that part of the Alpine chain that was immediately contiguous. This was a geographical area in which the plate-tectonic approach encountered typical difficulties.

The north Italian Po Valley is enclosed here by a U-shaped mountain chain formed in the west by the Maritime Alps, in the south by the Apennines, and in the north by the Alps. An arc of mountains like this confined to such a narrow space cannot be explained on the basis of plate tectonics even with the best will in the world— unless, of course, one is prepared to take refuge in arbitrary hypotheses. During the course of his long investigations, Wunderlich took countless measurements of the earth's gravitational pull. In the regions he investigated, he discovered gravitational anomalies that suggested the existence of a whirling rotational movement in the earth's crust. As in all geological processes, this motion, too, occurred very slowly over millions of years. Lateral pressure as a result of such rotation would explain both the formation of the mountain chains in this region and their peculiar U-shaped pattern.

But how did such a rotational movement arise in the viscous crust of the earth, which slowly gave way under the impact of millions of years of pressure? Wunderlich provided an amazing answer: the rotational movement occurs in the earth in precisely the same way as it occurs in the atmosphere. As the earth rotates, gigantic whirls form in the atmosphere within a matter of days, as air flows over the earth's surface toward any particular point. During the process of cloud formation, these whirls can be clearly seen from satellite photos. They can also be reconstructed on weather maps as areas of low barometric pressure. According to Wunderlich's fascinating theory, the same process that takes place in the atmosphere, and is visible to our eyes because of its speed, also occurs in the lithosphere, when thermal convection currents from the earth's interior lead to extensive upheavals and depressions in the rocky crust. Because this process is extremely slow in the lithosphere, it is much more difficult to discern.

Investigations carried out in the Carpathians and in the Balkans led to the discovery of another one of these lithospheric whirls. Unfortunately, Wunderlich died in 1974 at the age of forty-six before he was able to complete his work. It is to be hoped that another geologist will soon be found who will take up the rotation theory and continue the work that Wunderlich began.

The most recent publications on the theory of the formation of mountains prove once again that every new explanation in science always gives rise to new questions and problems. At the end of 1977, Herbert Frey, an American astrophysicist, called attention to a related problem that had remained unnoticed until this time: The relatively thick and stable continental plates could only be transported by conveyor-belt movement on the outermost layers of the earth's crust because sufficient space was available. To express this more scientifically, plate-tectonic mechanisms could operate on our planet only because just 40 percent of the earth's surface is covered by continental plates. The remaining 60 percent of the earth is comprised of relatively thin oceanic plates that undergo constant transformation and can be easily penetrated by the heavy continental blocks. The theoretical presupposition for the plate-tectonic explanation of continental drift is the fact that the continental crust exhibits a 60 percent deficiency in matter. When the earth was formed five billion years ago, the crust comprised 100 percent of the globe. Where, then, did 60 percent of this matter disappear to, leaving the continental crusts to form only 40 percent of the earth?

As Frey pointed out, modern space research has shown that the moon's craters were formed largely as the result of impact. Mars and Mercury also exhibit surfaces strewn with craters. Apparently, at least the inner part of our solar system was subjected to massive meteor bombardment at a very early period. We can assume that this also occurred on earth, even though the original impact craters on its surface have largely disappeared because of erosion caused by wind and storms.

In this connection, Frey offers some interesting figures. The percent of the original crust shattered by a meteorite impact depends on the size of the body bombarded. The greater the heavenly body, the greater the percentage of crust destroyed. In the case of the moon and Mercury, the crust deficit caused by meteorite impact equals 30 percent. In the case of Mars, photos reveal a 40 percent loss. In the case of the earth, astronomers have calculated a 60 percent deficit.

This figure corresponds almost exactly to the conditions that geologists on earth have actually found. Thus, it is conceivable that the earth's oceans with their thin and constantly renewed floors are related to the Seas of the Moon (which have taken their names from the seas of the earth). One can at least say that the seas of both the earth and the moon originated in the same way. Perhaps the first chapter in the formation of mountains was written five billion years ago, when a massive cosmic bombardment occurred.

This is the picture as it exists today. It is the result of revolutionary geological discoveries, nearly all of which were made within the past two decades. The results of these most recent investigations appear to have provided us with answers to most of the questions that earlier generations of geologists sought for, in vain, largely because they lacked the sophisticated technological means necessary for a complete analysis of the earth's surface. Even today, however, many unresolved questions remain whose solution will, in turn, generate ever new problems.

One fact will undoubtedly remain true regardless of what discoveries the future may bring: No "orogenic phases" exist in the history of the earth—that is, epochs of active mountain formation cannot be interrupted by long periods of geological inactivity, as had been imagined until recently. Rather, the earth's surface is constantly in motion. Even today, forces are perpetually at work that cause the formation and decay of mountains. It is merely that our life span is too short to allow us to establish and reconstruct this process as a series of real events in the physical world. Therefore, we must be content to approach the formation of mountains indirectly and theoretically by using sophisticated, scientific techniques and by deducing the truth from them. □

Hans Reiner

To the Chimborazo in the Name of Science

They were misunderstood. They were insulted as being boasters and liars. But they had only wanted to satisfy a very human and natural curiosity—those early explorers who had been tempted to travel to distant places and who had sought to escape beyond the narrow intellectual and cultural horizons of their lives.

At the beginning of the fourteenth century, an Arab student of law, Ibn Batuta, managed to return after twenty-five years from a pilgrimage to Mecca. His reports about East Africa, Persia, India, and China, as well as his description of his ascent of the holy mountain of Ceylon, were rejected by his contemporaries as mere extravagant boasting. And yet, how he must have suffered from hunger, thirst, and cold as he made his laborious way over the high mountains. Apparently, he took those routes traveled almost a thousand years before, around 400 A.D., by the Buddhist monk Fa Hsien. These routes ran from southern China to India over the high passes of Tsung Ling (today called the *Karakoram).* The return trip took another fourteen years. The primary intention of these early explorers was not to investigate mountains; nevertheless, they were forced to cross over these natural barriers in order to see what countries, people, rivers, and seas lay on the other side of the world from which they came.

These early world travelers were not researchers in the later scientific sense of the word, nor did they set out to satisfy a desire for adventure. Their great service lay in bringing back to their own culture information about other cultures, countries, civilizations, and languages. The mountains that they saw and experienced on their journeys into unknown places often left behind the most lasting impressions. In later times, the high mountains themselves became more and more the object of scientific research. In pursuit of knowledge, scientists were prepared to endure the greatest hardships and to accept even the most life-threatening dangers.

There have always been people whose desire for adventure and excessive craving for knowledge drove them into unknown regions. A long continuum connects the first daring travelers to the natural scientists and geographers of the nineteenth century, whose intellectual and physical achievements still today inspire wonder and admiration. Most of these explorers followed paths to the unknown over the tops of mountains. And perhaps it was the mountains that made them able, through renunciation and suffering, to grow far beyond themselves and all normal expectations. Reports about their experiences and impressions moved their contemporaries deeply. They continue even today to exert a profound effect.

Pilgrimages to the distant East made by two Franciscan monks in the thirteenth century stimulated two Venetian merchants to risk a trip across the whole of Asia. Nicolo and Maffio Polo traveled as far as China, returning home to Venice after nine years. Following a very short stay in Venice, they set out once again, now accompanied by Marco Polo, the seventeen-year-old son of Nicolo. The journey led through Persia and Afghanistan, across the Pamir Plateau, through the Tarim Basin and the Gobi Desert, and on toward China.

Young Marco Polo became the model for almost all explorers to come. He had all those characteristics that a geographer must possess: courage, love of travel, an outstanding gift for observation, a talent for bargaining, and physical stamina. He also possessed a unique gift for learning languages: During his trip to the East, he mastered Arabic, Persian, Uighur, and Chinese. In addition, Marco Polo had the ability to retain all the impressions he collected on his journey, which he described many years later in the most vivid fashion. Kublai Khan, the Mongolian ruler of East Asia, took a liking to this talented young man. He entrusted him with high offices and sent him on missions. In this fashion Marco Polo became acquainted with a world that stretched from tropical islands to the mountains of Tibet. Seventeen years later, he returned to Venice. No one recognized him. They thought he was a fraud. His book, which was dictated when he was a prisoner of war and was later to influence generations of readers, only served to earn him the nickname "Mr. Marco Millions," the millionaire of exaggeration.

In the meantime, a fundamental change had occurred in European thought. Humanism changed man's relationship to nature. The university scholar and much-honored poet Francesco Petrarch stood on the summit of Mont Ventoux in 1336, simply because of his sole wish to see the world from above. His all-embracing intellect, his reputation, and his highly esteemed descriptions made his climb into an event of significance. But hundreds of years had to pass before these seeds began to sprout.

Horace Bénédicte de Saussure pitched his tent in 1787 on the glaciers of Mont Blanc. This was a resounding signal that could not be ignored and that found an enthusiastic echo. De Saussure had been extravagantly endowed by fate—with intelligence, love of adventure, and endurance, as well as with financial means. When at the age of nineteen he saw the summit of Mont Blanc, he swore to himself that he would climb it. Even though he was not the first person to climb this highest peak in the Alps, he was nevertheless the one who prepared the way for the age of mountaineering. Having placed his reputation as a scientist in the service of mountain climbing, his assault of Mont Blanc attained unexpected significance. Mountains became an object of general interest as well as of great yearning. After seven abortive attempts, de Saussure set out on August 1, 1787, with a large caravan. Food, trunks, warm clothing, bedding, ladders, and, of course, scientific equipment were dragged along. On the Grand Plateau, everyone huddled together in tents for the night. A clear and cloudless morning favored the final ascent to the summit. The uniqueness of the moment did not overwhelm him. De Saussure, the prototypical scientist, began by making various measurements: he observed the pulse and breathing of the climbers, determined the color of the sky, collected samples of the air in bottles, and took barometric readings. This took four and a half hours. In Chamonix, he was mobbed and cheered. His report caused a sensation and initiated the Alpine Age.

The gate to the mountains was thrown open by de Saussure. At the time that the ascent of Mont Blanc gripped the public imagination, Alexander von Humboldt turned twenty years old. Alexander, who was born in Berlin in 1769, was a frail child, but, together with his stronger and healthier brother Wilhelm, he had enjoyed an excellent education. His first passion was the collecting and classification of stones, beetles, and plants. When his health improved, he was able to attend several universities. As a geologist, he traveled to Bavaria, the Tyrol, northern Italy, and Switzerland. These trips strengthened his desire to undertake a lengthy research trip to the tropics. Various setbacks did not discourage him. The brothers inherited a considerable fortune after the death of their mother. Alexander von Humboldt put half of it aside for the trip. It proved to be an excellent investment. In 1799 he left the Old World and returned only after having become the scientific discoverer of a forgotten continent. With his extraordinary talent for precise observation and careful deduction, he became the founder of almost all the natural sciences. His scientific output, which is immense, provided a foundation upon which future generations of scientists were able to build.

It was mountains and, in particular, volcanoes that above all else attracted Alexander von Humboldt's interest. He paid a visit to Pico de Teyde [3,718 meters (12,198 feet)] on Tenerife, one of the Canary islands. Everything here gripped his imagination: air, sky, clouds, earth, stones, plants, and animals. The scope, depth, and power of this man's intellect are almost beyond measure. After he landed in Venezuela, he climbed a mountain named Silla [2,543 meters (8,343 feet)]. On Cotopaxi, he reached a height of almost 4,500 meters (14,764 feet). With his companion Bonpland, he penetrated to the Orinoco. In his reports the flora and fauna of the tropics appear in all their exuberant abundance. While searching for the source of the Orinoco, he stumbled upon a fork of the Amazon. On June 23, 1802, he reached what he recorded as 5,880 meters (19,291 feet) on the Chimborazo [6,287 meters (20,626 feet)]. He was particularly proud of this achievement and later jokingly called himself "the old man of the mountain." For a long time, his ascent of the Chimborazo remained the highest recorded climb. It contributed greatly to Humboldt's popularity.

He returned to Europe. In spite of the Napoleonic wars Humboldt's achievements caused a stir and attained worldwide recognition. The results of his investigations (written in Paris in French) comprise twenty-three volumes and were never completed. They still await definitive evaluation. At the age of seventy, he wrote *Cosmos*, a standard work intended as a coherent description of the natural world. Alexander von Humboldt, who died in 1859 at the age of ninety, possessed to the last moment a clear and unclouded mind. His spirit remains even today a living presence in the intellectual world.

In the first third of the nineteenth century, Franz Joseph Hugi, a professor in Solothurn, had just about written himself out on the subject of glaciers in the Bernese Oberland. Beginning in 1828, he made several attempts to climb the Finsteraarhorn. Bivouacking during fog and storm, Hugi calmly continued to write down his observations. An accident occurred on the summit. One of the mountain guides, who happened to be carrying a long

pole, slipped. With a leap, Hugi caught hold of the other end. Each man clung to his own end of the pole, hovering over a terrible abyss. At great risk to all concerned, the two men were saved.

An internationally famous zoologist, Louis Agassiz, lived as a university teacher in western Switzerland. Like others, he also felt drawn to the glacial mountains. He allowed himself to be lowered by ropes into crevasses, where he was able to discern and measure glacial movements. For a long time he lived in a primitive hut surrounded by eternal ice and snow in order to pursue the glacial research that eventually led to the discovery of the Ice Age. He also sacrificed his modest income in this endeavor. Debts drove him to America, where he received a chair at Harvard University. Eventually released from his financial obligations, he was able to continue his research and confirmed by scientific proof that the Diluvium was the Ice Age.

The brothers Schlagintweit established Munich's fame in the fields of mountain climbing and geography. In their youth, they astonished the world by their climbing successes and by their admirable scientific achievements. Hermann, twenty years old, had chosen the Ötztal Alps as his goal. He was accompanied by his brothers, who were almost still children. Together, they added drawings and panoramic views to their research reports, transforming them into a wonderful illustrated volume. Soon thereafter, they dedicated their energies to the Monte Rosa group, also with great success.

After the Schlagintweits completed their studies at the universities of Munich and Berlin in 1851, at the ages of twenty-six and twenty-three, the brothers' attention was called by Alexander von Humboldt to the Indian Surveyor-General's Office. By 1854, Hermann, Adolf, and Robert were working as geologists in India. One year later they were already in the Himalayas. There they measured and mapped out more than sixty glaciers. They penetrated as far as Tibet and there tested out their climbing skills on the Himalayan mountains. They reached the height of 6,750 meters (22,145 feet) on the slopes of Ibi Gamin [7,732 meters (25,367 feet)], thus exceeding by far Humboldt's world record. Adolf extended his journey to western Tibet, bivouacked in the Karakoram, and measured the Baltoro Glacier in 1856. Hermann and Robert also investigated portions of the Karakoram and, disguising themselves, dared to enter the completely unknown mountainous country of Kwen-Lun. In 1857, Adolf was mistakenly identified as a spy in Kashgar and beheaded. Hermann and

Robert returned to Europe and were showered with honors. Their scientific exploits were recorded in thirteen volumes (nine in English and four in German). With the publication of these works, the highest mountains in the world had been made accessible. In order to achieve this end, however, the Schlagintweit brothers had sacrificed their lives and health.

In 1885, the Swedish student Sven Hedin went as a private tutor to Baku, where he hoped he would be able to improve his miserable financial situation. This move was to shape the remainder of his long life. Within a short period of time, he mastered Persian and Tartar and took advantage of his residence in Persia to make an adventurous trip through the Iranian highlands. Having studied in Stockholm, Paris, and Berlin, he left Kashgar in 1894 and traveled across the Takla-Makan Desert in the Tarim Basin. The first expedition ended in a catastrophe. Hedin, nearly completely delirious, was the only member of his caravan to reach a water hole. But, before he drank the water, he measured his pulse (only forty beats per minute), in order to determine how water intake would affect a man dying of thirst.

That's the kind of man Hedin was. Burning with the urge to travel, he moved day by day from camp to camp with iron-willed persistence. In broiling heat, in snowstorms, and in the icy cold, he conscientiously carried out his measurements. He drew charts and sketches and gradually filled in the last blank spots on the map of the world. For him there were no obstacles—neither sickness, nor hunger, nor bureaucracies. When the hardship of a trip had been overcome and the superabundant results ordered and written down, a restless spirit drove him out again. Seven times and in all directions he crossed Tibet. He personified exploration itself.

He found ruined desert cities, solved the riddle of the wandering lake Lop-Nor, and made an abortive attempt to reach Lhasa dressed as a pilgrim. In the freezing winter months of 1906, he entered Tibetan soil via East Turkestan with a huge caravan of animals. Almost all the horses and beasts of burden froze to death. The caravan did not meet another human being for eighty days. The caravan crossed the 5,000-meter (16,404-foot) passes of the Transhimalaya, a mountain range totally unknown at the time. The temperature was 30° below zero Centigrade. At the border of Nepal, Hedin discovered the source of the Brahmaputra. Through arcticlike storms, the expedition once again crossed the Transhimalayas, the mountain range that today bears Hedin's name. In the Pamirs, the Mustagh Ata ("ancestor of the icy mountains") rises from craggy glacial masses. After four attempts, Hedin's expedition reached 6,300 meters (20,669 feet). In the cold tents, the mountain-sick Kirghiz porters groaned. Hedin wrote: "How strange is a night such as this on the edge of an endless universe whose dark vault stretches over and encompasses all the mountains of the world. In our tent we were nearer to heaven than are the mightiest mountain peaks of Europe, North America, Africa, and Australia."

At the age of seventy, still indefatigable, Hedin crossed the Gobi Desert with a staff of scholars from many disciplines. In 1935 he returned to Sweden. Like Humboldt, he almost reached the age of ninety. This extraordinary geographer belongs in the company of those last towering universal men whose intellectual and spiritual strength and iron-willed physical stamina permitted them to obtain a nearly total view of the earth. In the twentieth century, specialization began. Mountain climbers and explorers now diverged and went their own ways. □

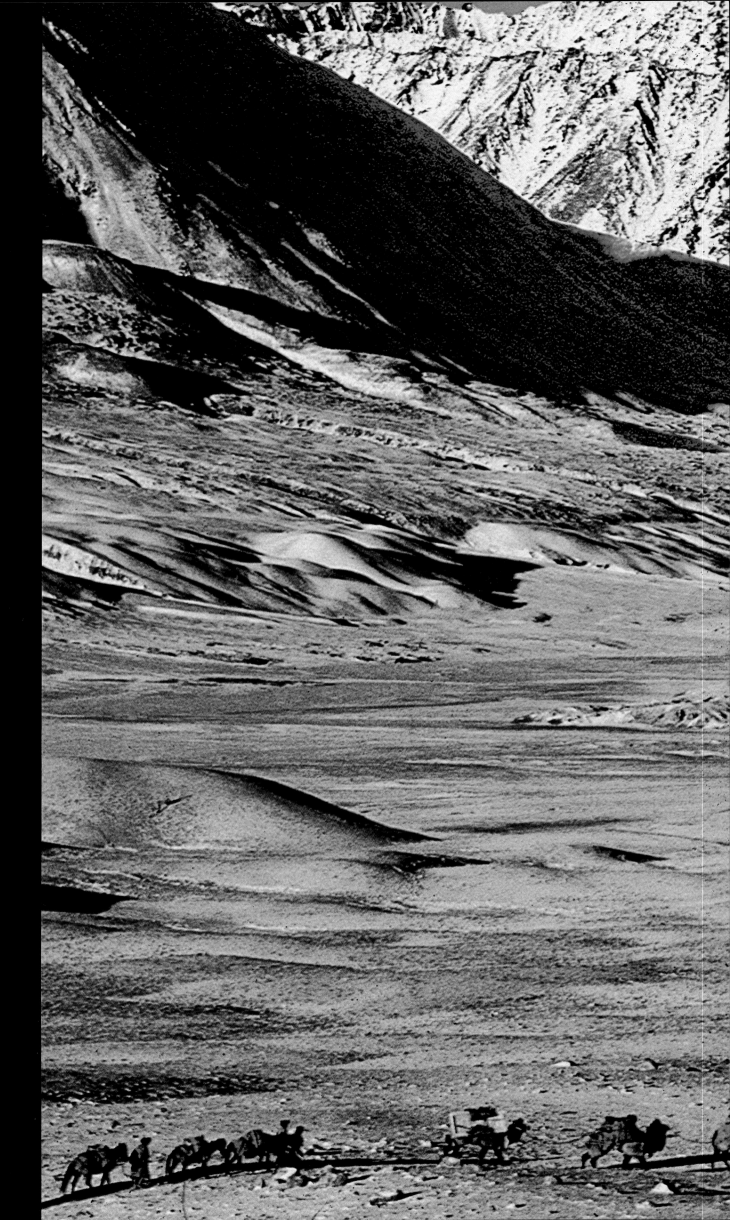

13

"The dome-shaped peak of Chimborazo once again appeared before us, this time quite near. It was a solemn and magnificent sight. The hope of reaching the summit of this mountain, which had been the object of our yearning for so long a time, gave us new strength. The topmost ridge of cliffs, which was covered here and there with patches of snow, became somewhat flatter . . . ." With these words, Alexander von Humboldt described his attempt to climb the Chimborazo. We know that the great scientist had to turn back on June 23, 1802 because of an impassable gorge. By then, too, he and his team had been weakened by mountain sickness.

14

More than 700 years ago, the young Venetian Marco Polo must have set out across Asia with his father and uncle along the same mountain plateaus of the Pamirs which caravans still cross today. In those days people regarded these inhospitable mountains as the "roof of the world."

In the seventh century, Siuan-Tsan (Huan-Tsang) described this mountain chain with the name "Pa-Mi-Lo." Marco Polo called it a "Pianura di Pamer." Scholars argue as to which designation is correct as well as what was meant. It has been proved that the word "Pamir" in the sense of "massif" means "roof of the world."

14

16

16

15

In the Soviet Union, the highest peak must be named for the greatest leader. In 1928, when a joint Austro-German-Soviet expedition climbed Pik Kaufmann in the northern Pamirs [7,134 meters (23,405 feet)], its name was changed to Pik Lenin, as it is still called today. Slightly to the south stood the high-est mountain in the range. The Soviet climber Yevgeny Abalakov climbed it in 1933. From that day on, the mountain was called Pik Stalin. Soviet history later demanded that the name of the proud summit be changed to Pik Communism [7,482 meters (24,546 feet)]. Stalin's bust was also removed.

16

Ice and glacial streams move slowly but steadily toward the valley. Boulde and rock debris have been forced up between the tw arms of the Kashkawulsh Glacier at the base of the Saint Elias range between Alaska and Canada. The glacier is constantly fed b precipitation which falls upon the 5,000-meter (16,400-foot) high mountai

17

the Pacific Ocean, not
from the Gulf of Alaska.
pite this water supply,
se two valley glaciers of
Kluane National Park
receding as are most of
other glaciers of the
ld. About sixteen million
are kilometers of the
h's surface are covered
glaciers. Four fifths of
n are located in the
arctic.

The Morteratsch Glacier
descends along the north
flank of the Bernina massif
in the Engadin. The Bernina
Railway brings one to the
edge of the glacier, 1,900
meters (6,233 feet) above
sea level. The peaks of ice
and snow glistening high
above the glacier are well
known to hordes of

mountain climbers:
Bellavista, Piz Zuppò, Piz
Argient, Piz Bernina. The
glacier comprises an area of
about 25 square kilometers
(9.6 square miles), only
1/60,000 of the surface area
of all the glaciers found on
earth. And yet the
Morteratsch overwhelms
one with its primeval might.

Wolfgang Nairz

Streams of Ice and Rock

The ice was a dirty shade of gray and was strewn with stones and gravel. It crunched underfoot as I walked, sounding like gnashing teeth. It even groaned. The summer sun beat down. Trickling rivulets of water formed as the ice began to melt. Here and there little streams gurgled down some hole to rejoin the roof of ice further down the mountain. Working their way toward the valley, these little jets of water made channels in the glacier's tongue, trying to form a regular system of canals. Far below, the melted water surfaced again, gurgling and bubbling through the glacier's outlet. Here, people stood on the moraine and gazed into the cavernous tunnel to regard the churning water—milky water, glacial milk, ice glimmering bluish as it dripped and melted. Higher up on the glacier, roped groups were making their way up the mountain in the care of a guide, who cautiously picked out the safest route. Sometimes this meant leaping over narrow crevasses. Sometimes it meant a detour. Finally, one reached the boundary fault at which point the path left the ice and continued up the rock cliffs. It was a typical summer afternoon on a small glacier somewhere in the Alps, a small glacier compared with the colossal streams of ice and rock found in Alaska, in the Himalayas, and in the icy wastelands of the Antarctic.

As ice streams flow slowly but steadily toward the valley, scientists are able to observe their changes. Thus we know that Alpine glaciers receded after 1927 but have gradually begun to advance again since 1974. Visible clues such as glacial fluting, smoothly buffed stone, and rock-strewn moraine tell us at a glance how far a glacier has advanced or retreated.

Glaciers move no more than 10 to 40 centimeters (4 to 16 inches) a day. Nevertheless, the constant pressure of the ice masses leads to the formation of new crevasses as well as to the collapse of already existing walls of ice. Therefore, unforgettable and rewarding though a hike over a glacier can be, the climber must observe the greatest precaution.

49

Almost one-tenth of the earth's surface [about 16 million square kilometers (6,177,600 square miles)] is covered by ice. This table presents a breakdown of this figure:

Antarctic regions	5,213,894 square miles
Arctic region (including Alaska, Iceland, and the Urals)	779,729 square miles
North temperate zone	20,270 square miles
Tropics	386 square miles
South temperate zone	4,734 square miles
Total glacial surface	6,019,013 square miles

In the Alps, glaciers cover approximately 3,600 square kilometers (1,390 square miles) making this region the largest single glacial surface on the European continent [2 percent of a total glacial area of 175,000 square kilometers (67,568 square miles)]. The Alpine glaciers rank second in area to the glaciers of the several Scandinavian countries, which together cover 5,000 square kilometers (1,931 square miles). Of the 3,600 square kilometers (1,390 square miles) of the Alps, approximately 2,200 square kilometers (849 square miles) lie in the Western Alps. The remaining 1,400 square kilometers (541 square miles) are found in the Eastern Alps.

The largest Alpine glacier is the Great Aletsch Glacier in the Bernese Alps, which covers a surface of more than 100 square kilometers (39 square miles). The largest glaciers in the Eastern Alps, with about 20 square kilometers of surface, are the Pasterzen Kees in the Hohe Tauern and the Gepatschferner in the Ötztal Alps. The glaciers of the Caucasus, the Himalayas, and the Pamirs are infinitely larger. The largest glacier of all is the Fedchenko Glacier in the northwest Pamirs, which is 77 kilometers (48 miles) long and covers an area of 1,350 square kilometers (521 square miles). The second largest is the Siachen Glacier in the Karakoram, 75 kilometers (47 miles) long, with an area of 1,150 square kilometers (444 square miles).

The term *glacier* was first used in the German-speaking regions of the Western Alps. In the Eastern Alps, two words exist to describe the streams of rock and ice. The term *ferner* is used in the Stubai and Ötztal Alps west of the Innsbruck-Brenner line, whereas the word *kees* is heard in the Hohe Tauern, as well as in the Alps of the Ziller Valley. The South Tyrolean term *vadrett*, or *vadretta*, has a Latin origin.

Reports dating from the sixteenth and seventeenth centuries tell us that individual Alpine valleys were flooded repeatedly by waters overflowing from dams formed by advancing glaciers. The most thoroughly researched glacial dam formation in the Alps is that of Rofental near Vent.

Here, the dam created by the Vernagtferner emptied out several times after 1599, the last floods occurring in the years 1845/1848. The lower end of the Vernagtferner lay diagonally across the main valley and dammed up the drain-waters flowing from the Rofenferner and the Hintereisferner, forming the Rofen Dam, almost 1 kilometer (3,280 feet) long and reaching a maximum depth of 140 meters (459 feet). Within the course of a single hour, the dam emptied out and, with catastrophic effects, flooded the surrounding land as far as the Inn Valley. However, it was not long before people recognized the value of glaciers as water silos. In Vintschgau and in the Valais, one can still discover the remains of old irrigation canals built high above the valley floor. That the interior valleys of the Alps have remained green and fertile despite meager precipitation is due largely to the presence of these glaciers.

The first representation of Alpine glaciation is found on Warmund Ygl's map of the Tyrol dating from the year 1604.

By the eighteenth century, the first studies of glaciers were appearing. In 1773, A. C. Bordier of Geneva was the first to suggest that glaciers be systematically observed. However, intensive work was not done until nearly a century later. In 1869 the Glacier Commission was founded. Now, systematic investigations of glacial changes were undertaken in the Western Alps under the auspices of the Swiss Alpine Club and the Swiss Natural Research Society, and in the Eastern Alps under the auspices of the Austrian and German Alpine Clubs.

After the foundation of the International Glacier Commission in the year 1897, glacial research was extended to regions beyond the Alps. The Alfred Wegener expedition of 1932/1933 brought back important information about the ice formations in the interior of Greenland. Extremely important contributions to glacial science were made by two men engaged in research in the Asian highlands: Richard Finsterwalder (Fedchenko Glacier, 1932/1933; Rakhiot Glacier, Nanga Parbat, 1938) and Philipp Christiaans Visser (Karakoram, 1938).

The work of the International Glacier Commission led to the founding of the International Commission for Snow and Ice, which devised guidelines for worldwide glacial observation and control. The first exact measurements of glacial movement were undertaken on the Mer de Glace. Today, countless measurements are constantly being made on numerous glaciers throughout the world.

The most characteristic type of glacier to be found in the Alps is the so-called valley glacier, whose source is nearly always high-lying snow fields. Such a glacier typically consists of two parts: the snowy firn fields (névé) above and the glacial tongue lower down. Several glaciers that originate in different snow fields can combine to form a single ice stream. A typical example of this phenomenon is the Great Aletsch Glacier. There are several other glacial types. Cirque glaciers (cwms) generally lie at the base of steep-walled amphitheater-shaped valley heads. In contrast, relatively thin sheets of glacial ice cover unbroken mountain slopes. In earlier times, these "slope glaciers," as they were called, would join up with valley glaciers and continue their course until throwback from the glacial tongue caused a reformation of the sloping ice sheets. A glacier that breaks over a steep escarpment or hangs down over a valley step without reaching the valley floor is called a *hanging glacier*. Plateau glaciers, which are quite typical in Scandinavia, are rare in the Alps. The most well-known examples of glacial plateaus in the Alps are the Übergossene Alm on the Hochkönig and the Marmolada Glacier in the Dolomites. Narrow, very steep glaciers that head down the valley in gorges or channels and are therefore called "gorge" or "channel glaciers" tend to extend below the snow line and are a variety of the valley glacier. Such glaciers are generally fed by avalanches.

Glacial movement is unique, a combination of gliding and the viscous flow characteristic of plastic materials. It is continuous, unrelenting, and very slow.

The velocity of glacial movement varies from a few feet to several miles a year. Small mountain glaciers move slowest. On the average, Alpine glaciers move approximately 60 meters (197 feet) a year. On some of the larger glaciers, movements of 100 to 200 meters (328 to 646 feet) a year have been recorded (Aletsch, Mer de Glace). The plateau glaciers of Scandinavia, as well as Arctic glaciers, move far more quickly. Although a velocity of up to 600 meters (1,969 feet) per year has been recorded in Scandinavia, the Great Karajak Glacier on the western coast of Greenland covers more than 7,000 meters (22,966 feet) a year. As a general rule, glacial velocity increases with the size of the glacier. It is also influenced by the angle of the slope.

Glacial crevasses are caused by fluctuation in glacial movement combined with unevenness in the subjacent surface. For example, if the rock bed of a glacier becomes steeper and thus causes the ice masses to move more quickly toward the valley, tensile stress builds up in the ice until a point is reached where the upper layers can no longer resist cracking. Transverse crevasses form, especially in the central portions of the glacial stream, which move at greater velocities. The crevasses are slightly concave in the direction of the valley. The wedge-shaped cracks rarely measure more than 30 meters (98 feet) in depth. If the glacier flows over a very steep escarpment, further disintegration occurs in any ice masses that have already been split apart by crevasses. In this way prisms and seracs are formed.

Longitudinal crevasses open up when a glacier flows into a wider bed from a narrow pass or if a bed becomes too wide as the result of a heavy thaw. This time, tensile stress builds up diagonally across the longitudinal axis and causes the ice to rip apart. Similar cracks, called radial fissures, also appear at the terminus of a glacier. Marginal crevasses form at the periphery of a glacier, because the ice stream tends to move with different velocities in the middle and at its edges. These cracks run at angles of 30° to 40° in two directions: up the glacier and toward its interior. However, they tend to confine themselves to narrow strips along the glacier's edge. A typical crevasse is the *bergschrund*. It is formed as moving ice tears itself loose from the higher-lying stationary ice and firn that cover the upper slopes. In other words, a bergschrund can be defined as a crevasse formed by shearing rather than by melting, which separates the dead ice and snow on the upper slopes from the rocky cliffs. This form of crevasse is also called a boundary fault.

Moraines are rubble deposits left behind on glaciers as a result of avalanches, mud flows, and landslides. In the upper firn fields, the rock debris is perpetually covered by snow and slides down with the snow onto the glacier. Moraine allows the observer to establish glacial high watermarks. Particularly striking are the submarginal or "bank" moraines that date from the last glacial high watermark around 1850. Shortly after this period, glaciers began a general retreat, which has continued almost unabated, with the exception of two short periods of advance around 1890 and 1920. Remnants of moraine left by these two advances are still clearly visible. Since 1930, however, glacial recession has been particularly noticeable and more or less continuous.

Debris that has hurtled into marginal crevasses or bergschrunds and rubble that already exists beneath the glacier or is churned up by its movement combine to form basal moraine.

Lateral moraines, which are found at the edges of the glacier, are preserved as submarginal or bank moraine when the glacier retreats.

Frontal moraine at the glacier's terminus often forms an arc and joins the lateral moraine. When the glacier retreats, the frontal moraine remains at the glacier's perimeter. The debris that comes down with the snow from the firn fields above lands as surface moraine in the melting zones of the glacier. Medial moraine is produced by the confluence of two or more glacial streams together with their lateral moraines.

Snow deposits on the glacier are gradually transformed into firn granules and ice. The glacier is fed by that zone on which greater quantities of snow fall than those that melt or evaporate. This zone lies above the snow line or, in specific reference to glaciers, the firn line. Where a glacier is surrounded by towering cliffs, the snow zone is usually concave. Glacial ice flows from the snow zone across the snow line and down into regions where melting and evaporation predominate. In the melting zone, glacial surfaces are usually convex, especially in Alpine glaciers.

The firn line shifts from year to year, partly as a result of changing climatic conditions. Snowfall, temperature, solar radiation, evaporation, heat emission, reflection, air moisture, and wind all play a role in determining the location of the snow zone. In short, its position depends on the local climate. If the snow line forms at a lower point on the glacier, the feeding area is enlarged and the snow deposits increase, while the melting zone shrinks and the water lost by melting and evaporation diminishes. Conversely, the firn line can retreat to a point high up on the glacier, especially during hot summers. In such cases, most of the glacier's surface becomes a melting zone, causing a massive loss.

Using the analogy of the budget, one can say that the glacier's total mass is determined by its revenues (in the form of heavy precipitation and avalanches) as balanced by its expenditures (in the form of evaporation and melting). The total mass of a glacier can be calculated if sufficient measurements are available. To compute the mass, any increases that occur both in the accumulation of snow and in the loss of snow and ice are critical. Measurements directed toward the accumulation of snow should take into account not only its height but also the water content of the snow blanket that adheres to the ice in the melting region. Measurements of precipitation and drainage complete the picture.

The mass of a glacier is inextricably related to prevailing climatic conditions. Since 1952/1953, constant measurements have been made on the Hintereisferner in the Ötztal Alps. In more recent times, scientists have been taking measurements on glaciers throughout the world in an effort to compile an inventory of the world's water supply.

From 1904 through 1909, Hess and Blümcke bored through the Hintereisferner at various places on the glacier, reaching a depth of 224 meters (735 feet). In 1926, the seismic method of measuring the thickness of ice was introduced. Seismic measurements have yielded the following maximal depths:

Hintereisferner	961 feet
Pasterzen Kees	1,053 feet
Aletsch Glacier	2,598 feet
Rhone Glacier	778 feet

At its deepest point, the ice covering the inland areas of Greenland measures 1,780 to 1,880 meters (5,840 to 6,168 feet.); in the Antarctic, maximum ice depth is said to reach 1,525 meters (5,003 feet) [T. W. David, 1914].

Mountain climbers, who think of glaciers only in terms of their beauty and the dangers they present, would do well also to remember that they are likely to grow ever more significant as water silos, which will bring life and prosperity to yet untold numbers of people. □

Structure of a Glacier

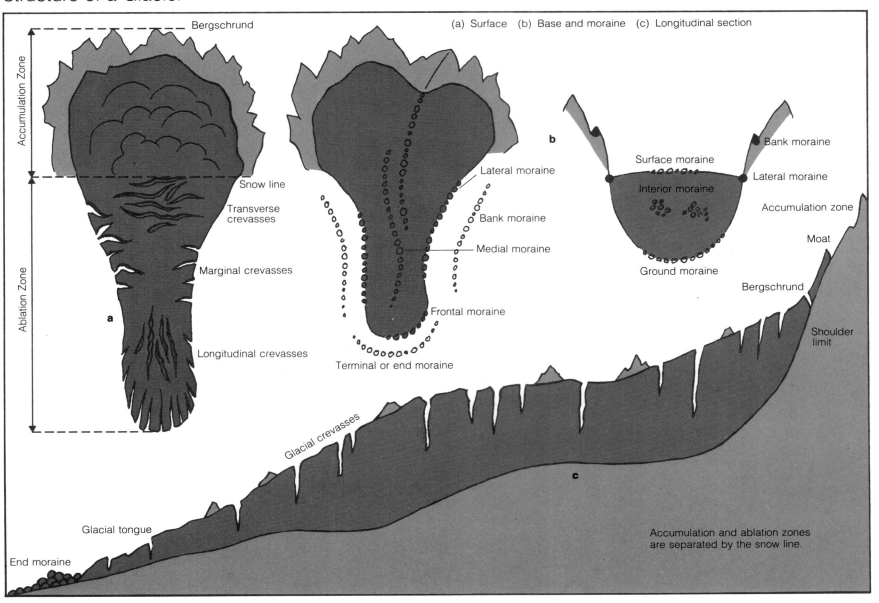

(a) Surface (b) Base and moraine (c) Longitudinal section

Bergschrund

Accumulation Zone

Snow line

Transverse crevasses

Marginal crevasses

Longitudinal crevasses

Ablation Zone

a

Lateral moraine

Bank moraine

Medial moraine

Frontal moraine

Terminal or end moraine

b

Surface moraine

Interior moraine

Ground moraine

Bank moraine

Lateral moraine

Accumulation zone

Moat

Bergschrund

Shoulder limit

Glacial crevasses

Glacial tongue

End moraine

c

Accumulation and ablation zones
are separated by the snow line.

53

Bruno Moravetz

Perhaps Goethe Arrived Only Three Months Too Late

On November 4, 1779, at about nine o'clock in the evening, Goethe wrote from Le Prieuré, a village in the middle of the Chamonix Valley:

> Here, too, it seemed to us as if the sun was drawing up to itself the faintest vapors from the highest snow-covered mountains and as if these very delicate mists were being dispersed by a gentle breeze across the whole sky like wisps of foam. Although I can recall having seen similar atmospheric phenomena at home during the height of summer, I never saw anything as transparent as this; never have I seen such a fragile web. Straight ahead, the snow-covered mountains from which these mists arose appeared before us. The valley started to climb, the Arve shot out of a rocky cliff, and we had to start the ascent itself. We climbed ever higher, the snowy mountains constantly visible above us to the right. We felt we were coming ever closer to a more powerful and mighty group of mountains. . . . It became darker. We approached the valley of Chamonix and finally entered it. . . . The stars appeared, one after the other. We noticed what seemed to be a light shining above the summits. . . . It was bright, though muted, like the Milky Way, but also more dense. For a long time this sight riveted our attention. Finally, as we changed our position, it appeared to soar above all the other mountain peaks like a pyramid made transparent by an inner, secret light. . . . Then we knew. This could only be the summit of Mont Blanc. The beauty of this moment was quite extraordinary. Illuminated by the stars surrounding it, glittering not like a star itself but with a more dense translucence, the summit of Mont Blanc appeared to belong to a different and higher realm. Here my description begins to become disordered and anxious. But, then, such a situation requires the efforts of two human beings: one who sees and one who describes. . . .
>
> Again and again one's eye and soul were drawn to the row of glittering icy mountains. When they finally lay before us in the purity and clarity of the open air, we knew that we would have to give up forever any pretension of striving for and capturing the infinite. Even the finite, which soared up ahead of us, could not be captured in thought or even through visual perception.

Goethe wrote the following lines on October 27, 1779, in Geneva at the end of a journey through the Jura Mountains that he made as the companion to his friend and patron, Duke Karl August of Weimar. The small company of travelers had ascended the Dôle, first on horseback and then by foot. A magnificent view over the ice-covered mountains opened up before them when they reached its barren summit: "As a vigorous living being begins to die away from the outside toward the heart, so each one of us slowly turned pale as he gazed out toward Mont Blanc."

Goethe was thirty years old, a man in the prime of life, powerful and trim. He was also devoted to the major intellectual currents of every period in European history. Barely two decades earlier, Jean Jacques Rousseau had recorded the impressions he had felt upon seeing a mountain landscape. In his novel *La Nouvelle Heloise* (1761), we read: "One is serious without being melancholy, calm without being indifferent; one is content simply to be and to think." Goethe, too, was able to recall the details of his trip through the Jura, the second of three trips to Switzerland. He described his impressions in many letters to Charlotte von Stein, as well as to Knebel, Lavater, and Merck.

On October 29, 1779, Goethe, who was preoccupied with problems in natural science, visited the famous natural scientist from Geneva, Charles Bonnet, on the latter's estate, Genthod. Here they doubtless talked about a certain professor of natural sciences, also from Geneva, named Horace Bénédicte de Saussure, since de Saussure was Bonnet's nephew. Three days later Goethe visited de Saussure in order to find out whether it was possible for the group to continue their journey from Geneva to the Valais through the Valley of Chamonix at so late a time in the year.

The sight of the ice-covered mountains made such an impression upon the companions of the Duke of Weimar (who was traveling incognito as a Count) that, according to Goethe, the mountains soon became the center of every conversation:

> When we came to Geneva, we heard that it was becoming ever more fashionable to see them. The Count was suddenly seized by a strange desire to redirect our route, so that we would have to go there too. . . . For this reason we visited de Saussure on his estate to ask for his advice. He assured us we could take this route without a second thought. Snow would not yet have fallen on the middle-sized mountains.

No doubt de Saussure also told the gentlemen from Weimar how much the first ascent of Mont Blanc had continued to occupy him for the past twenty years. He had visited the Chamonix Valley for the first time in 1760 and had offered a prize of 20 louis d'or (a French 20-franc gold piece) to anyone who could find a way to the summit of Mont Blanc and who would also show it to him. It is likely that Goethe, who was ever eager to undertake new adventures, inquired of de Saussure whether it would be possible to climb Mont Blanc now. (Goethe had made an adventurous climb of the Brocken Mountain in the Harz, neither hindered nor intimidated by storms or even snow drifts reaching up to his belly. That was in December 1778, less than a year before.) But as for Mont Blanc, Professor de Saussure probably discouraged the idea because of the lateness of the season.

De Saussure probably mentioned a few capable inhabitants of Chamonix who could assist the group in feasible excursions. Later, the aristocratic group of travelers did have two creditable guides to lead them through the valley. "One of them was a strong boy and the other, an older man, quite self-confident about his intellectual powers. He had been in contact with many learned foreigners and was fully informed about the nature and character of the ice-covered mountains." The man was named Michel Paccard. He was not, however, the Doctor Michel Gabriel Paccard, born in 1757, who was to reach the summit of Mont Blanc together with Jacques Balmat, a mere seven years after Goethe's visit. Goethe reported that his own guide, Michel Paccard, had already been guiding foreigners up the local mountains for the past twenty-eight years.

Goethe was probably greatly tempted to try to find a route to the summit of Mont Blanc in the company of such able guides, or, at least, to make some sort of assault upon this mountain. He had brought with him a copy of a book called *Description des glaciers de Savoie* (1773), which had just appeared a few years earlier. The book was written by Canon Marc-Théodore Bourrit of Geneva, who, along with de Saussure, was probably one of those "learned foreigners" whom Goethe's guide Michel Paccard had sought out to exchange ideas. For their part, the foreign scholars also had to turn to the Chamoniards to get their information.

Goethe's sojourn in the Chamonix Valley was not to be much more than a short excursion from Chamonix to the Mer de Glace in Montenvers. The party from Weimar, led by Michel Paccard and his nephew Victor Téssac, arrived there on November 5, 1779.

> Carrying food and wine, we began the ascent of Montenvers. The sight of the glacier surprised us. . . . There was not the slightest trace of snow upon its craggy surfaces. The blue fissures were glittering with great beauty. After a while the weather began to change and I glimpsed billowy gray clouds that seemed to hint at snow in a way I have never before seen. The peaks of the cliffs opposite us, as well as the peaks in the valley, are very jagged. . . . Such formations are called needles, and the Aiguille du Dru, which faces Montenvers, is just such a peculiar needle.

The gentlemen dared to venture out upon the glacier.

> It is a really magnificent sight when one stands on the glacier oneself and looks at all that massive ice pressing down and rent by strange fissures. But we didn't want to remain too long on this slippery surface, since we were wearing neither crampons nor shoes with studs. Moreover, our soles had become worn down and slippery from the long climb.

The next day Goethe left Chamonix and Mont Blanc. The letters he wrote in the early days of November 1779 do not resound with Bourrit's passion for "the free air of the highlands and for the beauty of the eternal snows." It was not until much later that Goethe assimilated and used his impressions from this as well as his third trip to Switzerland. In *Faust*, for instance, he wrote:

The panorama around me is fast becoming a paradise.
Look up! The gigantic mountain peaks are
Already proclaiming the most solemn hour.
They are privileged to bask in the eternal light
Before its rays fall upon us who remain below.

On November 6, 1779, Michel Paccard and his nephew Téssac led the gentlemen over the Col de Balme to Martinach/Martigny in the Valais. These aristocrats must have been very good walkers to have crossed this somewhat rugged terrain in only one day, especially since it was by then the beginning of November, when days were short to begin with. One week later, on November 13, Goethe arrived for the second time at the rebuilt monastery of the Capuchine monks on the Gotthard. (He had visited them for the first time in 1775.) The weather was bitter cold. Three years before, an avalanche had severely damaged the monks' residence. On January 14, 1780, the traveling party arrived in Weimar.

A selection of Goethe's travel descriptions, entitled "Letters from a Journey to the Gotthard," appeared in 1796 in the *Horen,* a periodical edited by Schiller.

Considered in the context of Goethe's total work, the "Letters from Switzerland, Part II" make a significant contribution toward an understanding of the poet as a human being. (Unfortunately, a note to the Berlin edition contains an error in Alpine history: it declares that de Saussure was the first man to climb Mont Blanc.)

As is now well known, the first men to have stood on the summit of Mont Blanc on August 8, 1786, were Jacques Balmat and Dr. Michel Gabriel Paccard, who had been practicing medicine in the town of Chamonix since 1783.

But then, perhaps Johann Wolfgang von Goethe might have been the first to reach the summit had these two skillful men, Paccard and Balmat, been there seven years earlier to guide him to the top and had the great man from Frankfurt and his companion, the Duke of Weimar, only reached the Chamonix Valley earlier, in July or August rather than in November of the year 1779. The year 1779 must have been a good year for mountain climbing, when one considers the fact that snow had not yet fallen upon the lower reaches of the Mer de Glace even as late as November. Johann Wolfgang von Goethe, just thirty years old, must certainly have felt challenged to climb Mont Blanc—less because he wanted to test or prove his physical powers in an athletic sense but rather because he yearned to satisfy his interest in the natural sciences.

One wonders how Alpine climbing might have developed had Goethe really arrived in Chamonix in August 1779—and not three months too late! □

Fritz Moravec

Selections from a Gallery of Greats

Mountain climbing means many things to many people. For some, climbing represents a search for experience; for others, it is a means of recuperating. Still others climb in order to test and measure their own physical and psychological capabilities. For mountain guides, climbing is a responsible profession that one can practice close to nature. Only recently has it been regarded as a competitive sport.

Many reports about climbers' experiences in the mountains focus on the difficulties of the particular climb. Since the 1920s, climbs have been measured on the basis of a fixed and ascending scale of difficulty. The endless controversy that has surrounded this scale demonstrates that it is not without its problems. Ultimately, climbing is not measurable—on this point the experts agree. A cliff in clear, dry weather presents quite different difficulties from those encountered during rainstorms or under fog, snow, or ice conditions. Since climbing is not measurable, a list of the world's greatest climbers is also meaningless. However, in surveying the great and most extreme climbs that have taken place in the history of mountaineering, one is able to put together a portrait gallery of "greats" who have made exemplary contributions in many ways. It does not matter whether their climbs took place in the Alps or in higher mountains upward of 4,000 meters (13,123 feet), where terrible weather and thin air significantly diminish the climber's physical strength. To put it slightly differently, a consideration of a selection of outstanding climbers can serve as a history of Alpinism itself. Men such as Whymper, Zsigmondy, Preuss, or Dülfer significantly influenced the development of Alpine climbing: first, because of their remarkable climbs; second, because of the knowledge they were able to bring back and give to others.

Experts disagree as to how long the so-called golden age of Alpinism lasted. Everyone agrees, however, that the period of the first great climbs ended in 1865 with Whymper's first successful ascent of the Matterhorn. Various dates are given for the beginning of this period. The year 1855 is often cited, because in the following ten years more than half of the highest Alpine summits were conquered. For other historians, the founding of the British Alpine Society in 1857 is so important that they date the period of the first great climbs from then. The year 1851 has also been regarded as a starting point, and with some justification. That year an Englishman by the name of Albert Richard Smith appeared in the Egyptian Hall in London to give a lecture entitled "The Story of Mont Blanc." His vivid descriptions set against a background of mountain scenery and accompanied by many illustrations of typical Alpine activities aroused great enthusiasm. For six years he publicized the Great White Mountain. Even Queen Victoria heard him lecture once.

Smith was the first lecturer who actually influenced the British to visit the Western Alps. At a time when most people regarded this region not only as remote but also as mystical and dangerous, Smith concentrated on its beauties.

A few incidents from the life of Albert Smith will help to make this Alpine pioneer more real. Already as a small child, he was obsessed with nature. Stones talked to him and he imagined the wildest storms. He could tell very dramatic stories about violent weather. His sister was his first listener.

Albert's father intended that he become a surgeon. But when Smith first saw Mont Blanc in 1838, he was so overcome by this massif that he decided to study in Paris in order to be near "his" mountain. The primary purpose of Smith's first lecture on Mont Blanc was to reveal this world to his fellow countrymen; however, he also wanted to earn the 2,437 francs that would enable him to finance his own expedition to Mont Blanc. This was the amount an ascent would cost. Smith lectured for years about Mont Blanc—about its rock formations, glaciers, dangers, flora, and fauna. He also spoke about climbing equipment and climbing techniques, although he himself had only been able to admire the highest mountain in the Alps from the perspective of the valley. Finally, in 1851, he stood on the top of the mountain of his dreams. When he died at the age of forty-two, he left his heirs a legacy of thirty thousand pounds earned from his lectures and publications.

A guided climb to the top of Mont Blanc cost a great deal of money. Only people of substance, such as scientists,

theologians, and lawyers, could afford it. In order to be admitted as a member of the highly respected Alpine Society, it was first necessary to meet a prerequisite: to have climbed a peak over 4,000 meters (13,000 feet). This was an expensive prerequisite. The British Alpine Society did not want to become part of a popular mass movement, as did later Alpine societies in Europe. The English club also did not feel that it was its mission to contribute to the exploration of the Alps. The loosely organized British society was simply there to permit those who felt a special interest in the Alps to meet once a year in order to gather information, exchange thoughts and experiences, and get to know one another. In the European Alpine societies, whole groups met frequently to discuss only one topic: mountain climbing.

Without devaluing the first ascent of Mont Blanc, I believe that the "Story of the Matterhorn" played an even more important role in popularizing mountains and mountain climbing. The tenacious struggle to conquer this pyramid-shaped rock awakened worldwide response. The first group of climbers were John Tyndall, Thomas Stuart Kennedy, Jean Antoine Carrel, and Edward Whymper. Whymper, who was not a professional mountaineer, was the central figure on the climb and the only one to reach the top. A skilled wood-carver, he had developed an artistic gift for painting in watercolor. The London publisher, William Longman, needed sketches from the Dauphine, from Mont Pelvoux. This was the way Whymper first became acquainted with mountains.

During his first visit to the Nikolai Valley (1860), he collected material for a planned volume, *Guide to Zermatt*. A year later he, too, fell under the spell of the Matterhorn. All in all, he made eight attempts to conquer it. He fell and was seriously injured during one solo climb. Nevertheless, he continued to pursue but one single goal: the conquest of the Matterhorn. His willpower was coupled with enormous egoism. At about this time, however, a wave of protest against mountain climbing broke out in England. Queen Victoria actually asked her Lord Chamberlain if such a dangerous activity could not be banned by law.

During the past hundred years, the idea of banning mountain climbing altogether has often been discussed, and there are many instances where it actually was forbidden by law. However, these restrictions were not founded in legal principles and, since they irrationally narrowed personal freedom, they eventually had to be revoked. Three examples come to mind. Shortly after the turn of the century, a climber fell to his death from the Raxalpe. At that point, the authorities in Vienna-Neustadt forbade anyone to climb the rock walls of this gigantic hellish valley. As an immediate reaction to this edict, three climbers from Vienna scaled the walls and opened the route, which was considered very difficult at the time, for the future. At the end of the 1920s, the authorities in Mödling closed the Mizzi-Langer Wall, a practice cliff in the Vienna Woods, which was used by everyone in Vienna who wanted to learn how to climb. After the Eiger catastrophe, authorities in the city of Berne considered closing off this "wall of death" to climbers. Once, for a short period of time, the climbing of the north wall of the Eiger was a punishable offense.

In the summer of 1868, Edward Whymper climbed the Matterhorn, together with his guide Jean Antoine Carrel of Valtournanche. Whymper's reconciliation with his mighty opponent, the Matterhorn, was certainly one of the few bright spots in his life. The climbing team of Whymper and Carrel endured. Twelve years later, they succeeded in climbing the highest peak in Ecuador, the Chimborazo. No matter what Whymper did, he was always criticized. People were particularly jealous when he was commissioned by the Canadian Pacific Railway to follow its route across North America and describe it in words and pictures. Everyone begrudged the wood-carver and artist this opportunity.

Today no one is disturbed when illustrated magazines capitalize on spectacular Alpine achievements. But when the athlete himself is paid for an extraordinary climb, people hold it against him. They do not consider how hard he had to train and how much money his preparation may have cost.

There seems to be a double standard, too. Everyone is used to the fact that Niki Lauda's racing costume looks like an advertising billboard. Yet, he risks his life in every car race. On the other hand, when Toni Hiebeler succeeded in scaling the north wall of the Eiger in the winter and generated publicity for this achievement, many thought he had acted dishonorably. Many in climbing circles also sneered when Reinhold Messner sold reports about his great Alpine achievements to illustrated magazines, when he traded his ideas for cash. Why should there be different standards for car racing than for mountain climbing? One would hope that the debate as to whether climbing is a sport or more than a sport has by now been laid to rest. Many demands are made on Alpine climbers who are out to set records or achieve new breakthroughs. But the news media lionize a single climber for just so long—just as long as he is successful!

Is not mountain climbing always being measured by standards different from those that prevail in other sports?

Why do people take it amiss when Reinhold Messner, one of the world's most successful mountain climbers, makes money by testing climbing equipment? At the Alpine Congress of 1977, when Messner was accosted on the subject, he replied: "I am not a professional mountain climber but a free-lance Alpinist. Through my various activities I earn the money I need to live on as well as the means with which to finance new expeditions." I was particularly impressed by Messner's proud and self-confident statement: "I would like to remain free and independent. Therefore, I refuse to be subsidized by Alpine Societies or other institutes."

Back to Whymper: at the age of 66, he wanted to brighten his last years by embarking on a happy married life. Perhaps because there was too great an age difference between husband and wife, this marriage became yet another burden for him and was dissolved within four years. He experienced no further high points in his life. The rest of his days were spent traveling back and forth between Chamonix and Zermatt, and it was in Chamonix that he died. He had rejected doctors and medicine and wanted to be alone in his last hour.

One ought to eliminate the word *victory* from Alpine terminology, for no man can conquer a mountain; at most he can conquer himself. If there was really a victor in "the battle for the Matterhorn," then it was the town of Zermatt. Within a few years, this quiet mountain village was turned into a center for tourism. The hotel king Seiler was largely responsible for this change. However, four human beings died on the descent from the Matterhorn. If Whymper and his companions had not been bound by a hemp rope but by a modern UIAA-tested synthetic one, which is supposed to bear the weight of nine men should they fall, there probably would have been seven deaths. I ask myself how the public and the press would have reacted to an Alpine catastrophe of this dimension. Would the climbing of high mountains have been condemned forever? Would governments have forbidden mountain climbing altogether because of the horror of so many deaths? Or would mountain climbing have become all the more interesting, given the possibility of such sensational accidents?

The hundredth anniversary of the first ascent of the Matterhorn was commemorated with an outdoor sound and light show as well as a television special. Searchlights illuminated the mountain, and the first historical climb was simulated. The terrible fall from the Matterhorn could only be presented as a spoken text. I myself had read the original report of the accident in the Munich *Allgemeine*

Zeitung of August 4, 1865. The report, describing how the bodies were found, was much less reticent than the sound and light show of one hundred years later:

> After a two-hour march through a landscape of a thousand dangers, Whymper and the search party finally reached the small plateau where the catastrophe had come to an end. Traces of blood, several human hands, scraps of clothing as well as the torn rope were discovered scattered about. . . . Twelve steps further on they came upon a flattened skull pierced by a diagonal bone that must have been the jawbone. A hand and forearm protruded through another pile of human remains. They identified the rough hand of the guide Croz by an old scar. They also discovered a fragment of his trousers. In the pocket was a wallet with six gold pieces and a rosary. The beads had been completely crushed. In another place the scattered remains of a third human being lay strewn about. These belonged to the unfortunate Hadow, as Whymper was able to tell from a few scraps of clothing and some beard fragments. Attempts to find the body of the fourth victim, young Lord Francis Douglas, were fruitless. Probably his body remained hanging on a jagged ledge.

Given a report like this, I had grave doubts about the propriety of the sound and light show.

After the first climb of the Matterhorn, which is considered a feat of "high Alpinism," the period of "difficult Alpinism" began. The goal was now no longer to conquer hitherto unclimbed high mountains but rather to seek out difficult routes.

During this period, climbers sought self-confirmation in objectively difficult regions. They took joy in danger for its own sake. During the first phase, guides were assumed to be a necessary part of every climb. Now the idea of ascending quite alone began to attract many followers. The motto of liberalism, "freedom for the individual," was now applied to mountain climbing. The Brenva flank of Mont Blanc and the Aiguilles of Chamonix were much sought-after goals. These were followed by several extremely dangerous ascents: the east face of the Monte Rosa, the north face of the Ortler, and the Pallavicini Gorge on the Grossglockner. At this time, a route was also found up the longest ascent in the East Alps: the east wall of the Watzmann. In the Sexten Dolomites, free climbs up cone-shaped rock cliffs were made, sometimes ranging in difficulty through Grade XII. Swarms of European climbers also began to seek out more distant mountain ranges. The Caucasus were relatively accessible, and in 1868 the English climbers Douglas Freshfield and C. C. Tucker reached the summits of the Elbrus and then of the Kasbek Mountains in the company of their French guide François Dévouassaud.

In the Eastern Alps, the practice of climbing without guides was dictated at first by financial necessity.

Although initially criticized, this new form of experiencing the mountains in solitude soon became the gospel of climbers in other Alpine regions. Many of the great climbers, such as the Swiss Johann Jakob Weilenmann and the legendary English climber Albert Frederick Mummery, who had once climbed only with guides, now became pioneers in climbing alone. Both in word and deed, they supported this higher form of experience. Mummery was the first to climb to the Zmuttgrat on the Matterhorn. His other "firsts" were the Grands Charmoz, the Aiguille du Grepon, and the Teufelsgrat ("Devil's Ridge") of the Täschhorn. He failed only once. This was in the year 1880 when he made an attempt to ascend the giant tooth of Mont Blanc, the Dent du Géant. At the place where he turned back, he said: "Absolutely inaccessible by fair means." These words have become the gospel for those climbers who for ethical reasons have rejected all technical assistance. Many attempts were made to climb the Dent du Géant, and many were quite peculiar. In 1875, French and Italian Alpinists attempted to shoot a rope over the gigantic tooth. Gusts of wind hindered the success of this effort. In 1882, the Sella brothers and their guides Daniel and Jean Joseph Maquignaz managed to reach the top of the Dent du Géant for the first time, although with the aid of ropes and iron pegs. Eighteen years later, a "pure" ascent up this rock obelisk was finally achieved by three climbers from Vienna: Thomas Maischberger, Heinrich Pfannl, and Franz Zimmer.

"Going it alone" introduced a new style into Alpinism, an even more intense way of experiencing the mountains. One of the most successful and daring guideless climbers was Baron Hermann von Barth. He had two professions: geology and law. His love of nature led him to study mineralogy. His legal mind revealed itself in the precise and systematic manner in which he set about exploring the Berchtesgaden, Chiemgau, and Allgäu Alps, as well as the Karwendels. He wrote several guidebooks to these areas and was, in general, an extremely skilled polemicist. He was fond of formulating his ideas in graphic phrases: "I refused to be dragged to the next summit like a calf on a rope."

Hermann von Barth represented the Langemarck ideology of Alpinism: he glorified the idea of death in the mountains. Once when his climbing stick slid away and fell over the edge of a cliff, he called after it: "Whoever comes with me has to be prepared to die." In his belief that mountain climbing represents a conscious search for dangers and a game of life and death, Barth was outdone only by the Viennese high school teacher Eugen Guido Lammer, who felt that man's confrontation with death in the mountains was the sweetest of all possible pleasures. In 1887, Lammer and August Lorria started up the west face of the Matterhorn. An avalanche swept them into the depths. Although Lammer was seriously injured, he later described this incident as follows: "I made this gruesome flight in a fully conscious state. And so I can report to you, my friends, it is a beautiful death. A needle prick hurts more than a fall from a mountain."

Lammer was masterful in his use of the ice axe, but he was just as masterful in his use of the pen and vigorously defended his activities. His book, *Fountain of Youth*, which is a collection of essays, is still considered to be one of the most significant works of Alpine literature. Lammer was an expert on rock and ice. Among his great climbs are the first ascent of the northwest face of the Grossvenedig, a traverse of the Mönch and the Schreckhorn, and solitary climbs of the Weisshorn and the Zinal-Rothorn.

A team made up of the Viennese brothers Emil and Otto Zsigmondy and Ludwig Purtscheller of Salzburg set out to solve some of the most difficult problems in the East and West Alps. They resolved most of them. The highly accomplished Purtscheller was also a much sought-after partner for assaults upon non-European mountains. In 1891 he accompanied Gottfried Merzbacher to the Caucasus, and in 1889 he climbed the highest summit of the Kilimanjaro massif, the Kibo, together with Hans Meyer. He was just as capable on rock as he was on ice, and during his career he reached the summits of more than 1,700 peaks in the Alps. He dedicated all his free time to mountain climbing. Nevertheless, he made it a point to encourage young people to discover the Alpine experience. To the company of mountain climbers everywhere, he left his guidebook, *A Tourist in the High Alps*.

As children, the Zsigmondy brothers hiked through the mountains that they later climbed. At a very young age, they were the first to climb the Feldkopf in the Alps of the Ziller Valley. This achievement made them famous. It was simply inconceivable for them ever to climb up a mountain attached by a rope to a guide. The stages of their climbing career may be traced by citing a few of their major achievements: the Kleine Zinne and the Croda da Lago; the east face of the Monte Rosa; the Zmuttgrat of the Matterhorn. Without guides, they conquered the cliffs and ice of the Western Alps, which had first been opened up by English climbers. After having succeeded in traversing the Meije together with Purtscheller, Emil Zsigmondy fell to his death on its south face—only days before his twenty-fourth birthday. Once again a tear in a rope caused the death of a young man.

That Emil Zsigmondy was a very sensitive storyteller is clear from the descriptions of his climbs in his book *In the High Mountains*. His teaching manual, *The Dangers of the Alps*, written with scientific thoroughness, has survived all the changing currents of Alpinism. Wilhelm Paulcke and Helmut Dumler have recently put out a new edition of the book, so that it now contains the most up-to-date scientific knowledge in the field. But its fundamental concept has remained unchanged. Zsigmondy wrote this first Alpine teaching manual at the age of twenty-three. He thereby became the spokesman of a humane concern: survival in the mountains, safety in the mountains.

Another eighty-three years had to pass before a second book of this type appeared. The Italian Gianni Mazzenga had lost a young friend in the mountains. This stirred him with a desire to help find a way to prevent fatal accidents. After an analysis of a whole series of disasters, he came to the conclusion that many of the deaths could have been avoided had the unfortunate climber and his teammate possessed even the most rudimentary knowledge of how to save themselves. His book *Safety in the Mountains*, written as a technical manual and founded upon concrete evidence, became a breviary for safety on rock walls.

The Austrian Paul Preuss has been more highly honored abroad than in his own country. The Italians have named the Kleinste Zinne the "Torre Preuss." The free-climbing movement, which has returned to the Alps from American centers of climbing, regards him as its guiding spirit. Finally, an Italian named Severino Casara, a lawyer from Vicenza, has written a biography of the climber, although he was not one of his contemporaries. A passionate admirer of Preuss, Casara first sought out all the places where Preuss had lived. After countless investigations, he drew together in his book everything worth knowing about this Austrian mountaineer.

Paul Preuss was born in Altaussee, grew up in Vienna, and studied in Munich. However, because of his insistence upon climbing "by fair means" only, he is said to belong to the Viennese School. While climbing alone on the north edge of the Manndlkogel in the Dachstein massif, he fell to his death. He was only twenty-seven years old. The irony was that he had already surmounted the most difficult part of this route. Within the space of a few years, he had managed to stand on more than 1,200 summits. His most significant "firsts" were the south face of the Grohmannspitze, the northeast wall of the Crozzon di Brenta, and the east wall of the Guglia di Brenta. The one aspect of Paul Preuss that is not generally known is that he was ahead of his times in his thoughts and wishes. For example, he realized the importance of training in preparation for a difficult climb. He underwent a substantial period of training before setting out to cross the entire Peuterey Ridge, including the south ridge of the Noire. He completed parts of the route alone. It was only many years later, in 1953, that Richard Hechtel and his teammates completed the project.

Casara calls his book *Preuss: A Legendary Mountain Climber*. It is a remarkable and uncommonly lively book. The author comes to the conclusion that Paul Preuss was the greatest climber of all times, and he supports his argument with concrete evidence. Many other mountain climbers had also completed magnificent tours, he admitted. However, Preuss alone had also mastered the most difficult degrees of rock climbing possible in his day and also without the aid of technical help. Citing the eyewitness reports of others, Casara adds that Preuss was not merely a good and capable climber, but that his movements were also harmonious. He appeared able to overcome difficulties without any effort.

Paul Preuss never used a piton in his life, and he even rejected the use of ropes. He firmly believed that every climber must be able to descend freely from each place he managed to reach in his ascent. He entered into a hot and very passionate debate over the question of using technological aids with the Munich School, particularly with the great technologist Hans Dülfer. However, it should be added here that this professional exchange of opinion in no way tarnished the personal friendship that existed between Preuss and Dülfer. Even Paul Preuss's strongest critics recognized his technical mastery, although they thought that some of his efforts were a bit mad. Paul Preuss was not only a climber, not just one who saw the mountains as merely a scaffold for some personal ascent. He possessed a deep feeling for nature, which is also why he chose to become a botanist. His childhood friend Alexander Hartwig wrote about Preuss: "His relationship to the mountains was quite different from that which prevailed among the other great Alpinists of his time. Battling, storming, conquering cliffs, smashing gaps into ramparts, winning, triumphing, scorning death—all these words and phrases taken from the language of war were totally foreign to his nature."

As Paul Preuss was simple in life, so he loved mountains simply. Mountain climbing was for him a simple and self-explanatory activity. And we mean here climbing in the highest sense, that is, overcoming the greatest difficulties by expending on rock and ice the greatest possible efforts. He climbed mountains as naturally as birds fly and fish swim. Whoever saw him climbing knew that here a young man was experiencing a pure naive joy in exercising a treasured natural gift. His climbing could best be compared with dancing: it appeared light and effortless, tinged with happiness. Elegance, absolute sincerity, inner freedom, and a total lack of unnatural inhibition characterize Preuss's every movement. Every movement revealed the dancing gaiety of his soul.

Was Paul Preuss, the climber, a genius? This is not a controversial subject today and can be left for discussion to those who are more expert in these matters than I. At any rate, in everyday life he was a simple, happy, and lovable man. I do not believe he had a single enemy. He was ready to take part in every kind of practical joke and remained a happy boy until the early years of his manhood. He kept extraordinarily busy in his profession and possessed an astonishing store of Alpine knowledge. All this helped him to develop into a successful and influential writer and lecturer. In the few years in which he was recognized as the best Alpinist of his time, he enjoyed an international reputation such as had not been the lot of any Austrian climber since Purtscheller.

But Paul Preuss, the model for generations of young climbers and the noblest representative of the Vienna School, exhibited one aesthetic flaw: his Jewish parents. It is for this reason that his name is only peripherally mentioned in Edward Pichl's book on Viennese climbers, which appeared in 1927. Does his ancestry continue to exercise an adverse effect even today? *Preuss: L'Alpinista Leggendario* has not yet found a single German publisher!

Hans Carl Heidrich writes in his book, *The Alps: Centuries of Adventure:* "Paul Preuss, a well-known solo climber not only rejected every aid in climbing as being unsportsmanlike but also rejected the presence of women in Alpinism." Preuss's so-called hostility to women has been denied by a female contemporary. Emmi Eisenreich, who had undertaken many extremely difficult tours with Preuss, told me: "Young Preuss was very charming and he admired women greatly." Casara, who describes several delightful episodes with women in his book, characterizes Preuss as a "cavalier of the mountain world."

Paul Preuss interpreted Mummery's precepts very strictly. Hans Dülfer, the master climber and inventor of many rope maneuvers, expanded upon them. Nevertheless, Preuss too supports the standpoint that safety is the highest commandment to be obeyed in mountain climbing. The presupposition for every climb is self-awareness, self-control, and knowledge of one's limits. He had good relationships with all the great mountain climbers of his day, such as Piaz, Leuchs, and Vallepiana. As noted above, Dülfer was also his friend. But when it came to the question of pitons, Paul Preuss knew no compromise. Preuss felt that these metal spikes not only revealed the weakness of the climber but also desecrated nature. In Preuss's view, the use of pitons represented such a virulent attack on nature that it was tantamount to cowardly stabbing the mountain in the back. This perspective quickly spread throughout Viennese climbing circles.

Munich was another center of Alpinism. The name of the high school student Georg Winkler deserves first place among the rock climbers of the period. Together with Alois Zott, he reached the western summit of Sass Maor in 1886 and a year later succeeded in being the first to climb the Vajolett tower, which today bears his name. Georg Winkler and Emil Zsigmondy also served as models for Paul Preuss.

The development of mountain climbing was abruptly broken off by World War I. In the Dolomites, the war was particularly merciless in winter. Many more soldiers (forty to seventy thousand) died in avalanches than from enemy fire. After the war, climbers gathered again in Munich and north Italy. They did not come together in Austria until much later.

Emil Solleder was one of the first to pit himself against the great faces. With Fritz Weissner, he climbed the north wall of the Furchetta and with Gustav Lettenbauer the northwest wall of the Civetta. Both ascents took place in 1925. The mighty northwest wall of the Civetta was at that time classified as the most difficult face in the Dolomites. Solleder's other successes are the east face of Sass Maor, the north face of the Rosengartenspitze, and the north face of Pala di San Martino. When Solleder stood beneath the 220-meter (722-foot) overhanging north face of the Grosse Zinne, he mused: "In a few years, someone else will probably come along who is even crazier than the rest of us. He will be the one to conquer this wall." Eight years later, in 1933, the mountain guides Emilio Comici from Trieste and Angelo and Giuseppe Dimai from Cortina d'Ampezzo found a route up the wall. They spent three days on this steep slope and used a great deal of equipment. In the Wilder Kaiser, the principal domain of Munich climbers, the most difficult rock climbs were executed, as well as in the Wetterstein range and in the Karwendels. Willi Welzenbach, Eugen Allwein, Willi Merkl, Alfred Drexel, and Karl Wien had specialized in the most extreme forms of ice climbing as well as in tours requiring a combination of various techniques. In 1924,

Willi Welzenbach and Fritz Rigele introduced a new phase into climbing, with their successful ascent of the northwest wall of the Wiesbachhorn: ice pitons were used for the first time on this great hump of ice. This method of forging one's way up extremely steep passages of ice with the aid of technical devices was soon employed in the Western Alps. The age of ice climbing was born.

The worldwide economic crisis and mass unemployment caused many climbers to take refuge in the mountains. It was a time of mountain "bums," and Hans Ertl, Anderl Heckmair, Franz and Toni Schmid, Sepp Brunhuber, Hans Schwanda, Hubert Peterka, Richard Reinagl, and Fritz Kasparek were typical representatives of this type. During the pioneer period of Alpinism, which was identical with the golden age of great guides, only wealthy individuals were able to climb mountains. Academics, civil servants of lesser rank, and students began to climb when dependence upon guides was abandoned. Now, in this period of economic depression, it was mainly members of the working class who accomplished the greatest feats in Alpinism. This was especially true in German-speaking countries.

It is impossible in this short survey to name every climber who contributed pioneer work to this field. A few will have to represent the many whose feats have been inscribed in the Golden Book of Alpinism. The goal of the 1930s was to solve the three great problems of the Alps. The brothers Franz and Toni Schmid cycled to Zermatt. In an effort to remain unnoticed, they secretly climbed the 1,100-meter (3,609 foot) north wall of the Matterhorn, and just as secretly they intended to cycle home again after their climb. But they were discovered and given a fitting celebration. Although a few German teams had joined in the struggle for the summit of the Walker Pillar of the Grandes Jorasses, it was finally conquered by the Italian climbers Riccardo Cassin, Gino Esposito, and Ugo Tizzoni. The gloomy, repelling 1,800-meter (5,905 foot) north face of the Eiger had claimed eight lives before Anderl Heckmair, Ludwig Vörg, Heinrich Harrer, and Fritz Kasparek succeeded in reaching the summit after a very dramatic climb.

The dreary economic situation as well as severe Swiss restrictions on entry visas (which lasted until 1950) forced the Austrian and German climbers to turn their attention to mountains in their own countries. The extremely difficult Dachl-Rosskuppe cutoff was conquered, as were the north face of the Lalidererspitze in the Karwendels, the west face of the Predigtstuhl in the Wilder Kaiser, and the southeast wall of the Schüsselkar in the Wetterstein massif.

Peter Aschenbrenner, Hias Rebitsch, Wastl Mariner, and Kuno Rainer from Innsbruck made many first ascents of Alpine summits in western Austria. Hermann Buhl from the Tyrol came somewhat later. Always reaching out for the most difficult feats, he quickly succeeded in conquering Nanga Parbat in what is now regarded as a legendary solo climb.

Swiss, French, and Italian climbers took the initiative in the Western Alps and in the Dolomites. The conquest of the west face and the southwest wall of the Petit Aiguille du Dru and the Grand Capuchin were highly regarded in climbing circles. The first climb of the northwest cutoff of the Cima su Alto in the Dolomites may be included on the list of epoch-making climbs of the period. A further goal was the constant search for a "direttissima," a direct ascent in the line of a falling drop of liquid!

In 1958, the Saxons Lothar Brandler, Dieter Hasse, Jörg Lehne, and Siegfried Löw attempted to trace such an ideal path up the north face of the Grosse Zinne: the first direttissima was celebrated. It was also condemned. The object of controversy was the use of hooks that had to be bored into the rock or ice. Now there was no longer anything "impossible," even in the realm of so-called extreme climbing. These four climbers from the Elbsandstein Mountains had proved that even overhanging smooth walls could be mastered. Five years later it was again Saxons who discovered a yet more direct route up the north face of the Grosse Zinne. In deepest winter, a seventeen-day battle of equipment took place for mastery of a "super-direttissima." Nevertheless, these new routes that were opened up with the aid of technological devices demanded less skill in free climbing than had the first ascents in the Dolomites. The southeast face of the Kleinste Zinne, the western Zinne north wall, and the southeast edge of the Torre Trieste (which Riccardo Cassin and his teammates had climbed between 1934 and 1935) all demonstrated characteristics typical of the sixth level of difficulty.

When one thinks of progress, of expanding the limits of extreme climbing, the first name that comes to mind is that of the Italian Walter Bonatti. It is well-known that he introduced the modern technique of piton-climbing into the Western Alps, a technique that had first been developed in the Dolomites. One of his landmark climbs was the east wall of the Grand Capuchin. He next climbed sixth-degree routes in winter, both in the Dolomites and in the Western Alps. He proved how much he could rely on his own abilities by undertaking these extremely difficult climbs alone. He took part in the successful Italian K2 expedition. He stood upon the summit of Gasherbrum IV. His solo climb up the north face of the Matterhorn in winter by a new route was probably the high point in his climbing career. It was also Bonatti's last climb.

For the thirty-five-year-old Walter Bonatti, the climb in winter of the north face of the Matterhorn represented a voluntary farewell to his career as a climber. The younger generation of "extreme mountain climbers" now begin their careers on the gigantic walls in winter. At the age of twenty-one, Alessandro Gogna climbed the north face of the Matterhorn and a year later, also under extreme conditions in winter, the north face of the Grandes Jorasses. At the beginning of 1978, the guide Yvan Ghirardini conquered all the most famous north faces of the Alps in winter and alone.

Beyond the Alps, the Englishman Chris Bonington and the South Tyrolean Reinhold Messner have set new standards for climbing all the mountains of the earth. Bonington's most spectacular achievement was the bitter and dramatic struggle for the Ogre summit in the Karakoram. Reinhold Messner with his companion Peter Habeler demonstrated Western Alpine style in its most perfected form on the Hidden Peak in the Karakoram. Messner is one of the best known and most publicized mountain climbers of today.

□

18

19
At the age of 17, Georg Winkler climbed the needle of rock which was later to bear his name. This high school student from Munich climbed one peak after another in the Dolomites, in the "Wilder Kaiser," and in the Valais. On August 16, 1888 after only four summers of intensive climbing, he was buried by an avalanche at the foot of the Weisshorn in the Valais. His body was not recovered from the ice until seventy years later.

18
The Vajolett needles of the Rosengarten group of the Dolomites soar aloft above the living larches, pines, and spruces like giant conifers of rock: wrapped in legends of King Laurin's realm, fantastic formations,

challenging spires of stone! The three south needles of the Vajolett group (of which there are six in all) are named Delago, Stabeler, and Winkler after the daring mountaineers who first climbed them.

Numerous routes traverse the flanks and edges of the Vajolett needles. But hardly anyone who today climbs the Winkler Needle knows anything about the young man who gave the rock its name.

20/21

Franz and Toni Schmid rode their bikes from Munich to Zermatt, arriving at the foot of the Matterhorn in the summer of 1931. Toni (22 years old) and Franz (26, left) wanted to climb the north face to the summit. They reached the top during a thunderstorm. The conquest of the north face of the Matterhorn was the first of three problems which still awaited resolution in the Alps.

In numerous books and journals, all the climbers of the period discussed the difficulties and how they could best be solved. The three problems were the north faces of the Eiger and the Matterhorn and the north wall of the Grandes Jorasses. The Schmid brothers were experienced, well-coordinated rock climbers. Having cycled to Zermatt in five days, they now climbed to the summit over snow, ice, and crumbling cliffs, constantly endangered by landslides. Even today many who reach the Hörnligrat shudder when they gaze over into the shadows of the north face.

22/23

In the 1930s mountaineers were dedicated to solving the remaining problems in the Alps: conquering high rock faces and great stone needles, crossing yet untraversed ridges. The Italian climber Riccardo Cassin (23), probably the most outstanding member of the "Ragni di Lecco" (a rock climber's guild known after 1946 as "the Spiders") achieved one of the most important successes of the period. Together with his comrades Ugo Tizzoni and Gino Esposito, Cassin reached the highest point in the Grandes Jorasses, Pointe Walker [4,208 meters (13,805 feet)], by way of a sharp spur 1,200 meters (3,936 feet) high, the Walker Pillar (22, center left). They spent three days and two nights on these rocks and ice. Twenty-five years later, in January 1963, the Italian climber Walter Bonatti and his partner Cosimo Zapelli were the first to climb the Walker Pillar in winter. Forty years after the first successful assault, yet another Italian mountaineer, Alessandro Gogna, ascended the Walker Pillar alone.

24

25

24/25

Ludwig Vörg, Anderl Heckmair, Fritz Kasparek, and Heinrich Harrer (25, left to right), the first conquerors of the north face of the Eiger were honored like heroes in the summer of 1938. This 1,800-meter (5,905-foot) wall of crumbling wet rock, covered with patches of ice, became known as "the wall of death." This conquest had significance for others than those who belonged to the small circle of mountaineers. The four climbers met near the foot of the Eiger to tackle the summit in a joint effort. For the political leadership of Germany, the successful climb was a welcome coincidence: July 1938 was a bare three months after the annexation of Austria. Now two Germans (Heckmair and Vörg) had conquered the most difficult route in the Alps with two climbers from the eastern frontier districts of the Reich (Harrer and Kasparek). This was reason enough to celebrate the four men who themselves were surprised by all the fanfare. Two of them are still alive: Heckmair, born in 1906, is still a passionate hiker; Harrer, born in 1912, is a well-known researcher and world traveler. Vörg died during World War II (1941) at the age of thirty. Kasparek, born in 1910, fell to his death in the Andes in 1954. The north face of the Eiger continues to challenge young climbers. Many of them have lost their lives there.

26/27/28

Annapurna I: the first 8,000-meter (26,245-foot) mountain to be climbed. Named after the goddess of nourishment and plenty, known respectively as Kali (the "black") or Durga (the "inaccessible" goddess) as well as Parvati ("the daughter of the mountain"), the Annapurna massif embraces several summits which drop off sharply to the south and dominate the landscape (26) with eternal ice and snow. Standing in the south, the view extends northwest past Gurkha and on to the massif.

In 1950 when the Kingdom of Nepal opened its borders to the West, a French expedition under the leadership of Maurice Herzog set out to conquer the north flank of the mountain. The team proceeded along the Kali Gandaki, regarded as the deepest gorge in the world [7,000 meters (22,965 feet)] and situated between Dhaulagiri to the west and Annapurna to the east. Since a mere thirty kilometers separated these two giants, the expedition turned its attention to Annapurna after an unsuccessful attempt to find a route to the summit of Dhaulagiri. On July 3, 1950 Maurice Herzog (27) and Louis Lachenal stood on the summit, the first men to have conquered a peak of over 8,000 meters (ca. 26,250-feet). Their clothing was inadequate for the bitter cold of these heights. The long descent through mountain storms, exacerbated by insufficient oxygen, so enervated the two climbers that they succumbed to severe frostbite. The team's doctor had to amputate frozen fingers and toes while the expedition was still encamped on the mountain. In a highly dramatic fashion the two critically ill men were carried off the mountain by Sherpas. The maneuver took nearly two weeks.

29

unset on the summit of an
,000-meter (ca. 26,250 feet)
eak in the Karakorum: the
hadows of night are
escending. The man on the
ummit of Broad Peak is
lermann Buhl. The picture
vas taken by Kurt
Diemberger at about seven
'clock on the evening of
une 9, 1957. The two
nountaineers belonged to a
mall expedition of four
vho, toward the end of the
limb, had to carry their
wn equipment and supplies
y themselves. The Balti
rters simply refused to go

on. Marcus Schmuck and
Fritz Wintersteller reached
the summit first. They were
joined a short while later by
Kurt Diemberger.
　Hermann Buhl (30), who
four years earlier had been
the first and only member of
the expedition to reach the
summit of Nanga Parbat,
met up with his teammates
below the summit of Broad
Peak as they were already
descending. Kurt
Diemberger returned to the
summit with Buhl, now the
first climber of two
8,000-meter peaks, and took

this impressive picture.
Three weeks later Buhl fell
to his death on the Chogolisa
when a snow-covered
cornice broke off during a
storm.
　Buhl's solo ascent of the
final 1,400 meters (ca. 4,600
feet) to the top of Nanga
Parbat is one of the most
impressive feats in alpine
history. The trip up and
back took forty hours. Buhl
had to spend an entire night
standing up, constantly
tormented by hallucinations
and tortured by cold and
hunger.

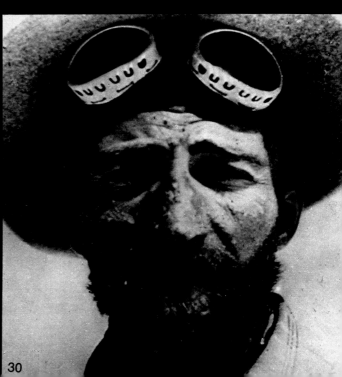

30

31

32

31/32

Footprints in the snows of
the Eiger summit: the first
winter ascent of the north
face, March 1961. Four
outstanding climbers spent
eight days and six nights on
the face before they
managed to reach the
sunlight of the summit
ridge. Toni Hiebeler (32,
right), Toni Kinshofer
(center), Anderl Mannhardt
(left), and Walter
Almberger accomplished

this highly esteemed feat
after long and thorough
preparation. Two years
later, in the summer of 1963,
Michel Darbellay of
Switzerland made the first
solo ascent and required
only one bivouac. In the
summer of 1964, the
German climber Werner
Bittner led the first woman
to the top of the Eiger. She
was Daisy Voog from
Munich.

33

33

Mont Blanc: the highest summit in the Alps. Though not a formidable landscape of rock and cliff, this snowy dome is nonetheless, at 4,807 meters (15,770 feet), the highest elevation in the Alps. It was climbed in August 1786 by a young doctor named Michel Paccard and his teammate Jacques Balmat, a crystal collector. The unpretentious Balmat became famous in Alpine history as the man credited with discovering a route to the summit. Many now believe that it was Michel Paccard who had investigated the possibilities and studied the route ultimately selected, carefully considering the dangers of sudden changes in weather as well as glacial crevasses. Countless routes and rock-climbing possibilities criss-cross the Mont Blanc massif. Needles (aiguilles), rock faces, ridges, and pillars provide one of the most varied climbing environments that nature has to offer. Less daring climbers can succeed here, too. The normal ascent of Mont Blanc proceeds along the Bosses Ridge (to the right of the summit). Mont Maudit [4,465 meters (14,648 feet)] lies to the left of Mont Blanc, separated from its neighbor by the Col de la Brenva (upper left). In the foreground, the Saussure aiguilles.

34

Walter Bonatti, an important alpinist, calls Mont Blanc, Monte Bianco, his friend. He has undertaken numerous tours of the greatest difficulty in this area.

One day in the winter of 1965 this perceptive Italian climber, truly one of the most extraordinary

members of an elite group of great mountaineers, decided to end his alpine career. Possessing a talent for rendering his experiences and observations into words and pictures, trained by years of climbing to make subtle distinctions, it was only natural that he would become a successful

reporter. He has traveled to the most remote places on earth to describe landscapes, people, and events. Although he has retired from climbing, he continues to visit mountain regions. Here, Walter Bonatti has climbed to one of the sources of the Amazon River, a small glacial lake

called Nino Cocha situated at the base of the Yarupa, located 4,796 meters (15,734 feet) above sea level. The lake is the source of the Rio Maranon which later feeds the great South American river.

35

36

Dhaulagiri: the Mont Blanc of the Himalayas. This was the last of the 8,000-meter (ca. 26,250-foot) Himalayan peaks to be conquered. In 1960 a Swiss expedition finally succeeded in reaching the summit by way of the northeast flank to the left (picture). The sole remaining challenge is Shisha Pangma in Tibet. Dhaulagiri is well known and feared for its bad weather. The mountain is a meeting place for cold air masses from the Tibetan mountains to the north and warm damp air which streams up from the south across the jungles of India. Snowstorms and avalanches have claimed the lives of many victims and have forced many expeditions to turn back ahead of schedule.

37

37

Many experts believed that it would be impossible to climb Mount Everest without supplementary oxygen, but in May 1978 Reinhold Messner climbed the highest mountain on earth without any technological assistance. His partner was Peter Habeler from the Ziller Valley, who had accompanied Messner on many extremely demanding climbs.

Messner was the first climber not only to have conquered four 8,000-meter (26,250-foot) giants but to have done so by way of difficult new routes or, as here on Everest, under extraordinary conditions.

Messner finances his climbs through his activities as a writer, photographer, and mountain cinematographer. His remarkable ability to give verbal expression to impressions and reflections makes Messner one of the most versatile and interesting mountain climbers of the present day.

36

The first human beings ever to enter the Thulo Kola or Wild River gorge leading to the south face of Dhaulagiri were members of an expedition led by the South Tyrolean climber Reinhold Messner. Here man is reduced in size to a tiny white speck. In the spring of 1977, when the feared monsoons hit the icy giant earlier than expected, Messner had to give up his plans for climbing the 4,000-meter (ca. 13,000-foot) south face and turn back

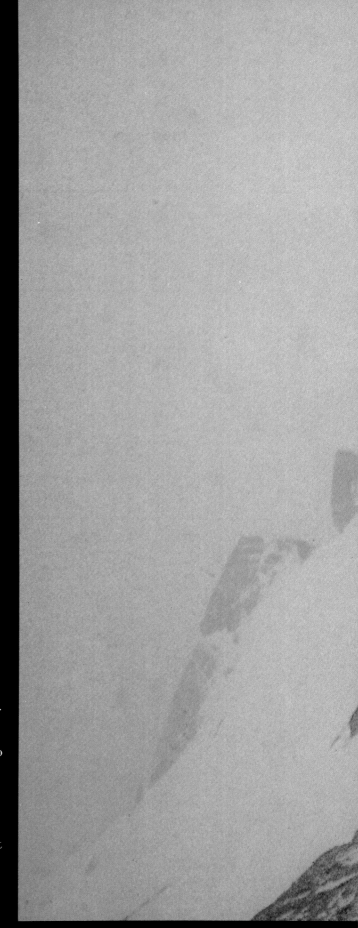

Doug Scott broke both legs near the summit of the Ogre Mountain [7,285 meters (23,900 feet), which is also known as Baintha, Brakk, or the Cannibal. He had to crawl for days on hands and knees. "When I recall the British expedition of 1977 to the Ogre Mountain in the Himalayas," he noted, "one person in particular comes to mind: the Balti porter Taki. After a 12-mile march with a 60-pound load on his back, Taki conjured up at least twenty-one eggs from the folds of his clothing. Not a single one was broken or even cracked. I haven't the faintest idea how he managed it. He performed this remarkable feat for a fee of thirty-one rupees but also to amaze us. I still can't imagine how on earth a man can make his way through such wild and rugged territory as a glacial moraine without damaging such a fragile load. In any event, Taki was far more careful than I could ever be. Eight weeks later eight other Baltis crossed the Biafo glacier and climbed up to our base camp on the Ogre. And with even greater care than Taki had expended on the eggs, they carried me down to the valley through the roughest landscape one can imagine without jostling me in the least."

39

40
Six climbers from England
assaulted the Ogre: a daring
enterprise in which Chris
Bonington also took part
(picture). As Doug Scott
was waiting for the

the edge of the Balti village
of Askole, he heard men
singing. "I have nothing but
admiration for these hearty
men with strong, individual
personalities who are

dedicate themselves to a
common goal. This
combination is what every
expedition needs if it is to
succeed."

Heidede Carstensen

Chris Bonington— His Comrades, His Mountains

Of one thing there can be no doubt: it was the British climbers who discovered the Alps, and, by conquering these peaks, they made the world take notice of high mountains for the first time. The history of Alpinism is at the same time a history of British Alpinism. Without the British, the history of mountain climbing as we know it would be inconceivable. From the winter sports playgrounds of the Alps to the Caucasus and Pamirs in Asia, from the gigantic mountains of the Americas stretching from Alaska to the Cordilleras and Tierra del Fuego, the British were there at the very beginning to explore and open up new routes.

There is no doubt that financial security was a significant factor in early British explorations. Trips to the distant mountains were very costly—not only in terms of material expense but also in terms of time. Moreover, the political situation favored British travel. The English occupied a worldwide empire in which one was able to travel all the way to India and still feel that one was journeying merely from one part of one's country to another.

The English concept of sportsmanship drove men to undertake the most daring Alpine climbs. Physical accomplishment was enjoyed for its own sake. For these reasons, the British took to the mountains almost immediately. The same attitudes prevail today among young British climbers, even though they lack the financial means of their Alpine predecessors. They still set out for the highest mountains in order to test themselves against the steep walls and exposed ridges. They pursue their personal goals with admirable self-control and inner perseverance. At the same time, their original ideas and bold plans cause large circles of mountaineers to sit up and take notice. The history of British Alpinism, which extends from Edward Whymper to Christian Bonington, includes an impressive number of enterprising, self-disciplined, and therefore successful men and women. Christian Bonington, his climbing companions, and their remarkable Alpine achievements may serve here as an example.

It is undisputed that Christian Bonington, born in 1943, is Great Britain's leading mountain climber. He is not only a prudent and experienced climber; he also possesses those characteristics that can ultimately transform a passionate mountaineer into an extraordinary expedition leader: a talent for organization, a democratic attitude, decisiveness, and a strong sense of responsibility for the welfare of a team that consists of the most varied individuals, whose strengths and weaknesses he strives to evaluate and utilize correctly.

Chris Bonington considers mountain climbing to be a matter of talent. At the age of sixteen, he began to test his own talent seriously. Since then, the list of his great climbs has become quite extensive: he was the first to climb Annapurna II [7,937 meters (26,040 feet), 1960], Nuptse [7,879 meters (25,849 feet), 1961], and the Freney Central Pillar in the Mont Blanc massif, also in 1961. In 1962, he was the first Englishman to climb the north face of the Eiger. He was the first to climb the middle Cerro Paine in Patagonia (1963), as well as the Old Man of Hoy (1966). In 1970, Bonington led his first expedition; it made an assault on the south wall of Annapurna. In 1972, he was in charge of equipping a British expedition to Mount Everest. The failure of this expedition was followed by many "firsts" in the Himalayas: the Brammah in Kashmir (1973), the Changabang (1974), the southwest flank of Mount Everest (1975), and the Ogre (1977).

Chris Bonington's friend, Doug Scott, had organized and led the Ogre expedition, but for both men this mountain almost led to catastrophe. During the ascent the difficulties often seemed insuperable. Two English and two Japanese expeditions before this had attempted to climb the Ogre (known in the vernacular as "Cannibal Mountain"), but landslides, gale-force storms, and steep, icy granite walls had prevented any expedition from reaching the summit. When Scott and Bonington arrived at the highest point that the Japanese team had reached the year before, it became clear that a frozen rock barrier and the last 245 meters (804 feet) to the summit presented even greater difficulties than they had anticipated. Their strength was almost gone. Exhausted by this killing climate, by the extreme height, and by his ceaseless struggles, Chris Bonington already had had to break off a final assault upon the summit from the southwest flank. This had happened two weeks earlier.

Nevertheless, in the late afternoon of July 13, 1977, he and Doug Scott stood on the summit of the Ogre [7,284 meters (23,897 feet)]—the first men ever to have reached the top of this giant. Four kilometers above the Biafo Glacier, a desolate and wild stream of ice, twilight was already falling as the two climbers prepared to descend. Scott set off first. It was necessary for him to lower himself by rope over the edge of a snowy ridge directly beneath the summit. It was a routine operation that any experienced Alpinist could do in his sleep. He placed a noose around a granite spur, pushed the rope through it, and threw both ends into the abyss below. As he began to lower himself, Scott noticed that the rope had become covered by a thin coating of ice and so did not lie properly against the cliff. For this reason, he landed at a point about 15 meters (49 feet) to the left of the best descent route. However, in the quickly falling darkness, he did not notice this fact.

He had the feeling that he was hanging helplessly at the most extreme point of a long pendular swing. And then—the catastrophe: Scott's right foot slipped on an icy spot. With a jerk, the pendulum swung to the right and headed straight toward a rock crevasse, carrying the stunned climber with it. Scott saw himself being hurtled toward a projecting granite ledge. He instinctively stretched out his feet in front of him in order to lessen the force of the impact. In the moment that followed he heard a strange grinding noise. What he felt was a searing pain in his ankles. He cried aloud. Bonington heard the cry above, and its echo penetrated as far as Mo Antoine, who was waiting for the two climbers in the camp below. When the rope finally stopped swinging, Scott secured himself with a piton. Bonington soon emerged from the darkness. "Is everything all right? Don't worry. You won't die."

The situation was more dangerous than anything they had encountered before: both Scott's ankles were broken. The right fibula was protruding. It would have taken too much strength to continue the descent in the darkness. It was clear to both men that they had to conserve their energy if they wanted to escape from the jaws of the "Cannibal." Using his ice axe, Bonington carved out a niche in the snow that would serve as a camp for the night. Half-lying, half-sitting, they spent the night at 7,224 meters (23,700 feet). Their greatest concern was to resist falling into a sleep of exhaustion, which, at −34° Centigrade, would have been fatal.

The next morning began an odyssey that was to last for two weeks. Following Bonington down a 65° snow-covered slope of snow and ice, Scott crawled on his hands and knees, holding fast to the steps and notches that Chris tirelessly cut into the ice. The next evening was spent in the camp with their companions Antoine and Clive Rowlands. But, on the following morning, a snowstorm broke loose and the small party was pinned down for two days at 7,000 meters (22,966 feet) without food. After the storm had passed, these exhausted men were able to descend only 160 meters (525 feet); they were then forced to spend the night in a snow cave. Scott had to fight against ever-increasing exhaustion, as well as moments of panic when he felt unable to follow quickly enough. His knees were scraped raw and his gloves were worn through. A gale suddenly blew up as the group stood on a 300-meter (984-foot) high spur. Bonington fell off. He broke three ribs and sprained his right arm. His condition was alarming: The shooting pains in his ribs increased with every cough and he had a fever. The next morning he collapsed in the tent and coughed up a yellow fluid. Was this pulmonary edema?

The Ogre had yet further difficulties in store for these men. Icy gusts swept over the cliffs for three days and forced the hungry climbers to remain in their camp at 6,400 meters (20,997 feet). On July 20, they dragged themselves to Base Camp II only to learn that it had been torn away by avalanches. There were now only two possibilities: to surrender and die on the Ogre or to drag oneself further in spite of illness and coldness. Scott crept like an animal over razor-sharp edges of ice and sharp pieces of rock. Through raging storms, centimeter by centimeter, he crept along the entire 7-kilometer (4.3-mile) stretch. Finally reaching base camp, the bruised and tattered climbers learned that their teammate, Nick Estcourt, had already set off on a three-day trek to Askole in order to mobilize help. The helicopter, which was to bring the two seriously injured climbers to Skardu, could not land because of mechanical difficulties. Scott was finally flown out, but Bonington had to wait another seven days in Askole.

After a four-year ban, the government of Nepal again issued permits to mountain climbers in the fall of 1968. At the time, Chris Bonington was considering the possibility of undertaking a large-scale expedition to Alaska, together with his friends Nick Estcourt, Martin Boysen, and Dougal Haston. When the news from Nepal arrived, the Alaskan plans were abandoned.

The south wall of Annapurna had long been Bonington's secret dream. "There is a route to the top," said Martin Boysen, after he had carefully studied photos of this face that had been projected onto a screen. "However, it is extremely difficult." This was quite true. The south wall was enormously high and enormously steep. Meter by meter, it was a challenge at every point. This Annapurna project was more difficult than all the other expeditions previously undertaken. Nuptse, which had been climbed in 1961, seemed a dwarf by comparison. But Chris Bonington, who characterizes himself as a competitive sportsman, was more attracted by the difficulties posed by Annapurna than he was frightened and repelled by them.

The first friend whom Bonington asked to accompany him was Ian Clough, with whom he had shared some of his most wonderful experiences in the mountains. The two climbers carefully put together a strong and promising team: Dougal Haston, Martin Boysen, Nick Estcourt, Mike Thompson, Tom Frost, Mick Burke, Pasang Kami, Kelvin Kent, and Dave Lambert as the doctor. Bonington's second-in-command was Don Whillans. On March 22, 1970, after eighteen long months of preparation, the Annapurna expedition set out. It consisted of twenty-one men, since a complete television crew was also accompanying them. What had been planned as a small expedition had grown into a mammoth undertaking. Materials, equipment, and food supplies were brought in by ship, by plane, and over land. When Bonington finally stood before his goal, feverishly yearning to climb, he found himself held up by administrative duties. But Don Whillans, the most experienced climber of the team, went on ahead. Having studied the mountain intensively, he had already worked out a preliminary plan. Base Camp should be established as near as possible to the base of the wall from which the ascent was to begin. He felt that the barefoot porters would not be persuaded to go further than this point on this sacred mountain. Don discovered that the rock wall was much more weather-beaten than he had anticipated. He also felt that the gorge, which ran through its center, was too difficult to climb. He thought that a route to the left of the gorge would provide more feasible possibilities. However, Whillans had also seen several landslides. He had even sighted yeti, the mysterious abominable snowman. At any rate, everyone saw its tracks clearly in the snow. Only Mick Burke tended to dismiss this possibility, regarding the footprints as bear tracks. The big questions were: Could one circumvent the ridge of ice by going to the left? How secure were the rocky ribs at the half point? Could one succeed in overcoming the wall? At first, the questions remained unanswered.

According to Bonington's plan, a nuclear group of four climbers would open up the first route and fix ropes in the difficult terrain. The rest of the team and the Sherpas would be divided into various camps and would also carry the load. As soon as the lead group became tired, it could stop to recuperate. The next group in the relay would take over the lead. In this way, every climber would have a chance to lead. Don and Dougal were the first pair to set out. In Chris's view, Don possessed a special feeling for the mountain, a combination of intuition, common sense, and experience. Dougal's excellent physical condition, stamina, and climbing skill ideally complemented Don's ability to interpret the peculiarities of the mountain. The other roped pairs were Mick Burke and the American Tom Frost, Nick Estcourt and Martin Boysen, and, finally, Bonington and Clough.

Aside from acclimatization, there were at first no other problems. (Of course, acclimatization has its own difficulties. No sooner has the body gradually adapted itself to a certain height than the misery begins all over again when the next level is reached.) Tenaciously and steadily, they worked their way upward. They climbed out of their sleeping bags as early as possible in order not to lose time. Dusk always fell much earlier than anticipated. Carefully, but at the same time viewing the possibilities from all perspectives, they worked out their route every day. It was extremely laborious. All too often, ice screws only took hold after many attempts. All too often, soft new snow lay over the rock and ice, and impeded progress. There were many places that should have been bypassed altogether in the interests of safety; for example, the "Sword of Damocles," a corridor along the route that was overhung by sharp, sword-shaped icicles. There was no alternative, however. One had to pass through.

Mick suffered for days from unbearable headaches. Chris almost fell into a glacial crevasse when a snow bridge collapsed beneath his feet. He was only superficially injured, but the wound later turned into a case of blood poisoning. On the way to the saddle, it began to hail. A wild snowstorm held them up for several days. Avalanches constantly crashed down the wall. At the end of April, Nick and Martin began the battle for the ice ridge, whose approach above Camp IV was blocked by seracs. It was only by making a tunnel 6 meters (20 feet) long and 60 centimeters (24 inches) high that they could reach the ridge. Progress was very slow, endlessly slow. It was extremely strenuous work. Large snow cornices, which could break off and fall at any moment, hung threateningly above them. On this difficult stretch of ice, Nick and Martin used snow anchors as well as Jümar stirrups fastened to safety ropes. Heart and lungs often seemed on the point of bursting. Martin's hands were chafed and raw. In their nightly broadcasts, both climbers asked permission to return to Base Camp in order to recuperate.

The ice ridge was more difficult than had been expected. The mountain consumed everyone. In May the climbers finally conquered the wall of ice. Although they used increasing amounts of oxygen, they became more and more worn out with each meter they climbed. The midday snows began ever earlier, and a general lethargy set in. Don and Dougal tried to conserve their energy for the climb to the summit; the others had the feeling that the mountain would destroy them with snowstorms, falling rock, and avalanches. Morale sank.

Don Whillans and Dougal Haston reached Camp IV, just below the summit. As furious storms howled outside, they waited (almost totally without food) for nine days. But their patience was rewarded: on May 27, 1970, at two o'clock in the afternoon, the final ascent took place and the summit was reached. The mighty south wall of rock and ice had finally been conquered!

After Mick and Tom had also reached the top, Bonington decided to clear the mountain quickly. Mike Thompson, Ian Clough, and Dave Lambert broke up Camp IV. Descending, they trudged along a narrow corridor of ice until they reached a kind of ramp. A thunderous crash was heard, and an enormous mass of snow came hurtling down from the glacier. Ian went ahead; Mike ducked into a small hollow and was covered by fragments of ice. When it was quiet again, Mike crept out and saw Dave quickly ascending with several Sherpas. Then they began to look for Ian. They found him at the lower edge of a field of ice debris. His death must have been instantaneous. It was exactly ten o'clock. Ian Clough was buried on Annapurna at the foot of a felsbank.

Like Ian Clough, Mike Burke was also to die tragically during a descent: During the 1975 British expedition to Mount Everest, he disappeared without a trace in a wild snowstorm near the summit, which had been reached by Doug Scott and Dougal Haston on September 25.

Everest: the Hard Way was the title Chris Bonington gave his book about his successful second assault of the world's highest mountain. The "hard way" referred to the steep southwest wall of Mount Everest, with its formidable icefall, a gigantic frozen waterfall on the mountain itself. The "hard way" also referred to the season of the year: autumn. A climb of this 8,848-meter (29,029 feet) peak in the autumn must take place between the end of the monsoons, which generally continue until the last weeks of September, and the beginning of the frigid mountain storms, which set in during the middle of October. Already, five very well-equipped expeditions had had to turn back from Mount Everest between 1970 and 1972 without having accomplished their goals. Why should this new attempt succeed?—ironically enough, because of the failure of the 1972 expedition. Bonington and his friends carefully analyzed the mistakes. They took improved equipment along: for example, more stable tents, which would better resist the murderous mountain storms. They also chose a more feasible route in order to surmount the great bank of rock upon which they had failed in 1972. Since Bonington also took along six members of the first expedition, the climbers thought they had a better chance of success. It was nevertheless the most murderous undertaking that any member of the team had ever experienced. They were exposed to the constant danger of enormous avalanches as well as to cataclysmic changes in weather. The extreme altitude was unendurable without additional oxygen; it also caused hallucinations. Finally, a combination of all these factors, but, above all, the frigid temperatures reaching forty degrees below zero, could plunge the weary climbers into a fatal sleep of exhaustion.

In the milky dawn of September 25, 1975, at about 3:30 A.M., Doug Scott and Dougal Haston made the final assault. Setting out with oxygen tanks from the last bivouac just below the south summit, they had to crawl on all fours as well as to support one another to prevent themselves from sliding down the slippery new-fallen snow in the fierce winds. In this manner, the summit of Mount Everest was finally reached. Together they set their feet down upon the highest point on earth and gazed out over Nepal and Tibet below. With the conscious realization that their goal had finally been reached, the two climbers surrendered to an overwhelming feeling of happiness, which lasted for several minutes.

When Chris Bonington was able to make radio contact and heard the news, tears filled his eyes: their efforts had been rewarded. Another climber also wept on Mount Everest: it was Martin Boysen, who first learned that Mick Burke would never return to the valley, and it was he who had to break this terrible news to Bonington. So a successful expedition returned to England, deeply shaken by the death of a friend.

□

Reinhard Karl

What Remains Is a Feeling of Emptiness

It may be difficult to believe, but the fact is that it was not until May 1978 that a German climber stood for the first time upon the summit of Mount Everest! Of course, Germans had already taken part in many expeditions to the world's highest mountains and even to Mount Everest itself. However, a student from Heidelberg, Reinhard Karl, was to become the first German to reach the highest point on earth. How did this come about?

The student was asked whether he would like to join an expedition to Mount Everest that was being organized under the auspices of the Austrian Alpine Society. In recent years, the youth's extreme climbs had aroused the attention of many members of the climbing guild, and he was now being offered an opportunity to go to Mount Everest as a reporter-photographer for a certain newspaper.

Climbing was something he knew how to do. At the same time, he was completely indifferent as to how his climbs were evaluated. In the summer of 1977, he had made a daring climb through the most dangerous cracks of the so-called "Fleischbank" in the Wilder Kaiser. Another student, Helmut Kiene, had accompanied him. Climbers in the Eastern Alps continue to debate whether these two students had achieved the seventh degree, which is the most difficult level of climbing possible. He didn't care. He simply climbed whenever the prospect presented itself. As mentioned before, he was primarily a student of geography at the University of Heidelberg.

Reinhard Karl possesses a healthy dose of common sense and is able to look at himself critically and honestly. He takes an extremely skeptical view of the way people make mountain climbers into heroes. When he speaks of mountain climbing as a form of work output, he is simply appropriating an industrial term that he feels reflects our times. On the one hand, climbing is largely a matter of personal satisfaction. On the other hand, it can be regarded as a phenomenon whose mechanisms do not greatly differ from those found among workers except that they have been internalized and stabilized. From this perspective, climbing as a sport is regarded not as a game but as a form of work.

Mount Everest became a place of pilgrimage. All nations wanted to raise their prestige by being able to announce that their climbers had succeeded in climbing the highest peak on earth. A long and tedious process of organization preceded every expedition. Each member of the party had to be carefully selected according to his capabilities and experience. Any member of the group who reached the top became a national hero. More often, however, he reached a hospital where frostbitten fingers and toes were amputated. Such was the likely fate—the tragedy and suffering—in store for the exhausted victor.

When I first thought of Mount Everest, my associations were as follows: frenzied exertion exacerbated by lack of oxygen, coldness, snow, storms, mountain sickness, frostbite, and, as a result of all of these individual phenomena, a kind of madness that reveals itself in the complete loss of objectivity and self-control. But then there is also the satisfaction of a profound desire to climb ever upward, to be on top, and to know that the world lies totally beneath one's feet. Complete surrender to the pure joy of going up—this is the driving force that guides every climb.

The conqueror of this senseless achievement enters upon a battle with windmills—too much action for so much nonsense. The situation is even worse on the large national expeditions. Here there is no room for personal decision, because one must submit to totally authoritarian leadership. Here one is forced to live among people with whom one has nothing in common. Here one is nothing but a little cog in a large climbing machine whose success is far more important than the ego trip of the single individual.

Climbing is masochism. That is why one often hears climbers express their joy that "it's all over." I am not one of those who says, "How good it is when the pain lets up." For me, climbing is like a trip into a dream world, a pristine world of light, pure colors, and romantic atmospheres. Like a marijuana smoker, I too feel as if I have left the planet earth behind. The abandonment of a worm's-eye perspective allows one to begin a journey to one's inner self.

In extraordinary moments one learns what one is. One discovers one's fears, weaknesses, and strengths. Of course, a "flight from the normal world into the realm of mountains" is also a search for adventure and danger and a desire for the unknown. It is partly a game.

The approach to Mount Everest, one's first experience of the heights, brings headache, apathy, and nausea. A process of acclimatization follows. My strength increases with the number of my red corpuscles. On this trip, my

chances for reaching the summit are poor: first come the Austrians and then the foreigners. The first setback occurs when a Sherpa is killed by a fragment of falling ice. Everyone is profoundly depressed. The repressed fear of an accident or even a death is suddenly present once again.

After a day of mourning and contemplation, we continue. The first summit team establishes Camp V at 8,500 meters (27,887 feet). The next day, the first Austrians stand on the roof of the world. They are Wolfgang Nairz, Robert Schauer, Horst Bergmann, and, representing all the Sherpas, Ang Phu, the sirdar. The next team to reach the summit is the pair Reinhold Messner and Peter Habeler, who made the sensational ascent without oxygen tanks. The expedition doctor, "Bull" Oelz, and I set out as the third team. On the first morning of our assault we meet Messner and Habeler at Camp III [7,300 meters (23,950 feet)]. They are descending from their successful but murderous conquest: snow-blind, totally exhausted, with cracked and swollen lips, and in a state of general debilitation. In spite of their torment, exhaustion, anxiety, and euphoria, their primary feeling is one of relief. They tell us about the summit and encourage us. "You'll make it too," they say.

We climb to the south saddle. Toward noon we stand on the highest pass in the world: Everest has moved from the realm of dream into a reality that can be grasped. For the past three months we have been living only in anticipation of the final few hours just below the summit. In my fantasies I had taken the last few steps to the top a dozen times: alone, in a group, in the best weather, during a snowstorm, in perfect physical condition, totally exhausted, struggling fiercely for survival, arriving in a state of absolute joy. These fantasies appeared almost every night in dreams or while I meditated during the day. The fear of returning without toes and fingers is not present in such fantasies. Somehow, one imagines oneself to be completely invulnerable. Such things could not happen to me! I will not allow them to happen! Now and then fear does break through, as occurred, for instance, when the Sherpa died. Sometimes, even the most powerful defense mechanisms break down, and my reason tells me: "That could have happened to you, too." When this happens, I am overcome by doubt and ask myself: "What is it that I have lost in this icy realm, in this refrigerator world, that has had such a chilling effect on my physical and emotional life?"

The south saddle is one of the most terrible places on earth: 35° below zero Celsius (−95°F), storms with winds up to 120 miles an hour. In addition, the air is so thin at

8,000-meter (26,246-foot) height that one can only survive here for a few days. "Tomorrow we will reach the summit." But how far we still are from the top! We must climb 900 meters (2,953 feet) higher, a colossal distance at this height. We settle comfortably into our tents, brew tea, and have a bite to eat. Bull tests the oxygen tanks; they register a pressure of 230. That provides about eight hours of oxygen—eight hours in which to transcend the limits of the human constitution, eight hours of borrowed time, eight hours of guaranteed survival, and, for us, the final eight hours of our Everest adventure.

It is bitter cold. Gathering all our belongings together, we retreat into our sleeping bags, our islands of warmth and refuge. At 3:00 A.M., I begin to melt snow. Bull is still sleeping deeply, aided by his supply of oxygen. We drink tea and choke down some chocolate. We turn on the oxygen system and check everything yet once again. We open our tent and are greeted by a blast of cold wind. Today is the big day! For three months the mountain above us has been the center of all our thoughts and wishes. We are not certain that we will succeed, but I am going to take my chances. I know I am capable of straining myself to the breaking point even when a situation is hopeless. In any event, this climb is going to be terrible. We feel no sense of release as we set out, but rather one of oppression. We ascend the steep couloir of snow that leads to the southeast ridge. I climb much too quickly. Bull is far below me. At the end of an hour, we are already 250 meters (820 feet) higher. Now, the snow is becoming deeper. I begin to doubt that I will ever be able to negotiate this brutally exhausting march through the snow. Three hours of frenzied work. We reach the final camp at 8,500 meters (27,887 feet). We cannot move. We can merely breathe. But then we get our second wind. We can make out the south summit.

Although I had been preoccupied with the limited amount of time available to us for the completion of the climb, I now push all doubts and fears aside. We'll simply keep climbing until we get to the top, no doubt slowly and with great effort, but nevertheless ever higher until we arrive. To the right, the mountain drops off 3,000 meters (9,842 feet) toward Tibet. We must be careful not to lose our balance in the storm. All at once, my air supply stops. My oxygen is gone. I tear the oxygen mask from my face and pant like a dog. But I recover. We change the tanks: 5 kilos (11 pounds) less weight to carry. Bull says, "8,600" (28,215 feet). Everything inside me has consolidated to form one simple command: "Keep going!" Step by step. All ideas and theories are gone. I do not experience a journey toward a world of light and absolute joy, as I had anticipated. Rather, a feeling of total emptiness takes possession of me. No special colors, no view; only footsteps in the snow. All in all, a trip of horror. At last, the south summit: 8,670 meters (28,445 feet). Near enough to reach the summit.

Emotions well up once again. We will succeed. The ridge covered with snow cornices looks fantastic. From somewhere in my head, words emerge: "Be careful. The ridge is dangerous." Bull climbs imperturbably ahead of me. I follow without fear. The Hillary Step, a steep, icy rise, is quickly conquered. Already we see the tripod the Chinese left behind as a token of victory. I am moving like a snail because my oxygen tank is not functioning properly. Although I breathe in with all my strength, I do not get enough air. We cover 10 more meters (33 feet), then pause just to breathe. The final meters. Bull waits 3 meters (10 feet) below the summit. "You go first," he says. "No, you." We take the last steps together arm in arm. We are on top. We embrace. It is noon. We are at the goal of all our hopes, just below heaven. An indescribable feeling of joy. We take photos of the summit, sit down, rest. The view is not particularly good. Way below in Tibet we can see countless 6,000-meter (19,685-foot) peaks. They all look tiny from here.

My reason tells me: "This is the highest point on earth and you are the first German to reach it." This fact leaves me cold. I couldn't care less. I have reached the object of great yearning. But the only reality now is this icy heap of snow, the fierce wind, the bitter cold, and my exhaustion. Joy slowly gives way to sadness and a feeling of emptiness. A utopia has become reality.

□

Guido Tonella

My Friend Walter Bonatti

Walter Bonatti: born in Bergamo in 1930; Alpinist, guide, photographer.

Thus reads a typical entry in Alpine reference works. Bonatti's great climbs, however, fill columns. But he is more than just a climber, more than just a photojournalist. Dino Buzzati, for years editor-in-chief of the *Corriere della Serra* and one of Italy's most important modern writers, confessed in a foreword to Bonatti's book about mountains, *I Giorni Grandi,* how difficult it was for him to describe Bonatti the climber, as well as Bonatti the man. However, Bonatti does not need to be introduced or sponsored—either as a mountaineer or as a writer.

When in February 1965 Bonatti set out upon his solo climb to the Matterhorn summit by way of the north wall, he was accompanied by three friends. This was a ruse designed to deceive all-too-curious journalists about the true nature of his plans. The excursion was disguised as a simple ski tour to the base of the north wall. The Italian journalist Guido Tonella, then living in Geneva, also came along. However, he knew exactly what Bonatti had in mind. Thus, Tonella is better able than any other writer to describe this great personality, even ten years after Bonatti's retirement from extreme Alpine climbing.

He visited Bonatti in Milan. Between the Matterhorn escapade and the present, Bonatti had become a well-known journalist, a writer as well as a photographer. The last time Walter Bonatti had addressed himself to problems of Alpinism, it was in a book that appeared in 1971. Only now, in conversations with Guido Tonella, was he to express himself again: he spoke with remarkable candor about some of the problems that were threatening to lead mountain climbing into a dead end. As he spoke, however, one also felt his never-flagging love for mountains.

89

When I was originally asked to write about Walter Bonatti, I had a few misgivings: the reason for my doubts was the title that now heads this article. Precisely because I am not a novice at reporting on mountain climbing and have interviewed many great Alpinists, I felt that it was presumptuous of me as a journalist to call Bonatti my friend.

However, a telephone call from Milan dispelled my doubts. "But of course you are my friend," Bonatti answered me with his beautiful, clear voice. "Come to Milan! You can finish your work in the quiet of my house." This episode not only guarantees the authenticity of the report; it also casts some light upon Bonatti's true character. Contrary to all those assertions to the effect that he is remote and reserved, the fact is that he is spontaneous, straightforward, and warm.

I would like to interject a little episode that occurred when I departed from Geneva for my highly rewarding visit with Bonatti in Milan. My grandson, who was nine-and-a-half years old, had to write a composition in school. The theme was to be taken from the words with which Bonatti described his climb of the Matterhorn in his book *I Giorni Grandi* [*Great Days in the Mountains*]. The description referred to his famous winter ascent (February 18–23, 1965) up a new route on the north face alone. When I asked my grandson why he hadn't told the teacher that his grandfather was about to meet Bonatti personally, he hesitated a moment and then announced that he hadn't wanted to contradict the teacher. It seems that while dictating the theme, the teacher had indicated that Bonatti belonged to the same race as did the heroes of Greek mythology. After this extraordinary achievement, he no longer existed among the living and had probably been taken by the gods of the mountains into higher spheres. When I told Bonatti this story and also explained to him that Nicolas's teacher had been very incapacitated by an accident, I saw that he was deeply impressed by this story. "In this one special case," he said, "I must agree with such an interpretation. My adventure on the Matterhorn can be regarded as a kind of transfiguration, which promises me a place in the Valhalla of Alpinists even during my lifetime. In general, however, it dismays me that people have dismissed me once and for all with the description 'Bonatti, the Alpinist' and cannot imagine that I am capable of doing anything else but climbing." Bonatti does not say this in order to provoke controversy. It is crystal clear to him that the profession of journalism, with which he has been occupying himself for the past twelve years since he retired from the Alpine stage, represents a logical progression from his climbing career. The mountains made Bonatti into the man that he is now. They influenced both his physical and intellectual development. They also provided him with a point of view that informs his reports of current expeditions, even to those regions that have nothing to do with mountains. This concept of continuity is a point which Bonatti repeats several times during the interview.

While looking for something else, he comes across a carton that contains equipment he used at the beginning of his career as an Alpinist. (But he does not take this opportunity to launch into a tirade against modern equipment.) Bonatti began his career in 1949 at the age of nineteen, when he pitted himself against the Walker Pillar with two friends from Monza. They followed the climbing route that had been selected by Riccardo Cassin in 1938. I was allowed to look at the contents of the carton: the remains of an old hemp rope worn bare by granite, a stirrup of hemp cord with iron treads drilled with holes, like a sieve, to make them as light as possible, a large, old-fashioned steel piton provided with a ring.

Another myth that sticks to me is the notion of Bonatti, the climber with superequipment! In 1955, I had devised a system for securing myself during a solo climb. This was necessary in preparation for my lone ascent of the Dru Pillar. I admit that my equipment improved a great deal in the period between 1949 and 1955. When I first started out, I mainly used materials from the army. Most important was ever better quality rope, first silk, then nylon. But I'd like to stress here that my partner Ghigo and I only had old-fashioned pitons when we made our first ascent of the east face of the Grand Capuchin in 1951. This kind of piton just cannot be compared with the variety of ultra-light expansion bolts that have been flooding the climber's market for the past ten years. I must say a word about the exaggerated reliance on equipment that characterizes climbing today. On a recent visit to Yosemite Park, I had an opportunity to prove that this development is taking place. There I witnessed an almost brazen use of every kind of climbing aid. This seems to be typical of American climbers, in spite of the fact that the American Alpine Club constantly preaches to us about the ethics of Alpinism. At the foot of the great wall of El Capitan, I saw how the rock had begun to crumble as a result of systematic boring with expansion bolts. As for me, here you see the only 'new' piece of equipment, which I used in 1951 on the Grand Capuchin: these two wooden wedges.

Walter showed me two gigantic wedges of ash wood, which bore not the faintest resemblance to all the superlight pieces generally used today.

I repeated the climb of the Grand Capuchin in the summer of 1976 with a 36-year-old climber, Angelo Pizzocolo, who also comes from the Monza clique. The repeat performance twenty-five years later was quite splendid. Unfortunately, we found several expansion bolts in the region of the three cliff overhangs, which cross the wall horizontally. Ghigo and I had taken the same route in 1951, using traditional means to conquer this passage. Does it need to be said once again? I am absolutely against the use of expansion bolts, which make holes in the cliffs and desecrate the mountain. For moral reasons alone, they should and must be rejected.

Bonatti's small collection of old pieces of equipment would make an impressive addition to any Alpine museum—and could serve as an example of how materials developed between 1949 and 1951. Before putting everything away again, Bonatti takes out the large bivouac sack that has always accompanied him—from the Walker Pillar in 1949 to the Dru Pillar in 1955. The material has been mended often, and burn marks are visible in many places.

Burns like this often occur when one tries to get a stove going without getting out of one's sack. But how else could I have managed during my five bivouacs? Here is a sailor's duffel bag that I also had on the Dru climb, so that I could rope up my possessions behind me. I had equipped the bag with removable straps so that it could be easily converted into an ordinary rucksack. And there is the old helmet I wore on the Matterhorn in the winter of 1965. I have saved all these precious souvenirs, not to stir up old polemics, but to prove how simple my equipment was and to show how such equipment corresponds completely to my traditional conception of what mountain climbing should be. Of course, these articles are also witnesses to episodes in my life.

Do I sense a little nostalgia in his words? Before I can ask the question, Bonatti defends himself:

While writing an outline for a more or less biographical work, I recently recalled a statement by Mark Twain: 'A good life is never logical.' I then noted that I myself belong to that class of people who are absolutely illogical. In our times, men strive for an easy life and pursue useful goals; in so doing, they lose their humanity as well as those ideals that slumber in every one of us. These feelings are exchanged for cold theories that make the individual into a slave of his so-called freedom and ambition. These ideas rob him of everything personal until all that is left is a long-drawn-out and oppressive fear of death. My statement that I am not a man of logic must be understood in this context and as a contrast.

Here lies the secret, the driving force, that has led Walter Bonatti to seek ever new horizons since 1965. This is the source of his never-ceasing desire to gain a larger perspective, to measure himself against new difficulties as well as against the unknown, to surpass himself, and to investigate the ultimate secrets of nature. This is the reason for the expeditions and reportage (more than 100 in twelve years) that have taken him to the most remote parts of the earth. He has been everywhere: on the gigantic glaciers of Alaska and even further east, in search of the land bridge between America and Asia, the mythological Beringia; in the deserts of Australia and on

this continent's magical dome, the Ayer Rock; in South America, from the source of the Amazon to the Aconcagua and even to Cape Horn; in Africa, on the Kilimanjaro and the Ruwenzori, surrounded by lions and without a weapon; in Ecuador, on the highest volcano of the earth; on Krakatoa as well as on the Niragongo; even in the Antarctic and at the South Pole. And this is only a small selection from a long list of his travels.

It should be added that on these expeditions Bonatti is particularly interested in making contact with wild animals in their natural habitat.

One way to rediscover nature is to rely only on one's human instincts. I have always been impressed with how wild animals live, and after a while I gradually succeeded, alone and unarmed, in entering into their midst. The wild cats can understand our intentions and react accordingly. I have systematically tried to reawaken in myself the remains of that latent primal instinct that lies dormant in all men. In order to make use of this instinct, of course, one must first get to know oneself.

These words remind me of a remark made by Michel Vaucher, Bonatti's partner on the first climb of the Whymper Pillar in August 1964.

What impresses me even more than his technical mastery is Bonatti's ability to feel instinctively the threatening presence of danger. He always succeeded in making the right decision at the right time, so that we stopped and waited until the danger had passed, whether this danger was in the form of a rock slide, a storm, or an avalanche. He succeeded in sharpening his natural instinct to such an extent that it has developed into a genuine sixth sense.

The American magazine *Argosy* called Bonatti a "Giant of Adventure," a title that had previously been bestowed on Hillary, Piccard, Cousteau, and Lovell. However, as already indicated, the motivating force that drove Bonatti to undertake his various kinds of expeditions was not merely the desire for an adventurous life. Rather, the impulses that inspired Bonatti to climb and travel are the same forces that gave rise to and continue to stimulate Alpinism itself. Therefore, Bonatti feels justified in evaluating the "adventurous" period of his life as one that at once provided him with an expanded perspective on world problems and also revealed to him a new dimension in Alpinism.

It was enthralling to watch him spread out before me the fascinating evidence of the past twelve years of travel. The things he showed me were impressive, from the point of view of both journalism and photography. Bonatti believes that photography is an indispensable addition to a written text. As he set forth his views, I had the feeling that he was taking stock of his own activities, almost as if he had found himself at a turning point in his life.

I hesitated to tell him what I was thinking. He might misinterpret my opinions and feel that I joined my grandson in believing—quite erroneously—that a man like this, at the peak of his fame, belonged in Valhalla and not on earth. Yet, one need only look at Bonatti to convince onself that, despite his graying hair, here was a totally vigorous man, a man fully alive both physically and intellectually. But, of course, he was born on June 22, 1930, and so can hardly be regarded as old! One thing is certain: this extraordinary human being is now standing on the threshold of a new and promising phase of his life. One can almost sense the dawn of great days to come. □

Reinhart Hoffmeister

Lyrics beneath the Summit Cross

A publisher once thought of establishing a prize for lyric poetry and of naming it for the poet Petrarch. It was first bestowed posthumously upon Rolf Dieter Brinkmann in a ceremony that took place upon the windswept summit of Mont Ventoux. This is the same Monte Ventoso that drew Francesco Petrarch from his hut in the Provençal town of Vaucluse 639 years earlier. At this time the great poet, philosopher, humanist, churchman, and lover was suffering from unrequited love for the unattainable Madonna Laura. The written evidence of this laborious mountain journey is regarded "in our circles" as the first literary work about mountain climbing—although it contains a few errors. It is a long epistle written in Latin to his spiritual adviser, Pater Denis Robert.

Anyone who reads this letter will observe how Petrarch held in check his enthusiasm for the snow-covered peaks. He had taken along the "Confessions" of the Church Father Saint Augustine (hopefully not all thirteen volumes!). Overcome by a feeling of joy in having surmounted the inhospitable stony wasteland of the mountain's summit, he began to study his breviary. However, after noting that his teacher criticized men for admiring high mountains, because in their enthusiasm they forgot God, Petrarch no longer delighted in his experience in the mountains.

The organizers of the 1975 Petrarch Prize commemorated the poet's climb by reenacting it, though in a more comfortable fashion. The bus with the jurors and guests stopped 100 meters (328 feet) below the summit. The party then began the final climb—on an easy path, naturally! Peter Handke, Bazon Brock, Nicholas Born, Hubert Burda, Michael Krüger, and all the others, accompanied by sweating cameramen, made their way up. But this ascent did not give rise to a new mountain book.

93

The first chapter of my (unwritten) mountain book is entitled "Similaun." In the years after the great slaughter, when we were attempting to come to terms in literature with the convulsions and violations of twelve years of Nazi rule, finding a way to survive by sweeping away the rubble of the past with words, a programmatic and pathetic motto occurred to me: "Everyone must cross the Similaun." Similaun—the mountain borderland between Italy and Austria, the pass leading from the Schnalser Valley to the Vent arm of the Ötz Valley, a snowy dome of firn, glittering brilliantly in the sun—had come to symbolize for me the abrupt transition from war to peace, from death to life.

It was April 1945. The war was almost over, and I was stationed in Mantua. Many of us began to engage in probing conversations. We no longer wanted to be charged up for war. We wanted to survive. Everyone in Frontier Reconnaissance Troop 374 wanted to go on living, even those who had yesterday sworn to "fight to the death for the Führer." And so it came about that a convoy of troops rolled northward with fraudulent orders "stamped" by the Chief Military Officer for Special Units. Our special unit vanished, not to be found by headhunters from the army or commandos from the SS. The men disappeared into the inaccessible Schnalser Valley, which is crossed only by one steep and narrow highway. The peasants of the village of Unsere Frau ("Our Lady") traded flour, butter, and eggs for bits and pieces of military equipment.

As the inferno raged during the last days of war before Germany surrendered, the path over the lower saddle of the Similaun seemed to offer the last chance for returning home. There were some Bavarians in our unit, and they were able to evaluate the situation. The south wall was steep and rugged, but it was easy to climb. So they said. The Bavarians had long since reached the Similaun hut and were enjoying a 38-egg omelet. Corporal Hoffmeister, whose left arm was still stiff from a gunshot wound, had meanwhile gotten lost in a cliff formation that he thought was a chimney. He had been born in the flatlands, and the Brocken was the highest mountain he knew. He was stuck—there was no going forward nor could he go back. At some point, those above discovered that a man was missing. They looked for him and finally pulled him by rope to safety above. Gripped by this experience, I thought I would entitle my book *Camaraderie in the Mountains*. I had been in uniform for three years but had not yet experienced the sense of brotherhood that is supposed to exist among fellow soldiers.

The unit commander, Lieutenant Werner Sarstedt, who was later to become a judge, ended the war in his own way. Here, at 3,019 meters (9,905 feet) above sea level, he simply disbanded the unit and climbed down the Nierderjoch Glacier toward the Samoar hut, which was still probably called the Hermann Göring House. His plan (which soon ended in disaster) was to meander home unarmed between American military outposts.

The end of the war on the Similaun: We sat in front of the hut with our legs stretched out in front of us and gazed into the bright sunlight. Drills and orders, hatred and struggle, and the indescribable pressure that had shaped our lives until this point were left behind in the valley, together with our weapons. Here everything was quite different. Without our weapons we felt ourselves delivered up to mighty nature, but our sense of powerlessness was salutary. The vastness of the sky, the endless mountain chains, and, above all, the stillness overwhelmed us. In the long years of war our ears had forgotten the sound of silence. Here we were removed from everything that had oppressed our youth, and we now began to talk, at first hesitantly, as if we had to learn all over again how to communicate. We spoke as we had never spoken before.

We were still angry that we had been ordered to fire on the garden at Mincio, where a young Italian had then senselessly died within days of the final capitulation. But we now wanted to speak about what lay ahead of us. Up here began our "new life." We would be free at last, and we tried to imagine what it would be like to be free. We took our hopes for a new and "happier" form of humanity, for a "glorious future," down with us as we descended into the Ötz Valley. The hopes we had dreamed of on our mattresses in the Similaun hut did not, of course, materialize, but that is another story for another time.

I tried to write down then what Similaun meant for me, but I could not complete my work. I had been trained as a reporter to describe in detail and without emotion "what is, what happened." I thus mistrusted recollection. I caught myself allowing feelings to suppress thoughts. Words could not express the effect the mountains had had on me, especially since they had acquired symbolic significance. Words were inadequate for explaining how mountains had changed my life. The result was that I had "fallen" for the mountains—first as a climber, then in later years as a devoted hiker.

I later discovered that many other, far better writers than I could not describe man's "experience" in the mountains. Others, whose typewriters should have gone out on strike, came up with such pretentious words as "mountain of destiny" or "death-defying effort."

Everyone who pits himself against a mountain and dares to take one more step breaks away from convention and thus from everything that is everyday, secure, and limited. He may be prompted by a mere desire for adventure, or he may feel the need to test his courage by placing himself at risk. Nevertheless, by participating in an unusual situation, he has agreed to engage in a debate with his inner self. One would think that this could provide a fertile field for writers and psychologists. However, if one surveys the literature of the past (and here I mean literature in its so-called higher form), one finds very few examples in which mountains and mountaineers have been treated.

The search for such a theme in contemporary literature is a hopeless one. Its absence may well reflect the existence of a profound disruption of the poet's relationship to nature. This is coupled with the modern writer's fear of the expansive words and feelings that would be required to describe men who have left the normal spheres of human activity and have embraced extreme attitudes.

This inhibition may seem strange to uncritical natures. Where others find no words because experience itself has dumbfounded them, many word acrobats—such as Guido Lammer in his lead article in the journal *The Mountain*—torture themselves and us with their "flaming thirst," "cold shoes," and "terrors of the mountain." Guido Lammer's essay "Suffering Becomes Joy," written in May 1923, is an example of climbing mysticism in all its arrogance. Its message has remained unchanged and is often repeated by officers of mountain clubs today. Lammer wrote:

> Sportsmen, especially we Alpinists, have been acting for many years as if we found pleasure in precisely that from which Philistines, or superficial spirits, flee, because for them it is painful. If we test our activities from the perspective of the Philistine, it cannot be denied that we pile hardship upon ourselves and do so voluntarily. Besides the difficulty of the climb itself, there are the pinpricks and whiplashes of the weather: burning hot sun, sunburn, torrential rains, wet feet, soaked clothing, vision blurred by swirling snow, winds that cut through the thickest clothing as if through a transparent spider's web, and, finally, the brutal, grizzly, threatening coldness. Up early, out of a warm bed into cold shoes, into the icy dawn, often hungry, often burning with thirst, for hours on end. And, to top off the physical agonies, there is the heavy burden of psychological suffering: the terrors of isolation, of getting lost, of disappearing in the fog—merciless threats, risk of death! Why all of this? Why?

This "why" is the eternal Gretchen question of mountain climbing. It is asked not only by "the Philistines down in the valley" but by everyone who strives to reach the top of a cliff. And not one climber, from Edward Whymper to Reinhold Messner, has been able to answer this question satisfactorily. Climbers probably have never wanted to answer this question, and they probably still don't want to. Only intimations of a solution are revealed. For, in the last resort, any attempt to analyze this "why" immediately uncovers the private self, which everyone who is not an exhibitionist at heart would prefer to leave concealed. Thus, even the most apparently honest confessions lack all conviction.

The wish to grasp hold of nature may be the primary motive that causes the climber to engage in a task that requires efforts far exceeding the demands of everyday human life. Let us examine these motives more closely: climbers regarded (and maybe still do regard) themselves as an elite, who, striving for the light, arise out of the lower depths of the dull masses of humanity. So said Oskar Erich Meyer, the self-styled Pope of German mountain-climbing literature of the 1920s. Meyer wrote in his book *Mountain and Man: Book of Prayer:* "Only he will be ennobled on the mountain who already possesses a noble heart. If the mountain has taken your deepest self onto itself, then you may ask it if you are noble." The Teutonic Superman rests within the heart of the German mountain-climbing hero! "German Alpine poetry reveals a passion and depth of feeling unknown in other nations," says Aloys Dreyer in his book about Alpine literature, a work that both stimulated and amused me.

In earlier times, there existed a whole crowd of God-seekers who, motivated by a "nearer-to-thee" feeling, took up climbing. Walter Flaig, yet another German chauvinist, uttered the following admonition: "Do not believe that the value of a climb can be measured in meters of rope or by the number of pitons used. Know that climbing is a cult, a religion!"

Pantheists from all nations, unite upon the heights! "Big mountains are a feeling," gushed Lord George Noel Byron, who, a hundred years ago, wrote his verse play *Manfred*, the first high-mountain drama. Byron was, like many Britons before him, a Wengen enthusiast. He prayed enraptured at the foot of the Jungfrau:

> Are not heavens, mountains, blue waves
> A part of me, as I am a part of them?

Max Haushofer regards mountains as holy places:

> And when, with your staff, you stand on the top of a ridge
> Where the terrors sit icy-haired,
> Where patches of fog blow past you,
> When you regard distant valleys below—
> Wave on high your brightly feathered hat,
> Let out a joyful shout and say:
> How beautiful the world looks so far below me!
> Only one stands on the top, and that one is I!

Heroism on a glacial crevasse; lyrics beneath the summit's cross!

To return to the question of motives: the primary external motive today is undoubtedly joy in athletic achievement. How does it look from within? Is climbing a way to self-knowledge? Does it represent the search for self-confirmation, a means of self-discovery through the expenditure of extraordinary effort, through showing what one still can do? It is perhaps a way of overcoming one's inner cowardice and of being alone with one's self. One study of the subject revealed that sensations of joy were typically felt particularly by male climbers (as is also the case in motorcycling). The following feelings were quoted: "Gripped by ecstasy, staking everything on one card"; "nervous tremor, as in a state of rapturous intoxication"; a kind of "being high is being free."

Friedrich Schiller, who never saw the Alps, proclaimed in his drama *The Bride from Messina:* "Freedom exists in the mountains." And this is certainly a sentiment that has exerted ever greater influence in modern times. Human beings take flight from their urban prisons of concrete, as well as from bureaucratic routine and technological order, and head for green pastures. They seek nature in its most pristine and wildest form. And because so-called progress pursues man with its highways and cable cars, one must climb ever higher if one wants to regain a feeling for life's richness. What is important is not what mountains really are but what the mountain world means to the climber.

In his story *The Lonely Man,* the Swiss author Alfred Graber treats a further theme that plays a part in the unconscious motivation of many extreme Alpine climbers: "And if I have to die someday, why should it not be in the mountains?" The desire to toy with death, the charm of daring to do something that cannot be calculated—might not the death wish be a motivating factor? Reading Toni Hiebeler's *Lexicon of the Alps,* one becomes oppressed by the many reports of the deaths of well-known climbers: lost, fallen, struck by ice, smashed by falling rock, disappeared, altitude sick—no one is left to die in an old-age home.

Walter Pause has written a fascinating and gripping book on the subject: *Death as a Climbing Partner.* Hermann von Barth said, "Whoever comes with me must be prepared to die." He made his most daring trips alone!

Back to literature: the classical poets reveled in and for nature. But Goethe alone proved to be an active admirer of mountains. Three trips to Switzerland took him as far as the Gotthard Pass, as well as to the summits of the Rigi and the Dôle. He watched with wonder the phenomenon of "Alpine glow" on the summit of Mont Blanc. Goethe's experience of the Alps was a source of "constant elevation and purification." His experience of the Harz Mountains, however, made a more lasting impression on him. The Harz, a mountain chain rich in myth and called by Novalis "the mother of mountains," was a favorite of romantics like Tieck, of German patriarchs like Klopstock, and of critical minds like Heinrich Heine. In the winter of 1777, Goethe traveled through the Harz and climbed the Brocken in the snow. Here, where "demons were said to dwell," the poet gathered the first impressions that were later to take shape in the Walpurgis Night scene of his drama *Faust:*

> The snow-laden ridge of the fearful summit,
> which superstitious folk had peopled with wreaths
> of dancing spirits—this mountain had now become
> for him an altar upon which he could fall in
> passionate gratitude.

Friedrich Hölderlin, already in flight from himself, worked for four months as a tutor for the merchant Gonzenbach in Hauptwyl in the canton of Thurgau. For this outsider, nature was necessary as an elixir of life: "If God Almighty has a throne on this earth, then it must be above these magnificent peaks." On his trip to Switzerland, Kleist once confessed to a friend that the Jungfrau Mountain (whose name means "virgin") was the only virgin he loved. Another pessimistic soul, Nicholas Lenau, cried out: "Alps, Alps, you shall remain beyond compare in my heart forever."

Nature, landscape, and the world of mountains appear as dominating themes in the works of very few poets. One of them was the Swiss theologian Albert Bitzius, who wrote under the name of Jeremias Gotthelf. His spontaneous joy in telling stories and his powerful language made him into one of Switzerland's most popular writers in the best sense of the term. His peasant novels *Uli, the Servant* and *Uli, the Landowner* failed completely and undeservedly, having been caught up in the backlash against "blood and soil" literature. The only works of real value in the mountain genre have been produced by writers from the Alpine lands. Germany's contributions here have been second-rate. Of outstanding literary achievement are the works of the Austrians Ludwig Anzengruber (in his village stories) and Peter Rosegger (the enlightened farmer boy), and the great Swiss writers Gottfried Keller ("I walk through the rocks and climb as high as the clouds upon my narrow path; in the Alps foams the white Rhine and my way is called 'via mala'") and Conrad Ferdinand Meyer (who on the highest peaks felt himself closest to God).

The more well-known and mysterious mountain climbing became, the more fashionable novels about mountains became. Edelweiss bloomed, forester's apprentices engaged in tragic battles with poachers, innocent maidens defended themselves against coarse villains, countesses fell in love with stable boys, young barons were permitted to court mountain peasants' daughters—and towering above these earthly scenes stood the eternally silent mountains, silhouetted against the evening twilight. Ludwig Ganghofer, Richard Voss, Rudolph Stratz, Georg von Ompteda, Ernst Zahn—they all exploited their readers' interest in mountains. Jakob Christoph Heer described the intrusion of technology upon nature in his novel *On the Shores of Sacred Waters*. In *Pilatus*, Heinrich Federer circumspectly portrayed the homosexual aspect of a friendship between male mountain climbers within the framework of an Alpine club. Of all those who wrote about mountains, the Welsh-Swiss writer Charles Ferdinand Ramuz, who died in 1947, probably possessed the greatest talent. In his novels *Avalanche on Derborence* and *The Great Horror in the Mountains*, the mystical connection that exists between the forces of nature and human fear leads to inevitable doom.

When the great classical period of mountain climbing began in the 1860s, a newer form of Alpine literature arose: books of "experiences." When one looks back today, it seems as if everyone who set out with a rope and ice axe also felt constrained to take paper and pencil along. Great bores set down their thoughts on paper, but involuntary humor was also produced. Great mountains were described as the "infinite cathedral of the Creator," arching high above the earth. At the same time, they were seen as petrified oceanic waves of rock. Mountain paths danced nimbly over stony cliffs; here and there some hero struck his faithful Alpine sword (ice axe) into a silver lock (glacier) in order to be able to meet God face to face on the bridge to heaven. The moon is a silver tear, glaciers are white lanterns, snowfields are shining shields, and snow cornices are overflowing breasts (in case you don't know, snow cornices commonly break off!). And, naturally, "mountain climbing is divine worship, a cult of the heights, a return to the sacred and pure sources of being" (Rudolf Haas in *Glittering Summits*). There is much here that is touching, but most of these works are unbearable.

In spite of the many significant, well-written books that have appeared in the past few decades, I still find Edward Whymper's *Experiences on Trips through Mountains and Glaciers* to be the most beautiful, the freshest, and the most exciting book ever to have been written by a climber. The book is finally to be reissued, but it will contain the illustrations of the first edition of 1872, which includes such scurrilous drawings as "Vertical Cross Section of the Snow

on the Summit of Col de Valpelline in August 1866." The London Alpine Club with its more than a hundred members had plotted the British offensive upon the unexplored Alpine peaks. The young illustrator became famous as the first man to reach the summit of the Matterhorn (July 14, 1865).

Edward Whymper's race against the Italian mountain guide Jean Antoine Carrel, who ascended from Breuil in the south, as well as the terrible catastrophe that occurred when a rope broke and four fell to their deaths, provided a whole series of writers with material. One example is Karl Haensel's book *The Battle for the Matterhorn*.

There are many more books in my mountain library. Herbert Tichy is represented by *To the Most Sacred Mountain in the World*, *The Paths of Man*, *Mountains and the Gods*, and *On Distant Peaks*. I have been fascinated by Tichy's life-style ever since our mutual friend Liselotte told me about some of his adventures. He spent seven years in China and in Tibetan monasteries, climbed three 6,000-meter (19,685-foot) and two 5,000-meter (16,404-foot) peaks in western Nepal all in one go, and was the first man to reach the summit of the 8,000-meter (26,246-foot) Cho Oyu.

On my shelf also sits *Annapurna: South Face*, an uncommonly straightforward book by Chris Bonington, as well as *8,000—More or Less*, a work describing the experiences of the doughty solo climber Hermann Buhl, one of whose great feats was the conquest of Nanga Parbat. Compared with Buhl's work, the official expedition book about "the fateful mountain of German climbers," *Nanga Parbat, 1953*, written by Karl Herrlighoffer, is long and boring.

Toni Hiebeler's books on the Eiger are also in my library, together with Harrer's *The White Spider* and Lehne and Haag's *The Battle for the Direttissima*. Gaston Rébuffat, mountain guide and writer from Chamonix, is represented with *Stars and Storms* and *On Cliffs and Firn*. There are also some works by the Himalayan scholar, Professor Dyhrenfurth, a book on the South Tyrol by Luis Trenker, which is better than his novels, and, yes, almost all of Walter Pause's books: *From Hut to Hut, On the Chalk Cliffs of the Alps, On Extreme Cliffs*. I greatly admire Pause's unpretentious and entertaining, descriptive style, which always stimulates the reader to reach for a guidebook to the mountains (if such a stimulus is needed). Pause's books, which contain suggested tours and routes, have won over many enthusiastic friends to amateur Alpinism.

To close the catalog of my collection, there are two more

writers whose contributions to Alpine literature are, in my view, very significant. The first is world famous for his books and deeds; the other has written only one thin volume and is dead and forgotten: Reinhold Messner and Leo Maduschka.

One can and must read Messner, this enemy of "hardware climbing" and large-scale expeditions. One must read his works not only because of his and Peter Habeler's spectacular climbs, without oxygen, of the two 8,000-meter (26,246 foot) giants Hidden Peak and Mount Everest—it is not only because of Messner's sportsmanlike posture in extreme conditions that his works are important but also because he is critical both of himself and of others. He reflects on what really happens "on rock walls." He does not spare himself and reveals his most intimate thoughts. Heroic gestures are repulsive to him. He is acquainted with fear and confesses to anxiety in borderline situations: *The Challenge* and *The Borderland of Death*. As has seldom occurred in this field, Reinhold Messner has gained a large reading public. His works are not mere "literature for specialists on mountains."

Nicknamed "Much," Leo Maduschka was only twenty-four years old when he died on the northwest face of the Civetta in 1932 when a sudden storm blew up. Some say he was on the way to becoming a truly great climber because of his first-rate intelligence. Others say he would have become the modern poet of the mountains. He earned his degree after having written a thesis on the subject "Problems of Loneliness in the Eighteenth Century." Four years after his death, friends published his collected descriptions, poems, and essays in a volume entitled *Young Man in the Mountains*. This is a book that revealed much thought and reflection. Although his style was not yet perfect in these writings, it showed great promise. A small local publisher recently put out a new edition of the work, but very few people know it. I myself value Maduschka's book, for it reveals much information about a young man and his mountains. □

Helmuth Zebhauser

Man Has Always Painted Mountains

Pictures of mountains and mountain landscapes have been drawn, painted, photographed, and filmed. Painters, poets, writers, and musicians have been stimulated by these beautiful primal landscapes that at once attract and repel the viewer. Artists have never ceased to look at mountains, to portray them, and to describe their own emotions upon viewing them. Pictures of mountain landscapes, whether by successful, well-known artists or by unknown painters, hang in many living rooms. There is a great demand for picture books, large-page calendars, and old prints depicting mountains. Mountains also appear on postage stamps. Not surprisingly, the postal system of Nepal has had all the well-known peaks of the Himalayas depicted on its stamps. They look like photographs in small format. Why did so many people attend an exhibition of Caspar David Friedrich's paintings in Hamburg, set up in commemoration of his birth two hundred years earlier? Was it only curiosity? Or did the public's interest in his work reflect a new yearning for a romantic world view? Perhaps it represented for those of us who inhabit cities of concrete mountains a desire to escape into an undisturbed, harmonious landscape.

It may well be that the great popularity of genuine folk music from the mountains can also be traced back to such a consciously unrecognized yearning. The concerts of the Mountain Choir of Trient are constantly sold out, and their phonograph records have sales in the millions. It is the mountains that have shaped this music: from the call of the shepherd, sounding from one pasture to another on the mountainside, to the simple song of devotion or the joyous dance of the yodeler. Mountain landscapes have stimulated man and awakened his imagination. Out of this variety of sight and sound, the artist created for himself, but also for others to whom he wanted to communicate his world, his image of the mountains.

The essence of Chinese landscape is "Shan Shui"—"mountain and water." Their best-known manual on landscape painting begins with the problems of depicting cliffs and trees. The earliest landscape paintings in China date from the second to the fourth centuries. By the eighth century, complex landscape paintings began to appear. A new system of strokes for the representation of cliffs and the shapes of the earth entered Chinese painting in the tenth century. Soon, ways were found to express the light and shade of the cliffs and the structure of rock, as well as its alignment and stratification. The Chinese grasped the mountain as an aesthetic phenomenon at a time when in Europe the conscious perception and depiction of this element of nature were still nonexistent. With Chinese landscapes, the mountain was brought into the realm of painting. To paint a picture was considered the highest spiritual realization of a particular theme, no less perfect a realization than could be achieved by writing a poem.

In the Western world, mountains were regarded at this time as inhospitable places or the exotic refuges of demons. To climb a mountain would have been a totally incomprehensible notion. The imagistic world of early Western man was determined by spiritual and religious preconceptions. In this world, there was no room for mountains. At the end of the twelfth century, however, artistic expression in western Europe underwent pervasive renewal and change. At the beginning of the thirteenth century, painters were freeing themselves from Byzantine formalism. Jacob Burckhardt wrote: "Italians were the first painters in the modern world who more or less perceived and enjoyed the shape and form of landscapes." Dante may be cited here as proof of the fact that the sight of landscapes made a great impression upon the medieval mind. He not only described morning breezes and distantly shimmering light upon a gently rolling sea; he also climbed high mountains for the sole purpose of gaining a wide perspective from the summit. He took delight in distant vistas.

The painter Giotto introduced a new dimension into the world, and a spiritual transformation took place in Europe. The new humanism liberated man and art from medieval traditions. In the last, Gothic phase of the great European quest for renewal and change, a new feeling for life itself emerged; natural and unrestrained contact with reality was sought and found. The third dimension was recognized, and the shapes and forms of landscapes were finally grasped. Mankind broke through to a new sense of unconditional freedom, to a new perception of spiritual relationships.

The birth of secular art begins with the golden miniatures produced in the thirteenth century, the century of Saint Louis (1226–1270). This phase ends about 1426 with the Limburg brothers, who realistically depicted worldly scenes in their book paintings. This is the period in which Giotto, Duccio, and Lorenzetti were active and in which techniques for the representation of mountains are discovered and refined. At the same time, Petrarch climbed Mons Ventosus (1336) and Fazio Delli Uberti (1360) described distant prospects from the Alverina Mountain, revealing a knowledge of mountain phenomena that could only have been acquired by climbing mountains.

Even before 1300, Giotto di Bondone (1266–1337) had painted a landscape in the church of Saint Francis of Assisi, in the midst of which Saint Francis is represented giving his coat to a poor man. Here the mountainous landscape is a very present reality, in spite of the fact that it has been simplified into a shorthand system of block formations. From this painting, it is only a short step to the "richly plastic concentration of trees and cliffs" in the work of Giotto. Within the span of a single generation, a transformation had occurred in man's concept of nature. In Assisi, there still prevailed a robust joy in the recognition, illustration, and perfection of the natural world. The joy of conquest was accompanied by a thirst for knowledge. Mountain landscapes provided a framework, an environment, a setting. In the later fresco *Joachim's Solitude* (Padua), nature becomes synonymous with feeling. Man and the cosmos work together in harmony.

Mountains and cliffs, each a kind of reduplication of Mount Sinai, symbolize the presence of God. The double summit of this sacred mountain passes through the imagistic world of the West as a symbol of God until the fifteenth and sixteenth centuries. During the Renaissance, no French court was more splendid than that of Bourges. Here, Duke Jean de Berry had commissioned priceless works of art. In the first quarter of the fifteenth century, the brothers Paul, Jan, and Hermann von Limburg founded a new school of realistic landscape painting. In their pictures, landscape is no longer mere background but is itself the center of expression. The Limburg brothers did not only use the shorthand block formation; they actually looked at mountains and drew them as they really appeared. As a result, people began to perceive the mountains as being real.

During the next two centuries, new and surprising ways of depicting mountain landscapes progressively developed. Simplified shorthand block formations were soon employed only to depict steep cliffs. Barrel-like mountains began to appear in the work of Simone Martini (1285–1344). Pietro Lorenzetti (1280–1338) made a distinction between steep flanks and gentle slopes. Ambrogio Lorenzetti (–1348) replaced block formations altogether with dome-shaped hills. Painters searched for and learned how to deal with landscapes and thus began to depict them realistically. Fra Filippo Lippi (1406–1469) worked at refining the newly won beginnings of realistic painting. In one picture, a cliff structure appears as a titanic pile; cliffs are heaped one upon the other like great stones. Nearby, other cliffs froth and foam in a fantastic manner. A green mountain chain shimmers in the background. Here, in a single picture, we find all the possible approaches to the mastery of mountain formations.

In the fourteenth century, man discovered nature and learned to look at mountains for the first time. A revolution in art began. Every new discovery in looking soon led to another. Ground waves, cliffs, and trees were recognized as elements of a landscape and perceived in realistic form. They soon acquired a spatial function. By the fifteenth century, separate elements were joined together to form a single, effective composition. A milestone in this development was a painting by the master Konrad Witz (ca. 1400–1445) dating from 1444. In his work *The Wonderful Catch of Fish*, Witz does not paint a landscape based upon some preconceived notion of the biblical Lake Genezareth; rather, he portrays a real, actually observed and realistically reproduced Alpine lake scene. He paints realistically, naively, and, at the same time, highly consciously; it is a wonderful catch of fish upon Lake Geneva. The area can be identified. Across the lake rise Mont Saléve, Môle, and Voirons. In the background are the steep, icy walls of Mont Blanc, which are rarely visible from Lake Geneva and therefore are seen only by careful, patient observers. Konrad Witz paints the landscape as it really is; through his eyes it appears in quite a new light. For the first time, too, the landscape is reflected in water.

Line perspective was next discovered, and the artist's method of viewing landscapes in perspective was heightened to create a grandiose plastic illusion of space. Andrea Mantegna (1431–1506), from Upper Italy, composed this space by arranging mountain groups. The viewer stands at a distance, as if on raised ground. The space falls precipitously off. Out of the depths the system of mountains is built up. The mountains are arranged toward the back in perspectively ever smaller rows; layer by layer, space is richly and dramatically ordered. In another picture, the Madonna stands in front of gigantic treelike, crystalline cliff formations. The cliff, which forms a background beyond which no view is possible, radiates light and stands there like a protective, commanding, and towering sign of God.

One of the greatest Renaissance painters of Venice is Giovanni Bellini (1427–1516). In the course of a long and productive artistic career, he refined the background landscapes of his paintings ever further until they, too, evoked feelings. Giovanni Bellini's inspired landscapes show mountains in their peaceful beauty. He concentrates on color rather than on drawing in order to create his artistic effects. Quite absent here are the rugged blocks of cliffs one finds in the early paintings, which were probably influenced by his father Jacopo (ca. 1400–1471) and by Mantegna. Poetry appears in all the elements of his landscapes. The clifflike, harsh earth structures are used only occasionally to provide a contrast with the pleasant, soft forms of the background landscapes. While Bellini introduced innovations into the rendering of landscape elements, man and landscape remained separate in his works. The human figure dominates the landscape. Nevertheless, landscape is seen as man's environment. It is harmonious but it remains in the background.

Next comes Giorgione (Giorgio de Castelfranco, 1478–1510). In his picture of the Palazzo Giovanelli in Venice during a storm, landscape dominates for the first time in Italian painting. The landscape seems to take up the whole picture—and what a landscape it is! Sensuously portrayed, manifold, metaphysically luminous, it determines the essence of the picture and enfolds the exposed human beings who also form part of the composition. Giorgione's last great work, the *Venus from Dresden*, remained unfinished. It was enlarged and completed in a masterful fashion by another student of Bellini, the painter Titian.

These two painters, Giorgione and Titian (1476/77 or 1489/90–1576), combined human figures and landscapes into an organic unit. This is their fundamental artistic achievement. The proportions of human figures and landscape elements are realistic: man, trees, mountains are in accord with each other. They all lie in the light of the same hour. They are all part of the same nature. The Venetian painters became aware of, understood, and represented the formal characteristics of landscape and rock formations ever more. They gave life to form; their mountain landscapes came alive, for these painters themselves lived in, looked at, and painted in the vicinity of the Dolomites.

Titian's method of painting, his ability to make distance and air visible, his comprehension of mountains and the effect of space in the Alpine world, all of this is an epoch-making advance compared with everything that had gone before. Here there is no longer landscape architecture; nothing is artificially fabricated. Titian submitted all his senses to that which is radiant, gloomy, deep, high,

101

distant; he heard the breathing of the landscape and was able to embody all this in painting. The painting *Ducessa d'Urbino* includes a landscape viewed through a window: beyond a hilly, tree-covered foreground, beyond a church tower that slowly melts into the evening darkness, the viewer's eye travels to distant blue-green foothills and green-blue mountains behind them. Above these peaks are cold and bluish evening clouds and the distant heavens. Perspective created by color conveys the landscape's depths.

Leonardo da Vinci (1452–1519) searched for the essence of mountains. With an eye for meteorological phenomena, he grasped and presented true perspectives of the Alps (Monte Rosa). In what is probably the most famous painting of a woman in the world, the figure is placed in front of a fantastic range of mountains. The landscapes in the background of Leonardo's great paintings, as, for instance, in the *Mona Lisa* or *Anna Selbdritt*, show an enormous "verticularization" of the mountains.

About 1500, the first wholly independent landscape paintings began to appear. Two significant events occurred. In 1492, Albrecht Dürer (1471–1528), using watercolors, painted the first pictures containing only landscapes. During his Italian trip of the same year, he made sketches of Alpine landscapes and mountains. He sought a total perspective, and nature itself was the sole frame of reference. His route over a mountain range stimulated the presentation of mountains. The Northern and the Italian ways of seeing the world were harmonized and made mutually inspiring. Around 1520, Albrecht Altdorfer (1480–1538), city architect and alderman of Regensburg, painted another independent landscape, of the Danube. The imagistic play and vision of the artists of the Danube School deepened and multiplied man's vision of landscapes.

The Dutch painter Joachim Patinir, also known as Patinier and Patenir (1485–1524), painted mountain landscapes from 1515 on. Here we find fantastic cliff scenes with towering rock formations. The vertical thrust of the mountains is contrasted with the horizontal landscape. With the work of Pieter Breughel (1520–1569), man's vision of landscapes achieves a world dimension. The seasons of the year are properly observed and realistically portrayed. Now mountains also appear in winter.

The baroque painters Nicolas Poussin (1594–1665), Claude Lorrain (1600–1682), and Gaspard Dughet (1615–1675) painted classical landscapes with mountains composed in an idealistic fashion. In the seventeenth century, topographers set out for the mountains. Mountain views

appeared and written descriptions of the Alps were illustrated. About 1800, an interest in panoramic views arose. The Swiss painter Escher von der Linth (1767–1823) painted one of the first mountain panoramas. It was an objective, unlimited rendition of the landscape as he himself saw it.

This new vision and the more refined and precise rendering of mountains correspond to developments in geognosy, a science of this period that was devoted to the study of mountains. Max Joseph Wagenbauer (1774–1829) was the first artist to go to the valleys of the Bavarian mountains in order to sketch them. He painted, among other works, the *Blue Gumpe* in the Wetterstein massif. Johann Christian Dahl (1788–1857), a Danish artist, painted the eruption of Vesuvius. In England, Joseph Mallord William Turner (1775–1851) gave form to his atmospheric visions. His paintings—fantasies of light, air, and color—show mountains in a way that had never been seen before: the paintings foreshadow aspects of German romantic painting.

Romanticism has often been deprecated and is still undervalued today. The landscapes of Caspar David Friedrich (1774–1840) have only just been rediscovered. His unusual rendering of landscapes reveals nature as a monument. The great exhibit in Hamburg (1974), which commemorated the two-hundredth anniversary of his birth, brought together 95 paintings and 137 drawings that had been widely scattered. His conception of art was all too clear: art should stand as "a mediator between man and nature." Landscape painting had become the expression of an all-encompassing pantheism. Romanticism created symbols for the loneliness of man, for his inferiority in contrast to the elemental forces of nature, as well as for the enigmatic, omnipotent power of God. Carl Philipp Fohr (1795–1818), the Heidelberg romantic, during his short lifetime painted mountain landscapes filled with his love for nature. His gift for drawing was combined with a passionate feeling for color. "A calm feeling for the sublime in the shape of the past" was for Goethe the romantic aspect of a region. Such a description defined the essence of a landscape as well.

If one is asked to comment on Swiss mountain painters of the last century, two great landmark painters immediately come to mind: Johann Jakob Biedermann (1763–1830), who painted at the turn of the nineteenth century, and Ferdinand Hodler, who painted at the turn of the twentieth century. There was also a highly varied, realistic genre (*Vedutenmalerei*) that arose as a direct result of enthusiastic travels through Switzerland. In the middle of the nineteenth century, Calamé, with his wild landscapes, became the most highly regarded painter in Switzerland. Barthelemy Menn (1815–1893) worked in immediate proximity to Calamé. Menn had studied under the great French painter Ingres and had followed him from Paris to Rome. Menn then returned to Paris and formed friendships with painters of the Barbizon School. Camille Corot said: "Menn was a teacher to all of us!" Hodler confessed: "Menn! I owe him everything." Menn's mountain pictures never have anything pathetic about them; the countryside, which is often bathed in light, reveals itself in quiet beauty. Mountains lie peacefully enveloped by a calm Sunday atmosphere. Johann Gottfried Steffan (1815–1905) and Gottfried Keller (1816–1890), the author of *Green Henry*, must be mentioned along with Menn. Their works reveal the beginnings of nature lyricism, which Adolf Stäbli (1842–1901) later developed and intensified.

Photography was invented in the middle of the nineteenth century. It was a technological response to man's profound thirst for realism. At this time, mountain painting developed in many directions. Alpine artists like Edward Theodore Compton led naturalistic mountain painting to extreme modes of expression. The major result of this tendency is to be seen in the illustrations of Alpine reports. At the same time, landscape painting, in general, attempts to make the fleeting moment stay, to capture the shimmering instant forever. Giovanni Segantini (1858–1899), the Italian painter who found his artistic homeland in the Engadine, paints hymnlike depictions of mountains in the clear light of the Alps. Using a segmented technique (in which the overall tone is achieved by the juxtaposition of individual daubs of color), he succeeds in conjuring up the glittering high mountains. Mountain chains and the measured world become the background, nature, and content of his pictures: pure landscape—and man in tension with it. His precisely constructed landscapes, the most powerful example of which is probably *Spring Meadows*, succeed more and more in achieving a direct and deeply penetrating view of nature. The greatest painter of the Upper Engadine is probably Giovanni Giacometti (1868–1933), who forms a bridge between Segantini and many other painters of our century. His landscapes are bright, colorful, joyous, and illuminated by the sun. He was able to render the colorful light that informs a landscape as no one had been able to do before.

The most significant and influential Swiss mountain painter is Ferdinand Hodler (1853–1918). In his early pursuit of technical perfection and as a mature painter,

Hodler encountered mountains as a fundamental experience. For him, landscape meant Swiss countrysides with lakes and high mountains, large picture formats, clear bright colors, and distant vistas. In the earlier works, high mountains appear broadly spread out and at a great distance from the viewer. In 1907 and 1908, Hodler approached the individual mountain. The idea of horizontal domination was given up, as were constructed compositions. The mountain stands there as it is, high and mighty in the middle of the picture. From now on, Hodler, the painter, was no longer fascinated by the mountain range but by the single mountain, by the summit. In 1911 in Mürren, something inside Hodler erupted like a volcano. Eighteen landscapes were painted quickly, one after another. "A frenzy of painting, of making shape out of color, overwhelmed him with primal force." The painter experienced the mountain with all its heaviness and with all its greatness and sublimity. Visually, he also brought the mountain much closer. The single summit became a web of ridges, flanks, and straight lines—variegated and complex giant, at times breaking formal rules and filling the canvas totally. *The Jungfrau of Mürren* and other paintings from this period present summits starkly outlined in brilliant light.

Hodler constructed pictures of individual style, using shapes and colors, contrasting heavy dark blue shadows in the niches of cliffs with warm green, red, and blue highlights. These pictures pass beyond a naturalistic motif to form a total unity encompassing the absolute essence and form of mountains. the *Breithorn* of 1911 is the most perfect expression of this unity of idea and form in the representation of an Alpine mountain. The picture of the *Jungfrau As Seen from the Schynigen Clearing* illustrates Hodler's typical rendition of that cosmic world feeling that has made him much more than merely a classical painter of the Alps and lakes of his Swiss homeland.

"How much is contained in Hodler's paintings: everything terrible and oppressive that lies within these cliffs and icy wastelands, these horrifying fields of stone and rubble; but also everything comforting and uplifting; everything about the mountains that makes the heart leap: Alpine meadows, the pure forms of their decay, the eternal, unfathomable, inconceivable purity of the radiant sky above—all this and much more we see." Along with his own epoch-making pictures of mountain ranges and mountains, Hodler served as an inspiration for future generations of Swiss painters.

To be able to speak with any degree of completeness about the mountain painting of our own century, one would have to enumerate and interpret a multitude of directions, schools, and forceful personalities. Lovis Corinth (1858–1925) painted the Walchensee countryside, the shimmering blueness of the lake, the mountains behind it, the reflected heavens, the sky, clouds, breezes—everything recorded with unmistakable brush strokes. Nature lyricism also emerged from the painting circle of Wilhelm Leibl. The painter Harrison Compton (1881–1960), much loved by mountain climbers, was the son of the Alpine painter Edward Theodore Compton. Harrison saw the mountains with the eyes of a man who actually walked through them.

The mountain landscape artists of the New Group (Lamprecht, Niederreuther, Meisenbach, and Maria Caspar-Filser) have since 1945 employed their own unique and powerful language to build upon the achievements of Oskar Kokoschka. We see their pictures in art exhibits year after year. Mention must also be made of Houwald and Hötzendorf, in whose pictures expressionistic and impressionistic elements live on. There is also Werner Gilles, who colorfully mythicized the mountain world, and Konrad Huber, his disciple. Painters like Segieth have continued the calm manner of the nature-lyricist Karl Haider.

A true survey of mountain art would not merely fill up a few pages but could generate a whole volume full of names and directions, of analyses of the most differing styles of expression, of seeing, and of perception. The art historian would have to speak of colors, inwardness, subjectivity, expressive power, gesture, style, broad, powerful language, ever-increasing abstraction, and of many other changes and tendencies in mountain painting. One would have to write of the ever-quickening ability of the human eye to grasp change, to change its own visual perspective. In this regard, one would have to take into account the advent of tourism in the mountains.

Western man has been making pictures of the mountains for seven hundred years. He has captured the essential form of mountains and given them identifiable names in his paintings. In this way he has conquered mountains and has banned their alien strangeness. □

In the fall of 1494 Albrecht
Dürer traveled from
Nuremberg to Venice by
way of Innsbruck and the
Brenner Pass, returning
home the following spring.
Dürer's encounter with the
mountains was recorded in a
collection of water color
landscapes. A self portrait
of the 27-year-old artist
(painted in 1498 and now
hanging in the Prado in
Madrid) shows a
snow-covered mountain
through a window. The
"Lament of Christ" (painted
about 1500, now in the Alte
Pinakothek, Munich)
includes an alpine landscape
of cliffs, distant
snow-covered peaks, a river
valley, and mountain
meadow (picture). These
elements do not serve as a
mere decorative background
for the main theme of the
painting. Dürer's
experiences in the
mountains on his first and
second trips to Venice
remained a powerful
influence on his work.

42

This section of "The Battle
of Alexander" shows how
Albrecht Altdorfer employs
a mountain landscape,
clouds, and the setting sun
not only for the background
but also as a dramatic
element. The battlefield
itself is a narrow plain
hemmed in by mountains, a
sea, and a small river.
Altdorfer painted the work
on wood and it took him
more than one year to
complete it. In 1529 he
delivered it to Duke
Wilhelm IV in Munich by
whom it had been
commissioned. In 1800 the
French seized the painting
and it hung for years in
Napoleon's dressing room in
St. Cloud. In 1815 it was
returned to Munich where it
has been hanging in the Alte
Pinakothek since 1836.
Friedrich Schlegel saw the
work in 1804. Asked to
comment on whether it was
a landscape, a historical
painting, or a battle piece,
Schlegel answered: "It is
everything at once and
more: it is a painting
entirely new and different in
style, a genre for itself."

44

Caspar David Friedrich, who lived and worked in Dresden, regarded art "as a mediator between man and nature." The strong expressive power which this artist's work possesses even today is largely the result of his feeling for the manifold moods of nature which was nurtured by much careful observation. Caspar David Friedrich's painting of the Riesengebirge, which he saw while on a short trip from Dresden, evokes a late fall mood. Its bare branches, valley fog, and hazy background produce feelings which the artist himself must have experienced and which are familiar to many a mountain climber of today.

44

The Swiss artist Ferdinand
Hodler painted mountain
landscapes both at the
beginning and the end of his
career. In between he
devoted himself to heroic
historical pictures, symbolic
allegories, and

lines of his Swiss mountain
landscapes have led to his
being regarded as the
founder of modern painting
in his country. Ferdinand
Hodler's "Lake Geneva
against the Savoy Alps" was
painted in 1907.

45

The summit of Nanga Parbat casts its shadow over the western landscape. This picture was taken at sunrise. Four climbers from Steiermark ascended the mountain alone in the summer of 1977. Making one last bivouac at 8,020 meters (26,312 feet) just below the summit, they set out again with the rising sun. The moon was still gleaming in the western sky but the sun's rays began to warm their frozen bodies. The shadow of the "Naked Mountain" lay over the landscape. Far beyond flows the Indus, which comes from Tibet and encircles this king of all mountains.

46

Nanga Parbat, Naked Mountain, also called Diamir, King of Mountains. This picture-book meadow lies on the north side of the mountain and can be reached by way of the Rakhiot Valley. Expeditions of the 1930s crossed this meadow on their way toward the mountain. The history of these expeditions is filled with tragedy. Some of their members died of exhaustion in mountain storms while others were buried in avalanches together with their faithful porters. The 1953 expedition also crossed this meadow. On July 3, 1953 Hermann Buhl reached the summit.

47

Cho Oyu: only 30 kilometers (18.6 miles) north of Mount Everest. The mountain has many Tibetan names: Turquoise Goddess, Great Head, Mighty Head, Godhead, the Head of God. Cho Oyu is visible from far away if one regards it from Tibet to the north. The view from Nepal in the south is blocked by other mountains. Cho Oyu was first climbed in 1954 by the Austrians Herbert Tichy and Sepp Jöchler who were accompanied by the famous Sherpa Pasang Dawa Lama.

48

48

Manaslu: in north-central Nepal on the border of Tibet. In 1956 members of an expedition from Japan were the first to reach the top. In April 1972, after his successful ascent up the south flank of Manaslu, Reinhold Messner brought back one of the two pitons left by the Japanese climbers in the rocks of the summit.

49

Lhotse: joined to Mount
Everest by its south saddle
at a height of nearly 8,000
meters (ca. 26,250 feet)
above sea level. The main
summit (left) is 8,501 meters
(27,890 feet) high. To the
right is Lhotse Shar [8,383
meters (27,502 feet)]. The

Swiss team of Ernst Reiss
and Fritz Luchsinger were
the first to climb it in 1956.
Two other roped parties,
Jürg Marmet with Ernst
Schmied and Hans Rudolf
von Gunten with Adolf
Reist, continued on to the
top of Mount Everest.

Bruno Moravetz

Because Mount Everest Is There— The Decade of the Highest Mountains

The south saddle of Mount Everest is the world's highest garbage dump. This is what Reinhold Messner said in the summer of 1978, and he was not the only climber to make such a statement. Situated at nearly 8,000 meters (26,246 feet) above sea level, the saddle lies between the base of the summit of the world's highest mountain and its satellite, Lhotse. Since 1952 countless climbers from all over the world have striven to reach this point, for it is from the south saddle that one tackles the final 900-meter (2,952-foot) ascent to the top. Climbers and Sherpas have had to carry essential equipment up to this height. For the most part, this equipment consists of oxygen tanks. Hundreds of these tanks are said to be strewn across the south saddle along the ascent route. The doctor and mountain climber Oswald Oelz observed that "whole areas are literally covered with yellow, red, and silver oxygen cylinders of all types." Having expended themselves to the point of total exhaustion, most climbers have shown themselves unwilling to carry down the equipment they have carried up. Willing or not, they are often unable to. Descents from the world's highest summit are usually more like flights or escapes. At this point, the climber is close to collapse, to complete exhaustion.

The so-called conquest of the 8,000-meter peaks and the large expeditions that followed the initial victories harmed not only the mountain, because of the garbage left even on the highest ridges and passes; in addition, the landscape at the base of these giants has also been damaged. Expeditions are seldom sufficiently concerned with a clean environment to do more than the minimal amount of tidying up when they leave an area. They also chop down trees, ruthlessly ignoring the fact that so few trees grow here to begin with. Perhaps man's attitudes will change. But, even if they don't, the problem may be resolved in the foreseeable future by a change in the pattern of mountain climbing: climbers are even now setting out in ever smaller groups to find new and difficult routes to the summit.

121

George Leigh Mallory, born in 1887, had a passion for mountains, although he was a teacher by profession. His first love was the Alps, and he undertook many difficult tours in the Mont Blanc massif, often seeking out new routes. One of his most noteworthy climbs was up the north face of the Aiguille du Midi, a spire of rock and ice that towers high above Chamonix. Like many others, he too was later drawn to the Himalayas, the highest peaks on earth. Mallory was a man in the prime of life when at the age of thirty-seven he left England for the third time, in order to find a route to the top of Mount Everest. He never returned. On June 8, 1924, he perished, together with his teammate Andrew Sandy Irvine, a twenty-one-year-old student from Oxford University, who had twice rowed on the Thames against Cambridge as a member of Oxford's famous "eights."

The geologist N. E. Odell, another member of this third expedition to Mount Everest, had reached Camp VI at 8,145 meters (26,722 feet). From here, when the clouds parted, he was able to make out two dark points on a white snowfield. The little spots appeared to be moving slowly toward the summit. Odell was not able to say just where they were or whether they reached the summit, for the clouds returned and obscured his view once again. Nine years later, in 1933, members of another British expedition to Mount Everest found Irvine's ice axe at the height of 8,450 meters (27,723 feet). Mallory and Irvine themselves disappeared forever. Three days before Mallory's and Irvine's final climb, Colonel Edward Felix Norton had reached the highest point yet achieved by any mountain climber: without the aid of oxygen he had climbed the northeast ridge to the height of 8,572 meters (28,123 feet). The summit was less than 300 meters (984 feet) away. Nearly snow-blind and totally exhausted, he had to give up and turn back as night was about to fall.

On June 2, 1953, nearly three decades later, a jubilant crowd cheered as Queen Elizabeth II was crowned in London. There was another reason to cheer besides the coronation: news had arrived from the Himalayas that on May 29, 1953, at noon, one of Her Majesty's subjects had reached the summit of Mount Everest. The New Zealander Edmund P. Hillary and the Sherpa Tenzing Norkay were now the first human beings in the world to have stood on the highest point on earth. Hillary describes the final moments as follows. He had just climbed over the back face of a very large chunk of rock. Now roped tightly to Tenzing, he "proceeded up a gently sloping snow ridge. Suddenly, we had reached our goal. It was 11:30 A.M., and we stood on the summit of Mount Everest."

In 1909, Robert Edwin Peary had reached the North Pole. (Some say Dr. Frederick Albert Cook arrived there a year earlier.) Two years later, in 1911, Roald Amundsen and his team were the first human beings to reach the South Pole. Now, the third pole had been conquered: The world's highest mountain had been assaulted and taken.

When the ill-fated expedition of 1924 returned to England, a requiem mass was held at St. Paul's Cathedral for the great climber Mallory and his young companion Irvine. George V, the King of England, said the prayer for the dead, and the priest chose a saying from the Psalms as the theme for his sermon: "Ascensiones in corde suo disposuit." God has enjoined man to aspire to the heights, to realize his potential, to reach for the limits of that which is possible, to uncover the essence of his existence, to discover the ultimate riddles of the world.

In 1924, George Leigh Mallory was already a successful, well-known, and highly regarded climber. As he was about to depart for Mount Everest for the third time, a reporter asked him how he could bear to repeat the agonies he had experienced two years earlier when seven porters had been killed by an avalanche and he himself had been forced to return to England with frostbitten fingers. Why was he returning to Everest again after all the struggle and deprivation? Mallory gazed intently at his interviewer and answered very seriously: "Why am I going to Mount Everest? Because it is there."

Kangchenjunga and Nanga Parbat lie far away from each other and represent, respectively, the easternmost and westernmost 8,000-meter (26,246-foot) peaks of the mightiest massif in the world, a huge chain stretching out for over 2,500 kilometers (1,553 miles) and sometimes achieving a depth of 250 kilometers (155 miles). *Himalayas* means the homeland of the snows. It is an ancient, sacred name for the mountain range whose summits, according to Buddhist and Hindu tradition, house both gods and demons. On the 1,500-kilometer (932-mile) stretch that separates Kangchenjunga from Nanga Parbat, twelve other independent mountain giants of 8,000 meters and more soar aloft. In 1852, Chomo Longma, the "goddess-mother of the land," was believed to be the highest mountain on earth. Known as Peak XV, the Surveyor-General's Office in India fixed its height at [8,839.8 meters (29,002 feet)]. Since 1955, its height has been definitively established at 8,847.6 meters, rounded off to 8,848 meters (29,028 feet). Peak XV received the now world-famous name of Mount Everest in 1856 in honor of Sir George Everest, who had been the head of the Surveyor-General's Office. (Sir George had retired more than ten years earlier.) The name Chomo Longma, Mount Everest's ancient Tibetan designation, was not known until later times. (Nowadays, the Tibetan name is appearing ever more frequently, as is fitting and proper.) Perhaps one day the abstract designation K2 for Chogori, the world's second highest mountain, will also disappear (K2 meant Contour 2 on a surveyor's map!).

Professor Günter Oskar Dyhrenfurth, a foremost expert on the Himalayas, entitled his history of the opening up of this mountain range *The Third Pole*. At first, only scientists journeyed to the Third Pole. Only later did climbers follow. Reconnaissance missions in the Himalayas belong among the most daring exploits ever undertaken by the world's explorers. Remarkably enough, one of the greatest intellects of his age, Alexander von Humboldt, triggered both the search for the magnetic South Pole and the exploration of the world's highest mountains. Three young scientists from Munich, Adolf, Hermann, and Robert Schlagintweit, investigated the Karakorams under the auspices of the Indian Surveyor-General's Office. This team of brothers, who were also skillful climbers, reached very great heights, crossed high passes, and brought back valuable information from the new and unknown world.

Before the Schlagintweits' time, officers of the Colonial Army had been busy making maps of the boundary areas of the Himalayas under the auspices of the British East India Company. Later, surveyors were systematically trained. These were the so-called pundits, whose "Great Game" was retold by the Nobel Prize-winning author Rudyard Kipling in his novel *Kim*. Among the surveyors were many Gurkha soldiers, who, though native born in Himalayan regions, had been called upon to defend Britain's position in India after 1815.

Toward the end of the nineteenth century, an officer by the name of Charles Granville Bruce was serving in a Gurkha regiment stationed in the northwestern part of India. When in 1895 Alfred Frederick Mummery, one of Britain's most outstanding Alpinists, wanted to join forces with Norman Collie and Geoffrey Hastings in an attempt to climb Nanga Parbat, Major Bruce placed two experienced Gurkhas at his disposal as guides and porters. With the aid of Ragobir Tapa and Gama Singh, Mummery wanted to reach the Rakhiot Valley from the Diamir side of the mountain by crossing the Diama Notch [6,200 meters (20,341 feet)]. Collie and Hastings waited in vain in the Rakhiot Valley for Mummery and his guides: in 1939, forty-four years later, firewood was found far above the tree line. It was believed to have been carried there by Mummery and his guides, who were probably killed in an avalanche.

Charles Bruce was himself an experienced mountain climber. Familiar with the local climate as well as with problems caused by high altitudes, he also knew the languages and peoples of the Himalayas. Twenty-five years after Mummery's death, he led several British expeditions to Mount Everest in a vain attempt to reach the summit. Before Mummery's assault on Nanga Parbat, Bruce had already been to the Baltoro region and the Chogori with an expedition organized by the Geographical Society and led by William Martin Conway. Mathias Zurbriggen, a guide from the Valais, was also along. Five years later, Zurbriggen was to make a solo ascent of the Aconcagua, the highest peak in the Americas.

The history of early exploration in the Himalayas and the opening up of this region to the West has been dominated by such personalities as Bruce (who later became a general and is regarded as the father of the Gurkha Mountain Guards) and Luigi Amadeo de Savoia Aosta, the Duke of Abruzzi. Alaska was the site of the Duke's first enterprise outside of Europe: he was the first to climb Mount Saint Elias [5,489 meters (18,008 feet)]. In 1900 he was a member of an expedition to the North Pole. In 1906 he climbed Mount Ruwenzori [5,119 meters (16,794 feet)] in Africa. In 1909 he joined a large expedition to the Karakoram. Vittorio Sella, the famous photographer of mountains, was among its members. In the Karakoram, the Duke explored the Baltoro Glacier and tried to find a route up K2. Turning his attention to the Chogolisa [7,654 meters (25,111 feet)], he reached the height of 7,490 meters (24,573 feet).

In the year 1899, the Englishman Douglas W. Freshfield began to explore the mighty Kangchenjunga massif, which lies about 2,500 kilometers (1,553 miles) to the east of Darjeeling. (Since its "discovery" in 1822, Darjeeling had become the summer vacation center for British officers and civil servants stationed in India.) In 1905, an unusual expedition set out from Darjeeling in the middle of a monsoon. The journalist Alistair Crowley had collected the funds, and the group included three Swiss climbers and Signor de Righi, an Italian hotel keeper in Darjeeling. On this trip, one porter fell to his death while three others, together with the young Swiss climber Alexis Pache, perished in an avalanche on the Upper Yalung Glacier. A spot above the Yalung Glacier on a hill 5,500 meters (18,044 feet) above sea level is now called "Pache's Grave."

Two personalities were later to emerge in connection with the conquest of Kangchenjunga. The first was a notary from Munich named Paul Bauer, who vainly sought a route up the (eastern) Zemu side of the mountain in 1929,

1931, and 1936. The second was Günter Oskar Dyhren-furth, who was born in Silesia but lived in Switzerland. Dyhrenfurth's international expeditions of 1930 and 1934 approached the mountain from the north and attempted to reach the summit by crossing the Kangchenjunga Glacier. The assault was unsuccessful. The first 8,000-meter peak was not climbed until June 3, 1950, when two French climbers, Maurice Herzog and Louis Lachenal, stood on the summit of Annapurna I [8,078 meters (26,502 feet)]. Within the next five years, human beings reached the top of Mount Everest, Nanga Parbat, Chogori (K2), Cho Oyu, and Makalu. But it was not until 1955 that an English expedition under the leadership of Charles Evans reached the main summit of Kangchenjunga, the mountain of "the five treasures of the eternal snows." George Band and Joe Brown had to wait just below the summit out of consideration for the religious feelings of the native population. According to local tradition, the god of wealth and prosperity dwells in this massif. There are five treasures associated with Kangchenjunga: gold, silver, copper, corn, and sacred books. Each treasure is preserved on one of the massif's five great summits.

Many religious views have played a role in the history of expeditions to the Himalayas. According to the Sherpas, who follow the Tibetan Buddhism of the lamas, natural catastrophes, such as violent mountain storms or av-alanches, which often take their toll of human life, mean that the god is angry. Nevertheless, the Sherpa porters, who are absolutely indispensable for successful assaults of the highest mountains, follow their masters with utter devotion, often to the point of self-sacrifice.

Willy Merkl had disappeared on Nanga Parbat in July 1934. When his body was found beneath the Mohrenkopf ["Moor's Head", 7,000 meters (22,966 feet)] in 1938, the corpse was covered by the frozen body of the Sherpa Gaylay, who had tried to protect his master. Willi Merkl had been the leader of the ill-fated 1934 expedition: at the beginning of July, a snowstorm took his life as well as the lives of Uli Wieland, Willi Welzenbach, and six Sherpas. Three years later, one of the worst catastrophes ever to occur in the Himalayas befell the third German expedition to Nanga Parbat: seven of the best Alpinists and Sherpas died in an avalanche. At midnight, a fatal mass of snow came plunging down the mountain, covering the tents as the climbers slept.

In 1924, General Bruce set out on the third British expedition to Mount Everest. Bruce was a man much admired by Gurkhas, Sherpas, Bhotias, and Tibetans. Bruce and his team, which consisted of members of the 1922 expedition, were honored in an unusual way: an Olympic medal in mountain climbing was awarded to the General as well as to all thirteen members of the 1922 expedition. (Only two more Olympic medals for climbing were awarded: Hettie and G. O. Dyhrenfurth received them in 1932. In 1934, Ertl, Höcht, and the Dyhrenfurths first climbed the western summit of Sia Kangri in the Karakoram. The conquest of this 7,314-meter (23,996-foot) peak represented at the time a world record for women climbers.)

Before 1924, Mallory, Norton, and Howard T. Somer-vell, attacking Mount Everest from Tibet to the north, had reached the height of 8,170 meters (26,804 feet). This was the first time any climber had reached a point beyond the 8,000-meter mark. Therefore, it was a record for the Himalayas in general, not only for Everest.

The Royal Geographical Society and the Alpine Club did not give up their attempts to conquer the highest mountain on earth. In 1933, Hugh Ruttledge led the fourth British expedition to Mount Everest. Climbing alone and without oxygen through newly fallen snow, Frank S. Smythe arrived at a point 8,572 meters (28,123 feet) high that Edward Felix Norton had reached nine years earlier. He, too, had to turn back.

Smythe later described a phenomenon that Hermann Buhl, likewise a solo climber, experienced after having spent a long period without oxygen in the so-called death zone [altitudes of 7,500 meters (24,606 feet) and higher]: hallucinations. Both climbers had felt they were climbing with a teammate. Buhl, who spent more than forty hours at this dangerous height during his conquest of Nanga Parbat, recalled having spoken with a nonexistent comrade. Smythe shared a biscuit with a companion who was not there.

Three more Everest expeditions by the British followed: the fifth in 1935 under the leadership of Eric Shipton, the sixth in 1936 under the leadership of Hugh Ruttledge, and the seventh in 1938 under the helm of Harold William Tilman, who gathered a team of men already experienced with the mountain—Smythe, Shipton, and Odell. Tilman had decided to do without tinned food. The main source of nourishment for the team was pemmican, which is meat that has been dried out Indian-fashion. Individual members of the team later reported that they had suffered terrible hunger.

When Nepal opened its borders in 1949, the first expeditions approached Everest from the south and west via Solu Khumbu, the land of the Sherpas. An American team arrived in 1950. Then followed a strange solo climber from Denmark, who had chosen the world's highest mountain for his first tour! In 1951, yet another large British expedition set out under the leadership of Eric Shipton. The team included two New Zealanders: Earle H. Riddiford and Edmund P. Hillary. Footprints, which were later known as yeti tracks, were discovered near Menlungtse [7,181 meters (23,559 feet)].

In 1952, a non-British team for the first time made an assault upon the mountain. A Swiss team arrived under the leadership of the physician Dr. Edouard Wyss-Dunant, the grandson of the founder of the Red Cross. The south saddle [7,986 meters (26,200 feet)] between Mount Everest and Lhotse [8,501 meters (27,890 feet)] was reached for the first time. The sirdar, or foreman, was the Sherpa Tenzing Norkay; he and Raymond Lambert inched their way up to the height of 8,500 meters (27,886 feet). The struggle was immense, because the oxygen tanks were not functioning properly. Just below the south summit the climbers had to turn back. A second Swiss expedition arrived in the fall of 1952 after the monsoons ended. The leader was Dr. Gabriel Chevalley, with Raymond Lambert once again as a participant. Other members of the team included Ernst Reiss and Norman Dyhrenfurth, the Swiss–American son of Günter Oskar Dyhrenfurth, who joined as cameraman. Lambert and Reiss reached the south saddle with Tenzing. However, they had to give up on the ridge [8,100 meters (26,575 feet)] because of mountain storms.

In the spring of 1952, the British headed north for Cho Oyu: this enterprise was to serve as a training camp for the 1953 Everest expedition. In fact, permission for the next assault had already been granted. Looking back, we can now see that what was joyously cheered on June 2, 1953, the date on which Queen Elizabeth II received her crown in London, was the British success in an endeavor that had been fought for during the course of three decades. At last, Edmund P. Hillary, the New Zealander, and Tenzing Norkay, the Sherpa, had succeeded in being the first human beings to step upon the summit of the highest peak on earth. John Hunt, a colonel on the General Staff, was the expedition leader. Many things had combined to make this success possible: a genuine collaborative effort by the climbers, the untiring assistance of the Sherpa porters, the sheer stamina and energy of Hillary and Tenzing, and, not least of all, the information learned from the Swiss expedition of the prior year.

Before Mount Everest was conquered, the French climbers Maurice Herzog and Louis Lachenal were the first human beings to stand upon an 8,000-meter summit. They conquered Annapurna I [8,078 meters (26,502 feet)] on June 3, 1950, though at the cost of permanent damage to themselves. Herzog, who was later to become State Secretary for Youth and Sports as well as mayor of Chamonix, lost several fingers and toes. For two weeks Sherpas carried the wounded climbers off the Annapurna massif. One of these Sherpas was Pasang Dawa Lama, who was to reach the top of a hitherto unconquered 8,000-meter peak four years later.

In the fall of 1954, Pasang Dawa Lama reached the summit of Cho Oyu [8,189 meters (26,866 feet)] with Herbert Tichy and Sepp Jöchler. On October 19, 1954, at 3:00 P.M., the group stood on top. The Sherpa proudly raised his ice axe with its flags of Austria and Nepal and made a military salute. Pasang Dawa Lama was one of six Sherpas to first reach the summit of one of the highest mountains in the world in the company of a sahib. Others beside Tenzing Norkay were Gyaltsen Norbu, who, with the Japanese climber Toshio Imanishi, was the first to reach the top of Manaslu [8,156 meters (26,758 feet)] in 1956, and Njima and Nawang Dorjee, who were with the team that first conquered Dhaulagiri [8,167 meters (26,794 feet)] in 1960.

Within a single decade—between June 3, 1950, and May 13, 1960—thirteen of the fourteen 8,000-meter peaks were conquered. Two Austrian climbers had each participated in two "firsts." Hermann Buhl from Innsbruck reached the summit of Nanga Parbat [8,125 meters (26,657 feet)] on July 3, 1953. Climbing under the auspices of an Austro-German expedition, Buhl alone made the final 1,300-meter (4,265-foot) ascent to the top. Kurt Diemberger from Salzburg was with Buhl when he reached the top of Broad Peak [8,047 meters (26,401 feet)] in the Karakoram on June 9, 1957, marking the second time Buhl had taken part in a "first" conquest of an 8,000-meter peak. On June 9, Diemberger stood on the summit twice: first with Marcus Schmuck and Fritz Wintersteller early in the afternoon and then again with Buhl much later in the day as the last rays of sunlight fell upon the mountain. As Diemberger was descending from the first climb, he met Buhl, who was heading for the summit, and decided to return with him. This Broad Peak expedition was one of the first small-scale expeditions to climb in these regions. The team, consisting of four outstanding Alpinists, reached the top without the aid of porters. Eighteen days later, Diemberger accompanied Buhl on his last climb. While attempting to reach the summit of Chogolisa [7,654 meters (25,111 feet)], Buhl fell off a wall during a storm when an ice cornice broke off. Three years later, Kurt Diemberger took part in the Swiss expedition to Dhaulagiri led by Max

Eiselin. A team consisting of the Swiss climbers Albin Schelbert and Ernst Forrer, the Saxon climber Peter Diener (then living in Switzerland), the Austrian Kurt Diemberger, and the two Sherpas Njima and Nawang Dorjee reached the summit of Dhaulagiri on May 13, 1960. The team and its equipment had been flown to the northeast saddle in a small airplane.

Austrian climbers as a group had the most "firsts" to their credit: Hermann Buhl (Nanga Parbat); Tichy and Jöchler (Cho Oyu); Fritz Moravec, Larch, and Willenpart [Gasherbrum II, 8,035 meters (26,361 feet)—July 7, 1956]; Schmuck, Wintersteller, Diemberger, and Buhl (Broad Peak); and Diemberger with a Swiss group (Dhaulagiri). After Annapurna I, the next French success was the first ascent of Makalu [8,481 meters (27,824 feet)—May 15, 1955]. Jean Couzy and Lionel Terray, who had been on the Annapurna I expedition, were the victors here. British and Swiss teams each had two "firsts": after Everest, the British conquered Kangchenjunga; after Dhaulagiri, the Swiss conquered Lhotse [8,501 meters (27,890 feet)—Ernst Reiss and Fritz Luchsinger reached the summit on May 18, 1956]. The Italians Achille Compagnoni and Lino Lacedelli conquered Chogori [K2, 8,611 meters (28,251 feet—July 31, 1954], the world's second highest mountain. Toshio Imanishi finally succeeded in reaching the summit of Manaslu [8,156 meters (26,758 feet)] on May 9, 1956, together with the Sherpa Gyaltsen Norbu. This was the fourth Japanese attempt to conquer the mountain since 1952. The first to reach the top of Gasherbrum I, also known as Hidden Peak [8,068 meters (26,469 feet)], were two Americans, Peter K. Schoening and Andrew J. Kauffmann. Only one more 8,000-meter peak, the lowest of the giants, remained yet unconquered: Shisha Pangma [8,013 meters (26,289 feet)]. Lying in Tibet, this mountain was inaccessible to Western climbers. However, a Chinese-Tibetan expedition led by its Chinese leader Hsu Ching conquered the mountain on May 2, 1964: nine members of the expedition stood on the summit.

The initial conquests of these giant peaks were cheered like battle victories. Their conquerors were honored, greatly admired, and even ennobled. Many of these ascents were repeated. As equipment improved, it became easier to climb at altitudes above 8,000 meters. Later expeditions did not have to find a route to the top. They could rely on information provided by the first team to succeed. Nevertheless, although many climbs were repeated, other climbers came along who sought out new routes on already-conquered peaks.

Many expeditions felt they no longer needed to bring along huge quantities of supplies and equipment. On the other hand, any number of enterprises set off for the highest mountains loaded down with materials. Japanese expeditions appeared to require the most: masses of food and equipment had to be dragged to Base Camp. A full-length television film was made of the Japanese expedition to Mount Everest in the fall of 1973. The expedition was termed "A Record of Human Existence on Mount Everest." For thirty days, fifteen hundred porters were busy transporting thirty-five tons of material to the Base Camp on the Khumbu Glacier. Eighty Sherpas were taken on for the ascent itself. They provided a support system for no fewer than forty-eight of Japan's best climbers. Six cameramen preserved this spectacle on film. The Japanese also filmed the remains of a helicopter that had crashed near the Mount Everest Base Camp a few months earlier.

An Italian expedition led by the industrialist Guido Monzino set up its tents at the foot of the world's highest mountain. Monzino spared no expense: the expedition could afford two helicopters, and its leader had shortwave radio contact with Italy.

The age of large and costly expeditions is probably past. The smallest expeditions had already reached the summits of 8,000-meter peaks in the 1950s: the Austrians Herbert Tichy and Marcus Schmuck had, respectively, conquered Cho Oyu in 1954 and Broad Peak in 1957. The future probably belongs to small groups of outstanding climbers. Chris Bonington has already led such groups up the highest mountains by new routes. Reinhold Messner, from the South Tyrol, climbed Hidden Peak with one companion, Peter Habeler. He plans to reach the top of Nanga Parbat alone.

There have always been men who climbed the giant peaks alone: the Englishman Mummery, who disappeared in 1895 on Nanga Parbat, has already been mentioned. Another loner, a romantic of the somewhat scurrilous type, was Maurice Wilson, a former captain in the British army, whom G. O. Dyhrenfurth mentioned in his book *The Third Pole*. In 1933, Wilson flew to India in a small plane. His original plan was to land it on Mount Everest at the highest possible point and cover the last stretch by foot. Naturally, he was not permitted to do this. Indeed, he was warned not to cross the borders of Nepal or Tibet. Nevertheless, he decided to sell his plane and spend the winter in Darjeeling. He set out at the end of March 1934. One pony carried his baggage and he was accompanied by three Sherpas. Wilson himself was disguised as a Tibetan. In rapid marches, he reached the height of 6,400 meters (20,997 feet) sometime in April. The Sherpas refused to go on. Wilson went alone. A year later his body was found.

During the period between 1950 and 1960, the decade of the 8,000-meter peaks, forty-four men, including six Sherpas, had stood on thirteen of the world's fourteen highest summits. Four years later, in 1964, nine Chinese and Tibetan climbers stood on the top of the fourteenth giant. The physical and spiritual achievements of the men who first stepped upon the highest, seemingly unconquerable peaks of the "third pole" deserve our full respect. These climbers rank with the Norwegian explorer Roald Amundsen, who first reached the South Pole on December 14, 1911; with Frithjof Nansen, who crossed the interior ice of Greenland from coast to coast in 1888; with Alexander von Humboldt, who sought to reach the summit of the Chimborazo; and with Sven Hedin, who spent years traveling the length and breadth of Tibet. They rank with these and many others whose explorations and research contributed so greatly to man's knowledge of the world. They rank, too, with those who risked everything for the sheer joy of great adventure.

But we must also remember those who sought possible routes, yet did not reach the top. And, above all, we must remember the dead. The graves, too, are testimonials to an idea, to courage, to the willingness to search for new worlds. There are many graves and graves of all kinds: graves of rock debris, graves of eternal ice. They stretch from "Pache's Grave" at the foot of Kangchenjunga at the eastern end of the colossal Himalayan massif to the stone monument above the "Fairyland Meadow" of Nanga Parbat in the west, which contains a memorial tablet to all those climbers and porters who fell, who died, who were buried under avalanches of snow and ice, and who—like Mummery, Mallory, Irvine, and Buhl—simply disappeared.

These men climbed the highest mountains on earth in cold and storm, reaching the limits of their strength, ready to bear deprivation, willing to exert themselves to an unimaginable degree. They tried and tried again. They finally succeeded. They stood upon the great summits of the world—"because," as Mallory had once said in reference to Mount Everest, "it is there." Because—these great mountains are there.

□

Guido Tonella

Teams That Transcend National Barriers

Guido Tonella declared a temporary holiday from his work in honor of his seventy-fifth birthday. In Geneva, he was busy preparing a lengthy description of the years just after World War II when the idea had first arisen of forming multinational climbing teams. His holiday was to be spent in a rather special context: he was going to participate in the annual Engadine ski marathon, which takes place in St. Moritz in early March. Many enthusiasts of all ages assemble every year for this event. As he later confessed, not without a certain sense of justifiable pride, this was the most beautiful birthday he had ever celebrated. Tonella received the applause of almost ten thousand men and women when the fact of his seventy-fifth birthday was announced over the loudspeaker before the beginning of the marathon.

This man from Geneva—born in Italy, white-haired, physically fit—was a passionate skier and mountain climber and had friends in all corners of the earth. As an Alpine journalist and historian, he was the first person after World War II to perceive that it was now high time for all those who loved the mountains to share their joy and take part in climbs together, irrespective of their differing nationalities. Unfortunately, his idea has not yet been completely accepted even today, more than thirty years later. Here and there, questions of national prestige raise their ugly heads. Nevertheless, at first all-European and then international teams began to be formed, although not without some difficulty.

It was only after Tonella had completed his contribution to this book that he learned of the death in Vienna of Norbert Biely, the founder of the High Alpine Group Bergland and a staunch defender of the idea of international teams. In memory of this man, we should strive all the harder to encourage the development of all-European and international groups.

If I recall correctly, I first employed the idea of a European team in September 1947—to be exact, in an article for the *Corriere Lombardo* in Milan. Its editor, Dino Buzzati, who has since died, was not only a well-known writer but also a passionate mountain climber. He asked me to write a commentary on the highly regarded second climb of the north face of the Eiger by the Frenchmen Louis Lachenal and Lionel Terray. This second ascent (July 14–16, 1947) occurred almost nine years to the day of the first successful climb by the Heckmair team. The year before, another important event had occurred: two Frenchmen, the veteran climber Edouard Frendo and the young Gaston Rébuffat, had ascended the Walker Pillar by way of the Cassin route.

Those were exciting times. The idea of Europe lay in the air, and thus it was not surprising that as a journalist I gave free reign now and then to a certain lyrical tendency, such as when I wrote the following lines: "The rust-covered pitons that had been once knocked into the vertical faces of the Grandes Jorasses and the Eiger by such men as Heckmair and Cassin, by Frendo and Rébuffat, by Lachenal and Terray, reveal not a trace of their national origin. These glorious pegs could do no worse than provide safety for an all-European team."

I repeated this passage word for word in 1949 in my preface to Anderl Heckmair's book *The Three Final Problems of the Alps*. (By the way, Heckmair and I are old friends; we first met in July 1938 on the Eiger Glacier, as he was returning from his grandiose first climb. We then learned quite by accident that we had both taken part in 1934 in the second Trofeo Mezzalama, a high Alpine race across glaciers.) To return to the preface of Heckmair's book: before concluding my thoughts concerning all-European climbing teams, I was forced to take a decisive and vehement stand against an idea that had been advanced in France. It had been asserted that the successful German and Italian conquests of the 1930s could only be explained by the political climate that was dominating these countries during that decade. The ascents of the north face of the Eiger and of the Walker Pillar in 1938 by German and Italian climbers were linked to the rise of the fascist temperament. It was even insinuated that the astonishing climbing achievements of Germans had been nothing more than an expression of their aggressive and warlike spirit.

I felt compelled to oppose this assertion, for I had myself always resisted the temptation to confuse political history with the history of Alpinism. It was for this reason that I wrote the following lines to Heckmair (please excuse my self-quotation once again): "Doesn't the mere fact that others have followed your lead, climbed your routes, and adopted your techniques provide you with the best answer to the question of whether your conception of climbing was the correct and healthy one?" In concluding my preface, I noted thoughts that had been preoccupying me even before I had the inspiration concerning European teams—namely, that the Alps do not separate but rather embrace us in a single unit. This fact should give all of us European mountain climbers a feeling of unity.

Perhaps it was due to Heckmair's fame or to the success of his book, or perhaps the words of my preface fell upon fertile ground; at any rate, the clarion call to a unification of all Alpinists found an immediate echo among the reading public. The concept of a European team—that is, my idea of a team, if I may be so bold as to say so—outgrew its infancy far more quickly than had been expected. It soon won international recognition. When Heckmair's book was published in France in 1952, my whole preface was adopted in spite of its rather polemical tone. The book was translated by Loulou Boulaz, the famous mountain climber from Geneva, who, like Heckmair, was also one of the well-known personalities of Alpinism in the 1930s. That my preface was retained strikes me, first of all, as a typical example of fair play that permeates French Alpinism. Second, it may reflect the fact that the elite of French climbers—Frendo, Lachenal, Rébuffat, and Terray, all mentioned in the book—have unanimously endorsed my position.

All these publications made me a popular figure to some extent throughout the Alpine world, not only in German-speaking countries. It is clear that this popularity is not solely the result of my personal efforts: the idea of a united Europe was in the air and had already begun to take root in general terms; it was only logical that it would eventually be applied to Alpinism in particular. Nevertheless, even today, after thirty years, I must admit without false modesty that I am filled with pride whenever my name is linked with the idea of European teams. Sometimes I catch myself thinking that my life as a climber has been justified by the support I was able to give to the development of international Alpinism by articulating and refining the concept of European teams. It would be wrong to consider these remarks as an expression of my excessive egoism. If I speak here of my efforts on behalf of international climbing, it is because I am firmly convinced that the camaraderie that exists among climbers of various nations is one of the sustaining and fundamental elements of Alpine ethics.

The principle of a fraternity of Alpinists is the point around which everything else revolves. Having remained true to my original concept that a spiritual unity exists between Alpine countries and unites climbers from these lands, I have merely expanded the idea in the direction of an international brotherhood of mountain climbers everywhere.

My ideas have gained sympathetic support from Egmond d'Arcis. In 1932, he founded the UIAA (International Union of Alpine Associations) and set out immediately after the end of the war to rejuvenate the organization. He succeeded comparatively quickly, for Germany (that is to say, the German Alpine Club, DAV) was reaccepted for membership as early as 1951. (Germany was one of the original six founding members of the UIAA.) Even at this time, it was clear that the UIAA was moving in the direction of continuing internationalization. My motto "Climbers of all lands, unite!" (a paraphrase of the familiar Marxist slogan "Proletarians of the world, unite!") did not strike my friend and teacher d'Arcis as being in the least revolutionary. He thought it fit in quite well with recent tendencies in the Alpine world.

I was invited to participate in the work of the UIAA and joined as the delegate from the Italian Ski Club (FISI). The first representative of the Italian Alpine Club (CAI) was Count Ugo di Vallepiana, who died in January 1978 at the age of 87. I would like to take this opportunity to mention a few of the count's contributions to international Alpinism. His successful youthful climbs on the Mont Blanc massif anticipated the idea of European team efforts. First, there was the second climb in 1911 to the top of the Brouillard Ridge in Mont Blanc in the company of Hans Pfann from Munich. Second, there was his ascent in 1913 of the Pic Gamba and the Innominata, together with his friend from Salzburg, Paul Preuss. The history of international Alpinism is also unthinkable without the contributions of Pfann and Preuss.

I later became a member of the Permanent Bureau of the UIAA and was entrusted with editing its bulletin. In this capacity, I served under various presidents, who followed one after another upon the death of the organization's first president, Egmond d'Arcis: Dr. Edouard Wyss-Dunant, Albert Eggler, Jean Juge, and the present officeholder, Pierre Bossus. One might be tempted to say that Bossus could have given somewhat more active support to the idea of European team climbing if he really believed in it as much as he says he does.

Let us now put aside the subject of my efforts and consider one important fact. To quote d'Arcis: "The UIAA is neither an international superclub nor some kind of international tribunal. It is first of all a connecting link, a clearinghouse, and is thus dedicated to establishing and strengthening friendly contacts between climbing clubs of various countries. . . ."

In this sense, the UIAA has performed an indisputably great service and will continue to do so. And in the perspective of the ever-growing fraternity of Alpinists everywhere, this is the goal of us all. The UIAA's Commission for Youth, which was created about twenty years ago in response to suggestions from the DAV, has been particularly successful with its youth camps and meetings for young guides. These activities have drawn participants from the most varied mountain regions both in the East and in the West. In this way, contact has been established between the climbers of the younger generation and the older Alpinists whose duty it is to guide them.

One must not overlook the work that goes on behind the scenes, without fanfare, and often in the shadow of some other event. There is, for example, the International Mountain Film Festival of Trient, which inspired Lothar Brandler's film *A European Team*. At the annual festival of 1958, which coincided with the twentieth anniversary of the first ascents of the north face of the Eiger and the Walker Pillar, a reunion took place that was attended by nearly every climber who had conquered these mighty walls. This moving event is a milestone in the history of the international brotherhood of mountaineers.

Let us also not forget the various discussion meetings that were organized during the Trient festival. Topics of general interest to international Alpinists were debated. One such topic was "Why Alpinism?"—one of the themes of the 1965 meeting at which I was a discussion leader.

Most climbers answered this question by emphasizing the camaraderie that arises in a team as well as by citing the friendships that are born as a result of sharing one's passion for the mountains.

There is also the joy of belonging to a circle of people who, belonging to different nationalities, perhaps do not all speak the same language but nevertheless feel the presence of a profound spiritual tie uniting them all. The French mountain climber Guido Magnone summarized these feelings succinctly: "The idea of European teams is emerging once again."

I must confess that I do not consider myself to be one of those people who ascribe a kind of magical power to mountains, as if man could become a better person through mere contact with them. I am rather of the opinion that mountains only let us discover and develop those characteristics we already possess. If we approach the mountains with a pure heart, driven by the need for spiritual exaltation, then the intensity of our mountain-climbing experiences can be strengthened by a magical hand. But it is only in this sense that one can assert that mountains improve man.

I would like to quote one other answer to the question "Why Alpinism?" It was suggested to me by my friend Kurt Maix, who has unfortunately since died. "Friendship is the most beautiful gift the mountains can give to us. A friendship begun in the mountains will last a lifetime, because there we get to know each other thoroughly and without the masks that we wear in everyday life. The great advantage of climbing is that we not only learn about ourselves but also about our friends. The laws of the mountains are often pitiless, but, precisely because they serve to create friendships, they are good laws."

You will understand that I welcome all efforts that make use of Alpinism to encourage friendship among climbers of all nations. I am thinking particularly of the High Alpine Group Bergland, formed within the Viennese section of the Austrian Alpine Club (OAV). My old friend Mathias Rebitsch of Innsbruck has informed me that this group has set itself the goal of cultivating and intensifying the idea of all-European teams (and, even beyond this, of international teams). The first advocate of the idea of a European team would like to take this opportunity of sending his best wishes to all those who are dedicating themselves to this effort.

□

Anderl Heckmair

Matterhorn, Eiger, Grandes Jorasses

In the fall of 1976, a few weeks before his seventieth birthday, Heckmair and his wife, who is an expert on Alpine flora, led a group of people on a hike in the Allgäu Mountains. Pointing to examples along the way, Heckmair explained the geological makeup of the area in an informed and lucid but not at all academic manner. His pace seemed slow as he walked uphill with short, regular steps, but those not used to hiking had to work hard to keep up with him. He was wearing a small backpack with a rain jacket in it, although the warm autumn sun was shining from a blue sky.

It was one of the excursions that the mountain guide Anderl Heckmair still makes occasionally with guests vacationing in Oberstdorf. He had a ready answer for every question, often in the form of a joke or a humorous anecdote. Those who were with him may not have been aware that they were in the company of one of the most accomplished mountain climbers of the 1930s. But Heckmair, a short, wiry septuagenarian, does not care. He is content to live in his mountains, to hike with his wife ("No more climbing!"), and to take extensive trips to see the world. He also does some writing. Here his manner is modest yet powerful. He expresses his views with an authority derived from long experience in the mountains, and his opinions are respected by layman and expert alike.

In his preface to Heckmair's book *The Last Problems in the Alps*, Guido Tonella writes: "In our universal admiration for Anderl Heckmair, we European mountain climbers have a unifying bond, knowing that the Alps do not separate us but bring us together."

At the close of the eighteenth century, interest in exploring and climbing the peaks of the Alps was high everywhere in Europe. It was at this time that Belsazar Hacquet, a Frenchman who worked as a scientist in Laibach, traveled to the Eastern Alps. In 1779 he came to Heiligenblut, where he did some preliminary exploring that later led to the first ascent of the Grossglockner. In his book *Unterricht für Bergreisende* [*Lessons for Mountain Travelers*], he recommended poachers as guides because they always knew a way out of danger; besides, a traveler would never go hungry in their company. He also urged that mountaineers chisel a sign into the rock of summits they had climbed so that later climbers would believe that they had reached their goal. On the basis of information gathered by Hacquet, Prince-Bishop Count Salm-Reifferscheid provided the financial backing needed for solving the "Grossglockner problem."

In 1799 the Kleinglockner [3,783 meters (12,411 feet)] was first scaled. Only from the top of this mountain could one see that an even higher peak lay behind it. In the following year this second peak, the Grossglockner, which measures 3,798 meters (12,460 feet), was first climbed by the brothers Martin and Josef Klotz, together with twenty-six carriers and five carpenters who went along to erect a cross on the summit.

Now there was no stopping. Every peak represented a problem just waiting to be solved. Well-to-do Englishmen who could afford to hire local guides played a major role in exploring the Alps. Together with their guides they scaled peak after peak. On account of this new sport, the English dubbed the Alps the "playground of Europe." It was only natural that the native mountain population, particularly the guides, wanted to conquer mountains on their own, not in the pay of foreigners. Climbers would seek out the easiest route, and when they reached the summit would leave a sign of their victory, either a pile of rocks or some other marker. Surveyors climbed mountains to make maps, and many ascents were made for scientific reasons. One of the mountains that excited scientific curiosity was the Zugspitze, the highest peak in Germany, which was first climbed in 1820.

The most famous of all the mountains in the Alps is the Matterhorn. In 1860, Edward Whymper, a twenty-year-old English painter and engraver, came to Zermatt and became fascinated with this mountain. The Matterhorn has two peaks 80 meters (262 feet) apart from each other, the Italian one [4,476 meters (14,684 feet)] and the Swiss one [4,477 meters (14,688 feet)]. It is not the highest mountain in the Alps, but it is the most dramatic. It has four faces

and four ridges, and each approach presents its own problems. The first assaults on the Matterhorn were made as early as 1857, although it was the general opinion that this mountain could not be climbed. Those who nevertheless tried were considered utter madmen. Whymper was one of them. He hoped to find a guide and partner among the Italians, who had already made some preliminary explorations. The first attempts were bound to fail, and they resulted in a bitter competition between Whymper, another Englishman John Tyndall, and the Italian team of brothers, Louis and Jean Antoine Carrel. Whymper reached 3,855 meters (12,647 feet), Tyndall 3,960 meters (12,992 feet), and the Carrel brothers 4,032 meters (13,228 feet).

On July 14, 1865, Whymper, together with his partners and Swiss guides, succeeded in reaching the Swiss summit by way of the Swiss Ridge. But on the descent one of his companions fell and dragged three of the others down with him. Fortunately for the other members in the party, the rope ran over a ledge and broke. The accident was later investigated, but no one was indicted. If Whymper had used a better rope, the whole party would have plunged to their deaths. The equipment and techniques used in Whymper's time cannot be compared with today's. To us it seems inconceivable that seven men would tie themselves to the same rope on a difficult climb. After this widely publicized accident, climbers went to the opposite extreme and did not use any rope at all. On the ascent the guide would follow behind his party, and on the descent he would go ahead.

Three days after Whymper's success, the Italians reached the top of the Matterhorn by approaching it from the south side. The next challenge was to reach the top by way of the two remaining ridges. First the Zmutt Ridge was mastered by the Englishman Albert Frederick Mummery and two guides in 1879. This left the Furggen Ridge, which Mummery also attempted, but he could not conquer the last rise. This obstacle was overcome after several tries by Guido Rey. He had two guides climb the Matterhorn by way of the normal route and lower a rope ladder down to him. In this way he was able to clamber up the last few meters of the Furggen Ridge.

After the ridges were conquered, the four faces of the mountains remained as a challenge to climbers. The first of these to be scaled was the dark and forbidding north face. The brothers Franz and Toni Schmid from Munich first conquered the Matterhorn via this route on July 31, 1931. This success spurred the Italians on to try the south face, which they mastered on October 15 of the same year. On

September 17, 1932, the east face was scaled. But it was not until August 13, 1962, that the fourth side, the west face, was conquered. Now all the major problems the Matterhorn posed were solved. But climbers worked out another thirty-five different routes to the top, one of which is so unusual that it deserves special mention.

An Italian by the name of Carrelino, a descendant of the famous Carrels, had the idea of circling the entire mountain at an altitude of about 4,000 meters (13,123 feet) and on September 25, 1941, he carried out his plan. Starting at the Swiss Ridge, he first crossed the east face over to the Furggen Ridge, then the south face to the Italian Ridge, then the west face to the Zmutt Ridge, and finally he traversed the north face just below the overhang. He reached the Hörnli Ridge at the lower end of the second fixed rope.

In the heroic period of mountain climbing before World War I, the period when the Matterhorn was conquered, climbers discovered new challenges all over the Alps. The Dolomites, too, offered almost unlimited opportunities. Many Italian and South Tyrolean guides figure prominently in the history of first ascents. Some guides even named previously unclimbed peaks after their wives and girl friends—Punta Frida and Punta Emma are examples—or "sold" peaks yet to be scaled to clients, as in the case of the Santerspitze and the Euringerspitze.

Improvements in technique and equipment brought about great changes in mountaineering. Pitons and carabiners were introduced for belaying. Hans Dülfer, a music student from Dortmund studying in Munich, did pioneer work in developing new techniques based on the use of pitons, but his primary aim was still to improve the safety of the advance climber. It was inevitable that controversy should arise between proponents of modern climbing techniques and those who rejected any use of hardware, like Paul Preuss, who stated: "To drive a piton into the rock is to violate the mountain." But the generation of climbers active after World War I used pitons as a matter of course, and with the help of this device previously impossible problems could be solved with relative safety.

The period between the two World Wars was the second Golden Age of mountaineering, and it was in this period that I came of age as a mountain climber. I easily mastered what were at the time considered the most difficult faces on the Wilder Kaiser and in the Dolomites. After climbing the Civetta and Sass Maor as well as some other peaks in the Dolomites, I returned home to the Wilder Kaiser region, where I became acquainted with Gustl Kröner, who had already done some extremely difficult ice-climbing on Mont Blanc. It was at about that time that the phrase "the three last problems in the Alps" gained currency. These three problems were the north walls of the Matterhorn, the Grandes Jorasses, and the Eiger. We thought that between the two of us we had just the right combination of skills to attack one of these problems, and we decided to team up. We picked the Grandes Jorasses as our target because I liked its name best, even though I had no idea where this mountain was.

Gustl Kröner had at least seen the mountain of our choice, which is in the Mont Blanc area. We did not want to tell anyone about our plans, because people would have thought we were crazy. For this reason we set out in 1931 on bicycles. Two climbers from Munich joined us on the trip. They were going to Zermatt, where they wanted to try their luck on the north face of the Matterhorn. Gustl and I went on to Chamonix and made the Leschaux hut our headquarters. At the first opportunity we started climbing the gully between the Whymper Spur and the Walker Spur, but a sudden change in weather drove us back. The bad weather that summer foiled all our attempts to conquer the north face of the Grandes Jorasses. Our one triumph came when we managed to climb the north wall of the Grands Charmoz vertically in a few hours.

During that same year the north face of the Matterhorn was first climbed by the Schmid brothers. Our friends Leo Rittler and Hans Brehm, who had bicycled with us from Munich, were disappointed that someone else had beaten them to that climb, and they decided to join us at the Leschaux hut. We happened to be away on another tour when they arrived, and, when we came back, they had set out for the north face of the Grandes Jorasses. They made the same mistake we had made by choosing the approach through the gully. They, too, were surprised by bad weather, and an avalanche carried them down the mountain. We had the sad task of recovering their bodies. At this point we decided to give up for this year but were intent on trying again later. We were not the only ones with this project in mind, and in 1935 Rudolf Peters and Martin Maier, both members of the Munich climbing group to which Rittler and Brehm had belonged, conquered the north face of the Grandes Jorasses. But the real problem, the Walker Spur, a pillar leading up to the highest peak [4,208 meters (13,805 feet)] of the Grandes Jorasses, had not been solved. In 1932 Rand Heron, an American, and Armand Charlet, a famous guide from Chamonix, had attempted to scale the Walker Spur, but they were defeated by the difficulties at the lower end of the actual pillar.

After the Grandes Jorasses had been conquered, only one of the three "great problems" remained, the north face of the Eiger. The first assaults were made in 1935, the same year in which the Munich team scaled the Grandes Jorasses. The first party to set out had advanced as far as the third ice field by the fourth day, when a change in weather cost them their lives. The summer of 1936 proved to be a dramatic one in spite of the fact that authorities had issued a prohibition against climbing the Eigerwall. No less than three parties met at the foot of the mountain to try the north face. The first of these had to give up after one member was killed and another seriously injured on a training tour. The two remaining parties, one made up of two Germans, the other of two Austrians, decided to combine forces. They started the climb on the western half of the north face, and, in gaining the first ice field by way of a rope traverse, Anderl Hinterstoisser, a German, found the correct approach. But this party, too, was forced back by bad weather when they reached the third ice field. On the descent, Hinterstoisser fell to his death, and the two Austrians, Eduard Rainer and Willy Angerer, were killed by falling rocks. Several attempts were made to rescue Hinterstoisser's companion, Toni Kurz, but after four nights spent on the side of the mountain he too died before the eyes of the rescuers, who were unable to reach him. The year 1937 was relatively uneventful in terms of climbing the Eiger. That year I myself approached the foot of the north face for the first time with the firm intention of climbing it, but the conditions were so unfavorable that I turned back. It was not until 1938 that I, together with Ludwig Vörg from Munich and the two Austrians Heinrich Harrer and Fritz Kasparek, met with success.

On July 20, 1938, Vörg and I reached the bottom of the north face around noon, early enough so that we would be able to bivouac on top of one of the pillars at the foot of the wall itself. When we reached that point, we found the backpacks of another party that had turned back. The night was as bad as could be, and by morning the mountain was covered by a thick fog, so that we decided to leave our things behind and descend. Suddenly, a figure emerged from the fog, followed by a second. While we were introducing ourselves to each other, a second party arrived. We stuck by our decision to go back, however, because I had no intention of exposing myself to the objective dangers with six climbers in the wall. In addition,

I did not believe that the weather would break. But by the time we were sitting in Alpiglen and watching through the telescopes, only one small cloud was still lingering at the top of the mountain. We noticed with surprise that only one party was moving slowly in the rock wall. The other party had been forced back when a falling rock hit one of the climbers. Now we felt free to follow the first party. We started out at night and reached the bivouac, where we had left our gear, by five in the morning. Around noon we caught up with Harrer and Kasparek in the second ice field. Together with them we climbed the rest of the way. Now the third and last problem was solved.

But what does it mean, the last problem? Routes had been found up the three walls in the Alps that had until then defied climbers. But there were still plenty of problems. A mere eight days after our ascent of the Eiger north face, Riccardo Cassin and his companion climbed the Walker Spur, which leads to the highest peak of the Grandes Jorasses. But, in the stir that our triumph on the Eiger created, this feat went unnoticed.

After World War II, equipment and techniques were further refined, and bolts, rope ladders or *étriers*, and ice screws came into use. Now no obstacle remained insurmountable. In the 1950s, climbers, using these new devices, began to find new routes proceeding as directly as possible from the bottom to the top. These are the so-called direttissimas. Another outlet for the desire to open up new frontiers is to climb even the most difficult routes in the winter. This used to be an impossible undertaking, but modern clothing made of synthetic fibers and down offers protection even against extreme cold. In the winter, the objective danger of falling rock is largely eliminated, because rocks fall only when water entering fissures freezes at night and cracks the rocks, loosening them so that they break free in the next thaw.

It did not take long before the three famous north faces in the Alps were conquered in the winter. In 1961, a party led by Toni Hiebeler first climbed the north face of the Eiger in wintertime. In 1962, a team of no less than seven climbers from Germany, Italy, and France succeeded in the first complete wintertime ascent of the north face of the Matterhorn. And in January of 1963, the famous Italian climber Walter Bonatti and his companions scaled the Walker Spur.

The direttissima routes also presented new challenges. The first experiments in executing these direct climbs were made on the north face of the Zinne. On the western side of the Zinne, the largest overhang in the Alps, which juts out horizontally for 36 meters (118 feet), was conquered with the aid of all the technical devices available to the modern climber. Needless to say, direttissima routes were explored and found on the north faces of the Matterhorn, the Grandes Jorasses, and the Eiger. The first vertical ascent of the Eiger took place in the winter. Englishmen, Germans, and an American competed in this struggle, which lasted thirty days. The climbers used fixed ropes in places where repeated ascents and descents were necessary. One of these ropes broke, and the American John Harlin plunged to his death. After this tragedy, the Englishmen and the Germans combined forces and finally reached the summit in the midst of a raging storm on March 25, 1966.

But further challenges were sought. In the summer of 1969, a Japanese team set out to scale the Eiger by way of its most difficult overhang, the so-called Rote Flüh. This enterprise turned into a regular battle of material and was executed in the expeditionary style that had already been used in the direttissima ascent. The Japanese carried 1,000 kilograms (2,200 pounds) of equipment with them, including 250 bolts, 200 pitons, and a total of 2,400 meters (7,874 feet) of rope. The cost of the venture was 80,000 marks, or about $40,000. The team spent a whole month on the mountain. After overcoming the enormous difficulties of the Rote Flüh, the climbers left their camp at the foot of the wall behind and battled their way up to the summit. Everybody, including one woman, arrived at the top without injury.

In my opinion, all the mountaineering problems of the Alps have been solved. But who knows what the future will bring? Expedition-style climbing will have to find new problems in areas outside of Europe. Climbing in the world's highest mountains has followed a similar course to that in the Alps. In the Himalayas, too, the highest mountains were scaled first by way of the easiest routes. Now the fourteen 8,000-meter peaks have been conquered. The next challenges are their lesser neighbors, as well as the ridges and walls of the giants. But in those altitudes the objective dangers are much greater than in the Alps.

There have always been those who have questioned the sense of exposing oneself to hardships and mortal danger in an enterprise that seems totally useless. But mountaineers have never been dissuaded by their arguments. Different climbers may give different reasons for their actions, but, in the last analysis, most of them would agree that what motivates them is the deep inner satisfaction they feel after winning a battle against one of the world's towering giants.

□

51

50-53
To climb mountains, to seek
the most difficult routes, to
ascend them through storm
and wind, ice and snow,
exposed to avalanches and
landslides; to have a goal, to
measure oneself, to take
stock of one's physical and
psychological limits; to
reflect upon the
senselessness of such
torture and yet not to give
up. To take delight in having
achieved one's goal. Then to
wait, to fall into a half-sleep,
to hope and pray the night is
over. Nights—hungry,
thirsty, freezing; tied to a
cliff, upon a narrow ledge,
high on a wall. To try to

sleep, to huddle tensely until morning, hour after hour. To ponder, to weigh, to wonder how best to go on, how to reach the top. All at once a snowstorm descends, the wind whips clouds, ice crystals, and moisture round the tiny human beings. Not to give up, nott to surrender, not to disappear into the storm. To have courage, the courage of despair, to hope perhaps to find salvation, a safe place, warmth, security. But one is not alone. The team suffers together, strives even further . . . together.

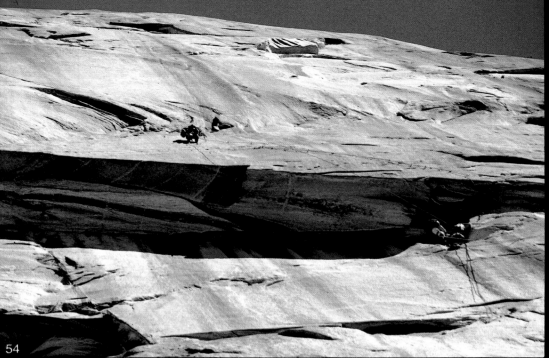

54/55/56

Climbing in the Yosemite: steep, almost flat walls, cracks, overhanging ledges. The brilliant California sun beats down hotly. Every drop of water has to be carried up together with food and sleeping bags for the cold night on these cliffs above the National Park. For many, the experience represents more than the conquest of a difficult route. For many, it is an escape from the ordered world of social involvement—bold, playful acrobatics over the abyss, a special form of self-expression. It is a test of courage—for oneself, for one's friends. To affirm oneself, to seek content for one's life, to find it . . . perhaps!

57

Ice climbing: iron crampons fastened to one's boots, secured to a partner by rope. Step by step, hold by hold—every movement must be carefully weighed. Cold is forgotten. Danger lurks everywhere. One false step and the climber can plunge to his death below. If an ice block breaks off, it will hurl him off the mountain, killing him. Up! Out!

58

On the summit: Lenin's head cast in steel. This 7,134-meter (23,405-foot) mountain giant in the Pamirs has been named for the Soviet leader. It used to be called Pik Kaufmann. Allwein, Schneider, and Wien made the first successful ascent in 1928. In the 1970s camps were built for the use of climbers from all over the world. Dozens have climbed to the top. They are rewarded with numbered commemorative plaques. For speical jubilees tablets are placed on the summit. In other lands, one sees crosses on the mountain tops . . .

58

Fritz Moravec

A most unusual story appeared in a Turkestan newspaper in the year 1889. In the seventeenth century, a military unit from the great Chinese Empire had stopped to rest in the high-lying Markan-Su Valley in the eastern Pamirs. Here, the emaciated horses were to recuperate in the good pastureland of the valley. Unfortunately, a winter snowstorm broke out unexpectedly early and trapped the soldiers in the rocky basin. The horses had no more food. One after another they died or were slaughtered. The soldiers eventually died, too. The unit commander's last orders were to hide the treasury and the booty, which had been taken earlier, in a cave. This grotto was located on a precipitous rocky wall 120 meters above the valley floor. The soldiers sought in vain to climb the brittle, crumbling cliffs. No one succeeded. A few fell off and died.

Someone finally thought of a way to climb the wall. Some soldiers cut pieces of flesh out of the dead horses and pressed the flesh, which was still warm, against the rock, where it soon froze to form steps. A kind of ladder of frozen flesh provided the necessary hand- and foot-holds for the climb. The treasure could be hidden. So much for the report of 1889.

News of the hidden treasure reached a Khirgiz prince. He, too, ordered his men to build a ladder of frozen horseflesh, in order to reach the cave. But, this time, the method did not work. At the beginning of the twentieth century, a few men reached a cave and found empty chests. Later, a Khirgiz shepherd found a silver goblet at the foot of the wall. With the aid of modern equipment such as ropes and pitons, Soviet climbers entered one of the cliff caves of the area. Under rock debris they found a piece of jewelry dating from the Hu-Wang Dynasty.

Competitions above the Clouds: Mountain Climbing between the Caucasus and the Pamirs

145

In Dürnstein, the Pearl of the Wachau, crowds of vacationers and weekend guests roam about from the time the apricot trees blossom until vintage time. Here, high above the Danube, is a fortress where Richard the Lionhearted was said to have been held prisoner for seven years. Dürnstein nearly achieved notoriety as an Alpine sports center. The first rock-climbing races were planned for the fall of 1977. This was to be the first competition of its kind to be held outside of the Soviet Union and was to take place on the rock walls of the Urgestein cliffs, which are used as a practice ground by many Austrian climbers. For many Alpinists, the fact that the conservative, hundred-year-old Austrian Alpine Club was ready to organize a climbing race was a sensation.

The Soviet Federation of Mountain Climbers had been trying to internationalize the sport of speed climbing ever since 1970. They had even sought to make this sport part of the Olympic games. It was a sport that the Soviets themselves had developed to perfection, and they supported their proposals with reasons. Competitive rock climbing is good because it demands great ability and the highest form of readiness to act; it evokes great enthusiasm in spectators, and it is not dangerous, since the climber is secured by a steel cable. Few people were interested, however, and the adherents of classical mountaineering damned competitive rock climbing out of hand.

There is no doubt of the fact that rock climbing as a sport shares many elements that characterize mountain climbing. However, there is a fundamental difference. In traditional climbing, safety is the first commandment: the first thing a novice learns is, Thou shalt not fall! In competitive rock climbing, time is the single most important factor; falls are expected and prepared for. Nevertheless, it is also true that mountain climbing involves a certain amount of competitive spirit; at least subconsciously, the urge to be first is a motivating force. The desire to be the first one to stand upon a yet unconquered summit is still active, as it always has been in every epoch of mountain climbing. In the Alps, rules and precepts to govern extreme rock climbing were never formulated. Nevertheless, there was always competition as to who was the best climber or who really belonged to an international elite. As for the much-feared publicity that would accompany the sport of rock climbing, why should this be so much worse than the publicity that even the most ordinary mountain climber seeks when he gives lectures and shows films or slides at club meetings or other gatherings.

In the Soviet Union, climbing for the sake of climbing has had a hundred-year-old tradition rooted in folk custom. Here, one climbs to prove oneself as well as to show others what one can do. In Siberia near Krasnoyarsk, there are many cliff turrets 8 to 10 meters (26 to 33 feet) high that in past days used to attract young men to undertake exhausting and risky climbs. The style of these men was often most provocative. They wore thickly cushioned clothing and wrapped a long scarf around their middles to aid them in climbing and also to secure themselves during both the ascent and the descent. These young fellows engaged in fierce competitive struggles, because the winners—like those who climbed the maypole—always found favor with the girls. In the USSR, the sport of competitive climbing began as a kind of "self-help" enterprise.

In 1945, Ivan Antonovitch was the director of a climbing camp in the Caucasus. He was exasperated by the lack of quality his instructors demonstrated in the area of rock climbing. In order to stimulate better performance in this sport, he devised a set of rules and established prizes. The climbers were always secured by a rope from the top. Competitive rock climbing quickly gained momentum. In 1947, the first interregional competition took place in the Crimea. Competitive climbing is now supported by the government, and All-Union championships have taken place since 1965.

Visitors from western Europe were invited for the first time to the fifth All-Union Championship in the fall of 1971. It took place in the Jaila massif in the Crimea. The Soviet athletes, performing their routines with breathtaking speed, demonstrated incredible technique—above all, in parallel and solo climbing. Team climbing, which is a variant of rock climbing in general, approaches the traditional form of mountain climbing as it is practiced in the Alps. When they performed in pairs, the Soviet climbing stars did not exhibit the same degree of polished perfection that they had shown when climbing alone. Nevertheless, observers raved about this form of Alpine sport with its emphasis on results and records. They believed that rock climbing as a competitive sport provides valuable training for mountain climbing. Their enthusiasm did not, however, succeed in overcoming the opposition of traditional climbers.

The first international championship took place on the rock walls of the Jupszara Gorge in the western Caucasus in the fall of 1976. Climbers from eight countries, including Germany and Austria, were invited to participate in individual and team races. The climbing conditions were unfavorable. It was raining, and the cliffs, which were partly covered by moss, were very slippery. The team representing the German Alpine Society was made up of Sepp Gschwendtner, Reinhard Karl, and Helmut Kiene. The Austrian team included Erich Lackner and James G. Skone. Both teams placed impressively high in the competition. Lackner and Skone encouraged the Austrian Alpine Club to organize a similar rock-climbing competition.

The climbing races never took place in Dürnstein as planned, not because of the protests of conservative mountaineers but because there were too few participants. Only five climbers wanted to test their accomplishments in the sport by engaging in a race of this kind. Nevertheless, one may dare to suggest that the time is not far off when the public will be able to attend competitive rock-climbing races in the Alps as well as in the Caucasus. After all, the amateur ski tours of the past grew and developed into the professional parallel-slalom races of the present. Industry has shown time and again how it can awaken this or that sport out of its sleeping-beauty phase and transform it into big business. The new passion for cross-country skiing is a notable example. "Sleepers" can also become box-office attractions.

Mountain climbing in the Soviet Union can be regarded as a new sport, if one disregards a few isolated undertakings that took place during the nineteenth and at the beginning of the twentieth centuries. The sport developed from two roots. First, an unverified report claims that the eastern summit of the Elbrus was reached as early as 1829 by the Circassian climber Killar Hashirov, a member of an expedition organized by the Russian Academy of Science, and by the Caucasian military commander, General Emanuel. The main summit [5,633 meters (18,481 feet)] was first conquered in 1874 by the English climbers Frederick Gardiner, Crawford F. Grove, and Horace Walker in the company of the Matterhorn guide Peter Knubel. Second, in the last quarter of the nineteenth century, Georgians began to take an interest in the mountains of their own homeland.

In 1877, the first climbing clubs or Alpine circles were formed in Tiflis. The members all came from the privileged classes. In 1895, the Tourist Club (ROT) was founded in Moscow but was not officially recognized until 1901. Its seven hundred members were high-ranking civil servants and scientists. After the October Revolution, students and workers could also join the various mountain-climbing clubs.

Today, the conquest of the Kasbek [5,047 meters (16,558 feet)] by two Georgian student groups from Tiflis in the year 1923 is regarded as having given birth to Alpinism in the Soviet Union. Professor E. Nikoladse reached the summit with eighteen members of his group. A. Didebulidse reached the top of this 5,000-meter (16,404-foot) peak with seven young people. (The Kasbek was first climbed by the Englishmen Douglas William Freshfield, Adolphus W. Moore, and Comyns C. Tucker, together with François Dévouassoud from France.) It is interesting that even this first tour reveals a trait that typifies Soviet climbing: it is a collective endeavor. In 1923, too, another group succeeded in climbing the Avatcha volcano in Kamtchatka.

A golden age of Alpine exploration and achievement began. In 1926, the Tourist Association was founded. It did not conform to the preconceptions of governmental officials either as to its organization or as to the activities it undertook. Therefore, a new society was formed two years later: the Proletarian Association for Tourism and Excursions (OPTE). That the government regarded the club as a very important organization can be seen in the fact that it appointed State Attorney-General Nikolai Vassilitch Krylenko as its President. Krylenko, himself a passionate climber, was Lenin's comrade in the great struggle and also the first High Commander of the Red Army.

The next important development was the organization of a separate mountain-climbing section within the OPTE. This section was given a great deal of independence. Krylenko appointed Vassily Loginovitch Semenowski as the head of this section. Semenowski, a diplomat and accomplished climber, had been arrested as a high school student because he was a follower of Lenin. Escaping to Switzerland, he had trained as a mountain guide. Semenowski applied the knowledge he had acquired in Switzerland and shaped the basic training system to be introduced and used in all the climbing schools of the Soviet Union. Instructors for these schools were soon trained in the central Caucasus, in the Besengi region. A so-called workers' faculty was now trained in rock and ice. In 1930, Semenowski wrote the first Soviet Alpine teaching manual.

Two accidents that befell solo climbers led to the strict regimentation of mountain climbing. In 1929, the climber Selheim froze to death on the summit of the Elbrus. In 1934, Nastenko fell from the north summit of the Uschba [4,694 meters (15,400 feet)]. Only group climbing was henceforth permitted.

In the beginning, those who wanted to attend a climbing school had to pay for the journey as well as for room and board. Only professionally qualified workers could afford it. Most of the students were technologists. By the summer of 1934 nine climbing schools were operating in the Caucasus, and the courses were all fully booked.

The Austrian Franz Sauberer, a trained lathe operator, arrived in the Soviet Union with a contract in 1928. A large group of climbers lived in Kharkov, and the climbing club worked together with the Academy of Science. This collective was especially interested in Tien Shan. In 1931, the first conquest of Khan-Tengri [6,995 meters (22,949 feet)] was made. The expedition leader was Pogrebetzki. Such experienced climbers as Tyurin and Sauberer were included on the summit team.

Toni Zak from Vienna had taken part in a 1930 trip to the Caucasus as a member of the Alpinists' Guild of the Society of Friends of Nature. In Naltchik, he met Semenowski, the leader of all Soviet mountain climbers. Soon thereafter, Zak moved to Moscow, where he worked as a foreman in an automobile factory. He also joined a climber's club. In 1932, Krylenko undertook a reconnaissance mission to the Garmo Glacier in the Pamirs. The purpose of the trip was to identify a mountain that was supposed to be higher than Pik Garmo [6,595 meters (21,637 feet)]. The results of a 1928 Pamir expedition, undertaken by members of the German and Austrian Alpine Clubs as well as the Soviet Academy of Science (under the leadership of Rickmer and including Eugen Allwein, Erwin Schneider, and Karl Wien), had exposed the riddle of the Garmo Glacier. The Krylenko expedition discovered the mountain whose 7,482-meter (24,547-foot) height makes it the highest peak in the Soviet Union. It was appropriately named Pik Stalin in 1933. It was given an equally fitting name in 1956: Pik Communism.

In the year 1953, another expedition set out for this 7,000-meter (22,966-foot) mountain. The purpose of the expedition was to conquer the summit and set up a self-operating meteorological station just below the summit. Three climbers found themselves in the front line for an attack upon the summit: Getye had a heart attack and had to remain in camp; the expedition leader, Nikolai P. Gorbunov, remained behind on the summit spur; Yevgeny P. Abalakov alone reached the top. The group found itself in great difficulty during the descent: Abalakov had become snow-blind, Getye's heart condition had not improved, and Gorbunov was frostbitten. Zak set out with two porters from a lower camp and met the summit team at 6,400 meters (20,997 feet). The men were brought down to the glacier camp. The two Austrians Sauberer and Zak were distinguished with the title "Master of Soviet Alpinism."

After the failure of the socialist revolution in February 1934, many Austrian members of the defense league arrived in the Soviet Union. These included such climbers as Franz Berger, Gustav Döberl, Ferdinand Kropf, Hugo Müller, Hugo Soell, Rudolf Spitzer, and Ernst and Fritz Tränkler. They soon found themselves employed in the climbing camps of the Caucasus. These foreign teachers probably gave new dimension to the Soviet Alpine training program. Ferdinand Kropf, who helped to found the Soviet Mountain Rescue Service, became the head of this organization after World War II.

In the year 1937, the Proletarian Association for Tourism and Excursions was placed under the authority of the trade unions. This transfer brought along organizational and financial advantages. The climbing camps in the Caucasus were now equipped with stable buildings that could be used in the winter. Group excursions were paid for, and the trade unions also assumed two-thirds of the cost of room and board. In the summer of 1937, Alpine training centers already existed in the Adil-Su Valley, in the Besengi massif, and in the Baksan Valley of the Caucasus; they also operated in the Altai range and in the Pamirs. In 1977, more than twelve thousand people took part in climbing courses. Besides the regular, planned program, Alpine collectives, so-called Alpiniads, were held. In the summer of 1935, more than two thousand people are said to have climbed the Elbrus, more than fifteen hundred climbed the Kasbek, and more than a thousand climbed the Pik Komsomol [6,930 meters (22,736 feet)], a spur of the Pik Pobeda [7,439 meters (24,405 feet)] in Tien Shan. For West European climbers, such Alpinistic mass movement is difficult to imagine.

Everyone interested in mountain climbing must take part in an Alpine training program. The title "Alpinist of the U.S.S.R." was authorized by the Central Executive Committee and introduced in 1937. The training program includes Alpine theory, first aid, and orientation on the slopes, together with a long hike to a previously determined goal. The course concludes with the ascent of a mountain of the difficulty of I(b). Only those who have passed this course and thus qualify as an "Alpinist of the U.S.S.R." are eligible for further training in a climbing camp.

The course participants are given uniforms and proper equipment in the camps. Class III is the first level. A three-week period of basic training includes ascents of difficulty II(b). The following year, a successful student can go on to class II and later to class I.

From the very beginning, climbing training in the Soviet Union was regarded as a system of physical strengthening.

The training programs developed and changed on a unified basis. Through central control, climbing could become a mass affair, while the risks of accident could be kept to a minimum.

But even a climber who belongs to class I may not set out on a tour as and when he wishes. Before each climb, the group must submit its proposal and plans to close investigation (usually in accordance with standards fixed by the climbing schools). It must also report to control posts maintained by the Mountain Rescue Service. Goal, planned route, and estimated return are entered in one report. If weather conditions are uncertain, the head of the Mountain Rescue Service, a salaried professional, does not permit the tour to proceed. The Mountain Rescue Service is also attached to the trade unions, which pay for the training of the rescue squad, for the costs of administering the service, and for the services of the director.

Climbers can work their way up to the rank of "Master of the Sport" after completing many tours of grade V(a) [heights of 5,000 meters (16,404 feet)] or IV(b) [6,000 meters (19,685 feet)]. A person who has climbed a yet unconquered peak or who has distinguished himself as an expedition leader can earn the title "Special Master of the Sport." More than 600,000 Soviet citizens have completed some Alpine training. More than a thousand Alpinists have earned the title "Master of the Sport."

In a society like that of the Soviet Union, the striving for records is consciously carried over into the realm of sports. However, because mountain climbing is not an Olympic sport nor one in which world championships are held, it is not greatly subsidized. All sports are driven by competitive spirit, which can be fostered by a process of selecting the winner. Therefore, a state championship has been held every year since 1947. There are many participants.

The winner is selected on the basis of such factors as the greatest height achieved as well as the difficulty of the routes and traverses if the tour is a new one. A jury decides which achievements deserve a gold, silver, or bronze medal. Alpine championships take place to a certain extent in a stadium that lies above the clouds. Therefore, mass participation plays a significant role.

Thirty-three climbing groups (more than two hundred Alpinists) competed in the twenty-second State Championship in 1970 in the Caucasus, the Pamirs, and Tien Shan. Two teams won gold medals in the technical difficulty category. One of them, a six-man group of student athletes from Moscow, climbed the 1,650-meter (5,413-foot) northwest wall of Pik Jagnob [4,248 meters (13,937 feet)] in the Gissar chain in the Pamirs. It took nine days (actual climbing time, eighty-six hours). The average gradient of the wall was 87.5°, and more than half the climb led over vertical and overhanging cliffs. The extreme difficulty of this climb could only be mastered with the aid of three hundred rock pitons and thirty-one bolts.

The other team, made up of five climbers from Leningrad, climbed the 1,410-meter (4,626-foot) west wall of Pik Bodchan [5,305 meters (17,405 feet)] in eleven days. Climbing time was sixty-six hours. The west wall has an average gradient of 80°. The climb was made more difficult by the fact that the team had to carry along half a liter (1 pint) of water per person per day.

Five more Alpinists from Leningrad won gold medals for technique and for height reached. They completed a first ascent of the northeast wall of Pik Engels [6,510 meters (21,358 feet)] in the southwestern Pamirs. They spent twelve days on the wall, which is almost 2,000 meters (6,562 feet) high and has an average gradient of 75°. For the combined mastery of the peak's steep slopes, rock, and ice, 143 hours of climbing time were required. No fewer than 355 rock pitons, 30 ice pitons, and 80 bolts were used.

One group qualified in the massif-traversing category. The six climbers (student athletes from Moscow and power plant workers) required six days to climb the north wall of Pik Tadshikistan [6,565 meters (21,538 feet)]. They then traversed all six summits of the Schachdara chain in the southwestern Pamirs. The total climb took fifteen days.

Very exact records have been kept of the climbs of the four 7,000-meter peaks of the Soviet Union. In the summer of 1971, seventy Soviet Alpinists climbed Pik Communism [7,482 meters (24,547 feet)], fifty climbed Pik Korshenevskaya [7,105 meters (23,310 feet)], thirty-four stood on the summit of Pik Lenin [7,134 meters (23,405 feet)], and twelve reached the top of the Pik Pobeda [7,439 meters (24,406 feet)] in Tien Shan, the most inaccessible of these peaks. In 1966, the Alpine historian Razek had recommended that prizes be give to those who climbed all four of these 7,000-meter peaks in the U.S.S.R. By 1975, eighty-two Alpinists had received the award, an honorary pin depicting Pik Communism. For the past several decades, all kinds of other Alpine awards have been given, usually pins depicting the particular mountain just climbed. These pins are eagerly sought.

In the U.S.S.R., special jubilees are always the occasion for great events. To commemorate the thirtieth anniversary of the founding of the Soviet Union, eighty-seven climbing sections sent five hundred Alpinists to the Caucasus. Ninety-two summits were reached. Three hundred climbers are said to have reached the top of Pik Lenin in 1967 in honor of the fiftieth anniversary of the U.S.S.R. This feat took place in the context of an Alpiniad in the Pamirs. Climbers from nine countries participated. On the occasion of Lenin's one-hundredth birthday in 1970, climbers from fourteen countries convened at an international camp for Alpinists at the foot of Pik Lenin. Since 1976, a subdivision of the Federation of Mountain Climbers has been attempting to make contact with climbers from all over the world. It has also organized international climbing camps in the Caucasus and in the Pamirs.

Soviet Alpinists who visited the Eastern and Western Alps have demonstrated that their climbing standards are comparable to those that prevail in the West. Back in 1965, Chergiani and Onitchenko conquered with amazing speed the east wall of the Grand Capuchin, the west wall of the Dru, and the north wall of the Grandes Jorasses (the Walker Pillar). Soviet equipment, which used to be heavy and awkward, has improved. The Masters of the Sport now use a special brand of pitons and carabiners made of ultralight titanium.

As has occurred elsewhere in the world, so, too, in the high mountains of the U.S.S.R., the period of exploration has given way to "difficult Alpinism." The only first climbs left in the Caucasus, the Pamirs, and Tien Shan are on remote, highly inaccessible mountains. These tours are extremely difficult and take several days, requiring not only perfect technique but many men. When such collective undertakings are planned, several factors motivate the participants. The primary wish is doubtless to become a Master of Alpinism. There is also the desire to conquer virgin territory. Finally, the mountain experience itself plays an important role here as it does elsewhere—even among climbers who have the title of master!

□

Elmar Landes

Mountain Climbers Are Children of Their Age

Reports concerning the dangers and horrors of mountains go back as far as two thousand years. Xenophon had marched across the wintry mountains of Armenia and back again in the company of mercenary troops who served Cyrus, the king of Persia's son. He took careful note of the dangers of winter, particularly the danger of freezing to death; he knew that one should never rest in the snow even if exhausted, for "movement creates warmth and suppleness." That was in the year 400 B.C.

A mere seventy years later, an army marched from Macedonia to the Indus, as far as the mountains surrounding Nanga Parbat. Alexander the Great had his soldiers undertake highly skilled Alpine feats as part of realizing his ambition to become "the King of Asia." His father, Philip II, had had units of his guards trained for mountain warfare. On one occasion, three hundred of these guards had to climb a steep cliff at night in order to seize a mountain fortress. For this task, they employed the iron pegs of their tents as climbing aids. Although nearly a hundred soldiers fell to their deaths, their surprise attack on the enemy succeeded. During his eleven-year-long campaign, Alexander was the leader of a whole expedition that included, among others, scholars who sent back reports and observations to Alexander's teacher, Aristotle.

The fact that mountains formed natural barriers between peoples and countries forced men to find ways and means of overcoming and conquering them. Everyone recalls Hannibal's crossing of the Maritime Alps with soldiers and elephants, as well as the mighty military expedition of Ghengis Khan, which reached as far as Central Europe. Henry IV's entourage, in the winter of 1076/77, also suffered great hardship in its struggle to cross the Alps on the way to Canossa.

151

The history of mountain climbing is—at least in terms of years—not very old. Therefore, many of the representatives of various periods in its development are still alive. Moreover, the beginnings of the Alpine tradition do not lie so far back in the past that they have ceased to affect us today.

Anyone who writes about the history of mountain climbing must realize that he will miss its essence if he neglects to perceive the life that surges beneath the chronological sequence of events that constitute its external history. Moreover, he should always bear in mind the fact that the history of mountain climbing—like every other aspect of human development—has not occurred independently of all the other historical events affecting human life at a particular time. Thus, the history of mountain climbing forms part of the general history of an epoch, irrespective of whether its phenomena run in harmony with or in opposition to the predominant currents of the times. The following attempt to trace the origins of particular developments in the history of mountain climbing in terms of major currents in general history can only be undertaken here in a very rudimentary fashion. One can only offer a scanty collection of phenomena from the vast collection of materials that exist on this subject, the bare bones of the theme, as it were.

On August 8, 1786, Jacques Balmat and Dr. Michel Gabriel Paccard became the first men ever to stand upon the summit of Mont Blanc.

During the same period, James Watt developed the steam engine, with its piston rods and centrifugal regulator. In England and Germany, the first attempts were made to light the interior of houses with gas. The cultural landmarks can be listed briefly: classical music (Haydn, Mozart, the early Beethoven); the rococo; the age of enlightenment; the age of sentimentality and of *Sturm und Drang* (Goethe's *The Sorrows of Young Werther*, 1774, and Schiller's *The Robbers*, 1782); also, extreme pietism and echoes from the Middle Ages (the last decapitation of a witch in Switzerland in 1782—shades of Gretchen's tragedy in *Faust!*). Goethe experienced these cultural currents in the form of violent personal "conversions." He became an enigma to his generation, a chameleon. His life already demonstrates the "discontinuity of modern man," and in his crises are reflected the revolution that was taking place in the order and structure of the Christian West. Goethe recognized "tragic man": "Two souls (Mephistopheles/ Faust!) are housed, alas, within my breast!"

In 1865 Adolphus Moore, Horace Walker, and G. S. Matthews, along with guides from Anderegg, opened up a route to the summit of Mont Blanc by way of the Moore Spur on the Brenva flank. A decisive factor in the development of mountain climbing during this period was the industrial revolution, for it provided the means that made it possible for ever-increasing numbers of foreigners, especially Englishmen, to visit the Alps, the so-called playgrounds of Europe. Naturally, not everyone could afford regular visits to these resort areas. Climbing became to a great extent—as is the case with sports in general—a privilege of the wealthy class. To this class belonged the English members of the first team to ascend the Matterhorn: Lord Francis Douglas, the clergyman Charles Hudson, and Douglas Hadow. Edward Whymper may serve as the exception that proves the rule. His Alpine journeys were made possible by an English publisher, to whom Whymper sent pictures and reports of his climbing activities.

The first ascent and the events that led up to it allow us to draw some noteworthy conclusions concerning the relationships that existed between the gentlemen climbers and their guides. It is well-known that Whymper and Jean Antoine Carrel wavered between thoughts of loyalty to each other and the demands of their individualistic competitive spirits. Finally, the Italian government itself intervened in order to maintain its national prestige. Michel Croz from Chamonix, who was the lead guide on the climb until the catastrophic descent, and Whymper regarded each other more as partners than as rivals. However, they raced each other up the last few meters to the summit. On the other hand, the two other guides on this first ascent of the Matterhorn, Peter Taugwalder and his son, from Zermatt, embodied the more typical local guide, who subordinates himself totally to the wishes and initiatives of his gentlemen employers.

For many historians of climbing, the first ascent of the Matterhorn in 1865 signalized the end of the golden age of Alpinism, of the striving for yet unclimbed peaks.

The industrial revolution was not the only significant occurrence to give permanent shape to the nineteenth century. A myriad of events literally tumbled one upon the other in this century of great change. They can only be outlined here. Napoleon took possession of the inheritance of the French Revolution. At the beginning of the nineteenth century, his claims to power and to European domination kept the whole continent in a state of suspense. There was also another, darker side to the industrial revolution, for the avalanchelike explosion of large-scale industrial enterprise destroyed other forms of livelihood. New perspectives on economy and manufacture were directed toward the unlimited expansion of production and industrial growth. This led, on the one hand, to euphoric speculation and, on the other, to an existential anxiety. Next, we have the 1848 February revolution in France, the March revolution in Germany and Austria, and the publication of the *Communist Manifesto* by Marx and Engels.

In 1859, Charles Darwin's work *On the Origin of Species by Means of Natural Selection, or the Preservation of Favoured Races in the Struggle for Life* appeared in London. With this work, Darwin at once established the theory of natural selection and gained general acceptance for the theory of evolution. At the same time, the natural sciences were discovering means with which to prolong man's life: Robert Koch discovered the tuberculosis bacillus in 1882 and the cause of cholera in 1883.

In the midst of these revolutions, the collapse of the Christian world order of the West was accelerating. No new order was able to stem and ameliorate the crisis of consciousness that thereby developed. This led to the corresponding and ever-increasing sense of discontinuity felt by modern man. This discontinuity expressed itself most clearly in the art and culture of the later part of the nineteenth century.

During the second half of the nineteenth century, a change took place in the style of mountain climbing that coincided with the spiritual crisis caused by the disintegration of the Christian cosmology. Some people tend to view these two events in terms of cause and effect. In any event, climbers from the cities, which were crucibles of cultural development, began to loosen their ties to the local guides. An example is provided by the Zsigmondy brothers, who placed the greatest value on climbing without the help of guides. (Emil fell to his death from the south face of the Meije in 1885.) Those who see the rejection of guides as an effect of general spiritual discontinuity should recheck their facts, for other developments also occurring at this time tended to show man's need for a new religion. In the last decades of the nineteenth century, the urge to go-it-alone spread among climbers as never before (for example, Hermann von Barth, Georg Winkler, Robert Hans Schmitt, and Albert Frederick Mummery; Mummery, accompanied only by two Gurkha porters, fell to his death in 1895 during an attempt to climb the Diamir flank of Nanga Parbat). A heroic-mythical approach to climbing mountains was cultivated by young Eugen Guido Lammer. He wrote: "Even when I was a boy, the province of life seemed to me to be most remarkable at its outermost limits." This attitude unmistakably characterized his solo first climb of the northwest face of the Venedig in 1891, the first traverse of the Olperer-Fussstein ridge in 1884, and the first climb of the east face of the Hochfeiler—always alone. Highly suggestive in connection with the quotation from Lammer is the title and subtitle he gave to his collected writings: *Fountain of Youth—The Mountain Journeys and Elevated Thoughts of a Solitary Pathfinder.*

Last but not least, there exists sufficient written evidence from these years at the turn of the century to prove that for many individuals mountain climbing took on the aura of a substitute religion: the mountains were an altar of light over the swamps of the lowlands.

There is much evidence to show that many a pilgrim to the altar of light felt himself to be a better human being. This may seem surprising, when one considers climbing in terms of the individual and his team. On the one hand, climbing provides an opportunity for the individual, who does not live in harmony with himself or his environment or who believes his potential has not been tapped or challenged, to test his mettle: in the mountains he can probe such human qualities as his spirit for adventure, his decisiveness, his prudence, and his tact; he is also given a chance to submit his own capabilities and his own success to proper evaluation. However, none of these factors is independent. If one is climbing with a team, one's own urges and needs must be tempered by the needs of one's comrades and may not conflict with theirs. That mountain climbers nevertheless indulge in eccentric cultlike orgies of self-exaltation at the expense of their comrades may speak volumes about their character: such behavior certainly does not bespeak the climber's having become a better human being.

Karl Greitbauer's book *The Figure of the Mountain Climber—Alpine Activity in Light of Psychology* provides us with a key to understanding some of this kind of eccentricity. Greitbauer sees mountain climbing partly as an endopsychic reaction of resistance to feelings of inadequacy. The mountain itself symbolizes resistance. By climbing it, one overcomes, resists, one's feelings of inferiority. In 1895 Sigmund Freud and Josef Breuer published their studies on hysteria. Toward the end of the nineteenth century, psychologists came ever more to the conclusion that feelings of inadequacy shaped and determined the human personality. All of this supports Greitbauer's thesis.

We are reminded once again of Greitbauer's thesis when we investigate the golden age of climbing, that is, the period of extreme Alpinism between the two world wars.

The development that took place at this time will become clearer if we first take a look at one other political event that occurred during the nineteenth century.

In 1871 the German armies were victorious over the French at Sedan. This victory was the most important precondition for the success of Bismarck's political plan to unite all the German states into a single nation. Not only did national euphoria express itself in monuments (the Armenius monument in the Teutoburg Forest in 1875 and the Niederwald monument near Bingen in 1885); it also shaped people's emotions—and, naturally, also those of the climbers who were citizens of the German Reich. Hans Dülfer was the first to climb the east face of the Fleischbank and the west face of the Totenkirchl by direct ascent. Even before World War I, Dülfer had reached the Fifth Degree of Alpine difficulty; his successes ushered in a new phase in the sport of climbing. Like some other climbers who embraced the national cause, Dülfer died as a volunteer in the battle of Arras in 1914.

The pathos of nationalistic resurrection at the conclusion of the world war in 1918 was diminished, if not transformed into its opposite. Hitler fanned the flame of national chauvinism once again during the twelve years of his rule. Between these two periods, however, lie the turmoil and confusions of the postwar years. Revolutions and conditions not unlike civil war broke out in large cities; in 1922 the Soviet Socialist Republic was founded; the Weimar Republic was established under the presidency of Friedrich Ebert (1919–1926); a worldwide economic crisis and mass unemployment spread. Unemployed climbers tried to deal with the economic situation and the other problems of these times in their own ways. They simply roamed about in the mountains. One of them, Anderl Heckmair, wrote about this period in his book *My Life as a Mountain Climber*: "First, I had to endure the winter. I had, of course, already registered with the unemployment office. But the unemployment check was barely enough for subsistence, let alone for trips to the mountains. Many climbers from our club 'Hochempor' ('high up') did not have much better luck. We finally renounced the inadequate subsidy altogether and settled into our ski hut on the Spitzing. Weekends, those who still had jobs would provide us with sufficient provisions to last the week. Thus, we survived, for better or worse."

Misery and deprivation provided the fundamental stimulus for the solution of the three last great problems of Alpinism during the following decade. First ascents were made of the north faces of the Matterhorn (1931), of the Grandes Jorasses (1935), and of the Eiger (1938). To this day, the 1930s are regarded as one of the great highpoints in the development of Alpinism.

Mass unemployment not only gave Austrian and German climbers an opportunity to work out great and beautiful projects in their dreams and fantasies; it also gave them time to realize their ideas. Hans Ertl and Walter Schmidkunz (as a ghostwriter) have described these years somewhat romantically as the time of the mountain vagabonds, producing the first best-seller on the Alpine book market. In reality, however, this misery usually expressed itself in unadorned despair, which finally made men ready to embrace National Socialist ideas as the new path of salvation and to welcome Hitler as the new messiah.

Hitler's attempt to interpret the successes of German and Austrian climbers as an expression of the superiority of the "master race" is touched upon in a critical review, published in the *Neue Züricher Zeitung* [the *New Zurich Press*] of December 22, 1973, of Toni Hiebeler's book *The Eiger Adventure*. The reviewer writes: "Toni Hiebeler's book is valuable as a chronicle of the mountain." What it lacks, however, is "a presentation of the history of this mountain and its climbs within the framework of a parallel development in intellectual history,. . . which definitely plays a role in Alpine history. Catchwords are decisive. In 1938, when it was first climbed, the Eiger's north face was associated with the master race; climbs after World War II were synonymous with existentialism."

The interpretations that such catchwords suggest are particularly illuminating from a Swiss perspective. There is no doubt of the fact that Hitler considered the 1938 Eiger success as a sign of the German master race's superiority and exploited it as propaganda. The climbing and expedition literature of 1938, as well as of the few years preceding the Eiger success, reveals that a significant number of Austrian and German climbers identified with these values and felt and acted in a corresponding manner. However, it is doubtful that the consciousness of belonging to a "master race" really played any part in the first successful climb of the north face of the Eiger, let alone a decisive part. As is well known, the two leading minds of the climbing team, Anderl Heckmair and Fritz Kasparek, both belonged to the so-called mountain vagabond period. Anderl Heckmair confessed in the book mentioned previously that until his Eiger success during the summer of 1938, which was indeed a turning point in his life, he had lived for more than a decade without a permanent home or a steady job. It is difficult to see how such circumstances could provide fertile soil in which the consciousness of belonging to a master race could take root and flourish.

In another chapter of his book, Karl Greitbauer takes issue with existentialism and its meaning for climbing. Man becomes conscious of existence, of true being, in peripheral situations—war, sickness, death—in other words, at the opposite edge of all existence, at the borders of not-being, of nothingness. Climbing as the locale of many borderline situations leads to an existentialism of action. From this perspective, one may well ask whether existentialism did not also play a role in the first ascent of the Eiger north face. If existentialism has any meaning for mountain climbing at all, then it certainly played a role in postwar attempts to scale the north face of the Eiger. Climbing was a reaction to being "driven by the impersonal mechanisms of daily life." And postwar industrial society, no matter by what economic system it was governed, recognized more clearly than ever before the fundamental problems of modern human existence. The salutary act of escaping from routine on a climb such as that of the north face of the Eiger could be intensified by the mass occurrence of borderline situations at the outer edges of life.

A number of other climbs in the Alps provide this borderline atmosphere, some even to a greater degree. Nevertheless, the north face of the Eiger is the one that is still the most sought after. Ever since the publication of Anderl Heckmair's *The Three Final Problems of the Alps* and Gaston Rébuffat's *Stars and Storms*, the Eiger has ranked with the Walker Pillar and the north face of the Matterhorn as one of the three faces that one has to have climbed in order to be accepted by the guild of climbers as a first-rate mountaineer. Because of the exciting history of its climbs, as well as its location immediately above Grindelwald, the north face of the Eiger has captured the attention of the mass media as has no other mountain. In this way, the Eiger has become a concept even to nonclimbers. Seen against this background, the constant flood of climbers to the Eiger north wall has provoked increasing criticism. It would seem that, despite all their talk of existential factors, postwar climbers even in their leisure time are motivated ever more by the very thing that most repels them: the impersonal mechanisms of everyday routine. This is particularly true to the extent that this mass movement to the Eiger is stimulated by notions of national prestige, ambition, career advancement, and climbing rank.

With these observations we have jumped ahead in our presentation of historical events in chronological sequence. Let us go back a bit. The end of the Third Reich in 1945 at first brought with it a new version of the age of mountain vagabonds, this time even more greatly tinged by romanticism. This cultural phenomenon revealed once again the unmistakable connections that exist between times of political crisis and the desire to climb mountains. Hermann Buhl is the best-known representative of this vagabond life-style. His teammate Martin Schliessler describes it as follows: "Tattered equipment, not much to eat, hardly any money, but a great deal of time; that was the stage where we called ourselves a brotherhood of good-for-nothings and ascended the great faces of the Alps." The consequences of this period were once again great new mountain tours, above all, in the region of the Northern Chalk Alps. During the decades that followed, these tours lost none of their reputation for difficulty and were just as sought after as the great climbs of the 1930s in subsequent years.

As early as 1945, Rébuffat and Edouard Frendo repeated the ascent of the north pillar of Pointe Walker on the Grandes Jorasses by way of the Cassin route. Lionel Terray evaluated the climb as the first great achievement in French Alpinism. In the first three chapters of his book *The Conquerors of the Useless* (which appeared in German under the title *Before the Gates of Heaven*), Lionel Terray presents abundant and noteworthy evidence to prove that this resurgence of interest in climbing toward the end of the war and during the first years of peace coincided with a period of "time when France, having suffered one of the most severe shocks in its history, was once again seeking to establish a fragile equilibrium."

When compared with the classical period of the mountain vagabond phenomenon, the period that followed the end of the "Thousand-Year Reich" was very short and disappeared within a few years. Western Europe recovered from the chaos of World War II with extraordinary speed. The "economic miracle," particularly in Germany, became the catchword that described European development during the postwar years. The fact that people amost immediately forgot the date of the spectacular first landing on the moon (July 20, 1969) illustrates the breathtaking speed of technological advance today. Achievements in science, for instance, in atomic research and in biology, are immense. No single individual, even a genius, can survey it all. In countless specialized areas of science, research seems to be pursuing the most hidden secrets of nature. Nevertheless, no one seems able to ban his primal anxiety, which now finds expression in great concern for environmental pollution and for conservation of the earth's natural resources.

Let us return to our discussion concerning the motives that caused so many climbers to tackle the north face of the

Eiger. I believe that the mass number of climbs of this wall just after World War II can be traced less to existential attitudes than to the fact that climbers of this period increasingly felt driven by the routine mechanisms of everyday life. This suspicion is supported by the Alpine literature that has appeared since 1945. One example will be mentioned here. Walter Pause's first book *With Happy Eyes* appeared around 1950. Its contents express the author's own unbounded joy that he was one of the lucky members of his generation to have survived the chaos of war. Like them, he was now ready to live his new life to the full—particularly in the mountains. In 1957/58 the first volume of his *Hail to Mountains* appeared. This was the first of a series of volumes that presented and outlined the one hundred greatest tours in the Alps. The books were widely circulated and often reissued. Since their publication, climbers of all degrees—from hikers to extremists—have measured the value of a tour by whether or not it is mentioned by Pause!

When I look at this historical phenomenon, I feel overwhelmed by a sense that the people of the developed countries of the earth have found a new center in their common hope for endless growth. On the one hand, this hope has been nourished by a constant rise in the standard of living as well as by perpetual technological advance. On the other hand, this concentration on growth has resulted from man's ever-increasing inability to find a cultural orientation. This striving for a new center, a new mean, a new norm, has left its imprint on everything—from everyday customs to the means for self-expression. It has affected mountain climbing, too.

Remarkably enough, climbers now concentrate on a few particular areas or a few definite tours, either because Pause has suggested them or because rank-consciousness has decreed that certain climbs must be made. Besides this, a parallel development has taken place in Alpinism in which technology has become an end in itself. This is symbolized by the expansion bolt, much used by rock climbers. How bizarre this may become is illustrated by one episode on the great northwest wall of the Western Zinne. During the mid-1960s a young American climber by the name of John Bruce Timpleton Brice was seized by a passionate desire to place a ladder of pitons once and for all on this imposing cliff. He had a special type of bore-piton fabricated, whose use demanded great technical skill on the part of the climber. First, a preliminary hole had to be made in the rock with the aid of a drill. Then a rod-shaped screw shaft had to be driven into the hole. A flat metal plate was placed above this. This plate contained an opening through which one could attach one's carabiners.

The plate was then to be firmly fixed in place with the aid of an appropriate screwdriver. It was Mr. Brice's intention to have the last man on his rope unscrew the plates again so that those who wanted to climb later would have to apply to him for the necessary hardware if they wanted to use this route. The plan never succeeded. Although Mr. Brice made an attempt to carry out this project, it failed partly because the technology was too difficult. The fiasco was embarrassing, because Mr. Brice and his comrades had concluded a contract with a television station. After the failure of their experiment, they were not simply permitted to go home—even if in disappointment and anger. In order to perform their contract, they had to climb the Swiss route to the top of the Western Zinne.

A few years later a team of brothers, Rudolf and Gerhard Baur, did succeed in pumping hardware into the Zinne. Gerhard later admitted quite frankly that this was no landmark achievement in the history of rock climbing but rather a successful demonstration of how bore-pitons could be used. In later years, Gerhard Baur's climbing achievements placed him among those young mountaineers for whom such bolts and pitons had already lost their fascination. This is the group that follows Reinhold Messner's Rousseauistic call, "Back to the Mountains," and regards free climbing without technical aids as the ideal for which one should strive. The sham successes that these climbers have renounced—the conquest of walls by means of artificial ascending devices, such as pitons, bolts, and ladders—have all been replaced by new goals. These climbers are now trying to master routes formerly conquered only with the aid of technical devices by using the pitons that have been left in the rock only for safety purposes and not as a climbing help. In order to achieve these goals, this new generation of climbers has come to recognize the need for rigorous training such as that engaged in by athletes in other disciplines.

Who knows where this development will end or even what role mountain climbing itself will play in the future? It is impossible to say what forms climbing will assume or what motives will drive it on. One thing is apparent: Alpinists skilled in extreme forms of climbing seem to be turning away from an ever-increasing reliance on climbing equipment. This revulsion appears to be running parallel to a general feeling of doubt regarding contemporary materialism. One way or another, we are all feeling the shock that comes with the knowledge that not everything is "do-able" and that clear limits have been placed on the idol of growth at whose feet we have worshiped for too long a time.

□

Hermann Huber

Yosemite and "Free Climbing"

In the spring of 1977, the climbing clan of the Yosemite National Park in California at first looked pleased. Several weeks later, almost the whole guild of extreme mountain climbers burst into broad grins—at least to the extent that they took any interest at all in Anglo-Saxon climbing: the center of the "cliff-climbing scene" in California was said to be embroiled in a strange scandal. Marijuana was allegedly involved!

Somehow or other, the boys from the Valley (as the Yosemite is called by its natives) had gotten wind of the fact that a plane carrying narcotics had crashed into a nearby lake. Three climbers set off to find it. It was winter and the ice had already frozen over the plane. They hacked holes in the ice and liberally helped themselves to the forbidden cargo. When they returned to the Valley with sacks of marijuana, something like a new gold rush began. The "mine" was exploited for about a week. In addition to the contraband, a human body, some money, and a notebook (probably belonging to the "smuggler boss") were found. Then a helicopter from the customs office appeared—and the gold rush was over!

The cleverest and most hardened of the Valley boys got rid of the drugs at a great profit. One bought a car. Another, who was poor and generally hungry, bought himself a $6.96 steak every night. Jim Bridwell, the patriarch of the mountain-climbing clan, after having spent many monotonous years in the Yosemite, was finally able to realize his dream of taking a trip to Patagonia.

In its historical and contemporary context, this episode is not really so unusual. "Yosemite climbing" appeared as a new concept in mountaineering toward the end of the 1960s and quickly spread to Europe and the rest of the world. The high standards of performance were set not least of all by a group of young climbers who had broken with society in order to push their personal experiences to the extreme. Here, on the big walls of the Valley, they pushed their excesses toward the edge of an abyss. Often, their daredevil exploits were undertaken under the influence of drugs.

The famous saloon in Fairbanks, Alaska, is gone. The pioneers of yesterday have long since passed over into another world. Billy McPhee, former owner of the Pioneer Saloon and Hotel for gold diggers, is also dead. But a few men yet living in this town of twenty thousand people at the end of the Alaska Highway still know stories dating from these early times. Wild and crazy stories they are, often connected with the mountains to the south of Fairbanks and with the rivers that had once washed gold down from the high peaks. The mountains of this Alaskan region are very high. The Athapaska Indians call the highest mountain of them all "Denali," which means "the big one." The Eskimos, who saw this mountain from its coastal side, designated it as "Tralaika," which also means "the great one."

One day a man arrived who had been tempted by Alaskan gold to travel across the Klondike, first to the Tanana River and later up the Chena. At the fork of these two gold rivers a settlement had arisen, which was later named Fairbanks. Upon his arrival, this man began to sputter a lot of big words about one Mr. William McKinley. That was in the year 1896. McKinley was then governor of Ohio but was seeking to become president of the United States. For some reason, the gold prospectors began to refer to the big mountain as "McKinley." As often occurs, if a person says something often enough, the words stick. This is how Mount McKinley got its name.

There was another topic of conversation in the town's saloon—a visitor from the East Coast who had been roaming around the valleys and climbing in the local snow and ice. That was in 1903. The man was Dr. Frederick Albert Cook, and he returned three years later. Cook himself claimed that he reached the very top of Mount McKinley. He probably also took photographs. We know that several men had been employed to carry up enormous pieces of equipment. The men themselves could not know that Cook only imagined that he had reached the summit. By the time they approached the top, they were all so breathless and exhausted that they couldn't know anything for sure. They coughed and spat, and their heads seemed about to burst. They were overjoyed when they could finally descend and breathe again. No one in the valley wanted to believe that Cook had reached the top. Then, fifty years later, Bradford Washburn, who knew this mountain like no one else, was able to prove that Dr. Cook had taken his photographs while still far below the summit.

Controversy still rages about the achievements of Frederick Albert Cook. He had also sailed through the Arctic Ocean and had claimed to be the first man to reach the North Pole on April 21, 1908. That record may well be his even if he was not the first to climb to the top of Mount McKinley. Mr. McKinley, who became the twenty-fifth president of the United States in 1897, never saw the great mountain that bore his name. He had already been elected for a second term of office when an attempt was made upon his life in the fall of 1901. He was seriously injured and died two weeks later.

There are still other crazy stories about Mount McKinley, which is called "the world's worst mountain." Billy McPhee, the owner of the Pioneer Saloon and Hotel in Fairbanks, figures in one of them. It is said that he paid five hundred dollars to have six quite mad gold diggers outfitted with coats, food, drink, boots, and woolen clothing. These six men wanted to travel up the river valleys, which issued from the great mountain and from its glaciers, in order to find out just how high the big mountain actually was. No doubt they really wanted to search in secret for the source of the gold that was washed down by local creeks and rivers and was sometimes panned along the sandbanks below by lucky prospectors. And so they set off. Very soon, fistfights broke out and three members of the party returned to Fairbanks. Only Pete Anderson, Charley MacGonagal, and Billy Taylor trudged on. They cursed the snow and the howling storms and were miserably cold; they gasped, coughed, spat. But, nevertheless, they continued to creep on. They dragged with them a long pole, which they wanted to place on the top of the mountain as proof that they had been there. This was in the summer of 1910. Three years later, on June 7, 1913, the archdeacon of the Yukon, Hudson Stuck, and his companions Harry Karstens, Robert Tatum, and Walter Harper discovered the pole (just how firmly the three earlier pioneers had rammed the pole into the snow and rock of the summit is revealed by the fact that it was still standing in 1913 and remained standing for several years after that). Two Athapaska Indians, Johnny and Elias, who had been baptized by the archdeacon, carried food, drink, furs, and ropes for Stuck's team. This group went further than the summit with the pole. They stood several hundred feet higher on the highest summit of Denali, or Tralaika, or Mount McKinley. For Mount McKinley has two summits: the first group of climbers had reached the northern summit, which is about 259 meters (850 feet) lower than the south summit (the main one). Today we know that Mount McKinley at 6,193 meters (20,318 feet) is the highest mountain in North America.

About the time that Archdeacon Stuck and his companions were climbing Mount McKinley, a man by the name of John Muir was roaming through the strange and wonderous landscape of Alaska. What he had already done further south in California, he sought to achieve here. He wanted to persuade the men who were responsible for the land that they ought to preserve the natural wonders of the territory they governed. It should be their aim, he argued, to see to it that the landscape remained unspoiled, that it was left in the same condition in which it had been created by nature during the course of thousands of years. He wrote numerous newspaper articles advocating this point of view. As a result of his efforts, gigantic national parks were created. One of these Alaskan parks, which encompassses 7,850 square kilometers (3,030 square miles), surrounds Mount McKinley. Created in 1917, it today attracts visitors from around the world, who come to experience nature in its untouched state as well as to climb America's highest mountain. Many paths lead to the top, and many climbers have since reached the summit of this frightful mountain.

The ridge which the gold diggers Pete, Charley, and Bill climbed and from which they eventually descended in more or less good health has been called the "Pioneers' Ridge." Thus, as one climbs today, one is reminded of the past.

A long time before the interior of Alaska had been discovered and the gold rush had begun, a Danish ship captain (Vitus Bering) in the service of the Russian czar had sailed northward along the coast. He discovered that America and Asia were not connected but were separated by a sea. In 1741, he sighted from his ship a colossal mountain rising up near the coast and called it Mount Saint Elias. News that the sea captain had discovered this great mountain and had entered it upon his map did not reach St. Petersburg until many years later. In the fall of 1741, the ship was stranded on the reefs of an island near the Kamchatka Peninsula opposite Alaska. The captain died of scurvy on this island, which now bears his last name, as does the passage he discovered between Asia and America: Vitus Jonassen Bering.

Thus, the history of the high mountains of North America is closely tied to the activities of researchers and adventurers who dedicated their lives to a search for the ends of the world as well as to a quest for gold and other riches. It is possible that the pioneers from Fairbanks, Alaska, who persuaded Billy McPhee to finance their trip to the top of Mount McKinley were aware of the statement made by Dr. Frederick Albert Cook after his first trek through this area: "Rich rewards await the man who conquers this mountain. But he must be prepared to endure suffering, renunciation, and hardship to the highest degree!" Perhaps they were tempted by Cook's reference to "rich rewards," which to them could only have meant gold. No one will ever know. Dr. Cook himself could not have foreseen the wealth of adventures and experiences that this mountain and this land were to provide.

Not far from Mount McKinley, on the northern border between Canada and Alaska, there rises the second highest mountain in North America, Mount Logan [6,050 meters (19,849 feet)]. McKinley and Logan are the northernmost mountains in a chain that stretches from Alaska to the volcanoes of Mexico—Popocatepetl, Ixtaccihuatl, Citlaltepetl, and Pico de Orizaba. Seven thousand kilometers (4,350 miles) separate the peaks in the north from those in the south. In between soar countless magnificent peaks of the Rockies, the coastal chains, and the Cascades.

The Indians of North America, like the peoples who lived in Alpine valleys or inhabited the mountainous regions of Asia and South America, regarded the mountains as wild, alien, and sometimes sacred. The settlers who moved to the Golden West were not interested in summits but in mountain passes leading to California. The only kinds of people who climbed mountains and made their way laboriously to the summit were surveyors, researchers, and, later, European Alpinists, particularly British "gentlemen," whose names had become famous because of their activities in the Caucasus and the Andes. As was also the case in the Alps, the next wave of visitors comprised the sportsmen, who were interested in pitting themselves against the steep cliffs and ice walls of this new territory.

One of these early climbers was Fritz Wiessner, born in Dresden, who had matured and developed his skills in the Elbsandstein mountains of Saxony. After having completed many tours in the Alps and reaching the Sixth Degree of difficulty, he emigrated to the United States at the end of the 1920s. It was Wiessner who encouraged young Americans to climb. He stimulated their enthusiasm for mountains, and, on the cliffs of the Appalachians in the East, he showed them how a courageous climber can succeed in scaling even the sheerest walls in safety. He became famous among American climbers when, accompanied by his friend William House, he conquered the most difficult 4,000-meter peak in the world during the summer of 1936: Mount Waddington [4,042 meters (13,261 feet)] in the Cascades, also known as Mount Mystery. Sixteen men had previously tried to climb this last of the unclimbed mountains of North America. Wiessner and House succeeded after twenty-three hours of unbroken climbing. They became famous and much admired throughout the United States.

Because of his skill as well as his concept of climbing that eschewed the use of technical aids except for safety purposes, Fritz Wiessner of Dresden, resident of Stowe, Vermont, as of 1928, was largely responsible for kindling the flames of an idea that later developed in the Yosemite National Park of California. After a period of decline, a return to the pure sport of rock climbing without the use of hardware has reemerged in full force throughout the climbing world today. Before the Yosemite school of climbing existed (Yosemite is an Indian name pronounced "Yo-sem'-it-ee"), the Valley was explored by members of the Sierra Club of San Francisco, founded by John Muir. These climbers had developed a style that was completely independent of the influence of the European Alpine tradition. In the 1930s, they were attracted by the difficult problems posed by walls. At the same time, they cut themselves loose from conservative attitudes in climbing which prevailed in large parts of the world, attitudes that were characterized by an ever greater rejection of climbing aids.

A milestone in this initial period of sport climbing was the conquest of the Upper Cathedral Spire in 1934, one of the striking granite towers on the orographic left side of the Yosemite Valley. It was members of the Sierra Club who in 1939 climbed the extremely difficult Californian cliff named "Shiprock" [500 meters (1,640 feet)]. The impact of the war caused an almost total cessation of climbing activity. On the other hand, new equipment had been developed for the United States mountain troops (who played a little-known but significant role in the conquest of Italy in 1944). Decisive innovations appeared, such as nylon cord, lightweight carabiners, and the first profile pitons (at first made only of soft iron). This revolutionary equipment, which was as yet unknown in other parts of the world, was available at very low cost to American climbers at the end of the war and stimulated the independent development of climbing techniques in the western part of the United States. The local centers of activity were Tahquietz Rock, a small area possessing the best type of granite and ideal weather conditions (located in the greater Los Angeles–southern California area), and the Yosemite Valley of central California, with its inexhaustible reserves of virgin land.

Yosemite's granite has been rubbed smooth by glacial movement; thus, the walls of this area remained unclimbable with the usual equipment. In 1945, John Salathé appeared: he was a blacksmith from Switzerland who did not begin his climbing career until he was forty-five years old. He set new standards. Stubborn willpower, combined with his gift for designing and making technological aids, helped him and his equally tenacious partner, Ax Nelson, to reach their goals. Salathé quickly realized that the conventional all-purpose piton made of soft iron was not suitable for use upon the cliffs of Yosemite. Repeated use quickly deformed these pitons into lumps of iron. From the axles of old cars, he forged excellent steel pitons in lengths and strengths appropriate for the conditions of Yosemite. Because of the natural absence of hand- and footholds, the routes planned by Salathé required so much equipment that the pitons could not be left in the cliffs but had to be withdrawn and used again at the next stage of the climb.

Except for practical necessity, American climbers feel a sense of responsibility for leaving the mountain in the same condition in which they find it.

Salathé was the first to cross the psychic barrier of the one-day climb, and he extended his tours to five days, which, of course, required repeated bivouacs. He also replaced the double-rope technique used throughout the world for difficult rock climbs with a refined single-rope maneuver that has remained a characteristic feature of American climbing style. Salathé's greatest successes and landmarks in this first period of extreme climbs are the southwest face of the Half Dome, accomplished in two days (1946), and the Lost Arrow Chimney, in five days (1947). In addition, there was the north wall chimney of Sentinel Rock, which Salathé climbed in five days (1950) along with Allen Steck, who, after Salathé's departure from the scene at the beginning of the 1950s, became a central figure and an "old master" in the guild of California climbers. A large number of the most prominent climbers of western America were present at a party held in May 1976 to celebrate his fiftieth birthday. Around 1950, Steck also made countless climbs of the most difficult routes in the Alps, particularly in the Dolomites. Here he was accompanied by the Viennese climber Karl Lugmayer.

The climbers from Southern California, whose advanced techniques had been perfected on the Tahquietz, arrived in Yosemite after 1955 and solved many of the problems that then still existed. The mighty 700-meter (2,297-foot) granite wall of the Half Dome was conquered in 1957 by Royal Robbins and his friends in five days.

As the great classical period began, men like Robbins, Yvon Chouinard, Tom Frost, and others from the south of this sunny land played a significant role in the development of the Yosemite Method of Big Wall Climbing, with its emphasis on climbing ethics. Soon, a new goal emerged in the Yosemite: El Capitan, a gigantic and unique granite monolith whose smooth rock walls towered 1,000 meters

(3,280 feet) above the valley floor. Despite all the refinements made in climbing hardware, El Capitan was a nut that simply could not be cracked.

In 1958, after many attempts, El Capitan was conquered by way of the Nose, the striking southeast pillar whose noble form towers up into the heavens. Many climbers had struggled for a direct route to the summit. Warren Harding, a man of unbelievable strength and endurance, finally succeeded. Today, at the age of fifty, he still likes to scale rock faces and hang on walls never before climbed, if necessary even for weeks at a time. Warren Harding probably has more steep-wall bivouacs to his credit than has any other climber in the world. The ascent of the Nose required forty-five days of climbing, punctuated by various types of traverses, rappels, and ascents on fixed ropes. Twelve days on the wall itself were necessary. Harding spent the last night preparing a row of bore-pitons leading to the overhang that led off the wall, while his companion tried to doze as he lay cramped up in his sling.

Opinions vary concerning the beauty and value of this kind of activity. If nothing else, it does reveal how man can adjust himself to unusual circumstances if he is physically and psychologically prepared. In 1971, Harding conquered the Dawn Wall (Wall of the Early Morning Light) to the right of the southeast edge of El Capitan. The climb required an enormous amount of technological aids—bore-pitons, rurps, skyhooks, rivets, bashies, blobbies, and anything else the Devil had invented. Harding had to spend a full thirty-one days and nights on the wall. There was no fixed rope to the bottom, and no additional supplies from below were hauled up. He thereby set a rather unique record. At the same time, Harding revealed himself to be a notorious crank, who had deliberately set himself apart from the new climbers whose ethical principles demanded the use of as few technological aids as possible.

Such a demand may seem absurd in view of enterprises like these. Nevertheless, what "clean climbing" means in practice will be unforgettably impressed on anyone who climbs in Yosemite today or, indeed, anywhere else in the United States where native experts are at work. The technological assaults of the late 1950s and early 1960s may have been necessary for the discovery of routes up the huge walls—of which there are now fourteen on El Capitan alone. Today, however, free climbing, even under extreme conditions and especially on shorter stretches, predominates, and this requires a sharp curtailment in the use of hardware. One must see or experience for himself what the grades 5.10, 5.11, or 5.12 mean here. Most good European climbers would find it difficult to complete these routes as

lead climber. In general, free climbing in the Alps has thus far reached only the level of 5.9, although isolated instances of 5.10 climbs have recently begun to appear.

Solo free climbing has reached dizzying heights. Royal Robbins, who climbed the Muir Wall on El Capitan in nine days, is a member of the avant-garde in this discipline. From time to time, however, young unknown climbers emerge out of the blue and climb the most difficult walls alone, mastering them in quick, skillful attacks. The number of accidents has remained surprisingly low. The big walls, which were first conquered between 1955 and 1970, are now attempted by means of the cramp-wedge technique, a technique that took only a few years to perfect. Pitons, which in time damage even the rock of Yosemite, which is as hard as iron, are only used as a last resort (some have remained in the walls as fixed pins).

In 1973 the Nose was climbed without the use of a hammer. It was the first such climb, and the hammer was left behind in the Valley. The normal climbing time for this much sought-after and supposedly easiest route on El Capitan is four days. Jim Bridwell and his comrades completed the tour in the unbelievably short space of a day and a half. Nevertheless, even today, many good climbing teams cannot overcome the great difficulties of these routes. In 1969, the ratio of success to failure on the big walls was approximately 1.8 to 10.

Climbing virtuosi like Charlie Porter, Steve Sutton, and their friends have opened up a few hair-raising A4 and A5 routes on the big walls with the aid of technical devices. (The small pitons and cramp wedges can barely hold in the almost nonexistent fissures of these rock walls.) One should not condemn these daredevils for their continued and expanded use of aids. They have chosen a razor-sharp sphere of activity, and their use of hardware has nothing to do with an attempt to "make things easy." There is probably not a single climber from Europe who would dare or even want to repeat their routes on El Capitan, routes such as the Shield, the Mescalito, or the Pacific Ocean, whose conquests were largely stimulated by a search for transcendental experience. This is an American tradition that began back in 1964 with the Yosemite pioneers Royal Robbins, Yvon Chouinard, Chuck Pratt, and Tom Frost. They spent nine strenuous days without ties to the Valley, climbing and hammering their way up the North American Wall, thereby setting a standard that made this almost purely technical tour the most difficult one in all of America at that time.

To get back to classical extremes, the opening up on El Capitan of a second route, named the Salathé Wall in honor of the "old master," by Robbins, Frost, and Pratt is regarded as perhaps "the greatest rock climb in the world." This route, which follows the most natural line up the center of the face, demands hard piton work but also offers many difficult and varied free-climbing possibilities on the platens, cracks, and chimneys of the cliff. (The author personally climbed this route in May 1976 with its first conquerors Royal Robbins and Scott Stewart. It took four days.)

Although America's leading climbers may come from Colorado, the Pacific Northwest, or from the East Coast, they have all grown up with the standards set in the Yosemite Valley. They have also been through the hard school of the big walls.

An interesting event took place in May 1976 in the Elbsandstein cliffs of Saxony. The occasion was marked by a distinctly competitive spirit. The old master Fritz Wiessner arranged for a comparative demonstration of free climbing as it had been developed by the exponents of the two best rock-climbing schools in the world. Only the most difficult free climbs were selected. The happy-go-lucky boys from America, including Henry Barber and Steve Wunsch, who had undergone quasi-professional training for the event, showed the Saxon top-drawer athletes on their own soil what Americans nowadays mean when they talk about rock climbing. The exhibition was impressive and resulted in mutual respect.

The techniques, strategies, and equipment (including Chouinard's ice equipment) that were developed in California have now been tested out in the Alps, as well as on other mountains of the world. The hardware has passed with flying colors. The testing grounds were the Robbins-Hemming route on the west wall of the Petit Dru (1962) and the south wall route of the Aiguille du Fou, opened up in 1963 by the Americans Gary Hemming, John Harlin, Tom Frost, and Fulton. These two routes rank among the most difficult granite climbs in the Alps. Countless routes that were believed unclimbable without the aid of pitons were reconquered, and new "firsts" were achieved: specifically, the first totally free climbs in which such tools as cramp-wedges, pitons, stirrups, and carabiners were used only for safety but not as ascending aids.

The definition of free climbing, at least on shorter stretches, is strictly construed. Once a climber uses a carabiner as an actual aid, he has forfeited the right to call the climb a "free climb." The relevant position or even the whole rope length is deemed "artificial." In Europe, the standards are quite different. One can speak of oneself as a free climber as long as one refrains from using étriers. A striking example of the intensity with which the new wave of American free climbers pursue their sport is revealed in a 1976 climb made by Jim Eriksen from Colorado. After several attempts, he nearly succeeded in freely climbing the original route up the northwest wall of the Half Dome, whose first successful ascent in 1957 had required a large amount of hardware even for a Big Wall Climb. He roped himself down the 700-meter (2,297-foot) high wall several times, whenever it appeared that he could not get any further "by fair play."

One may ask what such developments as these have to do with mountain climbing. The answer is that free climbing represents a zenith in the sport of rock climbing, which itself has unquestionably become a significant branch of the rapidly growing tree of life that encompasses mountain climbing as a whole. It is undeniable, of course, that this constant striving to intensify the difficulties reveals a far greater degree of competitive spirit than is found among mountain climbers of the Alps.

The point is to "push oneself to the limits." This motto has a higher value in American climbing than in central European Alpinism. Anglo-Saxon puritanism may well have contributed to the strict self-discipline that American (and British) climbers have imposed upon themselves in their pursuit of climbing as a sport. Self-discipline has never been regarded as a symptom of decadence. Climbers everywhere can therefore profit from the spirit that pervades American rock climbing even if some of its aspects appear exaggerated and even if one believes that the pleasure to be derived from the mere act of climbing with a good friend on a beautiful day is more important than the level of difficulty achieved. When all is said and done, the American spirit is to be applauded, because it has resulted in placing greater value on the way a climb is made than on the fact that it has been done.

In passing, I should add that climbers on the other side of the Atlantic treasure a glorious day in the mountains, whether easy or difficult, no whit less than do climbers anywhere else in the world. □

Christine Schemmann

Women Are Not Frogs and Men Are Not Eagles

In the Year of the Woman, which has been celebrated in various forms and discussed throughout the world, two women climbed the highest mountain on earth. One woman came from Japan and the other from Tibet. Women now climb on all the mountains of the world. In their clothing as well as their movements, they are indistinguishable from men. It is by now obvious that members of the weaker sex, who are considered the equals of men in many respects, can take or leave any activity they please. The climbing achievements of women have earned respect and admiration. Nevertheless, here and there one also meets men who would prefer to see women only on marked and charted hikers' paths.

An article on women's contributions to Alpinism was felt to be an essential part of this book. Although mountain climbing in all its aspects has largely been shaped by men, nevertheless, to give a complete picture, the active, if relatively small, role that women have played in its development deserved mention. In this regard, women's passive role could not be overlooked. There have been countless women who have accompanied their brave husbands to the starting point of some extreme tour, masking their anxiety with a smile. All too often, those left behind have been mothers. Should one not consider the many women at home who have had to come to terms with their sorrow when they learned that a husband or a son had had a fatal accident, would not return, had disappeared in the mountains? Should one not reflect on the profound hurt experienced by these wives and mothers when someone came to break the sad news as gently as was possible? Or when friends returned with a coffin?

Just as there are days to commemorate fallen soldiers, in Alpine countries on mountaintops there are also often memorial ceremonies dedicated to those who have died in the mountains. The mothers, widows, children come. Not a sign of heroic transfiguration is to be seen. Only memories remain. We should also remember this.

163

Her head was empty of thought. The little gray cells had gone on strike. Her brain was subordinate to the compulsion to go on, to take just one more step, and then just one more after that. She was aware of nothing more. She gasped and tried to listen to an inner voice. Could she perceive a danger signal from within? Now, so soon before the end? Breathing was painful. Sirdar Ang Ensing proceeded one step ahead of her and at the same pace. Despite the physical strain, the Sherpa was swimming in a state of euphoria. He was now accompanying the first woman to the summit of the world's highest mountain. Only a hundred steps more, and then 8,848 meters (29,029 feet) was reached. It was accomplished.

On May 16, 1975, at 12:30 P.M., Junko Tabei, a Japanese woman from the province of Fukushima, about two hours from Tokyo, stood on the top of Mount Everest. The victor was a climber from the Far East, born in 1940, mother of a little girl just turned three. Here in the land of the classical Alpinists, in Hillary land, British hearts stood still for a fraction of a second: a woman on Mount Everest! The Japanese climber looked around and gazed at all the summits below. So this was it; this was the goal. "It's finally behind you." No jubilation, no tears. She felt empty, a mere shell. She reflected and again thought: "It's over; you did it!" Joy came later. So did satisfaction. And fame. The world only learned of Phanthog later. On May 27, 1975, at 2:30 P.M. Peking time, eleven days after Junko reached the summit, a lady from Tibet stood there too, together with eight men who had ascended from the north.

In the same year, 1975, two Polish women, Anna Okupinska and Halina Krüger-Syrokomska, reached the top of Gasherbrum II [8,035 meters (26,361 feet)], the first team of women to conquer an 8,000-meter peak. Two different women from the Polish expedition formed a mixed quartet and conquered the highest yet unclimbed summit: Gasherbrum III [7,952 meters (26,089 feet)]. They were Wanda Rutkiewicz and Alison Onyszkiewicz, née Chadwick, born in England and married to the expedition leader. Twelve months earlier Japanese women stood on the top of Manaslu [8,156 meters (26,758 feet)]. In 1934 a Swiss climber was the first woman to set her feet on the summit of a 7,000-meter peak: Hettie Dyhrenfurth. The peak was the western summit [7,315 meters (23,999 feet)] of Sia Kangri (Queen Mary Peak) in the Karakoram.

Things did not always succeed. In July 1974, eight Russian women died descending Pik Lenin [7,134 meters (23,405 feet)] in the Pamirs, when a violent storm broke loose barely 400 meters (1,312 feet) below the summit. Five years after its first conquest by Herbert Tichy and Sepp Jöchler, Claude Kogan led a women's expedition to Cho Oyu [8,189 meters (26,866 feet)]. The graceful Parisian died in a snowstorm, together with Claudine von Stratten from Belgium and two Sherpas. Search parties found torn and empty tents. Two women Alpinists had vanished in the Himalayas. But, like all women climbers everywhere, they knew exactly what they were in for.

Whenever women climbers had accidents, the press would foam at the mouth: It is irresponsible for women to expose themselves to such things, they sermonized. But this attitude is now a thing of the past. Even from the point of view of statistics, fewer women die in mountain-climbing accidents than do men. Every woman who had pitted herself against the mountains of Europe and other summits of the world or who has made her way through labyrinthine underground caves knew the risks involved and accepted them. What, then, tempts her to pin her life on a rope or on the blade of an ice axe? Nothing, really, that distinguishes the mountain climber from the woman who takes up sport parachuting, car racing, or white-water boating. It is the desire to engage in pure pleasure as a complement to her professional or domestic duties. She seeks a little adventure; she is eager to discover her physical limits; she wants to feel the satisfaction that comes from knowing that her body is functioning well. Finally, she, too, yearns for the "extraordinary experience."

At 5:00 A.M. on July 29, 1972, they stood in front of the hut on the Leschaux Glacier. Ahead of them rose the steep walls of the Grandes Jorasses on Mont Blanc. Only a few clouds and scraps of fog were to be seen. Their destination was the Walker Pillar. A teenager from Allgäu shook the sleepiness from her limbs. Her stomach settled. Reinhild Natterer was going to follow her friend in a spirit of controlled calmness. At the age of thirteen, she had been taken ill with tuberculosis. The desire to break free, to get higher, to get further, to have friends, to have pride, to have something to show for herself—all these wishes must have taken root during the year she spent in the sanatorium, a year that seemed to grow ever longer. At seventeen, she climbed the Matterhorn. She was now about to tackle the Walker Pillar, one of the most difficult tours in the Alps—the Rébuffat Niche. The view below was mostly air and little rock. Then came an ice-coated overhang and some black cliff platens. Then a good place for the night. The girl squeezed herself into her bivouac sack. The sun set over the famous Aiguilles of the Western Alps. It grew cold. "My God, if only my mother could see me now," she thought. "Ladies first," said Georg

59/60/61

Mount McKinley: 300 kilometers (186 miles) from the Artic Circle, more exposed to storms than any other mountain in the world. Called Denali, the Great One, by Indians who regarded it with awe, its first discoverers were not professional explorers, insisted Archdeacon Hudson Stuck in 1913 after the first ascent of the Great Mountain. They were not rock climbers or scientists but missionaries, simple amateurs. The Archdeacon climbed to the summit accompanied by his young assistant Robert Tatum. They were joined by Harry Karstens, a vigorous man who lived in Alaska and was accustomed to storms and bad weather. Sixteen-year-old Walter Harper, a half-blooded Indian devoted to Stuck, was a fourth member of the band. Stuck was probably the spiritual leader of the group but, as he later reported, Harry Karstens was the real leader when the team came face-to-face with the difficulties and dangers that faced them. Mount McKinley subsequently became the goal of climbers from all over the world: still storm tossed, still the Great One.

62/63

Camp-bound: climbers can be forced by storms to remain in camp for days on end as here on Mount McKinley. Those with sufficient skill can build igloos, dome-shaped Eskimo huts made of blocks of snow. Here one is at least moderately protected from the violence of the weather and the unbearable cold. Inside an igloo the snowstorm becomes tolerable, particularly if one's clothing is warm enough. In this region the climber must carry everything on his own back: equipment, clothing, food, even fuel. It is true that daring pilots in small planes land on the nearby glaciers to drop off climbers and their gear. But from there each one must go on alone, often heavily laden. When the storm is howling outside, it is often difficult to keep the gas fire burning. Preparing a cup of soup or tea becomes a chore. Then, suddenly, the curtain of clouds parts, the blanket of white disperses. The path to the summit lies ahead.

64
The summit of Mount
McKinley: the vast
stretches of Alaska lie
below. Many a climber has
already stood here in the
light of the midnight sun.
The mountain, named after
a president of the United
States, was christened by a
man in search of gold. Gold
prospectors were the first to
stand on these heights. As it
later turned out, this early
group only reached the
North Summit which is
slightly lower. Gold is still
mined in Alaska. And not
far from the Great Mountain
flows black gold—carried by
pipeline to the coastal ports.

66

65

65
Women no longer lag behind
men in mountaineering
accomplishment, even on
the highest mountains. In
ever-increasing numbers
they are climbing the
steepest rock walls, though
admittedly often
accompanied by men. Helga
Lindner has triumphed over
the most difficult rock
climbs, usually roped to her
husband.

66
The Polish alpinists Wand
Rutkiewicz and Alison
Onyszkiewicz-Chadwick
climbed Gasherbrum III i
the Karakorum in the
summer of 1975. At 7,952
meters (26,088 feet), this
was the highest yet
unclimbed mountain.
Gasherbrum I (Hidden
Peak) is only a little
more than 100 meters high
(26,469 feet). Its mighty
northwest face was
constantly in view as the
Polish climbers ascended
the steep ice flanks of
its neighbor.

Geisenberger, the next day, when the two reached a point 2 meters (6.5 feet) below the summit. He allowed her to go first. The pounding heart, the difficulties, and the many moments of anxiety were now forgotten. A dream had become reality. She was eighteen years old, and with the back of her hand she brushed away a few tears.

Nadja Fajdiga was one of the most successful climbers of the so-called middle generation. She is still remembered, even though Alpine stars are born and quickly die. (Loulou Boulaz, a Swiss climber from the Waadtland, also belonged to this group and was perhaps its senior member. She had not merely followed men on difficult climbing tours; she had climbed many of them first—for example, the south wall of the Marmolada or, in 1941, the north wall of the Zinal Rothorn. She was also on Cho Oyu.) Nadja Fajdiga was from Yugoslavia. Already top class at home, she suddenly appeared in the West toward the end of the 1950s. People were soon very much aware of her presence. She was beautiful and interesting and, beyond that, a "specialist in rock faces." She appeared to crack the hardest nuts with a kind of playfulness—for example, the west face of the Dru, the north wall of the Grands Charmoz, the Brenva Pillar. And in the Dolomites—the Solleder route on the Civetta, the Comici-Dimai path up the north wall of the Grosse Zinne, the steep cutoff of the Pala di San Martino.

In July 1963, the ambitious woman from Yugoslavia and her friend Ante Mahkota arrived in Zermatt. They reached the base of the north wall of the Matterhorn on the twenty-fifth. Nadja wanted to be the first woman to climb it. Italian and German climbers were just then on the north wall. The Italians were in trouble and needed help. For the Germans, the climb was also not proceeding according to plan. Then one member of the group was seriously injured by falling rock. That was that. The two women from Yugoslavia left the route on the Hörnligrat shoulder and alerted the rescue squad. For Richard Lentner, however, help came too late.

Two years later, on July 14, 1965, Yvette Vaucher and her husband inscribed their names in the history book of the Matterhorn's north face. Finally in 1977, an all-women team, Anna Czerwinska and Krystina Palmowska, reached the top.

The Stegers are still active: Paula at the reception buffet of her hotel and Hans as a ski instructor for the winter guests—both in the seventh decade of a full life. In the breakfast room hangs a letter, written in the hand of Albert I of Belgium, stating that his grandson Baudoin was coming. In the 1920s and 1930s, Paula Wiesinger, later Steger, had led royalty on the rope. Leopold III, Albert's son, had also been there. "What was it like to climb with kings? Did one act differently with royalty?" The old lady thought this notion amusing. "Of course not. We called the old king 'Herr Réthy' and Leopold 'Father.'" Now she laughed. "That sounds peculiar, of course, but it has to do with the figure of the king in card games. Around here, that card is called 'father.' And you can be sure we played a lot of cards while waiting for decent weather."

Wiesinger's story begins in 1928. At that time she had won fame first as a plucky high diver and then as a ski racer, becoming a world champion in 1932. She had been working as a clerk in a business establishment in Bozen when she met Hans Steger, a cabinetmaker and mountain climber. He soon discovered that this girl had real dash, much more than his climbing colleagues at home. He tested his discovery on the Preuss Niche on the Kleinste Zinne. Their second tour together was admired beyond Alpine circles. They had made the first direct climb of the northeast edge of the Zinne, and, right after that, the north pillar of the Einserkofel in the Sexteners. In the South Tyrol and in Italy enthusiasm was overflowing; it was almost too much. Everyone was talking about "La Paola." She was soon the first person to climb the east face of the Rosengartenspitze. A year later, in 1930, she was the first woman to climb the northwest wall of the Civetta. Paula Wiesinger likes to reminisce. She likes to remember their popularity. I now see two old people on the Seiseralm, hand in hand for fifty years. One could call them "a team for life"—if this weren't such banal kitsch.

The iron was corroded by rust. The wooden handle had also suffered; it was bleached by the sun and was brittle. One is tempted to blow on it and would not be surprised if the whole thing disintegrated. This pick belonged to Eleonore Noll-Hasenclever, who was killed by an avalanche in August 1925 on the Weisshorn. Since that day, it has been lying on top of her grave in Zermatt. Young people often gather noisily near the village cemetery, but when they see the old graves they become quiet. There is the monument for Lord Francis Douglas and Charles Hudson from Edward Whymper's team; the tombstones of Franz and Bernard Biner; father and son Taugwalder; Johann, Petrus, and Augustin Gentinetta; Alexander Burgener—all leading mountaineers of the first generation. The young people pause, perhaps, in front of Noll's grave because of the ancient ice axe. Could this name mean anything to them?

The Stegers were the first great mountaineers from the working classes. Before this time, the early Alpinists had been ladies and gentlemen: well-established persons, usually rich.

Eleonore Hasenclever from Remschied was the last of that generation when she left the scene at the age of forty-five. In 1899, with the great guide from the Valais, Alexander Burgener, she began her career by climbing the Matterhorn and afterwards pursued everything that was interesting, bold, and expensive—all the way to the Aiguilles of Chamonix. Then came the Dolomites. Two decades later, accompanied by Burgener's son, she was the first woman to climb the east wall of the Monte Rosa—downward!—descending it from the summit. Hasenclever was also one of the first climbers to renounce the help of guides. In 1913, she paired up with a female doctor and was thus one of the first to form an all-women team.

Women like this did not climb behind men. Moreover, the stronger sex often put obstacles in their way. Today one might say that some of the mountain guides were afraid of losing their jobs. They sometimes sabotaged Mrs. Noll's enterprises, for example, by blocking the bedroom door. Once they even cut her rope.

Once upon a time there was a woman who did not curtsy to a prince. Indeed, the prince bowed to her and to all the other members of Rickmer's expedition. The woman slept under silk sheets and ate in the Prince's house at his own table. And lived through a Caucasian fairy tale. This was in 1903, the year of the first climb of the Uschba. A unique event occurred: Bekerbi Dedaschkeliani, the ruler of a thousand-and-one-nights realm, presented a woman with this highest of mountains, the Matterhorn of the Caucasus, the Uschba.

The deed of the gift burned during the last war when the Alpine Museum in Munich, which housed it, was hit by a bomb and reduced to ashes and rubble.

Cenci von Ficker from Innsbruck was only two years older than Eleonore Hasenclever. She crossed Samarkand and Turkestan generally in the company of her brother and the legendary Rickmer. During the first climb of the Uschba, there was only time for three on a rope to reach the summit. Without complaining, she gave up her place and remained just below the summit. Wearing snowshoes, she was the first woman to stand on the top of the Venediger. She knew the 4,000-meter peaks of the Western Alps as well as the famous routes in the Dolomites. She later climbed with her husband, who had fought and won honors on the Sexten Rotwand during the mountain war. The Sild tower is named for him. Cenci later climbed with her sons. One died and two were killed

during the last war. By then, Hannes Sild was long since dead.

Cenci Sild lived to the age of 78. She died on August 26, 1956, a lonely old woman.

Eleonore Hasenclever and Cenci von Ficker were still sucking their thumbs when a British woman succeeded in "shocking all of London," as one biographer put it. On the British Isle, Alpine fever had broken out in the wake of Whymper's Matterhorn adventure. Hundreds of English gentlemen flocked to the continent and left their traces everywhere in the Alps. They had grown used to the achievement of Lucy Walker, the sister of Horace, who gave his name to the Walker Pillar in 1868. This young lady had been sent to the high mountains as a cure for her rheumatism. The doctors believed that the air in these regions would have a healthy effect. Six years after Whymper, she stood on the Matterhorn—a very athletic achievement. But what Elizabeth Witshed of Killincarrick did went too far. A daughter from a good family, suspected of having tuberculosis, was now frolicking about in a Swiss ski hut with two men. Shocking! They said she even bivouacked. This person then wrote her first book, *The High Alps in Winter*. The year was 1883 and she had just turned twenty—a truly remarkable personality. Normally, she bowed to tradition and wore a skirt. But on the edge of civilization, such scruples were rejected. She put on trousers and mastered the great tours—113 in all, and many during the winter.

In 1883 Elizabeth was the first woman to succeed on the Dent du Géant near Chamonix. In the Berninas, a good ten years later, the list of her credits increased with the first winter ascents of Crast' Agüzza, Piz Zuppô, the middle summit of Piz Palü, and, finally, the Morteratsch. At least, this is what Martin Schocher's tour book says, although it is also noted that "the Morteratsch summit was not quite reached because of snow storms." Next to Christian Schnitzler, Martin Schocher was her favorite guide. The man from the Engadin was greatly impressed by the energy of this Englishwoman. Schocher's son Bartholeme recalled in January 1978: "My father always used to say, 'She was not a woman. No, she was a horse!'" Miss Witshed wore out three husbands and bobs up in Alpine literature as Mrs. Main, Mrs. Aubry Le Bond, and Mrs. Fred Burnaby. There is no doubt she was a woman! Martin Schocher was wrong to voice such doubts.

The iron-willed Elizabeth formed the Ladies' Alpine Club in 1907, because the members of the London Alpine Club, the oldest in the world, refused to admit women. It wasn't until the middle of the 1950s that the relationship between the clubs relaxed. Members met for tea, which was recorded in the annals of the all-male club as a memorable event. On March 31, 1975, the clubs were merged. After long discussions, everyone agreed that "all are equal before the mountain." The Ladies Alpine Club was founded purely as a matter of necessity and self-defense. Other such clubs followed. In England, perhaps the most exclusive was the Pinnacle Club, which was open only to the most accomplished climbers, the so-called "Sestogradistes." Even today, there are tests that must be met: climbs in rock and ice under the most demanding conditions. These women are incredibly proficient. No wonder that English girls were the first to emerge as solo climbers on the mountains of the world.

In Switzerland the National Alpine Club is still taboo for women. But women had already emancipated themselves in 1918. Everyone who can prove she is a woman can join the Swiss Women's Alpine Club. One need not pass any other test.

Even in the most tolerant republic that ever existed on German soil, outdated prejudices still remain. The great German Alpine Club has three groups that are still closed to women. They are called Berggeist ("mountain spirit"), Hochland ("highland"), and Bayerland ("Bavaria"). No one cares. The gentle sex has long outgrown such petty warfare. Occasionally, someone makes an issue, but, before she knows it, she's in the corner, like Red Iris not long ago.

The women who climb with men friends or husbands or with each other are more or less quite ordinary people despite their brilliance on rock and ice. And they do not waste their energy on feminist clichés. Although they are able to reach the Seventh Degree of difficulty in the pursuit of their Alpine hobby, they have nothing against wearing lace or spraying themselves with "Aimé de la Nuit" from Paris when the mood strikes. The bluestocking type is outdated. There are no more mountain witches. With very few exceptions, these women are not horses!

Karl Greitbauer, who is probably the only psychologist to have specialized in mountain climbers, explained that the reason women undertook extreme Alpine climbs was their wish to adopt and excel in man's accomplishments as a reaction to the feminine role that they were forced to play in life and that they regarded as inferior. It is unbelievable that such a view could be put forth as late as the end of the 1950s.

Greitbauer's view, not based on evidence, is as peculiar as the thesis propounded by a young doctor from the respiratory department of the University Clinic in Mainz. This doctor said that the fetuses of pregnant women not used to high altitudes could be expected to show brain damage because of insufficient oxygen at heights of 2,000 meters (6,561 feet) above sea level. Evidence shows that women climbers' children are not retarded. The libido of these women is also quite in order. Interpersonal relationships on the rope are as complicated or uncomplicated as they are anywhere else. Of course, literature delights in pointing out "transfigured partnerships for life." But there are also triangular relationships as well as every other variety. If the women themselves are asked, they are quite straightforward. Some, like Inge Rost, a highly regarded extreme climber from the Saxon climbing school, declares that erotic tensions on a tour are absolutely inappropriate. Others, such as Erika Heimrath and Christa Sturm, prefer to climb with men. "As a matter of course, they take on a protective role, simply because they are physically stronger." In this regard Irmgard Dobler adds: "This is particularly important if one has children. Every time a stone breaks off, a shudder goes right through one. One wonders what will become of the children if anything happens. . . ." Edith Bednarik, an expert high-Alpine cave explorer, believes that, if a woman is fully engaged in something, she is often a better partner.

Jürgen Winkler, a first-rate photographer of international repute, hit the nail on the head when he remarked: "It's clear that if one glows with passion for a person, one keeps glowing on the rope. . . ." (Winkler's specialty is mountain climbers.) The large and small problems of living together naturally turn up in the marriages of women climbers. One of these is the fact that when young women become mothers they usually abandon or at least greatly curtail the wild freedom formerly enjoyed. This is not necessarily true for their husbands.

Felicitas von Reznicek, the daughter of the composer Emil von Reznicek, is one heart and one soul with the best female Alpinists in the world. The Baroness was born at the time the Society of Suffragettes was formed. She went to school before World War I, when Emmeline Pankhurst was arrested by London Bobbies at a demonstration and imprisoned. She was fifteen when Hedwig Dohm, "the bravest woman in Bismarck's realm," died.

At the end of the 1960s, Felicitas von Reznicek formed the wittiest Ladies' Society for top-class Alpinists that the world had seen since the days of Mrs. Main, alias Mrs. Le Bond, alias Mrs. Burnaby. Men were allowed to join but only if they could follow behind a female leader on a Fourth Degree rope climb. If necessary, they could stumble up grade III—"For what is life without men?" said the Baroness, a much sought-after bridge partner in old Berlin. The rendezvous Hautes Montagnes on the ice cap of the Titlis, high above the Engelberg near Lucerne, was christened with fifty bottles of champagne. "I would love for once to take off for the mountains cackling and screeching like a bird," she said indignantly in her Swiss home, gazing adventurously at the woman who was interviewing her. "It is ridiculous to make distinctions. As if women were frogs and men were eagles. . . ." Frau von Reznicek knows where her thoughts would take her if she began to meditate on female Alpinists. As a young girl she worshipped Noll-Hasenclever and went first hiking and then climbing with her in Zermatt—though within limits and without ladders to the stars! She is a woman of great imagination, the author of twenty novels, biographies, and UFA film scripts. "What does this war between the sexes really mean? Of course, girls are ambitious. But aren't men ambitious too? Of course, these's competition, but it is no teeth-gnashing struggle!

"They say that when women engage in Alpinism it is only a substitute for bad luck in love." Reznicek nods in recognition. She has heard this before. "Possibly true, but for men too."

The year 2000. Only two decades remain until this magic mark is reached. Will the mountains still be our mountains? Or will they be talked to death, used up, made desolate, laid bare? From the beginning of time, we have constantly removed ourselves ever further from our origins, from nature.

The year 2000. "This petty sexual distinction will not count even in the highest mountains of the world." The Baroness spoke quite confidently. "There will be many more top women Alpinists, and they will have far more opportunity to train. Distances are even now no longer of significance. Polish women have already reached the summit of Gasherbrum II without oxygen, porters, or Sherpas. It caused no great sensation! A generation to be envied," she said contemplatively. "Young girls pile into old cars with boys who also love mountains, drive hundreds of kilometers, and set up tents somewhere. This would have been unthinkable in my day. . . ."

Women are not frogs and men are not eagles. And women are equal not only before mountains. They are free to take flight into tender dreams or into the world of high adventure. Alone and on eagle's wings. They can do whatever they like.

□

Franz Berghold

Why the Air Is So Thin on Mountaintops

It was the sixth night I had spent in my tent. We were accompanying Reinhold Messner's expedition to the south face of the 8,000-meter (26,246-foot) Himalayan peak Dhaulagiri and were now at Base Camp, 4,000 meters (13,123 feet) above sea level. The weather had been bad for days—first it rained; then it snowed. The day before, the sun had shone for a while in the morning and the humidity had dropped a little. I decided to set up my tent all over again. First I patted down and smoothed the ground. Then I carried and rolled some rocks over to my tent site. The doctor warned me not to overdo it, but I felt quite well. That night mountain sickness attacked.

I had to pay the price for having engaged in so much physical exertion without sufficient acclimatization. My sleep was fitful and it was hard to breathe. I felt as if I would forget to inhale, as if I would simply stop breathing altogether. The hours until daybreak were frightful. I felt a little better when I could get up and move. However, a few hours later when I lay down inside my tent, the doctor had to give me oxygen. He examined me and decided that I would have to put on an oxygen mask and climb down to a lower camp. There was no alternative since pulmonary edema was a real possibility.

Two days later, as I rested at about 2,500 meters (8,202 feet), my breathing difficulty ceased. However, my lungs had become inflamed because of exposure to the wet snow as well as because of my recent descent through the Wild River gorge. I was taken to a hospital. Had this not occurred, I could have returned to Base Camp after a few days of recuperation in the lower camp. A doctor from that expedition prepared this contribution on the dangers caused by thin air on the highest mountains of the world.

Andreas was a very experienced Alpinist. I met him in the Oberwald hut, which stands among the mighty glaciers of the Grossglockner. Andreas had interrupted his summer in the mountains to take a two-week holiday in Venice with his family. On this day, he had just returned from the sea and immediately climbed up to the hut, which lay about 3,000 meters (9,842 feet) above sea level—an insignificant feat for a highly experienced climber and not worth mentioning. The next morning was glorious and we all headed toward the summit of the Johannisberg, about 3,500 meters (11,483 feet) high. Just before noon, it began to get humid and even with skis the ascent was strenuous. A change of weather seemed imminent, and we increased our pace. Suddenly, Andreas stopped and doubled up over his ski poles. He was unrecognizable. His face had turned ashen, his lips were blue, and his features pinched. He seemed years older. He could scarcely stand up and complained of unbearable headache and a burning sensation in the chest. He was afraid he would suffocate, and his breathing was, indeed, a spasmodic rattle, punctuated by weak fits of coughing. There was no doubt about it: Andreas was suffering from a severe form of mountain sickness, which threatened to develop into fatal pulmonary edema. We quickly built an emergency sled; it was a matter of minutes. There was only one way to save Andreas: we had to get him down to the lower Pasterzen Glacier as quickly as possible.

The rescue attempt was successful. Seven hundred meters (2,300 feet) lower, Andreas was over the hump. I was a very young climber at the time, and this was the first time I had been confronted with such a dramatic situation. The question kept going round and round in my head: how could such a thing happen, especially to a person who had spent half his life in the mountains? What is mountain sickness? Today I know a good deal more about it.

Every child knows that air gets thinner the higher one climbs. More precisely, it is the atmospheric pressure that decreases with altitude and therefore also the partial pressure of the oxygen component of the air. At 5,500 meters (18,044 feet), only half the oxygen we breathe at sea level is available; at 8,500 meters (27,889 feet) only one-third. Mount Everest is 8,848 meters (29,029 feet) high, nearly 9,000 meters. A mere 2,000 meters higher ends the 11-kilometer-thick (6.8-mile) layer of atmosphere that protectively encircles the earth. (The atmosphere consists of 21 percent oxygen, 78 percent hydrogen, and 1 percent noble gases.) As the atmospheric pressure diminishes with increasing altitude, so too does the temperature and moisture of the air. The temperature

both in his laboratory experiments of 1878 and on a later scientific expedition to the Andes. Ten years later, changes become ever greater, and radiation from the universe increases. We notice none of these physical facts, of course, when we fly through altitudes of 35,000 feet in comfortable jet planes. The cabins are pressurized to simulate the height of 2,500 meters (8,202 feet).

A quick glance at a demographic map shows that the human being was not made for high mountains. For millions of years, his biophysical mechanisms have become accustomed to lower environments or, more precisely, man has adapted to the lowlands. Only a few isolated peoples have formed settlements high up in the mountains, for example, the Indios in the Andes and the Sherpas in the Himalayas. But even these peoples cannot live higher up than 5,500 meters (18,044 feet). There are no permanent settlements at higher altitudes. Permanent acclimatization is impossible at greater heights because there is not enough oxygen. Here one can only survive for more or less temporary periods—at least, on one's own. Several factors distinguish the high-altitude climber from the pilot. For the Alpinist, oxygen deficiency (hypoxia) is not the only limiting factor. Several other deprivations also affect him to greater or lesser degrees. The most important of these is the loss of water and minerals, a loss whose critical effect has been largely ignored or underestimated. Strenuous physical work at high altitudes causes an excess water loss of from 1 to 3 liters (2 to 6 pints) an hour through perspiration and exhalation. During the course of a day, a total water deficit of from 10 to 15 liters (21 to 31 pints) can occur. This loss must be replenished immediately, if possible in the form of liquids with a mineral content.

Grotesque as such quantities may sound, they represent the bitter truth. The liquid must be restored to the body, however difficult it is to prepare drinking water at high altitudes. If the liquid isn't restored, the blood becomes thicker (hemo-concentration); the viscous blood begins to circulate ever more slowly at the peripheries of the circulatory system and, in places, comes to a halt altogether. This condition places an enormous burden on the cardiovascular system. It leads to a lack of energy, greater exhaustion, and susceptibility to frostbite and thrombosis. The worst danger is that the slow transportation of oxygen from the lungs to the cells can cause mountain sickness with all of its complications: pulmonary edema and brain inflammations, which are often fatal.

Man has not known these facts for very long. Paul Berth, a French scientist, was probably the first to investigate the effect of rarefied air on the human body, measurements of red blood corpuscles were made in South America. Nevertheless, many details were obscure until quite recently. Today, research in high-altitude physiology is leading ever more into problems of hormone balance. High-altitude medicine did not greatly advance until after World War II, when it gained momentum as a result of a general mass movement of people toward the highest mountains of the world. Research in this field was given particular impetus by the work of numerous scientists who participated in these various expeditions.

In Europe, a dense network of mountain railways and highways crisscrosses the high Alpine regions. Within a matter of hours, tens of thousands of people from the flatlands are catapulted up to heights of 3,000 or 4,000 meters (9,800 to 13,000 feet) without advance preparation and without being aware of the adaptive processes that the body undergoes at these heights. Therapeutic medicine has recently discovered the benefits of high-altitude climates. Remarkable successes have been documented, and mountain "cures" have led to the rehabilitation of many people suffering from heart and vascular disease. Finally, sports medicine has proved that high-altitude training is particularly effective for athletes such as long-distance runners.

When the human being climbs to the height of 1,500 meters (4,900 feet), an alarm system goes off: the cardiovascular system responds by increasing the systolic volume and the pulse rate. The latter is particularly dependent on altitude and can increase from 20 percent to 50 percent above that measured at home. The pulse does not return to its normal rate until the climber has become completely acclimatized. The volume of air inhaled decreases, while the rate of respiration increases. This causes changes in the gas content of the blood and leads to such symptoms of adaptation as headache, dizziness, and insomnia.

Finally, the blood corpuscles (erythrocytes) and their main component, hemoglobin—which is the actual oxygen carrier of the blood—respond to the oxygen deficiency by increasing in number (high-altitude polyglobulae).

Admittedly, the significance of red blood corpuscles for the mountain climber has been generally overestimated. An increase in the number of erythrocytes does not necessarily improve the blood's ability to transport oxygen, which is the critical factor. However, a very interesting substance is increased at high altitudes. It has the oily-sounding name "2.3-diphosphoglycerate" and is a substance that hastens the deposit of oxygen into the capillaries. Of all the physiological changes that the body undergoes, it is only the increase of this one substance that

remains for months after the climber has returned from the heights. It accounts for the feeling of well-being that many people experience for a relatively long period after their return from high altitudes. Everything else returns to normal. New acclimatization processes must always begin from the beginning.

The first adaptive reactions serve as a temporary bridge to the final stages of acclimatization. The duration and extent of the critical initial phase of the process depends on three factors: the altitude difference involved, the speed with which the new altitude was reached, and the length of time spent at the new level. These transitional reactions vary with each individual and are quite independent of the degree of preparatory training one has undergone. Clinical tests and medical examinations provide no clues as to how one will react during the process of acclimatization. Each climber must learn to observe his own reactions.

The alarm mechanisms gradually give way to the actual process of acclimatization. As already mentioned, permanent acclimatization is possible only for altitudes of up to 5,500 meters (18,000 feet); above this height, the body undergoes only a more or less temporary process of adaptation, which is accompanied by considerable losses of various substances. Modern expeditions to the Himalayas have been able to make use of this information. After two- or three-day rapid advances, the particular team involved returns to Base Camp to recuperate at levels below 5,500 meters (18,000 feet).

Breakdowns in the adaptive process become acute when the organism can no longer deal with the oxygen deficiency or the thickening of the blood. Clear warning signals appear, but these are usually overlooked or made light of. The symptoms are bad headaches, nausea, loss of appetite, loss of breath with the least exertion. If one ignores these signals and continues to climb, genuine mountain sickness breaks out. Now one is unable to breathe even if one is totally still. In addition, one suffers extreme headaches and exhaustion. Vomiting occurs, the face becomes gray, the lips become blue, behavior becomes irrational, and one cannot walk without wobbling. Under certain circumstances, this condition can quickly develop into possibly fatal pulmonary edema, accompanied by such symptoms as fear of suffocation, coughing fits with discharge, a burning sensation behind the breastbone, and raspy breathing. Only two things can be done: either the patient must be given artificial oxygen or he must be transported down to a lower altitude immediately.

Mountain sickness, pulmonary edema, and brain inflammation are not inevitable but are absolutely avoidable. One cannot overemphasize this, especially in view of the fact that in 1976 in Nepal alone, which is one of the world's great trekking paradises, nearly three hundred mountain hikers were stricken with severe cases of pulmonary edema. For many of these people, help came too late. It appears that neither Alpine Clubs nor commercial trekking or expedition organizations have taken sufficient responsibility in informing themselves or their members of the dangers. Still, it is only necessary to remember a few simple principles, yet ones which are largely ignored out of ignorance. First, the climber should undertake a six- to eight-week period of endurance training in advance of the planned expedition, paying special attention to his pulse and body weight. A thorough physical examination is obligatory. This should include ergometric analysis of the muscles as well as a careful checkup of the internal organs. The doctor should also investigate possible sources of infection. The greatest precautions should be taken to prevent outbreaks of diarrhea and infection at high altitude, since these conditions substantially interfere with the process of adaptation and increase the risk of mountain sickness. Climbing should proceed in stages, and the altitude difference should not exceed 600 to 1,000 meters (2,000 to 3,300 feet) per day. If possible, the climber should sleep at a lower altitude than the highest point reached during the day. There is one rule of thumb that each individual should follow strictly: Do not continue to climb if your pulse rate upon waking up is 20 percent higher than normal. The ascent can continue safely only when one's pulse rate has returned to normal.

Besides a balanced diet, the most important thing to remember is to drink, drink, drink—best of all, mineral drinks in powdered form. Warning: One tends not to be thirsty at high altitudes! And yet, despite the lack of thirst, climbers at high altitudes are nearly always at risk from fluid deficiency. The warning signals are noticeable daily weight loss and a reduced 24-hour accumulation of urine (the normal quantity is 1.8 liters (3.8 pints) over a 24-hour period; an accumulation of from 0.5 to 1 liter (1 to 2 pints) should be regarded as an alarm signal).

Today we know that the only way to encourage the adaptation process is to allow the body sufficient time to complete the stages of acclimatization to high altitudes and to make certain that the electrolyte-fluid deficiency is constantly repaired. In light of the frequent attempts to aid the process of acclimatization through medicines or decompression chambers (which are totally valueless for the Alpinist), the importance of the basic precepts cannot be overemphasized. Unadulterated reason is the only effective aid: he who knows the ground rules that prevail at high altitudes and obeys them will not be likely to encounter serious problems—high above the earth, where the air is so thin. □

Nicolas Jaeger

Where the Sun God Once Dwelled

"What kind of world was it—this unique and bygone realm poised so close to the stars? When and why did it perish? What demonic power forced the Indios into these icy, dizzying heights where storms often raged for days and temperatures at night sank to −20°C (−68°F)? Was it religious belief? Sun worship? Military necessity? The merciless command of the Incas who worked their couriers to death? Here, at a height of nearly 7,000 meters (23,000 feet), sacrificial smoke once rose up to the heavens while fiery signs blazed toward the stars, heralding war and misery across infinite spaces. . . ."

In the 1950s, the Austrian Mathias Rebitsch found walls, wood, straw, corn cobs, and silver figures of gods on Andean summits in the vicinity of Puna de Atacama. The artifacts were remnants of the great Inca civilization, whose realm once encompassed 1.8 million square kilometers (695,000 square miles) of the South American continent, an area almost as large as western Europe today. The backbone of this empire, so to speak, was a chain of mountains reaching heights of nearly 7,000 meters. Military outposts were established on the highest summits. The Incas scaled these heights in order to pray to the Sun God, to whom they sacrificed animals and even, perhaps, human beings.

It is not surprising that cultic sites were maintained in high places. The Indios were able to cultivate their high-lying parched fields and thus survive only because the gods in the mountains were gracious enough to send water down from the snows above.

The Inca empire is gone. No more smoke signals from the mountain tops testify to its greatness and power. The Sun God is no longer worshiped. Today, the Andean summits only attract mountain climbers, who often ascend by the most difficult routes.

At least three hundred years before the first successful ascent of Mont Blanc, men stood on the tops of even higher mountains in the Andes. In 1956, Mathias Rebitsch found Inca artifacts on the 6,000-meter (19,684-foot) Cerro Galan in the wild wasteland of Puna de Atacama, which forms a border area in northwestern Argentina where Chile and Bolivia also meet. He discovered silver statues of the gods in a cult site that had been covered by ice and snow for hundreds of years. Cult sites had existed upon the summit of Llullaillaco [6,723 meters (22,057 feet)] even before Columbus discovered America. Rebitsch was the leader of an Austro-Swedish expedition, one of the countless climbing groups that came to the Andes, particularly after the Second World War.

From the Caribbean Sea and the Sierra Nevada de Santa Marta [5,775 meters (18,947 feet)] to the archipelago of Tierra del Fuego, the Andes form the South American part of the Cordillera, a mighty chain of mountains that stretches across the western part of the double American continent for a distance of more than 7,500 kilometers (25,000 miles). The highest elevation between Alaska and Tierra del Fuego is the Aconcagua [6,959 meters (22,381 feet)], located on the border between central Argentina and Chile. The Inca civilization had its beginnings in the middle of the Andes. The ruins of Tiahuanaco on Lake Titicaca [3,812 meters (12,506 feet)] among others testify to the existence of this empire and its culture.

For hundreds of years, the mighty Andean giants of rock and ice, many of which are still active volcanoes, have attracted scientists and explorers. For the past hundred years, they have also been sought out by mountain climbers. For about one hundred years, and until the discovery of the Himalayan giant Dhaulagiri [8,167 meters (26,794 feet)], the volcano Chimborazo [6,287 meters (20,626 feet)], which Alexander von Humboldt had attempted to climb, was considered the highest mountain in the world.

Today, superlatives are still bestowed upon several of the Andes mountains. The Alpamayo [5,947 meters (19,511 feet)] in the Peruvian Cordillera Blanca, the Condoriri [5,648 meters (18,530 feet)] in the Cordillera Real, and the Cerro Fitz Roy [3,441 meters (11,289 feet)] in the National Park on Lake Viedma in southern Patagonia are each described as "the most beautiful mountain in the world." The Jirishhanca Grande [6,126 meters (20,098 feet)] in the Cordillera Huayhuash is regarded as the Matterhorn of South America, and the Morado [5,060 meters (16,600 feet)], the Matterhorn of Chile. Many say the Fitz Roy, a granite needle in Patagonia, is the most difficult mountain in the world.

More than sixty summits in the Andes tower to heights above 6,000 meters. More than thirty Andes peaks are higher than the highest mountain in North America, Alaska's Mount McKinley [6,193 meters (20,318 feet)]. Most of the high summits have been climbed in Venezuela, Colombia, Ecuador, Peru, Bolivia, and Argentina. Nevertheless, there are still many hardly known mountains that are and will become tempting goals for climbers from all over the world. Every year these climbers set out—for the South during the European winter, for central and northern South America during the spring and early summer.

Already in the eighteenth century, scientists had traveled from Europe to South America in order to survey the land. In 1737, Charles Maria de la Condamine and Pierre Bouguer, members of a group consisting of four French and two Spanish scientists, climbed several peaks in the Andes of Ecuador, including the Corazon [4,840 meters (15,879 feet)]. Scientists who brought back knowledge of the high mountains of South America were followed there by mountain climbers, as had also been the case in the Alps. By 1897, the highest peak in the New World had been climbed: the Aconcagua [6,959 meters (22,831 feet), though according to earlier measurements 7,130 meters (23,392 feet)]. The Swiss mountain guide Mathias Zurbriggen, from Saas in the Valais, was the victor. He went the last distance alone. Stuart Vines, his client, reached the top one month later accompanied by a porter. Together with Vines, Zurbriggen also climbed the Tupungato [6,800 meters (22,309 feet)], the third highest mountain in South America. British climbers came to South America in great numbers at the turn of the century. Such a trip was a costly affair, and one also needed a great deal of time. The names of the foreign climbers are well-known: Whymper with the Carrels; Vines and Edward A. FitzGerald with Zurbriggen; William Martin Conway with the Italian guide Daniel Maquignaz was particularly active, especially in Tierra del Fuego; Annie Peck with Rudolf Taugwalder and Zumtaugwald; Hiram Bingham and Comyns C. Tucker.

After the First World War, the Austrians and Germans arrived. They achieved a number of first climbs, mainly in the Cordillera Blanca. The cartographer Erwin Schneider was very active here, along with Philip Borchers, Erwin Hein, Arnold Awerzger, and Hans Kinzl. The first ascents were Huandoy [6,395 meters (20,980 feet)] in 1932 and 1936; Pucahirca [6,046 meters (19,835 feet)] by Schneider alone; Huascaran [6,768 meters (22,204 feet)]; and Yerupaja Grande [6,634 meters (21,765 feet)] in the Cordillera Huayhuash.

The Italian Count Aldo Bonacossa selected the "most difficult mountain in the world" as the goal of his expedition of 1937, whose participants included some of the strongest Alpinists in Europe. But he had to give up because of bad weather conditions: Pacific storms raged with tremendous force against the monolithic cliffs of Patagonia and covered the summits of the perpendicular granite needles with caps of ice. The Cerro Fitz Roy, called "Chaltel" by the Patagonians, was not climbed until 1952. After a great and tenacious struggle, two of the most outstanding Alpinists of the time, the Frenchmen Lionel Terray and Guido Magnone, reached the top. Ten years later, Terray, along with Magnone and Claude Maillard, achieved another "first": the Chacraraju in the Cordillera Blanca. In 1956, Terray had been the first to climb the western summit [6,075 meters (19,931 feet)]. Now, in 1962, together with his partners, he conquered the eastern horn of the beautiful double-peaked mountain.

Men from Switzerland, Austria, France, Belgium, Italy, America, Great Britain, Germany, and Poland made the 1950s into the period of great climbs in the Andes. In 1957, a German group under the leadership of Günter Hauser successfully climbed the Alpamayo, the "most beautiful mountain," following in the footsteps of Swiss climbers and a Belgian-French group that included Claude Kogan (who later died on Cho Oyu in the Himalayas). Toni Egger and Siegfried Jungmayr, members of an Austrian expedition, climbed the Jirishhanca Grande [6,126 meters (20,098 feet)]; in 1959, Toni Egger fell to his death from the Cerro Torre [3,128 meters 10,262 feet)], not far from the Fitz Roy in Patagonia. The catastrophe occurred after the controversial first ascent by Egger and the Italian Cesare Maestri. As the climbers were descending during a bad storm, a gigantic avalanche plunged Egger into the depths. A year before, Walter Bonatti had also made an attempt on the Cerro Torre.

As had occurred in the Alps and the Himalayas, climbers in the Andes were now tempted by new and more difficult routes to the top. The most daring of all were attracted to the towering, ice-covered, vertical granite needles of Cerro Fitz Roy and Cerro Torre in Patagonia. It was not the height of these peaks that made them difficult; the Fitz Roy is no higher than the Marmolada in the Dolomites, which hundreds of tourists climb every year. The difficulties were caused by the climate of the Patagonian highlands. Rain and snowstorms from the Pacific rage around the granite cliffs and through the glacial valleys. Only the most hardy of hardy mountaineers are able to endure sitting for days in a tent or crouching Eskimo fashion in an igloo waiting for short periods of better weather. The technical climbing problems are uncommonly great and, therefore, particularly challenging. Admittedly, the manner in which Cesare Maestri conquered the Fitz Roy is not everyone's cup of tea. Using a drill weighing 70 kilograms (154 pounds), he laid pitons on the tower, even in places where only moderately experienced climbers would not have thought of using them. English and American climbers who later followed him were amazed at this masterly use of hardware.

The period when men would climb at any price and by any means is probably finished in the Andes. Ice and rock climbing as a pure sport, with its thrills and variety, is more popular than ever. The mighty south wall [2,000 meters (6,562 feet)] of the Aconcagua, which is partly covered with snow and ice, was successfully climbed for the first time in 1954 by a French expedition under the leadership of René Ferlet. For the Alpinist, the mountains of the Andes offer countless interesting climbing goals. Aside from Patagonia, where the most exciting adventures still await Alpinists from all over the world, there are several reasons why climbers are attracted to the South American Andes: the mountains are less than 7,000 meters (23,000 feet) high, so that supplementary oxygen is not necessary; there are hardly any administrative obstacles; the climate is extremely favorable; and, finally, there are countless summits over 5,500 meters (18,000 feet) high and, therefore, there is plenty of room for many, many climbers. This is why tours in the Cordillera Blanca, the Cordillera Huayhuash, and the Cordillera Vilcabamba and Vilcanota of Peru as well, as climbs in the Cordillera Real of Bolivia, have become so popular.

One of the most extraordinary expeditions of recent times took place during the summer of 1977 in the Cordillera Central. It was led by the French physician and extreme climber Nicolas Jaeger, from Paris, who had already made a name for himself with his extreme solo ascents. The team consisted of John Bouchard, a student from the United States, Dennis Ducroz, a high-mountain guide and filmmaker, René Ghilini, an Italian student living in France who was also a passionate kite flyer, Bernard Prud'homme, an engineer and guide, and Marie-Odile Meunier, a French gallery owner living in the United States. A Peruvian porter, Felipe Mautinho, who had been accompanying expeditions since 1951, was hired as an assistant and porter. He recruited mule drivers for the transport of equipment into the mountain valleys, guarded the camps, and helped move the equipment from the camp to the snow line.

In an informative documentary report, Nicolas Jaeger wrote about this 1977 Peruvian expedition to the 5,000-

and 6,000-meter peaks of the Cordillera Blanca, which contains thirty summits of more than 6,000 meters (20,000 feet). Jaeger's report, which is sober and objective, although it also reveals the personal involvement of a passionate mountain climber, exemplifies the down-to-earth goals advocated by the younger generation of highly skilled Alpinists. His style is not marred by pathos or, indeed, by any discernible feeling; nevertheless, it reflects the profound and lasting experience of its author.

The 1977 Peruvian expedition to the Cordillera Blanca broke with the traditional style of most of the Andes expeditions: a great number of ascents were made in the purest possible Alpine style. There was no advance technical preparation. Roped teams consisted of two or three climbers; often solo climbs were made. The entire expedition was rarely assembled in any one place at the same time. The team consisted of climbers of all ages, educational levels, and nationalities. There was even one woman in the group. Since René Ghilini, the youngest member of the expedition, was a passionate devotee of kite flying, some among the group also occupied themselves with this sport.

It is obvious that difficult climbs on mountains of 6,000 meters, with little or no support from others, demands, first of all, excellent training, techniques of proven reliability, and sufficient acclimatization. Above all, one must have a thorough knowledge of the particular risks involved and be ready to accept them. Naturally, a team that is hanging alone somewhere on a mountain can hardly count on help from others. Each individual's preparedness and skill are thus the most important prerequisites for a successful climb. On the other hand, fast climbs reduce objective dangers to a minimum, because such climbs allow one to select routes previously rejected by large but cumbersome expeditions.

The remarkable capacity for endurance exhibited by Meunier, the only woman in the group, deserves particular mention. She succeeded in two climbs. The second, directly up the south wall of the Chacraraju [6,075 meters (19,931 feet)], proved to be the most technically difficult tour of the whole expedition. The route required five bivouacs: two at the foot of the wall because of bad weather; one just beneath the summit; and the last on the summit ridge, again because of bad weather. At the end of this difficult tour, Marie-Odile Meunier's physical condition was still excellent.

René Ghilini (only twenty years old) also conducted himself with distinction. He accomplished great feats at high altitudes and proved to have extraordinary powers of resistance. The expedition's leader, Nicolas Jaeger, had been an extremely successful solo climber on the most difficult routes of the Alps for a decade. Except when making films, he climbed the 6,000-meter Andean peaks alone, not because he was a misanthropist but rather because solo climbs allowed him to deepen his experiences. In the Alps, he selected ever more difficult solo tours. Climbing new routes in a free style alone at 6,000 meters on difficult terrain, without security or any possibility of rescue, became a kind of game for him—a game that, while heightening his sensibilities, allowed for no mistakes. During his long bivouacs, this solo climber steeped himself in the magnificence of the Andes chain. When he was not climbing, he supervised the medical and physical needs of the team.

The group was under way for about four months—from the beginning of May to the beginning of September 1977. The first base camp was erected in the middle of May on one of the world's most inaccessible stretches of land, the Alpamayo Valley [4,550 meters (14,928 feet)]. It took three long, arduous days of walking to reach this wild, high valley at the foot of the beautiful Alpamayo. In spite of the bad weather—storms every afternoon—several climbing successes were recorded: the Quitaraju by way of the north wall; the Alpamayo (twice) by way of the southwest flank; and the Santa Cruz Sur (south) by way of the north ridge and the northeast wall. René Ghilini and Bernard Prud'homme climbed to the summit of Quitaraju [6,110 meters (20,046 feet)], a beautiful and massive mountain ridge running in an east-west direction. The climb, which involved a very difficult ascent of a steep, sun-drenched glacier on the north side of the mountain [climbing grade D-*difficile* ("difficult"); altitude difference 600 meters (1,968 feet)], took four hours.

The most beautiful mountain on earth, the Alpamayo [5,947 meters (19,510 feet)], is a snow-covered pyramid with four ridges and four faces. A sharp crest, 100 meters (328 feet) in length, forms the summit, whose highest point lies at the southern tip. Nicolas Jaeger was the first to conquer the Alpamayo alone. He reached the summit by way of the southwest flank, crossing a beautiful snow-covered glacier. There is a 400-meter (1,312-foot) rise between the moraine at the glacier's terminus and the summit ridge. Jaeger surmounted it in two and one-half hours. René Ghilini and Bernard Prud'homme reached the summit one day later.

Five days later, Nicolas Jaeger also succeeded in climbing the highest point in the northern massif of the Cordillera Blanca: the Santa Cruz Sur [6,259 meters (20,535 feet)]. Swiss climbers, Frederic Marmillod and Ali

Szepessy (1948), had been the first to climb this mountain, following a route up the northeast gulley and, on the upper section, across the north ridge to the summit. The north ridge route confronts the climber with a sequence of cliffs, snow, and ice. From the saddle that lies between Santa Cruz Sur and Santa Cruz Chico to the summit there is a rise of 700 meters (2,297 feet). Jaeger needed a total of five and one-half hours for the ascent. At the same time, Ghilini and Prud'homme made first ascents of the northeast flank, tracking an elegant route over the glacier. The climb took nine and one-half hours and covered a rise of 750 meters (2,460 feet).

After these early successes, the group left the Alpamayo Valley, traveling south through Huarez, to the west of the Cordillera Blanca. A second camp was set up in the Cojup Valley. Nicolas Jaeger also made several solo ascents here. One was the first climb of the glacier-covered southeast flank leading to the lonely summit of the Ranrapalca [6,168 meters (20,236 feet)]; the route, classified as TD (très difficile ["very difficult]), took seven hours. Several days later, John Bouchard, Ghilini, and Prud'homme reached the summit by a new route over the east ridge. On Pucaranra [6,147 meters (20,167 feet)], Jaeger (once again by himself) opened up an extraordinary route across the snow-covered northwest ridge. Some very difficult (TD) passages were discovered in the course of the 650-meter (2,132-foot) rise. This solo climber also made an assault on the Palcaraju [6,274 meters (20,584 feet)], which closes off the Cojup Valley in the north. He reached the Palcaraju Oeste [6,110 meters (20,046 feet)] by way of an interesting route to the main summit across the snow-covered southeast ridge. The climb took only five hours in spite of its great technical difficulties. From here, the route to the main summit by way of the summit ridge was easy. Descending on the same route, Jaeger had to rappel several times.

A third camp was erected at the southern foot of the twin-peaked Chacraraju [6,075 meters and 6,000 meters (19,930 feet and 19,685 feet)], which had first been climbed by the unforgettable Lionel Terray in 1956 and 1962. From here, John Bouchard and Marie-Odile Meunier climbed for three days across the south face, bivouacking twice. Twenty-eight hours of pure climbing were required for the 800-meter (2,625-foot) rise from the end moraine to the summit. Marie-Odile Meunier was the first woman to reach the top.

Nicolas Jaeger made the first solo ascent of the mighty Huascaran [south summit 6,768 meters (22,204 feet); north summit, 6,655 meters (21,884 feet)], following a route over the northeast ridge of the south summit. This peak had been first climbed in 1932 by an Austro-German expedition (Borchers, Willi Bernard, Hein, Hermann Hoerlin, and Schneider). Jaeger required fourteen hours for this tiring route, which involved a rise of 1,350 meters (4,429 feet) from the saddle connecting Huascaran South and Chopicalqui to the summit. This was certainly a high point of the expedition.

There are still several tempting peaks (all about 20,000 feet) to climb in the Cordillera Blanca: Huantsan (6,395 meters), lying in the southern part of the chain and reachable only after a very tiring march; the Huandoy, with its four summits (6,395 meters, 6,356 meters, 6,166 meters, 6,070 meters), each of which offers steep rock faces; Chopicalqui (6,356 meters), an elegant snow-covered pyramid lying very close to Huascaran; Chinchey (6,222 meters); Copa, with its two summits (6,188 meters and 6,173 meters); Hualcan (6,125 meters), characterized by a large summit plateau and offering yet unclimbed, vertical rock faces to the north and east; and the six peaks of the Pucahirca, which form a long dome-shaped ridge (the summits ranging between 5,900 and 6,046 meters high). Besides these, there is a series of other interesting summits, all just under 6,000 meters in height.

The Huascaran was the scene of a terrible event not long ago. In May 1970, an earthquake killed twenty thousand people within a matter of minutes. Ten thousand tons of rock and ice broke loose from the west face of the north summit and plunged down the mountain. The town of Yungay was completely buried, as was the camp of a Czechoslovakian expedition that had set out to climb the Huascaran.

Access to the mountains of the Cordillera Blanca is simple and fast. There is a paved road 420 kilometers (261 miles) long from Lima, and one can also easily fly there. From Huarez, one can either drive a rented car or make use of the famous-infamous "colectivos." The latter are cars that move constantly through the valleys and pick up anyone who is willing and able to pay. It is not too difficult to find donkeys, mules, or horses (and their keepers). It is also relatively easy to engage porters, as long as one is not planning to climb too high. Fuel, however, is a problem. It is best to provide one's expedition with bottled gas (for use in the base camp) and with handy, lightweight cartridges (for use on bivouacs and in the high camps). Food can usually be bought in the larger towns. However, there was no powdered coffee, condensed milk, or any vacuum-packed food to be found in Huarez in 1977. It is advisable to bring the necessities from Europe.

Base camps are best established at heights between 3,800 meters (12,467 feet) and 4,000 meters (13,123 feet). Because the transport route is relatively short, it is feasible to carry and set up a large common tent and smaller sleeping tents with field beds, kitchen equipment, gas cookers, gas lamps, and collapsible basins for washing. Of course, one must also bring along sufficient equipment required for Alpine climbs: pitons, crampons, ice axes, rope, bivouac tents, down sleeping bags, gloves, snow goggles, and . . . and . . .

The South American Cordillera, the Andes, that stretch from the Carribean Sea to Tierra del Fuego, will doubtless attract ever more mountain climbers and probably more high-mountain trekkers too. Most of the highest summits have now been climbed. However, many mountains are still waiting to be discovered. It will not be long before whole groups of people from everywhere in the world will follow in the footsteps of the courageous first climbers. Aconcagua and Illimani, Huascaran and Tupungato, Chimborazo and Cotopaxi, Alpamayo and Condoriri—they will soon be experienced by thousands of people, either from the summit or simply from the distance during the course of a hike through high mountain valleys. Groups will come even to Patagonia in order to experience adventure in the stormy winds of the Pacific. The mountains of the earth have come nearer to us—even the lonely, legendary, and mysterious mountains of the Andes.

□

Herbert Tichy

They Came from Far Away

The image is unforgettable: two men are carefully guiding a strangely dressed couple through the chaos of Viennese traffic. It is the Sherpa Pasang Dawa Lama and his second wife Yang Chin. They had been invited to Vienna by Herbert Tichy and Sepp Jöchler the year after the first successful climb of Cho Oyu. With his ascent of Cho Oyu, Pasang Dawa Lama, the Sherpa sirdar, won not only a wager but also his second wife.

In Lukla, on the way to Cho Oyu, Pasang, who was already married, had become acquainted with the Sherpa girl Yang Chin ("precious stone"). He was absolutely set on marrying her, although he already had sons who would have made more appropriate husbands. Since Sherpa marriage laws permit a man to have a second wife, Pasang decided to marry again. However, he either could not or would not pay the customary settlement to the bride's parents. Nor was he prepared to work off the obligation. He therefore made the following suggestion to his prospective father-in-law: he, Pasang Dawa Lama, would be given Yang Chin for nothing if he managed to climb Cho Oyu with the sahibs; if he did not reach the top, Yang Chin's parents could keep their "precious stone" and he would pay them one thousand rupees in compensation for the loss sustained. Well, Pasang climbed Cho Oyu with Tichy and Jöchler and on his return to Lukla celebrated his second marriage. Pasang called his friends Tichy, Jöchler, and Heuberger, and his father and mother. The wedding was a feast. A year later the married couple arrived in Vienna to pay a visit.

Herbert Tichy has come to know the Sherpas as few others have. For this reason, he becomes reflective when he considers a rather unpleasant development that is taking place in Sherpa lands today: ever-increasing, ever more commercialized tourism.

The Sherpas have achieved something that distinguishes them from every other small people in the course of history. A few decades ago, they were just another of the many tribes that form the Central Asian racial mix. Today they are world famous, much beloved, and highly respected. Our grandfathers had to learn the fact that Mount Everest, not Gaurisankar, was the highest mountain in the world. Like Mount Everest, the Sherpas have today become an international household word. "I am not a Sherpa," a tourist might well protest if his rucksack has been too heavily loaded. Now he has to learn that "Sherpa" does not mean "high mountain porter"; Sherpas are "people from the East."

It all began in the early 1920s. At that time, the English were trying to climb Mount Everest and needed porters. There were many Sherpas living in Darjeeling, the point of departure for the British expeditions. The Englishmen hired these Sherpas, who revealed themselves to be true pearls of mountain climbing. They are not only strong and powerful porters as well as excellent Alpinists; they are also extremely friendly people who possess all the qualities that we value in the West. They are a happy folk, and even terrible misfortune cannot destroy their equanimity. They are more intelligent than most of the other natives and are able to think ahead. They are honest, trustworthy, and, whenever necessary, forceful and courageous.

At first, their good reputation spread only among mountain-climbing specialists. Later, Sherpas became the darlings of the whole world. Two phenomena were responsible for this. First, Tensing Norgay stood with Hillary on the top of Mount Everest. Later, Sherpas assisted in the conquest of other 8,000-meter (26,246-foot) peaks. Second, hundreds of thousands of people from all over the world were lured to Nepal to participate in the increasingly popular sport of trekking. In the history of the conquest of the Third Pole, it would be hard to find an example of a Sherpa's having left his sahib in a moment of danger in order to save his own life. On the other hand, there are many examples of how they sacrificed their own lives in order to help a dying friend or at least not to abandon him to solitude.

Probably I am not the right man to write an impartial account of the Sherpas. I have known three generations of them and have spent many months in their company—a stretch of time that was of immeasurable value to me. In 1936, I went with Kitar to the holy mountain of Kailas in Tibet and, on the way there, we tried to climb the Gurla Mandhata [7,728 meters (25,354 feet)]. I can still hear Kitar's voice as a storm threatened to tear our tent from the ridge and fling it into the depths. "The Gods," he muttered, not exactly calmly but also not in panic. Only once did I witness an occasion where a Sherpa lost his nerve. On the Cho Oyu, a hurricane had destroyed our tent, and it looked as if we would not be able to make our way back to safety. Pasang cried out again and again: "We will die, all of us." But in spite of this fatalistic and pessimistic prediction, he devoted all his effort and skill to the welfare of his companions, concentrating wholly on the retreat. We all came safely down.

The plan of attacking Cho Oyu arose during my first crossing of western Nepal, together with Pasang, in 1953. I have forgotten many details from that time, but the evening on which we first seriously thought about climbing this 8,000-meter mountain will always remain fresh in my memory.

We had pitched our tents in front of a peasant's hut on a field that had just been harvested. We were chewing on sticks of sugarcane and warming ourselves in the faint winter sun. Pasang, sitting next to me, cleared his throat and threw me an embarrassed look. I knew from experience that he was about to make a request. After persuading me to buy a goat, an act that was not too difficult since the Sherpas were not the only ones who were hungry, he asked me without a long introduction:

"Another high summit?"

This high summit had already often been the subject of our conversations. I'd like that, I said, but it was a question of money and of obtaining permission from the government of Nepal. Neither obstacle appeared to be a problem for Pasang. "Cho Oyu," he said, "a very high mountain, but a mountain we can do."

I shook my head doubtfully. "Next year Cho Oyu," Pasang insisted.

I nodded. Adjiba brought the cooked liver of the goat.

"We are going to climb Cho Oyu," Pasang said to him.

"Ah," said Adjiba and cut a pumpkin into small slices.

Barely one year later we really were standing upon the summit of Cho Oyu, my friend Sepp Jöchler, the Sherpa Pasang Dawa Lama, and I.

I have had only good or, rather, the very best experiences with Sherpas and cannot regard them without favorable bias. But also I have met many tourists who have returned from trekking trips in Nepal, and there is not one among them who has not raved about the Sherpas. Since the observations made by these transient visitors agree entirely with the conclusions of expedition members, it is clear that the positive characteristics ascribed to the Sherpa people really exist. We are not dealing here with

68

69

Children who have never seen a mountain might well imagine one to look like the Alpamayo in the White Cordillera—at least, this is how its first conqueror Günter Hauser expresses the fantastic quality of this mountain peak. The tropical sun beating down meets damp air rising up from primeval forests to form the cathedral-shaped south wall with its fine ridges of perpetual snow (firn). In 1936, news and pictures of a nameless mountain in the Alpamayo Valley made their way to Europe. In 1948 a Swiss team attempted to climb it but plunged off when a snow-covered cornice broke away. They survived the fall with bruises. In 1951 a group of French and Belgian climbers tried again. In the shadows of approaching nightfall, they believed they had reached the summit. In reality it was still 200 meters (656 feet) away and 80 meters (262 feet) higher. It was not until June 1957 that Günter Hauser, the leader of a German reconnaisance mission in the Andes, reached the 6,100-meter (20,012-foot) summit of the mountain of his dreams!

67/68

Climbers from all over the world search for new routes on the 6,000-meter (ca. 19,700-foot) peaks of the Andes. Although the summits have been conquered, their steep walls of ice and rock still attract the Alpinist. In two summers, the French climber Nicolas Jaeger opened up many new routes, for example, on the south wall of Chacraraju and on the Huandoy in the White Cordillera.

70

Patagonia: the
southernmost tip of South
America. A windswept
stormy landscape between
the Pacific and Atlantic
Oceans; a landscape of
glaciers and bizarre
monoliths whose vertical
tips are coated with ice.
Damp air from the Pacific
blows toward the massif,
discharging its
precipitation. To the east
begins the Patagonia Steppe
where rain hardly ever falls.
The Cerro Fitz Roy (middle)
at 3,441 meters (11,289 feet)
towers above everything
surrounding it. Its proud
neighbor, the Cerro Torre
(left), whose ice cap lies in
the clouds, is 3,128 meters
(10,262 feet) high. Many of
the best rock climbers in the
world have tested their
skills on the steep faces and
pillars of this mountain.
Many have had to turn back
short of their goal because
snowstorms arose and ice
formation made further
climbing impossible.

72
Alpacas on the high plateaus
of the Cordillera Vilcanota:
domestic animals bred by
the Indios.

71
Pushed up by forces from
the core of the earth, split
and cracked from the
constant alternation of heat
and cold, molded by wind
and water, ice and
snow—such are the
mountains seen here.
Though no changes appear
to occur, the landscape is
changing constantly. Ice
masses, perpetually fed by
new-fallen snow, plunge
down the steep slopes of the
Jirishhanca Grande [6,126
meters (20,098 feet), center]
in the cordillera de
Huayhuash of Peru. The
melting ice feeds the glacial
lake, the mountain stream,
the river. Water from the
mountains brings life to the
environment.

73
In the middle of a small
mountain settlement,
Spanish conquerors built
their church facing out upon
the peak. The first
inhabitants of South
America were forced to
worship the god of their new
masters. Their own gods,
who had come from the sun
retreated into the
mountains. In the course of
time, ancient religion and
modern faith coalesced.
Local churches contain
many representations of
Christian saints with
ancient Indio features.

74

75

Winds carry moisture from the Pacific Ocean in the west to the Andes peaks where it falls as snow. On the Chilean side of the range, a few smooth slopes provide a modern paradise for winter sports. The area near Aconcagua is particularly favored. Aconcagua itself is 6,959 meters (22,831 feet) high and thus the highest point in the Western Hemisphere. In 1966 the World Skiing Championship was held in Portillo. The hot southern sun, whose rays hit the earth at a nearly perpendicular angle, has caused these strange needles of ice to form both on the Horcones Glacier and on the northwest flank of Aconcagua (76/77) just below the summit. Drifting snow blown by the west wind forms huge overhanging cornices; the sun's rays create bizarre formations of snow. Even on skis, it is often exhausting to climb through the granular icy snow of these peaks.

76

77

A view across the countless Andean peaks on a beautiful, cloudless day compensates the climber for the rigors endured on the way to the summit. Wild, crevassed ridges covered with ice and snow stretch as far as the eye can see. Here, only the highest peaks have been climbed. Many precipitous rock faces, many ridges with snow-covered cornices will yet lure generations of climbers to their midst. There are still many discoveries to make and many unnamed mountains to climb.

The proud Yerupaja Grande [6,634 meters (21,764 feet)] in the Cordillera de Huayhuash: the second highest summit in the Peruvian Andes. In 1950 two Americans climbed for two months until they

reached the summit via the south ridge (right). Germans and Austrians had already visited the Cordillera in the 1930s. In 1936 the Tyrolean guide Arnold Awerzger and the well-known cartographer

Erwin Schneider reached the 6,000-meter mark. El Toro, the Bull's Head [6,121 meters (20,081 feet)], rises to the left, separated by a saddle. It is also known as Yerupaja Chico.

The Cordillera Real: the
Royal Cordillera. One must
bow before the "sublime
beauty and grandeur" of this
mountain range in the
highlands of Bolivia. The
British opened up this
territory before the turn of
the century. They were
followed by Austrian,
German, and Swiss
climbers. Illimani, Illampu,
Haucana, and
Chearoco—mysterious
names, many passed down
from ancient times when the
first inhabitants of this land
approached the dwelling
places of their gods filled
with awe. Today
experienced guides lead
Alpine enthusiasts to the
top.

82

83

82-85

In the high mountains of the
world everything is
transported on foot. Were it
not for the local porters it is
doubtful that any of the
highest summits could have
been climbed. In the
Himalayas the Sherpas have
accomplished incredible
feats, often climbing up to
the highest camps with the
heaviest loads. Young
women, Sherpani (84),
frequently carry loads as far
as the base camp. Boxes,
barrels, and baskets,
supported by a head strap
are lugged up the mountain

after days of hiking along
the valley floor. The
Sherpanis often walk
barefoot even through the
glacial snows. For many
inhabitants of the
Himalayas and the
Karakorum, employment as
a porter has become an
important source of income
and the men are often called
upon to assist the countless
expeditions which arrive in
these regions. However,
unpleasant incidents also
occur. All too often the
porters become dissatisfied
with the original wage

agreed upon, refuse to go
on, and strike. When large
expeditions arrive,
hundreds of people carry
tons of material up the
mountain. A large column of
porters could very likely
represent a cross section of
all the numerous tribes
which inhabit the area. The
poorest mountain peasants
call themselves coolies. For
miserable wages they must
carry loads of up to 30
kilograms in addition to
their own provisions: some
rice or barlay for chapatis, a
few potatoes. They may

bring along an old jute sack
or a blanket made of yak
wool in which they wrap
themselves as they huddle
around the campfires on cold
mountain nights. Only those
who accompany the climbers
to the high camps must be
equipped by the expedition
with proper clothing, snow
goggles, crampons, ice picks
and whatever else is
necessary for survival at
these altitudes. New shoes,
however, often pinch; feet
worn flat by so much labor
seldom fit into climbing
boots.

86
Namche Bazar: the principal
Sherpa settlement in
Khumbu, 3,400 meters
(11,154 feet) above sea level.
There are approximately
25,000 Sherpas in the world.
Migrating from eastern
Tibet in the sixteenth
century, they traveled south
across the Nangpa-La, a
mountain pass situated at
5,716 meters (18,753 feet),
and settled in the Khumbu
region at the foot of Mount
Everest. Sherpas practice
Tibetan Buddhism and
every house contains a
"gomba" or place for
religious worship. The
people are mainly farmers
and cattle-breeders. Some
are traders. In recent times
young men have begun to
migrate to cities in search of
work. Sometimes
employment as a mountain
guide is available. When
expeditions come to climb
the giants, the young men
take jobs as porters.

the transfigured perceptions of Europeans in a holiday mood.

The Sherpas come from the districts of Solu Khumbu and Pharak, to the south of Mount Everest. The Darjeeling Sherpas (numbering about eight thousand), who started things rolling, are only immigrants; they have never fully lost their connections with the homeland. Solu Khumbu is a mountainous region. The highest village, Pangpoche, lies at about 4,000 meters (13,000 feet) and the highest pastureland at about 5,000 meters (16,500 feet). The Sherpas prefer not to form settlements below 2,500 meters (8,200 feet). Like their most important domestic animal, the yak, they only feel well in air as thin as that which wafts across the highest peaks in the Alps. They follow wedge-shaped mountain ridges that stretch toward the south, but they leave lower-lying lands to other local tribes and make no attempts to settle there.

Thus, the Sherpas inhabit a magnificent and isolated landscape (at least they did so before the sport of trekking became so popular). Their activities as shepherds, traders, and even as farmers offer them much solitude. People engaged in lonely occupations are generally peaceful people. When Sherpas reach a house or village, they also expect a hospitable reception, and they always receive one. The Sherpas are daily thrown upon one another, and this may well be one of the reasons for the friendly atmosphere that still characterizes the Sherpa villages of today.

The fourteen thousand Sherpas are divided into about two dozen clans. Each group has equal rights and none tries to dominate the rest. The knowledge of belonging to a community welded together by blood ties probably provides each individual with a feeling of security. This in turn creates a feeling of self-assurance, and it is precisely this self-assurance, which is never pushy, that makes the Sherpa into such an agreeable partner. The Sherpas are a tiny people, a small tribe. It is not that each one knows everyone else personally, but, somehow, they have all heard of each other or have a great uncle in common. This feeling of belonging, which is characteristic of small groups and island people, serves to insulate against confusion and encourages a happy disposition.

The main reason for the Sherpa's tolerant nature seems to me to lie in their religion. They are Buddhists (or, more correctly, Lamists) and so believe in reincarnation. Present-day life is only a tiny link in an infinite chain of being. In every life, the acts of the preceding one are rewarded or punished. Naturally, everyone attempts to collect as many pluses as possible for his next reincarnation. Every visitor to the Sherpa lands is struck by the great tenderness with which children are treated. Warning slaps or real spankings are unthinkable—sometimes to the visitor's indignation. This behavior by the adults does not arise solely from their great love for children; it also arises from their conviction that it is a sin to cause children to cry. And who wants to make a mess of one's next life because of some child's tears in this life?

Interestingly, Sherpa children learn to walk very late—often not until the age of four. This is an astonishing fact, considering that the Sherpas are a people who later largely earn their livelihood with their feet. The smallest children are carried on the backs of their mothers or older brothers and sisters. Later, they are allowed to crawl. But they are not helped to stand upright or to walk, and there are no devices to make the learning process easier. As Pasang once put it: "Long rest, then very strong."

To return to the influence of the belief in reincarnation upon the Sherpa's character, he does not only try to avoid committing sins himself; he also regards the evil actions of his neighbor without self-righteous anger. He does not demand earthly retribution. He feels pity for the poor neighbor who has just cheated and stolen. How wretched the poor man will be in the next life. He may even be an animal! Such an attitude nurtures an almost sympathetic understanding for the weaknesses of others and allows a feeling of brotherhood to arise among the travelers who are journeying together through numberless existences toward a distant goal (Nirvana?). (One might object that hundreds of thousands of Buddhists and Hindus also believe in reincarnation without having constructed a harmonious social order. One need only look at the rigid caste system of the modern Hindus.)

Perhaps the positive and unique position of the Sherpas can be explained by the fact that for four centuries (from the period of their arrival from Kham in 1533) they have been left alone and subject to no authority from outside. The power of the Lama cloisters of Tibet did not reach across the Himalayas, and the central authority of Katmandu was only superficially and very faintly visible. But even these facts do not really provide an answer. Migrating over a stretch of more than 100 kilometers (62 miles) from Kumaon in the west to Sikkim in the east, Mongolian Tibetan-speaking peoples came across the ridges of the Himalayas and eventually settled on the south slopes of the massif. Like the Sherpas, these people are also Buddhists and live independently outside the pale of any external authority. Nevertheless, how different they are in every respect from the Sherpas! When one is with the Bhotias of the Indian Himalayas or of West Nepal, one feels well. When one is with the Sherpas, one feels happy. At least, this has been my experience.

Ethnologists may find an explanation for the special qualities that characterize the Sherpa people in genetics. The Sherpas do not come simply from Tibet but from the region that today is called Szechwan. Here, China and Tibet have been battling for sovereignty for many centuries. Barbarians from the south (Lolos, Miaos, and Liaos) intermarried with the Sherpas, and even the influence of Turkish blood from Turkestan can be proved. Thus, the Sherpas are a veritable melting pot of races. Perhaps a unique combination did occur. I have my own explanation, however; it is one that has nothing to do with the shape of the skull, blood type, or genetic makeup. At the same time, it is one that would also be unable to withstand scientific scrutiny.

Accident caused the Sherpas to end their long wanderings in one of the most beautiful landscapes of the world, in a place where heaven and earth meet, in a country whose grandeur simply cannot be surpassed. Just as the peasants of the Alps hardly see the beauty of their native mountains, so, too, the Sherpas seem hardly aware of the beauty of the Himalayas. Once I happened to get into conversation with a Sherpa as we both regarded Dhaulagiri from the north. The view is unforgettable. "Where would you like to live?" I asked him. "In Calcutta," he answered with great conviction. Calcutta is perhaps the ugliest, most overcrowded city in the world—and this Sherpa had already been there!

But even if the Sherpas are not consciously aware of the uniqueness of their environment, they are not able to escape its influence. It is well-known that shoppers are influenced by musical stimulation. The Himalayas provide constant visual stimulation for the Sherpas. Perhaps this helps them to fulfill the commandments of their religion so easily and so well. Thus, their admirable temperament is not a purely personal achievement but is one partly determined by environmental conditions.

However surprising it may seem, potatoes have been as important in forming the Sherpa character as has been the influence of Buddhism. Potatoes are the most important source of nourishment for this people, and their lives are unthinkable without these modest tubers. I recall a time in Solu Khumbu when there were potatoes for breakfast, lunch, and dinner: sometimes peeled, sometimes with salt, sometimes served with a sharp sauce, sometimes merely hot. Without potatoes we would have starved.

Potatoes were first introduced about 1850. There are many old men still alive who recall other old men having told them that potatoes were first introduced when they were young men. In his book *Himalaya Journal*, Sir Joseph Hooker writes that in 1848 in the vicinity of Kangchenjunga "potatoes had just been recently introduced from English gardens into the capital city of Nepal." At about the same time, the potato probably reached Solu Khumbu as well. There, it caused as complete a transformation in the local way of life as did the introduction of the sweet potato into Polynesia. (Fishermen there suddenly realized that far more nourishment could be derived from an acre of land than from the sea and all their boats.)

Until that period, the Sherpas grew buckwheat, barley, and wheat, as well as Indian corn and millet in the lower lying areas. They were also forced to breed cattle and engage in trade in order to eke out an existence from the barren land. The potato changed the entire economic structure. The sandy earth and the short summers were favorable for potato crops. An acre of potatoes provided far more nourishment than an acre planted with buckwheat. The battle for daily survival lost its severity. Energies were released. Suddenly there were people who had free time, even after a day's work in the fields or among the cattle. They had no idea how to fill up their leisure hours since the only things that had previously occupied them were the struggle for survival and the cultivation of their religious beliefs. People with time to spare now became lamas or painters and sculptors who engaged in various forms of religious art.

Buddhism dominated the life of the Sherpas for hundreds of years. However, most of the temples and other religious structures were built only within the last eighty or one hundred years. Before this, time and energy had to be applied wholly to the search for food. Now, there were idle hands that could be used to turn the prayer wheels or the pages of sacred books. Religion now occupied a central place in the lives of the Sherpas; it was both splendid and joyful. Christoph von Fürer-Haimendorf reported in his excellent book *The Sherpas of Nepal* that in 1836 there were only 169 households in all of Khumbu, but in 1953 there were 596. Thanks to the potato, there was a population explosion.

We know that "Sherpa" means something like "eastern man," since the tribe wandered out of eastern Tibet. This fact gains support from most of the religious legends of the Sherpas, as well as from the hypotheses of scientists. In 1965, Michael Oppitz, who was working for the Thyssen Institute, found old Tibetan documents in Solu that treat not only religious themes but also describe the migration of the Sherpas. The most important document is called "Ruyi." It was probably written between 1500 and 1530. *Ru* means *bones* or *clan*. Thus, it is a report about the bones, that is, the ancestral history, of the Sherpas.

The four protoclans of the Sherpas (Minyagpa, Thimmi, Serwa, and Chakpa) originally inhabited what is now the province of Szechwan, east of the Yangtze, whose landscape is similar to that of the Solu Khumbu. Apparently, the migration was precipitated by fear of the Mongols, who had been penetrating ever further south from Kukunor ever since the days of Ghengis Khan. Religious reasons may also have played a part. The reformed "yellow-caps" of Tsongkhapa exerted great pressure upon the followers of the old Bön religion. Thus, the Sherpas began their 2,100-kilometer (1,300-mile) march. In Tingkye, southeast of Shigatse, they thought they had found a new homeland. However, peace was short-lived.

If fear of the Mongols caused the migration to begin, fear of the Moslems drove the Sherpas ever further on. Sultan Sa'id Khan set out from Kashgar with an army and headed for Kashmir and Ladakh. The Sherpas thought it wise to move further south. According to the "Ruyi," this must have been around 1533 when a group of perhaps twenty or fifty Sherpas crossed over Nangpa La. On the southern slopes of the Himalayas, they found "an area that was hidden, empty, uninhabited, and covered with virgin forests. . . . There were no people. The rivers had no bridges and the cliffs no steps."

The Sherpas lived undisturbed for four hundred years and developed their own unique characteristics. In order to avoid inbreeding, they were not permitted to marry within their own clan. Otherwise, there were few prohibitions. Sherpa women enjoyed a remarkable degree of equality (especially when compared with the women of neighboring India). Marriage is a long-drawn-out, ceremonial business. It can take years to proceed from the initial proposal to the consummation of the marriage contract and the wedding itself. The feelings of the couple themselves are more important than the wishes of their parents. A wife can have several husbands, and a husband several wives. This notion of marriage is largely determined by economic factors. Emotional inhibitions are unknown. Nevertheless, only about 8 percent of all Sherpas are not monogamous. Bearing an illegitimate child does not bring disgrace or scandal, and divorces are easily arranged on a rational and economic basis. The Sherpas seem to have been able to deal with the complex, often burdensome relationships that exist between husband, wife, child, and family. What we in

the West are laboriously struggling to achieve through legal reform, the Sherpas have already achieved by natural, rational means.

Compared with us, the Sherpas have one decisive advantage (or disadvantage, depending on how one views such things). Excessive emotions are alien to them, and crimes of passion are unknown. The betrayed husband does not reach for his gun. The mischief maker gives the cuckold a few rupees, a symbolic token of repentance, and the whole matter is settled. If the affair involves a lama, who is highly respected in Sherpa society, or a friend of the family, all he has to do is buy a jug of beer (which Sherpas like to drink at the drop of a hat).

If a wife has borne no children after three years of marriage (sometimes five), the husband can obtain a divorce. Childlessness is always considered to be the fault of the wife and never that of the husband. Norman Hardie tells of a woman who, after four years of childlessness, was cast out of her husband's house. She retired to a convent, where she became pregnant a few months later.

Since 1950, two events have fundamentally changed the lives of the Sherpas: the occupation of Tibet and the advent of tourism. In earlier times, trade across Nangpa La was very important, particularly for the Sherpas of Namche Bazar. Cloth, paper, sugar, cereals, flour, and dried fruits were transported to Tibet. Salt, wool, silverware, and coral were brought back. Today, the Nepal-Tibetan border is closed. Only the shepherds of the border region may engage in limited crossings. Nangpa La is no longer a trade center. But the Sherpas are able to make up for the losses in trade by gains in tourism.

They have been torn out of their splendid isolation. At the airport of Lukla, several hundred tourists often wait for an overdue airplane to make its daring landing. In Khumjung, the Japanese have built a modern hotel—with a fabulous view of Mount Everest at correspondingly fabulous prices. In UNESCO, concern has been expressed regarding environmental damage and pollution. A Bara Hakim or "governor," appointed in Katmandu, resides in Namche Bazar. The face of the Great Chairman beams down from the walls of many a Sherpa house. Transistor radios are common, and the advantages of a common language will soon become clear to everyone in Lhasa. Perhaps the attractions will cancel out the fear of the new order in Tibet. On the positive side are electricity, schools, hospitals, streets, wristwatches, and enough food. On the negative side are dissolution of the cloisters and the fight against Buddhism.

Sherpas have also discovered trekking. Not every

Sherpa is a daredevil who wants to distinguish himself on an 8,000-meter (26,000-foot) mountain; most prefer the safe but nevertheless lucrative walking tours. This is not surprising in view of the considerable toll that conquests of the high summits have taken of Sherpa lives. Very few families have been spared. Nearly everyone in Solu Khumbu has cause to mourn for a relative who has died in the mountains. Mostly it is the youngest and most active relatives who do not return.

Soon the Sherpas will be taking over the trekking business themselves and offering their own tours. This is only just, since the Sherpas are after all at home in Nepal. Will their admirable personal traits begin to suffer? This is a real danger. There is little doubt that tourist money will bring latent bad qualities to the surface. Twenty years ago, for example, begging was unknown in Katmandu. Today, hordes of children more or less demand a contribution.

Namche Bazar will soon be a second Katmandu. Earlier, it was considered inexcusable not to trust a Sherpa absolutely. Now, instances are known where Sherpas have liberally helped themselves to expedition property.

I asked a friend, who has lived among the Sherpas for a long time and who still spends a great deal of time in Nepal, for his opinion. "There is no doubt that the Sherpas have been changed by the influx of tourists as well as by the inflation caused by expeditions," he wrote from Katmandu. "The Tyroleans used to be pretty decent folk, and they have also changed a lot." Things could be worse, I thought. After all, one can still get on quite well with the climbers from Tyrol. But my friend must know what he was talking about: not only is he knowledgeable on the subject of Sherpas—he is also a Tyrolean! ☐

Bruno Moravetz

Reinhold Messner— Taking His Own Way to the Top

Although Reinhold Messner has been called the world's greatest mountain climber, it must be admitted that Alpine achievement cannot be measured in such terms. We can at most evaluate, compare, and weigh each climber's accomplishments. On the other hand, Reinhold Messner is surely one of the most successful mountaineers of the 1970s not only because of the number of his extraordinary climbs and the way in which he executed them but also because his fame has spread so far.

Violent controversy immediately broke out upon his return to Europe from Mount Everest in the spring of 1978. Without the use of additional oxygen he had just climbed the world's highest mountain "as mountains used to be climbed in the old days, when the assistance provided by modern technology was not yet available." This great climber would now commercialize himself, people said, as if the noble profession of mountaineering could never be more than a noble pastime. His critics would count the number of his television appearances and of his publications and hold them against him!

Messner has never been reluctant to express his views or even his most personal feelings. Whenever he felt himself attacked—and he has been attacked a good deal—he has always defended himself against false assumptions, insinuations, and even slander. Much of what he has said has been misunderstood. Moreover, whether consciously or not, many of his critics have also distorted his statements. Nevertheless, Messner's plans and projects have been the source of great interest to ever-widening circles, and this is what should concern us here.

The sensationalism surrounding Messner's achievements may well have had its source in the climber's own statements, which express ideas that transcend traditional notions of mountaineering. He has said, for example: "Climbing has provided me with various experiences— romantic ones, visionary ones, the joy of achievement, and, not least of all, the experience of having to exert my utmost strength upon the mountain."

On one occasion Reinhold Messner was climbing in the Himalaya with his friend and partner of many a difficult tour, Peter Habeler from Mayrhofen in the Ziller Valley. The two men were forced to surrender to the force of nature as they encountered an ice-covered wall of rock jutting abruptly skyward ahead of them. Regarding this experience, Messner noted: "The decision to give up was not difficult. And so we gave up."

Messner chooses to regard himself as a free-lance Alpinist for several reasons: "First, so that I can maintain complete independence in all my mountaineering endeavors; second, so that I can climb how, when, and where I wish; and finally, so that I need to be responsible to no one and can thus avoid all external pressure to succeed. . . ."

Messner comes from the Villnöss Valley in the South Tyrol, a mountain valley bordered by the Dolomite remnants of the Geisler group. Messner's heritage, then, consists of a landscape of rock pinnacles that nature herself has chiseled over the millennia into nearly symmetrical towers whose steep walls rise more than 500 meters (1,640 feet) above the valley floor. An old house, which was once built for the vicar and later used as a school, stands at the end of the valley on a little promontory together with the Church of Saint Mary Magdalene. The house has thick stone walls, so necessary in this inhospitable mountain region as a protection against frigid temperatures and storms. Inside the house is a rattling staircase worn down by thousands of children's footsteps. Old furniture fills the rooms: a chest in which perhaps a great grandmother once stored her Sunday clothing; a table that Messner got from a mountain farmer who had kept it in his pigsty, where its crudely fashioned surface provided storage space for pails of feed not yet ladled out. One wall contains a bookcase, stuffed full with Alpine literature, including a dozen volumes written by Messner himself. These lie side by side with works by Goethe, Kant, Marx, Mao, Brecht, and Grass. My host could have been an architect, a profession for which he had studied. With his fine-boned, narrow hands, sometimes chapped and torn from gripping onto cliffs, he could also have been a surgeon. However, he could just as well have been a pianist or a painter.

Outside the house lies a plot of meadowland filled with colorful wild flowers, as well as a garden in which lettuce, chives, and carrots have been planted. A fence separates this garden both from the narrow path winding up into the mountains beyond and from adjacent pastureland. This fence prevents the cattle that graze nearby from getting to the herbs and also keeps any all-too-curious onlookers away. Faded Buddhist prayer flags from Nepal wave on long hazelwood posts near the fence. Two or three Lhasa apsos frisk about the little meadow garden and across the narrow vegetable beds in whose earth the very stones themselves appear to grow like plants. These little woolly dogs used to be kept and bred in the Tibetan monasteries of the lamas. In Messner's garden they now bark at anyone who strolls along, yelping in a high-pitched playful treble.

Not only traditional Tyrolean furniture fills the rooms of the house; there are also stools from Pakistan, prayer rugs from Afghanistan, and blankets from the Andes—souvenirs brought back from many visits to the mountains of the world. A small study contains a typewriter, a telephone, and bits of office equipment. For several years Messner's wife also occupied this room, busily planning lecture tours and corresponding with people from all over the world—governmental authorities in Nepal and Pakistan, mountain climbers from Japan, and manufacturers of mountaineering equipment from Germany, Austria, and Italy who sought and continue to seek Messner's valuable advice. She typed out many handwritten manuscripts, notes often jotted down on stormy days inside a tent pitched way up in the highest mountains. She also transcribed the many sentences, thoughts, or formulations that Messner had recorded on tape. Unfortunately, Frau Uschi no longer works in this house, neither in the study nor in the modern, well-equipped kitchen across the hall, where she had prepared so many meals when guests arrived—and visitors to the home were many and frequent.

Messner's wife could not endure life within this house. She was unable to remain permanently at the side of her ever more restless husband, and so she left him. Messner had just returned from a trip to the Himalaya that had ended in defeat upon the south face of Dhaulagiri in the spring of 1977. Having had to resign himself to failure, he had come back to a state of "black loneliness." He thought he no longer had the strength to continue upon his chosen path—to reach the highest summits by the steepest routes, up the most formidable and forbidding mountain walls. But in spite of everything, he overcame these difficult days, days that were filled with self-questioning and torment. He surmounted these days and weeks and eventually returned, as he later put it, to the "white loneliness" of the mountains.

Reinhold Messner, the great Alpinist, was born in 1944 and studied surveying at the University of Padua. For a time he was a teacher of high school mathematics. This very Reinhold Messner was to give new life to Alpine climbing throughout the world in the 1970s.

He now runs a climbing school during the summer

months when the Dolomite cliffs are warm and seductive, tempting man to merge his whole being with the rocks. Now, when the spacious Alpine meadows, speckled with color, shimmer and sparkle with the flowering blossoms of a transient mountain summer, Messner devotes his energies to a dozen mountain guides. Having thus been taught themselves, these men in turn lead others into the mountains. The clients of these guides frequently come from distant cities and often from the flatlands. The guides must teach them how to reach the summits of these cliffs as well as how to leave behind their fears and inhibitions and dare to pit themselves against the precipitous walls. Sometimes, of course, the guides must act to restrain a sudden burst of reckless exuberance or excessive self-confidence, holding in check bravado that transcends the bounds of reason.

In the fall when the first snows lie like confectioner's sugar upon the craggy peaks and in the glacial hollows, when the frost-covered meadows glitter in the cold mountain nights, it is then that Reinhold Messner sets off upon his lecture tours, traveling throughout his homeland and on to other German-speaking countries, to Scandinavia, and to Japan. In the lecture halls, he may well find himself standing in front of men who already know firsthand the profound feelings mountains can evoke. But his audience may also be composed of those who are merely curious, people who have heard of this man, read of his exploits, or seen him on television. For Reinhold Messner is not just another mountaineer speaking about his adventures and observations in the mountains: he is the one and only Reinhold Messner himself!

Walter Bonatti, who had never met him personally, dedicated his book *Great Days in the Mountains* to Reinhold Messner, whom he characterized as "the young and last hope of great classical mountaineering." Bonatti knew Messner only from reports of his exploits in the Alps and other mountains of the world. In 1973, when Messner published his paperback book *The Seventh Degree* about the most advanced type of mountain climbing—its techniques, the training required, and the experiences one encounters—a storm broke out in the ranks of professional mountaineers. Messner questioned much that until that time had apparently been accepted as the immutable credo of mountain climbing. To the extent that mountaineering is pursued as a sport, Messner now demanded that the climber voluntarily renounce any superiority over natural difficulties granted him by the devices of modern technology while at the same time striving to overcome ever greater hurdles. Messner had always abided by this precept and continues to follow it. The climber must approach the mountain honorably and by fair means. Pitting his own strength against the mountain, he must discover his true worth and recognize the limitations of his own abilities. These were and are the challenges Messner threw into the arena to be picked up by mountaineers ever eager to debate such matters.

Messner's climbs, both in his native mountains and on those of every other continent of the world, caused many people to shake their heads, for Messner often chose to tackle the most difficult routes by himself. He often astonished the world with the speed of his ascents and with the sureness and elegance of his climbing style. Many people found disturbing his unfailing instinct for that which was possible. Mountaineers began to divide into two camps. There were those who were unable or unwilling to understand Messner's activities and his opinions, making little effort to do so. Such climbers criticized his exploits often without a factual basis and in a devious fashion. The other group, among whom were many of the youngest climbers, began to follow him, guiding themselves by his opinions, pursuing his routes. These mountaineers devoured his publications and sought and obtained his advice. There are already some among Messner's adherents who appear to have surpassed their teacher with new, yet more difficult routes and variations. The "Seventh Degree," the breakthrough Messner demanded as a culmination of the six established levels of climbing, each one of which is itself graded according to nuances of difficulty, has been achieved not only on the slippery granite walls of Yosemite National Park in California but also in the Alps, the Wilder Kaiser, and the Dolomites.

The great test has now also been passed on the giant mountains of the world: the Himalaya, the Hindu Kush, the Pamirs, the Caucasus, and the Andes. In these regions, the difficulties caused simply by the steepness of the rock faces are intensified by ice, avalanches, and mountain storms. Thus, climbing in the thin air of 4,000-, 7,000-, and 8,000-meter (13,000 to 26,000 feet) peaks demands more training and a higher degree of psychological preparedness. What is required at these heights is naturally even more necessary on a peak like Mount Everest (29,028 feet). The most important prerequisite of all is an emotional readiness to turn back, to break off, to give up, to accept a so-called defeat, a defeat that in these mountains really signifies the victory of more powerful nature over man.

Reinhold Messner has become the symbol of modern Alpinism, first of all, because of his intellectuality. Throughout the world he has become the most well-known Alpinist of the 1970s. Although he himself does not speak of his exploits as adventures, because this word has been trivialized by so much usage, his adventures and those of a few kindred spirits are exceptions in a world where most men need guided tours and where derivative experiences are for sale. Messner's adventures, by contrast, are of a unique kind and cannot be repeated. Nevertheless, it is no surprise that this man has become the center of publicity, for in addition to an active mind he also has a gift for rendering experiences, thoughts, and feelings into words. No wonder, then, that newspapers, magazines, and television networks have pursued him as a "subject." In the 1970s, it should be noted, ever more people have become interested in mountaineering and in the search for meaning in the mountains. Hiking and even the most advanced forms of rock climbing in the Alps and in the great mountain ranges of the world have found ever more adherents, and the trend is likely to gain momentum in the future.

Literary critics, who have generally shown little interest in literary efforts emanating from the Alpine world, have recently begun to study Messner's writings seriously, analyzing the style of his works and his gift for uninhibited expression. But for these skills, too, Messner has been reproached in many mountaineering circles.

Reinhold Messner's climbs can no longer be taken in at a glance. Every spring before the monsoons come he spends two or three months in the Himalaya. He has already stood upon the summits of three out of a total of fourteen mountains that tower more than 8,000 meters (26,000 feet) above sea level. On three more of these peaks he had to turn back prematurely, a not unreasonable act, considering the circumstances. Carefully and with great deliberation, he weighed the external factors and recognized in these great mountains a force far stronger than the tiny human being (as he has always described man in comparison with mountains and with nature).

On three more of these eight-thousanders he tried out new routes: up the steep 4,000-meter (13,000-foot) Rupal flank of Nanga Parbat, up the equally high south flank of Manaslu, and up the northwest side of Gasherbrum I (Hidden Peak) and on to the summit. Messner undertook this last climb, whose difficulty equaled that of the north face of the Eiger, only in the company of his friend Peter Habeler. He had to turn back without reaching the summits of Makalu, Lhotse, and Dhaulagiri, rationally submitting to the forces of nature, voluntarily giving up on the steep flanks of these giants.

During the pre-monsoon period of 1978, however, Messner attempted to carry out what was probably his most daring plan, once again in the company of Peter Habeler, that comrade of so many an arduous climb. Under the auspices of the Austrian Alpine Society, he set out without oxygen tanks for the summit of the world's highest mountain, Mount Everest, also choosing an incomparably difficult route up the steep south pillar. This tour was to entail at least three days of the most strenuous possible climbing under the worst conditions, where the men would be exposed to crumbling ice-coated rock, threatened by avalanches, shaken by cold, and battered by mountain storms. On top of this, they would have to spend two nights in a tent they would have to carry up themselves—all this in the so-called "zone of death." No wonder, then, that the whole world, and not merely the smaller circle of Alpinists, fixed their eyes upon the progress and conclusion of this exploit.

The two friends were wonderfully well trained and functioned with perfect coordination as a team. And yet, when they looked up for the first time at the column of rock upon which they had intended to climb to the highest summit on earth, few words were needed to decide "no." This route, partly covered by ice, was too dangerous. It was too risky to accept such a challenge in the death zone with one's strength already diminished. And so they decided to follow the route that had been taken twenty-five years earlier by Hillary and Tenzing, the first conquerors of Mount Everest.

They started out twice. The first time Habeler was compelled to return to the base camp, weakened by a stomach upset. Messner, together with a Sherpa, climbed up to the camp on the southern saddle just below the magical 8,000-meter mark. A storm raged for two days, imprisoning him in his tent. When he was finally able to climb down, he was exhausted by a lack of oxygen as well as by a lack of food and water. Nevertheless, one week later Messner and Habeler were climbing once again. They pursued their ascent even though the weather conditions were not favorable. Each step of the way was torture. Finally, they were climbing on all fours, gasping for the little oxygen that was available at this altitude. Then— they stood on the summit! Messner snipped off a piece of rope that connected the two climbers and knotted it around the Chinese-Tibetan symbol for the summit that had been placed on top of Mount Everest three years earlier. Like every climber of the higher mountains, they took photographs, visual proof for those who would doubt or envy their achievement.

Peter Habeler descended almost immediately. Thoroughly exhausted by the altitude, almost at the end of his physical endurance, and plagued by cramps, he was afraid of suffering a stroke, as had befallen a Sherpa not long before. Climbing down, he slid across a snowfield and set off an avalanche, but managed to reach the southern saddle and the friendly welcome of a tent. Reinhold Messner followed somewhat later, only then discovering that he had lost his snow goggles, probably during the foggy ascent, when he had removed them in order to find the path. His eyes were sore; even in the fog the ultraviolet rays had had their effect. During the night he suffered violent pain and feared that he was going blind.

The two finally reached the bottom of Mount Everest and were home again in Europe a short time later. Soon, suspicion and nasty rumor began to spring up: perhaps the team had secretly provided for a jet of oxygen into the tent? Envy, grudgingness, and ill will are feelings that arise time and again even among the exalted ranks of mountaineers, some of whom always consider themselves to be so much better than the ones who reach the top!

"For mankind, it is totally unimportant whether such an undertaking succeeds or not, whether Mount Everest is conquered or not. What is alone significant are the experiences and feelings evoked by such a climb and then only for the climber who himself experiences them." Whenever Messner returns from the loneliness of the realm of rock and ice, he is happy to be alive, overjoyed to see trees, flowers, and grass once more. On expeditions he seldom travels with a group and usually climbs alone. To most people he seems forbidding, strange, and cold; to some he seems arrogant as well. He has his own convictions, has chosen his own way, and pursues it again and again. Nevertheless, though judicious and rational, he is also understanding and sympathetic. In conversation, he is quick to accept the value of other people's opinions.

He always says exactly what he thinks, as was the case in the fall of 1977 when he spoke to a group of mountain climbers, Alpine organizers, and reporters: with astounding matter-of-factness, he characterized the great faces of the Alps simply as advanced kindergartens for climbers. The Matterhorn, the Grandes Jorasses, and even the north wall of the Eiger, famed as a "wall of death," were no more than training and acclimatization grounds for those prepared to face the extremities of the mightiest walls of the highest mountains on earth. As he said, he was speaking from experience and from personal knowledge. Applying to the giant peaks concepts from the thirties describing the most difficult, yet unclimbed routes up the three highest north walls of the Alps, Messner said that only those who have experienced the physical and psychological self-discipline necessary to overcome the great problems of the past should dare to pit themselves against the so-called greatest problems of the present. This attitude also informs of Messner's considerations regarding the calculated risks to be taken on the most demanding climbs. The climber must know ahead of time the possible difficulties he will encounter, prepare himself emotionally in advance, and estimate his own abilities in light of these two factors. "Every ascent," he wrote in his book *The Great Walls* (1977), "is preceded by an idea in which success and failure, progress and retreat, expectation and disappointment alternate. . . ."

Twice, in extraordinary situations at the very outermost regions of human existence, Messner lost companions; there, friends close to him died in the loneliness of the mountains. This occurred once on Manaslu, on a storm-tossed plateau where two members of the group simply disappeared in an icy storm. The other episode occurred earlier during the descent from Nanga Parbat. On this climb, Messner and his younger brother Gunther had already crossed over to the Diamir side of the mountain, having reached the summit by way of the Rupal flank. Gunther, dragging himself down at some distance behind his brother, was suddenly plunged into the depths by an avalanche of ice. Mountain peasants from the Diamir Valley later found Messner himself, totally exhausted from days of aimless wandering and suffering with frostbitten toes, which subsequently had to be amputated. The peasants carried him off the mountain and back to humanity. At that time, Messner declared, he felt that he too had died. Although his body was not dead, his spirit, his will, and all his hopes were gone. "When I found myself again, a new spirit, a new will, and new hopes were born!" He also said: "It is not easy to escape from death. In the face of incessant danger I instinctively withdraw into myself and surrender to it in the same way that one lets go during states of intoxication or great fear. . . ." Reinhold Messner's ability to render in words what he has experienced, thought, and felt, his readiness to express emotions that border on the intimate and yet to do so without a trace of exhibitionism—this contributes in great measure to the man's uniqueness.

It is true, of course, that Messner recognized early on how important publicity could be for him. In conversation he is often able to retort with clever answers that are all too often provocative. He is ready to reenact certain situations. Many people smiled to themselves when he posed in the snow for an illustrated magazine, naked after a sauna bath. One branch of the Alpine world was shocked when Messner dared to let himself be filmed for television while climbing in glaring yellow pants. They didn't approve of his being photographed in a broad-brimmed slouch hat either. But Messner feels it suits contemporary times to let himself be pictured in such ways.

One well-known political television interviewer was totally captivated by Messner after an unexpected meeting with him. He was quite impressed by the special qualities of this strange species of mountaineer, a man so wholly unlike those wooden stereotypes of the "mountain man." This experienced television personality, whose everyday encounters are by no means restricted to unimportant and colorless individuals, admitted that it meant a great deal to him to have made the acquaintance of Reinhold Messner.

A free-lance Alpinist like Messner must naturally try to sell the results of his exploits to a large audience. As a lecturer he must seek to fill the halls, whether he chooses to tell a story, chat, or report and evaluate his experiences. "I sell my products to the highest bidder," he says without hesitation. He is, after all, a man of his times. He also knows that his physical activities will one day reach a biologically determined limit.

"I don't believe," he asserts, "that mountaineering will degenerate into a discipline merely aimed at breaking records. I am convinced, however, that the next generation of climbers will undergo far more rigorous training, not only to enable them to climb the difficult routes but also to obtain mastery over many objective dangers by relying upon the superior physical conditioning of their bodies. A thoroughly trained high jumper may at most win another competition; a thoroughly trained climber may thereby save his life."

Messner once said that he did not want to be the founder of a cult. Nor did he want to establish ultimate values or to set a standard for all times. Just as he himself did not rely on the traditional approaches and traditions of his predecessors, so he hopes that a new generation of climbers will not cling rigidly to his ideas. "Only that which is mysterious can be conquered and this is the mystery within ourselves. The impossible exists in concrete cases but the unthinkable never does. With this attitude I have reached what others conceived to be unreachable."

Reinhold Messner is an extraordinary phenomenon, not only in the world of mountain climbing; it is now beyond dispute that Messner already serves many as a guide to the future. It is clear that his influence will grow significantly in times to come. We may yet expect many observations, thoughts, and feelings from his pen, words pouring forth from behind the thick stone walls of the old house at the end of the valley beneath the Geisler peaks. ☐

Luis Trenker

Mountains Are More Than Beautiful Scenery

At the annual festival of mountain films at Trient, which is one of the climbing centers of Italy, masses of old and young people storm the movie houses. Special performances are scheduled for schools. Whenever mountain climbers arrive in Hamburg, Cologne, London, Paris, or in other cities far away from mountains to give lectures and to show slides or films, the organizers don't have to worry that unsold tickets will remain. Pictures, reports, and films with the mountains as scenery or as an important part of the action stir up interest everywhere. The organizers of these evenings have discovered again and again that their audiences do not consist only of people who climb mountains themselves. All kinds of people are now interested in mountain films. Some want simply to gaze at the realms that lie beyond their depressing urban environments. Others want to admire the graceful acrobatic technique of highly skilled climbers.

What are mountain films? First of all—presentations of untamed and untouched nature: beautiful, wild, pristine, real. Second—stories of human beings caught up in human activities. Hardly any mountain films are made today. What now wins prizes at the film festivals held in Trient, Les Diablerets in Switzerland, the United States, and elsewhere is nothing more than well-made film strips about this or that particular adventure in the mountains, usually involving daring rock climbs or the most difficult white-water maneuvers. Critical reviews do not have much influence on the success of a film.

There is not enough money available for the production of mountain films. Although television corporations could undertake such projects, other subjects are considered more important. Besides the lack of money, there is also a noticeable lack of quality in the scripts. Critics often remark that if you've seen one mountain film you've seen them all.

On a nasty day in 1923 when I was a student in Graz, I passed a small theater whose marquee displayed the promising film title *A Battle with the Mountain*. I entered the theater with much skepticism but experienced a surprise that transported me into a kind of ecstasy. What I saw was my own dream world: the silvery, snowy crowns of the Valais, sparkling crystals of ice, and a sun-drenched summit. My mood brightened and I was overwhelmed by a feeling of inexpressible joy and exhilaration, which grew with each image. Over the years, hundreds of thousands, if not millions, of people, have had similar experiences watching this or other mountain films.

Under the influence of my experience, I wrote to Dr. Arnold Fanck, the film's producer, and asked whether he would like to come to the South Tyrol in order to film the beauties of my native Dolomites. I offered to assist him. At first, his answer was negative. A little later I met him on the Walther Square in Bolzano. He was with Hannes Schneider, the actor I had so much admired in the film, as well as with several of his co-workers. I was happy to accept Fanck's invitation to work on his new film project as an all-round assistant.

Fanck became my teacher. Advancing beyond the basic concepts of photography, he pointed the way toward filming in the open air. Under his tutelage, I also learned how to select the most fitting visual images. At this time, I began to enjoy the warmth of friendship and comaraderie that prevailed within the small circle of like-minded mountain enthusiasts.

Our first headquarters was a windowless hut below the walls of the Tofana Group. Here, we slept in the hay and cooked our own spaghetti. Fanck asked me to accompany him on his daily search for suitable motifs.

The film's star came from the theater and was not an Alpinist. Our world was alien to him and much too strenuous. After much pressuring from Fanck, I took on the role myself. We each carried bits of the heavy equipment ourselves. Happy and filled with contentment, we worked all summer and winter. We finished what was to become the first film of the Freiburg Mountain Sport Film Corp., Ltd., in an attic studio in Berlin. It appeared under the title *The Mountain of Destiny* and was destined to be a great success.

A new style of photography in which actors without makeup were filmed in unadorned mountain landscapes proved to be successful. The public enjoyed a sense of the real and the genuine, which was now projected on the silver screen in place of the cardboard scenery they had been used to. I am describing the beginnings here, because the so-called Fanck School, as it was later called, was the basis for later mountain films. Asceticism, industriousness, patience, and tenacity were tributes that had to be paid for the privilege and joy of working on these films. All our energies and ambitions were focused on the mountain film.

One year after *The Mountain of Destiny* there followed a film financed by UFA. It was called *The Sacred Mountain* and was quite an ambitious film. In spite of the rather unbelievable love story injected into the film, critics in and outside of Europe praised this splendidly photographed silent movie for its dramatic scenes on storm-tossed walls of ice. Dr. Fanck, who created a number of great Alpine movies, tended to be a little one-sided. In his films, decisive action always took place amid falling avalanches, between demonic glacial crevasses, during storms, or on idyllic flowering meadows. The interplay of human beings was constantly neglected on behalf of the scenery. It is significant that Dr. Fanck entitled his biography *Directing Glaciers, Storms, and Avalanches*. He was clearly far more interested in the dynamics of mountains than in the interaction of living human beings. His greatest success was *The White Hell of Piz Palü*. The screenwriter Ladislaus Vajda and the director G. W. Pabst contributed greatly to this achievement, the latter particularly during the filming of dramatic Alpine scenes.

While Ernst Lubitsch's *The King of the Berninas*, which was filmed in the studios of Hollywood, was being booed in Zurich, Fanck's *Piz Palü*, which was filmed on location in the Berninas, was enthusiastically received by the public and the press. Here was something real: the close connection that exists between mountains and human beings who are desperate, suffering, and in danger served as a gripping unity that was sustained until the film reached its heroic and tragic conclusion. Fanck's *Storm over Mont Blanc* appeared in 1930 and *The White Dream* in 1932. Although both films were magnificently photographed, they did not achieve the intensity of *Piz Palü*.

In 1929 I produced *Son of the White Mountains* in the Monte Rosa area and in 1930, *Mountains in Flames*, set on the Dolomite front of World War I. German and French versions of the film were made. The English version, released by Universal Picture Corporation, had a worldwide success. A year later, *The Rebel* appeared. Financed by Universal Films, it was set in the Tyrolean mountains, in the Berninas and in the Jungfrau massif. *The Fire Devil* appeared a few years later. Eberhard Lutz wrote in the *Frankfurter Zeitung:* "This film contains radiant images and dramatic splendor that takes its dimensions from the overpowering mountain landscapes. . . . These dimensions grow by the second. Personalities disappear in the chaos of nature. The stillness of the mountain is suddenly transformed into anarchistic and raging passion; the change is grippingly portrayed."

In 1934, I filmed *The Prodigal Son*, which received a prize at the Venice Film Festival. This theme gave our mountain films new dimensions and new impulses. Many elements provided dramatic contrast: distance; geographical freedom; the grandeur of the Alpine world; the misery, bustle, and material wealth of the cosmopolitan city of New York; the anger of the icy giants at home; and the distress of the prodigal son who had been driven out of the mountains. His homecoming on Christmas Eve reconciled man, mountain, and valley.

In 1960, the critic Dr. Günther Groll wrote in the *Süddeutsche Zeitung:* "Thirty years ago *The Prodigal Son* achieved international fame as has hardly any German film since." "The man who made it," wrote the dramatist Deval in Paris, "is a genius." The critic Sacchi of the *Corriere della Sera* wrote: "The quality of the images is unsurpassable." An English paper noted: "A German film to be envied." So it was—once upon a time.

After the Second World War, in the 1950s, the French took up the theme of mountains. Pierre Tairraz continued the family tradition of his father, the photographer Josef Tairraz, who had died in 1902 in Chamonix. Together with the extraordinary guide Gaston Rébuffat, Tairraz led the mountain film to new heights with the documentary color film *Stars and Storms*, which was shown at the Mountain Film Festival of Trient in 1955. This film was followed in 1961 by their even more magnificent work *Between Heaven and Earth*, which again won the prize at Trient. Filmmakers learned to their amazement that not only mountain climbers were excited by a film like this; everyone was moved by the immeasurable richness and splendor of this matchless documentary film of the Mont Blanc massif.

A harmonious blend of Alpine achievement, direction, and personal statement form the epic *Les Etoiles du Midi*, a film made in 1958 by Marcel Ichac, together with Lionel Terray and Maurice Herzog.

Modern technology, having produced lighter and more wieldy apparatus as well as more sophisticated Alpine equipment, has made it possible for men like Terray, Ichac, Rébuffat, Tairraz, Languepin, and others to film the infinite beauty of the mountain world. With their films they have brought to the general public an appreciation for the ethical values that inform mountain climbing.

It is impossible to draw precise lines between the documentary film, the sports film, and the expedition film. The boundaries are constantly shifting. One of the most gripping documentaries of an Alpine expedition was Marcel Ichac's moving report *Victoire sur l'Annapurna*, which received many awards. This unique record of the first climb of an 8,000-meter (26,000-foot) peak in the Himalayas (1950) represents a high point in the presentation of intense experience and camaraderie in the mountains. The film radiates a classical greatness.

Hans Ertl's film about Nanga Parbat (1953) and Mario Fantin's film on the ascent of K2 appeared next. Other successful documentary mountain films were produced by Toni Hiebeler, Lothar Brandler, Wolfgang Gorter, and Gerhard Baur.

It is strange that American filmmakers, who are preeminent in the art, are hardly represented in this genre; before 1956, they made no Alpine films worth mentioning. In spite of the great financial means at their disposal, they have been unable to create a memorable work in this category. In 1950, a film about the Matterhorn was made. It was based on the novel of James Ramsey Ullman and was a flop. Authors, directors, and cameramen for whom mountains were alien arrived on the scene. However, they lacked the inner sensibility, the *sentimento della montagna*, that is necessary if one is to make a genuine and worthwhile film. Instead, they came to Switzerland and set up cardboard scenery at the foot of the Matterhorn, in front of which actors with equally little sensitivity mimed their roles with a hopeless lack of feeling. The premiere in Zermatt was greeted with boos and shouts of laughter. Norman Dyhrenfurth's 1975 sensation, *The Eiger Sanction*, did not fare any better, even though it cost five million dollars to produce.

The only American-produced Alpine movie that deserves to be called a mountain film is *Mountain of Temptation* (1956/57), with Spencer Tracy in the main role. It was based on MacDougell's novel, directed by Edward Dmytryk, and photographed by the excellent Austrian cameraman Franz Planer. Its Alpine scenes were photographed in the studio as well as in the ice world of Mont Blanc.

A clear distinction naturally arose between our work and those film strips in which Alpine scenes served only as a backdrop for the action. Although such films were called mountain films, too, the designation was erroneous and merely a means of creating competition within the industry. For a public who knew nothing about mountains and so lacked a critical perspective, any film that was set in the mountains was a mountain film. We always tried to clarify the difference. For us, it was very important to bring mountains into the action as a functionally dramatic element—mountains had to be more than beautiful scenery.

This was the case in the Alpine drama of the first conquest of the Matterhorn (1865) by Edward Whymper and his companions. *The Mountain Calls* (1937) was filmed in a German and an English version and may be counted as one of the classics in the genre of mountain films.

Intellectual movie critics take a condescending attitude toward the mountain film. Others, who recognize the ethos and the visual intensity of its effects, bring greater understanding to bear and ignore many weaknesses. Only he who is acquainted with mountains can understand their language and thus translate it into a film experience that can be reexperienced by an audience. We have not yet sufficiently recognized what possibilities exist for developing ethical values in the young by encouraging them to climb mountains. Television has not yet exploited this theme.

Do genuine mountain films exist today? The answer is no—apart from a few expedition films. Love for the mountains, however, has not diminished. More than ever, youth is looking for models and for action in the mountains—even without the aid of an exciting Alpine film! Of the several thousand films that were produced in Germany after 1924, only a few are remembered. Several of these are mountain film classics.

Germany was once the homeland of the mountain film. Its beginnings go back to Arnold Fanck's Freiburger School and to his cameramen Sepp Allgaier, Richard Angst, Albert Benitz, von Rautenfeld, and Hans Schneeburger. Mountain films not only brought the fairy-tale-like beauty of the Alps into the darkened movie theater; they also opened people's eyes to the noble grandeur of the mountains. Millions of viewers owe a debt of gratitude to the pioneering efforts of these men who dedicated themselves to mountain films, sparing themselves neither efforts nor danger in order to give pleasure to their fellow men.

Seven hundred years before Christ, the Greek epic poet Hesiod wrote:

You can buy worthless goods and evil everywhere,
The way is smooth and easy,
And near is the comfortable house.
But it takes sweat to reach the high summits,
For the lonely path to the immortal gods is long and steep.

□

Günter Hauser

Sir Edmund Hillary — A Life for the Sherpas

Again and again, even a quarter of a century after his great success, Edmund Percival Hillary is asked who was the first to reach the summit of Mount Everest, he or the Sherpa Tenzing Norkay. When they first returned after their victory, the two were cheered alike by the Sherpas and the people of Katmandu, the capital of Nepal. They were also received by Pandit Nehru in New Delhi. Here, however, Hillary was insulted. Placards on the streets and cartoons in Indian newspapers showed a caricature of a man standing on the top of a mountain and holding the flag of Nepal in one of his hands. With the other hand, he was busy hauling up a wriggling man tied to a rope, arms and legs stretched out in all directions. This other man was Hillary! The eternal question had been answered at the time: Hillary and Tenzing had reached the summit together. The struggle for victory was genuine teamwork.

This New Zealander, who was later knighted, did not take it amiss that the people of the Himalayan countries had expected one of their own, Tenzing Norkay, to be the first to reach the summit. Today, Hillary is greatly respected and much beloved in Sherpa lands. He is still busy trying to raise money privately throughout the world to help these people develop their country. It is his way of expressing his gratitude for the fact that he became a famous man in their country. He does not regard himself as a superman: "In the course of time, I have learned that a person of modest talent can experience the most wonderful adventures and that a timid soul can be successful. In a certain sense, fear became my friend. . . . I have stood on towering summits and have seen the world lying at my feet. I have also seen the sun's red ball come up over the horizon after a long Antarctic winter."

"When I woke up, I felt shattered and depressed. But a sense of joyful expectancy soon took hold of me. During the night the air had escaped from my mattress and I had lain on the hard ice. I opened my eyes reluctantly . . . our spacious tent was a wretched sight to behold. My tentmates were still asleep on the floor, which had become coated with ice. They were motionless. Oxygen tanks, rucksacks, spare clothing, rope, pitons, crampons, and ice axes were flung about helter-skelter. Chaos reigned. A typical morning at Camp IV. Life at 7,000 meters (22,965 feet) is not pure joy. . . . Now we were to begin the arduous ascent, which, if we were lucky, would end on the summit of Mount Everest. . . ." With these words Hillary describes his mood a few days before the first conquest of the highest mountain on earth, a conquest that, in 1953, transformed overnight this unknown beekeeper from New Zealand and the Sherpa Tenzing Norkay into two of the world's most celebrated men.

"It will probably be the most important day of my life, . . ." reflected Hillary. Even as this self-confident conviction took hold of him, other members of the expedition, including its leader John Hunt, were already making the first advances toward the summit from higher camps. With disarming candor, Hillary let us glimpse the human dimensions that surrounded the race to the top. He wrote that he and Tenzing resented the fact that they had been ordered to spend two days resting at Camp IV: "We absolutely wanted to be there at the beginning of the last, decisive phase. . . ."

On May 26, 1953, Hillary had to look on as Tom Bourdillon and Charles Evans reached the south summit [8,754 meters (28,720 feet)] of Mount Everest at 1:00 P.M., disappearing behind it in order to continue on up the ridge that led to the main summit. Hillary's competitive spirit is clearly expressed.

"It was a splendid achievement," he wrote. "They had now climbed higher than any predecessor. But, to my disgrace, I must confess that my joy over their success was dampened by a light undertone of jealousy and fear. Would they get to the main summit? They had already accomplished much more than I had expected. And it was possible that their reserves of energy were not yet used up. Tenzing was even more concerned than I was. He was sure they would reach the summit and was angry that no Sherpa had been taken along as part of the first assault team in order to share in its success. . . . Our ungenerous thoughts and fears did not become reality. At 3:30 P.M. Evans and Bourdillon emerged from the fog and descended the ridge."

What had happened to the much-praised "team spirit" of the expedition? Had egotistical ambition swept all of it away? Twenty years later, Hillary provided the best answer to all these questions: "When I read my diary now, I have the feeling that I was often irritable, restless, and ambitious on this expedition. I also inclined toward self-contradiction. Nevertheless, I remember mostly positive things: the people whom I admired and with whom I was able to laugh; the difficult tasks we surmounted together; and the feeling that each person had done the best he could in light of his temperament and skill. We were a good team, and it was team spirit that ultimately made it possible for Tenzing and me to reach the summit. If one shares the modern view that athletic competition demands ruthlessness and egotistical ambition if one is to win, it must be admitted that Tenzing and I came closest to today's mountain-climbing 'stars.' We wanted to reach the top, and no one else was jumping at the chance. Success, however, meant that we had to be as close to the summit as possible at the right time."

Sir John Hunt, the energetic organizer and leader of the expedition, has repeatedly and with justification described the conquest of Everest as a team enterprise. And yet, the best-planned expeditions fail if men like Hillary—men who are ready to risk all to win—are not available at the decisive moment. Many expeditions have failed just beneath the summit because no such men were there. Hillary and Tenzing had to expend superhuman effort just to get out of their sleeping bags at the highest camp [8,510 meters (27,920 feet)] just below the summit, where the predawn temperature was −30°C (−86°F). It was excruciating to do anything, because of the paralyzing effect of oxygen deficiency. But at 6:30 A.M. they forced themselves to get up, put on their boots that had to be first thawed over a primus stove, and head off into unknown, extremely difficult terrain. Finally, five hours later, on May 29, 1953, at 11:30 A.M., the unbelievable tension could be relaxed—at least for fifteen minutes. The two had reached the 8,848-meter (29,028-foot) summit of Mount Everest! They could not rest for very long, however. They faced a descent that was every bit as difficult as the way up.

Teamwork made this historic moment possible. But the final breakthrough that spelled success lay in the fact that one member of the team was a little stronger and a little more ambitious than the rest: that man was Hillary.

Where did Hillary get this energy, skill, and willpower? Born on July 20, 1919, in Auckland, New Zealand, the son of a journalist turned beekeeper, he faced a tough and

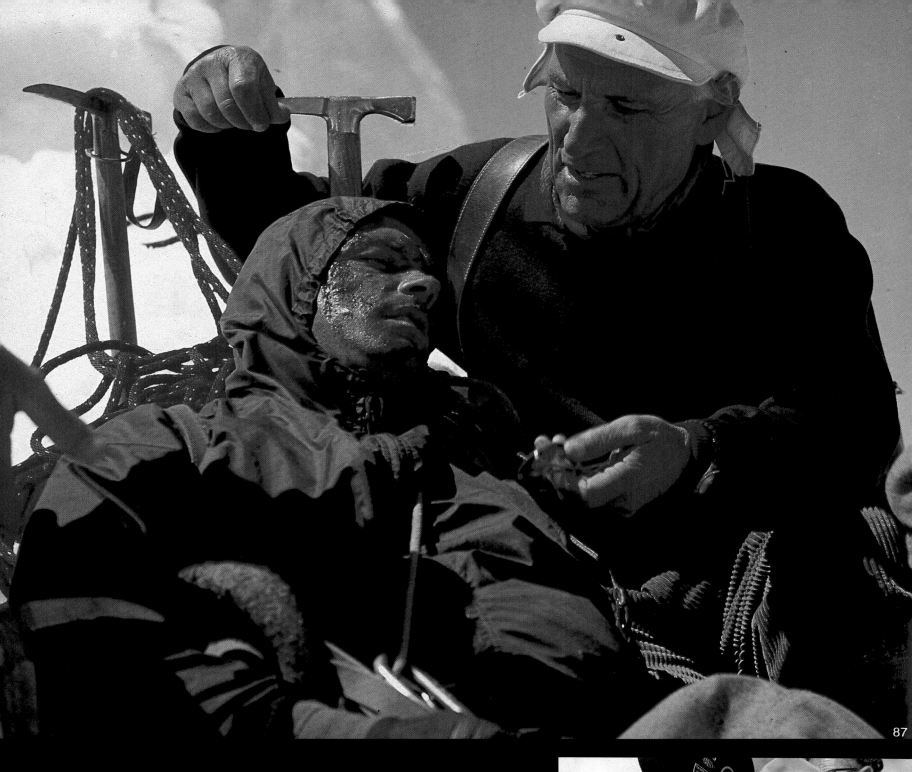

87

87/88
Luis Trenker: Who is not
familiar with this great
producer-director of
mountaineering films? And
who does not know the star?
The great epoch of feature
films set in the mountains
appears to be over.
However, Luis Trenker's
films still have many
admirers. Here, Trenker is
busy shooting a film about
the Eiger: "His Best
Friend." It stars the
well-known skier Toni Sailer

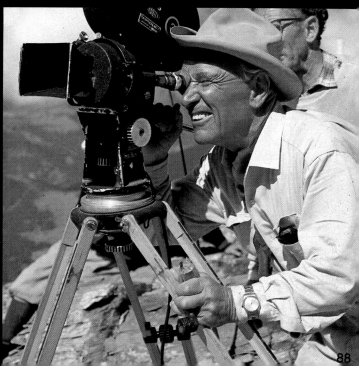

88

9/90
othar Brandler has
roduced documentary films
bout mountains, news
ports of daring climbs,
nd feature films with very
ealistic scenes set in ice and
ock. An extraordinary
imber, he is able to shoot
lm even in the most
ifficult situations.

91/92
Climbing acrobatics with
camera in hand high above
the Sahara: extraordinary
maneuvers on an
overhanging ledge in the
Hoggar. Films like these
bring the beauty of
mountains to those who will
never have a chance to reach
a summit, to experience it as
the ultimate reward for the
toils of an arduous climb. An
unforgettable sight: sunrise
over Mont Blanc (92).

Chomo Longma, Mount Everest, changed their lives: the New Zealander Edmund Hillary and the Sherpa Tenzing Norkay, the first conquerors of the highest summit on earth.

The date was May 29, 1953. After that each went his own way. Sir Edmund, who was knighted by Queen Elizabeth for his achievement, has worked privately and untiringly to

aid the development of the Sherpa people. Money which he has collected all over the world has been used to build hospitals, schools, and bridges. Tenzing Norkay lives in

Darjeeling where he heads a mountain climbing school for Sherpas and Indians. He also directs an art school in which traditional religious painting is taught. Tenzing heads dozy too

95

On the summit of Mount Everest in September 1975: Doug Scott stands next to the Chinese symbol for the summit, which was placed there four months earlier by a Tibetan-Chinese group which climbed the mountain

Haston took the picture toward evening after the two British Alpinists had reached the highest point on earth by way of the southwest flank. "This matter-of-fact, weather-beaten man," Scott

reference to the minutes the two of them spent on the summit of Mount Everest, "had a face which radiated happiness in the light of the setting sun." Haston died in an avalanche while skiing in Switzerland in 1977.

rigorous childhood. The family never had sufficient money, so that he and his younger brother were required to help their father with the bees after school and, indeed, during all their free time. Hillary traces his excellent physical condition to the fact that he had to run back and forth to the honey extractor thousands of times, carrying crates of honeycombs, each weighing about 40 kilos (88 pounds). A single harvest involves 20 to 60 tons! On the other hand, the child's involvement in the parental enterprise, coupled with the fact that his father was excessively strict, resulted in young Hillary's having very few friends. In addition, he was often plagued by a lack of self-confidence. Hillary's mother was the harmonizing influence in the family, and she provided a counterbalance to the father's all-too-strict nature. There were three children—Hillary, his younger brother, and a sister. It was the mother who saw to it that Hillary attended high school in Auckland, even though he had to commute there by train every day. She also insisted that both sons go on to the university after passing their high school final exams. The boys, however, did not pursue their studies but soon returned to their father's sixteen hundred beehives. When the war broke out in 1939, Hillary volunteered for military service. He tried to enlist in the air force but was rejected because of his agricultural obligations. Later, he harbored grave doubts as to whether there was any justification for killing human beings.

In 1944, he was recruited into the Royal New Zealand Air Force and trained as a navigator. This training was to stand him in good stead for his subsequent Antarctic expeditions. He used every available Sunday to climb the mountains in the vicinity of his training camps—first on the South Island and then on the North Island. Most of these climbs required arduous forced marches, and Hillary often climbed alone through the typical storms and snows that characterize the bad weather of New Zealand. All of this hardened him and improved his climbing techniques.

When Hillary returned home, he continued to work on his father's bee farm. After 1946, it became possible for him to spend more time in the New Zealand Alps, where he was able to undertake tours with the best climbers of his country, men who served as both partners and teachers. A high point of this period (1948) was the first climb of the southern ridge of Mount Cook, a climb that until then many had unsuccessfully attempted. His sister's wedding in London in 1950 gave him an opportunity to visit the Stubai and Ötztal Alps as well as the Bernese Oberland and Zermatt. Among the many peaks he climbed were the Jungfrau, the Monte Rosa, and the Lyskamm.

In 1951, Hillary received his first invitation to take part in a New Zealand expedition to the Himalayas. Its goal was Mukut-Parbat [7,242 meters (23,760 feet)], a mountain in the Garhwal Himalayas of India. This expedition had not yet been brought to its conclusion when a telegram from England arrived, inviting two of its members to join a British expedition to Mount Everest. It was to be under the leadership of the famous Eric Shipton. One of those invited was Hillary. One group from the Shipton expedition reconnoitered possible routes from the south. The other group, which included Hillary, explored a route to the east over the passes of Ama Dablam. One year later, in 1952, Hillary joined the team that climbed Cho Oyu [8,189 meters (26,866 feet)] in order to train for what was to be the final successful Everest expedition of 1953.

After the great success on Everest, the beekeeper from New Zealand found himself required to deal with a world that was new and unfamiliar to him. This world had first greeted him during the descent from Mount Everest. It appeared in the form of a telegram addressed to *Sir* Edmund Hillary: the Queen of England had knighted the conqueror.

There was no end to the honors and receptions that welcomed him first in England and then in New Zealand. Soon after his return, he married Louise Mary Rose, a music student eleven years his junior. She accompanied him on his lecture tours through England and the United States. On the side, he wrote his book *High Adventure*.

There have been many celebrities who later found themselves unable to cope with the endless honors they received. There is always a great temptation to rest on one's laurels and thus miss opportunities for further meaningful enterprises. For an expedition member, adventure can be a personal end in itself. There are many well-known climbers of the past who, still feeling the urge to succeed, have attempted to find some way to live on their bygone fame when advancing age caused a decline in their physical capabilities.

It is therefore interesting to trace the further course of the famous Sir Edmund Hillary's life. First of all, there was his family, one son and two daughters. Hillary devoted himself to them even though he did not have all that much time to spend in New Zealand. In later years, he frequently took his wife and children to Nepal, for example, to the main camp at Mount Everest. He also took them to other countries in order to enable them to share the beauties of his world. It must have been a terrible blow when his wife of twenty years died in a plane crash near the airport of Katmandu.

As before, Hillary continued to enjoy planning expeditions and bringing them to a successful conclusion. He led several expeditions to Nepal and made first climbs of a succession of important 6,000- and 7,000-meter peaks: Baruntse, Tamserku, Kangtega, and the beautiful Ama Dablam. He also organized a large expedition whose purpose was the study of human physiology at high altitudes. The group also tried to find yeti, the abominable snowman. Hillary's greatest post-Everest achievements, however, were in the Antarctic, where one of his expeditions succeeded in reaching the South Pole, using relatively primitive vehicles with chains. This was forty-six years after Amundsen's and Scott's first visit. An adventure of a special type was Hillary's first trip down the white waters of the Nepalese-Himalayan river Sun Kosi by jet boat. The expedition traveled from the Indian border almost all the way to Katmandu.

After his conquest of Everest, Sir Edmund Hillary exerted his best and most meaningful efforts in a realm that earned him not fame but deep gratitude. He undertook privately to gather funds to aid the development of Sherpa territory in Nepal. Year after year, and with his usual tenacity and persistence, he collected and still seeks donations for his assistance program. The sums Hillary obtains privately do not match those that states are capable of collecting. However, they are far more effective, since the aid that derives personally from Hillary and his friends comes straight from the heart and testifies to the sincerity of the individual donors. Over the years, seventeen schools have been built in the Sherpa's land south of Mount Everest. If one recalls that under the Rana (princely) rule there were almost no schools at all in Nepal until 1951, one realizes the significance of these new schools in the development of the country as a whole.

Water plays an important role in the mountain villages, and its effects are twofold. On the one hand, the deep, gorgelike valleys are dry for a long period of the year, causing widespread drought. On the other hand, the melting water of the glaciers forms wild mountain rivers that tear away bridges during the summer. To ameliorate the situation, Sir Edmund built water conduits, often many kilometers long. One of them leads to Khumjung, the main village of the Sherpa territory. Another leads to the monastery of Tengpoche. He also had stable hanging bridges built across the violent rapids. The monastery of Khumjung was provided with a new roof; this guaranteed the preservation of a valuable cultural monument. One of Hillary's most important efforts was the construction of the hospital of Kunde, which enabled the Sherpas to avail themselves of much-needed medical treatment. Today, another, even larger hospital exists.

With the assistance of many Sherpas who engaged in arduous manual labor, Hillary built what is now the busiest airport in Nepal. It is located in Lukla, which lies between Katmandu and Pokhara. He later harbored doubts as to the wisdom of this project. "The airport of Lukla has, unfortunately, hastened the advent of tourism and bureaucracy in the Everest region. One is already beginning to feel the so-called blessings of civilization on the Khumbu. Forests are being chopped down and refuse is piling up on campsites and in front of the monasteries. Children have already learned how to go begging. The Sherpas now have at their disposal a hospital and more than a dozen schools. There is sufficient employment to allow them to cope with the galloping inflation. But is this worth the losses? My conscience often bothers me. My only comfort is that the ancient life-style of the Sherpa people was bound to have been modified in any case, for very few societies can resist the temptations of civilization. We believe we have helped the Sherpas to maintain their individuality while enabling them to achieve a competitive position in the new society. If they have lost their traditional hospitality, their religious impulses, and their sense of community because of their contact with the West, do they really care? I have been told that foreign money is effective medicine in the treatment of such "'diseases'."

I discussed this complex problem with Sir Edmund, for it has been mainly tourists from German-speaking countries who have taken part in organized trekking and mountain-climbing expeditions to Nepal and who, therefore, populate the mountain valleys in rather significant numbers. We agreed that the negative effects of tourism should be kept to a minimum at all cost, but it is also true, we felt, that the dangers are no longer as great as we had originally feared. Both the Sherpas and their foreign guests have become more conscious of the environment. The highly developed cultural and religious traditions of Nepal are also so firmly rooted in its population that their ancient ways will be able to give unique shape to the modern way of life that is to come. It is no accident that everyone who visits Nepal is fascinated by the friendliness and tolerance of its people. We can truly say that in exchange for the modern civilization we have brought to the Sherpas we have been able to take back values of immeasurable human and cultural worth.

Hillary agreed that it is both false and romantic to regard the so-called underdeveloped countries of the world as idyllic when regarded from the towering ramparts of the highly industrialized societies of the West. Instead of making such comparisons, we should help to steer the development of civilization in those lands onto an appropriate and rational course. This, precisely, is the task that Sir Edmund Hillary has placed upon his own shoulders. All of his projects are rational. And just as rational was his successful attempt to block the Japanese construction of an airport on valuable Sherpa farmlands in Khumjung.

Sir Edmund has already achieved a legendary reputation that transcends the borders of Sherpa lands. He has also found followers who, in their modest ways, have helped to finance the improvement of dangerous road conditions and the building of schools in central Nepal. Hillary has become a model for many of us, but especially for the youth of the world. His deeds are a clear illustration of the fact that we need not passively participate in the ruthless striving for personal gain that characterizes contemporary industrial society. Rather, we can dedicate ourselves to solving the urgent and current problems facing the Third World—in ways that allow each country to develop according to its own inner needs.

Hillary's strength of will and pursuit of a particular goal transformed him from an unknown beekeeper into one of the world's most famous men. If we could pattern our own behavior after his, we would have a little less to fear from both the present and the future.

□

Joachim Hauff

No One Has Yet Seen the Abominable Snowman

In the middle of the south face of Manaslu, lying at about 6,000 meters (about 19,684 feet) above sea level, there is only ice- and snow-covered rock. This is a landscape devoid of flowers; there is not a sign of green. Nevertheless, it was here that members of an expedition caught sight of a colorful group of butterflies that must have been carried up to this height by the wind. The team had been living for weeks in this formidable landscape; now they experienced a moment of joy at this colorful sight. Other people have also reported a feeling of release when, after weeks or months in high mountains or in the icy world of Greenland, they caught a glimpse of the first bit of green vegetation, the first flower, or when they heard the first birdcall.

There may well exist a living being whom the inhabitants of the Himalayan highlands have described as the abominable snowman—a creature both gigantic and very shy. A Sherpa woman maintains that she met such a yeti several years ago. There are other descriptions, too, especially of the hair and footprints of this being, all having been reported by totally reliable people. In contrast to the yeti, there are animals that every climber knows; indeed, he can often spot them in their natural habitat, even from the windows of a gondola or cable car. When hiking in the mountains, many people take special joy in spotting a deer or chamois, and how wonderful it is suddenly to see an eagle circling above one!

Fritz Wiessner, who was born in Dresden and is now a citizen of the United States, was one of the most extraordinary climbers of the 1920s. In a recent interview, he reported one such experience that occurred during his first climb of the northwest face of the Furchetta together with Emil Solleder in the summer of 1925. When the two were just below the point where they could leave the wall, they suddenly heard a rustling sound: an eagle was circling around the two climbers, eyeing them curiously, for they had come too close to his refuge and had disturbed his nest. Wiessner said that this was one of the most unforgettable experiences he had ever had on his countless mountain tours.

It is repeatedly asserted that no one has as yet seen a yeti. People generally respond in the same way to the possible existence of this creature. "Oh, yes, the legendary snowman! The abominable monster who is making the Himalayas unsafe!" In the large Brockhaus encyclopedia of 1898 there is absolutely no mention of a yeti or a snowman. A recent edition of this work, however, contains an explanation as well as the photo of a footprint. More careful observation revives the old question once again; one begins to believe in the possibility of this ancient, legendary, and very controversial Himalayan creature. Even someone who is not a biologist can see that the footprint must have been made by a plantigrade animal.

Apparently there are two kinds of yeti. The American zoologist J. A. McNeely searched for the yeti in 1965. After evaluating eyewitness reports, wall paintings in cloisters, and various other descriptions, he came to the conclusion that the yeti is an apelike creature about 1.50 to 1.65 meters (4.9 to 5.4 feet) tall. Shaggy red-brown to gray-brown fur covers its whole body, leaving only the face visible. Large teeth fill a broad mouth, but there are no pronounced tusks. The long arms reach, apelike, to the knees and are used to support the lower extremities during rapid marches. Its feet are large and have five toes; next to three smaller toes, there are two large gripping toes.

The second type of yeti has been described by the ethnologists R. N. Wojkowitz and Dr. Michael Ward. This being is said to be 1.80 to 2.40 meters (5.9 to 7.8 feet) tall and to weigh about 90 kilograms (198 pounds). The footprint of this yeti is 35 centimeters (13.7 inches) long and about 15 centimeters (5.9 inches) wide. Further biological details are not available, since Ward has based his assertions almost entirely upon his interpretation of the footprints.

Does the yeti really exist or has some other creature left traces of its existence behind? Which of the mammals might this be? From the class of primates, it could be either an ape or a human being. Only one of these species would be able to produce the corresponding footprint. It could also be a relic from prehistoric times, the descendant of an apelike human creature known as the *Gigantopithecus*. These beings lived about one hundred thousand years ago at a time when the earth was covered by layers of ice. The ice masses withdrew, leaving behind some remnants in the form of glaciers. Could it not be that these creatures withdrew along with the ice, leaving behind descendants in the mountains? But then why are yeti said to exist only in the Himalayas and, more precisely, only in the eastern part of this gigantic range? This question can

be partly answered—at least in a speculative fashion. Since 1956, teeth have been found in south China that have been ascribed to the *Gigantopithecus*. South China and the eastern part of the Himalayas are not separate worlds. Therefore, the presence of this being in south China would support its presence in the eastern Himalayas. This theory does not, of course, explain its absence elsewhere. Furthermore, it is also possible that the so-called yeti is really an entirely different animal, perhaps a member of the small bear family. The bears suggest themselves because they too are plantigrade animals.

Let us turn for a moment to two of the most typical representatives of the small bear family. The giant panda belongs to this group in spite of the rather impressive length of its body [up to 1.50 meters (4.9 feet)]. The panda is the heraldic animal of the World Wildlife Foundation, and we are all familiar with its habitat. The Tibetan black bear, also called the blue bear in English-speaking countries, roams the mountains of Tibet up to altitudes of 4,000 meters (13,000 feet). These two types of bear have been selected here for a specific reason. An American expedition, which was searching for traces of the yeti in 1958, confirmed the assumption that two kinds of yeti exist. Admittedly, this expedition was unable to produce photographs of the yeti; nevertheless, after investigating the resting places and caves of the yeti as well as their hair and excrement, the scientists came to the conclusion that the two forms of the yeti just briefly described must, in fact, exist. One type supposedly lives in the rain forests between 2,400 meters (7,873 feet) and 3,600 meters (11,810 feet); the other lives somewhere between human settlements and glacier areas. The first zone corresponds to the natural habitat of the Tibetan bear. This is not to say that the yeti really is a Tibetan bear. The question is, rather, whether it could be possible for a second large mammal to share its habitat with the bear.

Sir Edmund Hillary, the conqueror of Mount Everest, led another expedition to the Himalayas in 1960. One of its purposes was to look for traces of the yeti. Hillary firmly denies the existence of this being. An animal of the magnitude just described, he argues, could not have permanently escaped the sharp eyes of the Sherpas, especially in the open slopes of the region. Now, the Sherpas do not claim that they have never seen a yeti.

Even Hillary's partner on Mount Everest, the Sherpa Tenzing, reported that he had had an encounter with this fabled creature. With one part of the expedition, Hillary visited every town and every cloister in which yeti fur, as well as scalps and skeletal parts, has been preserved. He even succeeded in acquiring several of these furs so that it became possible to conduct a careful scientific investigation. The most varied scientists identified these pelts as the fur of the Tibetan blue bear. The so-called yeti scalps, from which some scientists deduced the probable shape of the abominable snowman's head, were classified by Hillary's group as artifacts. With the help of wooden forms, they succeeded in reconstructing scalps from the fur of an antelopelike forest goat. These artificial scalps were almost identical with those allegedly belonging to the yeti. The skeleton of a yeti hand was carefully examined, and scientists came to the conclusion that it was the skeleton of a human hand. The bones that did not quite fit in with the skeletal form of a human being were identified as the bones of an animal, which had probably been placed into the skeleton by monks.

More serious problems presented themselves in connection with the footprints that were found. It was difficult to explain the 30-centimeter (11.8-inch) size. On the Ripimu Glacier, the expedition found footprints at a height of 5,500 meters (18,000 feet), which could also be followed over a relatively long distance. Where the footprints had not been exposed to the direct rays of the sun, their size approximated the footprint of a fox. Where the footprints had been exposed to the sun, they reached a considerable size through melting. However, while the phenomena of insolation (solar radiation) and ablation (melting) can explain the large prints in the snow, they do not account for those that were found in the mud.

Hillary believed that he also answered another question: a typical characteristic of the yeti foot was said to be its large toe, which is aligned at right angles to the remaining toes. Hillary has a picture of a Nepali with deformed feet; he used it to show that a toe like the one ascribed to the yeti need not be so unique. The big toe of the Nepali crossed over his remaining toes. If one bears in mind the fact that Nepalese mountain dwellers walk barefooted, even through these snowy regions, one can argue that the so-called characteristic feature of the yeti may well be quite simply the uncharacteristic footprint of a human being.

There appears to be a normal and rational explanation for every external characteristic that the Himalayan natives ascribe to the yeti. From this perspective, the yeti does not exist. But is the existence of this snow creature really so improbable? Let's reconsider the question for a moment. The first reports about this fabled creature reached us about forty years ago. Nevertheless, its existence has still not been confirmed. Can't there nevertheless be a few surviving members of a rare species of mammal whose timid nature has caused him to seek out a habitat in the remote valleys of the Himalayas that no man has ever entered? A hypothesis of this sort proved true once before, when the bamboo bear, or panda bear, was discovered. European scientists first heard about the panda during the middle of the nineteenth century. In spite of intensive exploration and research, the French missionary and zoologist Armand David was unable to find this legendary being. The first European zoologist to come upon a panda living in its natural habitat was the German researcher Weigold during the German Tibet expedition of 1913–1915, half a century after the first reports reached Europe. Before resolving the question of the yeti's existence, we should ask ourselves whether animal and plant life is actually possible at the heights involved.

A presupposition for the existence of every form of animal life is the existence of plants. Plant life in the Himalaya is divided into zones similar to those found in the Alps. Deciduous trees such as birches, sycamores, and oaks grow up to 1,500 meters (ca. 5,000 feet); next come bamboo forests, which, above 2,500 meters (ca. 8,000 feet) are replaced by unpretentious conifers and rhododendrons. Above 3,100 meters (ca. 10,000 feet) rhododendrons are no longer merely underbrush but comprise the major source of plant life. The rhododendron belt continues up to the height of 4,200 meters (ca. 13,800 feet), at which point the Alpine-like meadows and the arctic steppes begin. The plants here are quite similar to those found in the Alps.

A few indigenous mountain plants, such as the *Ranunculus glacialus*, grow even in the zone of the eternal snow. These flowers were found on the Finsteraarhorn even at a height of 4,275 meters (ca. 14,000 feet). A similarly unique plant is also to be found in the Himalayas. A member of the primrose family *(Androsacepolster)* grows in the Mount Everest region at an altitude of 6,350 meters (ca. 21,000 feet), that is to say, 2,000 meters (ca. 6,600 feet) above the snow line, which, with the exception of central Tibet, lies between 4,200 and 4,800 meters (ca. 13,800 to 15,800 feet).

Of the animals that inhabit the Alps, the Alpine chamois *(Rupicapra rupicapra)* should be mentioned first. This animal is distinguishable only in color from its relatives in the other high mountains of Europe. Both the male and female have horns that jut straight up from the head; only the points are bent into hooks. They also have yellow-white designs on the face and neck. The chamois live in herds and at altitudes of from 700 to 3,000 meters (ca. 2,300 to 10,000 feet). Plants and shrubs are the primary sources of food. This skillful climber has been hunted from time immemorial.

The ibex *(Capra ibex ibex)* is as good a climber as the chamois, if not a better one. It inhabits an area between the timberline and the eternal snow. Full-grown ibex bulls can reach a body weight of about 120 kilograms (264 pounds). The females are smaller and live with the kids in a separate flock. The two flocks only mix during the mating season (December and January). A newborn ibex can follow its mother immediately after birth but requires her milk for another six months. In spite of their mobility, they are an easy target for birds of prey.

Everyone knows the marmot *(Marmota marmota)*. This rabbit-sized plant eater is related to our squirrel. It is an awkward rodent and may be a remnant from the ice age. Marmots spend the winter asleep in holes 3 meters (10 feet) deep in the earth. The extensive underground system built by a whole colony also serves as a refuge in summer, a place of flight when a whistling sound warns of an approaching enemy. In spite of its shyness, the marmot is an endangered species in its natural habitat at altitudes of from 1,000 to 3,000 meters (ca. 3,300 to 9,800 feet).

Because of their constant body temperature, mammals have the best chances for survival. But a variety of cold-blooded creatures also live in the earth beneath the snow—for example, the ancient glacier fly *(Isotoma saltans)*. Plant and animal remains that drift in the wind provide its nourishment. This insect has also been observed to eat its own kind. Since the glacier fly is a wingless insect, it can only hop on the snow surfaces when it is forced out of the earth by too much melted water. It has specially designed hindquarters to propel it as it hops along.

High above the rugged surfaces of the cliffs is the home of the great birds of prey. The golden eagle *(Aquila chrysaëtos)* is about 1 meter (3.2 feet) long and has a wingspan of over 2 meters (6½ feet). It attacks marmots and young chamois and thereby helps to maintain natural selection in the animal world. A phenomenon that is taking place today has had its effect on the eagle. In earlier times, this bird had various habitats; however, it has been driven back by encroaching civilization and forced to seek a place to nest in extreme zones. The mountain jackdaw *(Pyrrhocorax graculus)* has experienced fewer difficulties from the pressures of advancing civilization. This black raven with its golden beak and red feet has even become a follower of human civilization and so can be spotted even in cities. The jackdaw lives on a mixed diet and possesses great adaptive abilities. It has almost completely driven the Alpine crow *(Pyrrhocorax pyrrhocorax)* from the Alps.

In the Himalayas, on the other hand, these two species still find their world in good order and can peacefully coexist at altitudes of up to 5,000 meters (ca. 16,500 feet). Another kind of Himalayan bird, which shares the crow's territory, deserves attention—the golden vulture *(Gypaetus barbatus)*, which resembles an eagle. Neck and head as well as the underside of the bird are covered with white feathers, and a black beard grows beneath its beak. The upper side of the bird is black and brown. Highly individual in its eating habits, the vulture only eats bones and can swallow a whole yak. Large scraps that it cannot swallow it lets fall from the air onto the cliffs until they fragment into smaller pieces. Because of its complete processing of bones, the vulture also provides a service by disposing of human corpses.

The vulture also finds yak bone in the slaughter pits of human beings who keep this type of ox *(Bos [poephagus] mutus grunniens)* as a domestic animal. The yak provides meat, wool, and milk and also serves as a beast of burden in heights of 4,000 to 6,000 meters (ca. 13,000 to 19,700 feet). The color of its fur varies between yellow, gray, and black, so that the herds appear colorfully variegated. The domesticated yaks have inherited their stamina and climbing ability from their ancestors, the wild yak *(Bos [poephagus] mutus)*, which have been almost totally exterminated in the last eighty years. The wild yak is black. Bulls reach a height of up to 2 meters (6½ feet). Except for height and fur color, the wild yak and the domestic yak are identical in appearance.

The yaks have their homeland in the Tibetan highlands. The blue sheep *(Pseudois nayaur)* lives in the peripheral mountains of Tibet and West Mongolia at altitudes ranging from 4,000 meters (ca. 13,000 feet) to the eternal snow. The bharal really is not a sheep but rather is related to the maned goat. The blue-black coloring that gives this animal its name appears only once—in its first winter coat.

When one thinks of the high mountains, one probably does not think of the large cats. However, one must revise one's ideas: between 2,000 meters (ca. 6,500 feet) and the eternal snow lives the snow leopard, or irbis *(Uncia uncia)*. In its powerfully built hindquarters and general body form, the irbis is reminiscent of the puma. It measures about 2.50 meters (8.2 feet) from the head to the tip of its tail. The fur color—basically varying between a whitish gray and dirty ivory—is similar to that of a leopard. The upper part of the body and tail are covered with large, faded-looking dark circles, which are filled in on the head and legs. This striking coloring provides excellent camouflage, for it makes the creeping animal look like a dirty speck of snow. The leopard's prey in this area are blue sheep, musk deer, pheasant, and domestic sheep. The snow leopard avoids man. If threatened, however, it will attack.

Finally, a word about the bamboo or panda bear *(Ailuropoda Melanoleuca)* mentioned earlier, whose appearance is marked by the characteristic black-and-white color of its fur. The panda feeds on bamboo, particularly young shoots. Its habitat stretches from Iran to Japan. In the Himalayas, it can be found in altitudes of up to 4,000 meters (ca. 13,000 feet).

This necessarily brief survey of the flora and fauna of the high mountains shows that plant life and animal life are possible even at extreme heights. We have seen that certain animals even in these areas have been driven back and survive only in small numbers. Perhaps there are yet places in the inaccessible high valleys of the Himalayan mountains where the legendary yeti can dwell. No one has seen him. But it is premature to conclude from this that he does not exist. □

Toni Hiebeler

To Climb a Mountain and Return Safely

In Alpine literature there is one book that deserves to be called a classic. It is a book about the dangers of the Alps, written nearly one hundred years ago by Emil Zsigmondy, a young doctor of medicine. Even before the end of the nineteenth century, second and third editions were prepared for publication by Ludwig Purtscheller and Emil's brother, Otto Zsigmondy. Later editions were edited by Wilhelm Paulcke, a professor of geology at the University of Freiburg and himself an important mountain climber and Alpine researcher. The 500-page ninth edition of 1933 contains a wealth of information derived from Paulcke's own experiences. In 1971, a handy abridged version appeared, which, despite its brevity, contains the most essential information about the dangers of the Alps and is a must for anyone who decides to take excursions into the mountains—the vacation hiker as well as the extreme Alpinist.

"Courage is a fine thing," Paulcke wrote, but "ill-considered bravado is stupid! It is better to make use of the experiences of one's predecessors and supplement courage with reflection, reason, and skill. Only he who always considers the consequences of his actions possesses true courage."

These words speak for themselves. It is no disgrace to be taught something. It is not embarrassing to purchase such a book. One should not set out for the mountains without having first familiarized oneself with the ABCs of climbing. Even beyond the study of a particular book such as Paulcke's, the aspiring Alpinist should seek help from the numerous climbing schools that exist throughout the Alps—so that one can better climb a mountain and return in one piece.

I come from the Vorarlberg in Austria. From the windows of my parents' house in Bludenz, one can see mountains belonging to three different Alpine groups: the Elsspitzen and Rogelskopf of the Lechquellen chain, the Dawennakopf of the Verwall, and a dozen summits of the Hüttenkopf massif in the Rätikon.

It was my father who first ignited the spark of my youthful passion for the mountains. He was a skiing teacher as well as a ski and mountain guide—always suntanned, athletic, and dynamic. I regarded him as the personification of "the father." I admired and worshiped him because he appeared to be occupied with something mysterious: he was constantly going off into the mountains with his rope, ice axe, skis, and rucksack. As a tot of six, I kept telling myself that my father would take me along when I got bigger.

But he had no time for me—ever! The fact that his clients, who were strangers, could go into the mountains with him while I had to remain behind made me into one of the most unhappy children for miles around. But by the time I was eight, I had decided to become a climber. I told my plans to everyone who asked me what I wanted to be when I grew up—my mother, my schoolmates, and my teacher. The latter tried to convince me that even a mountain climber needs brains, but I didn't pay any attention to him. I knew there were other things that climbers had to learn and these things were not in my school books. As a result, I was left back in the fourth grade, because of German grammar, which I hated. On the other hand, I knew by heart the names of all the mountains that surrounded Bludenz. And I knew that behind the mountains that I could see were many other mountains— much higher and steeper ones.

When I was nine years old, I could no longer accept my father's promises that he would definitely let me come with him someday. I wanted to climb a mountain now. My eyes were always riveted to the Hüttenkopf massif. Whether I was sitting in my classroom or running around outside, I was searching the heights for something that did not yet have a name. There stood the Kennerberg, whose craggy surface was interspersed with grass and dwarf pines. To the left was the broad lumpy dome of the Zwölfer. There were countless magnificent peaks to gaze at.

It was a Saturday afternoon and I had just returned from school. I said to my mother: "I have to climb the Zwölfer today." Instead of giving me an answer, she handed me a shopping bag and sent me out on errands. Tears of anger and frustration welled up. No one understood me and I was miserable.

I threw the bag and change purse behind the door of my house and took off, gripping my crude but sturdy shoes tightly under my arm. I raced off to the foot of the Hüttenkopf. I had escaped! I was free! I gasped. My heart was pounding! It was already late. I knew nothing about routes or paths. The forest was steep and dense, and not a soul was about. After a while, the woods seemed to become lighter. Soon I was standing on the Zalumwiese. Toward the end of summer, the steep grassy slopes of this mountain meadow are mown and the hay is gathered up into many small stacks to be stored away for winter. The way ahead was open from here to a point just beneath the steep craggy wall that connects the Zalumwiese to the Frauenalpe. Although I was beginning to get hungry, I could not admit it, since I had brought along nothing to eat.

Dusk slowly descended over the valley. Here and there tiny lights began to flicker. My luxuriant green meadow was transformed into a dark carpet. I had never spent a night away from my mother; I did not know what it was like not to sleep in a bed. Panting, I ran all the way up the steeply sloping meadow as if I wanted to escape from the oncoming darkness. I reached the upper Zalum hut as the last rays of daylight disappeared. The hut was open. I gazed down at the sea of sparkling lights in the city below. Somewhere to the right of the most dense cluster of lights had to be our house—the warm and comforting parlor, my bed, my mother. Feeling my way about in the darkness of the square room, I found some hay. It had the wonderfully pungent aroma typical of mountain grass. I dug myself in as best as I could and sank into a deep sleep. I did not wake again until the cold mountain morning drove me out of my nest. The new day dispelled my anxiety and oppression and filled me with renewed joy and expectancy. There was nothing I could do to still my hunger, so I just kept climbing.

I reached the edge of the Zalumwiese. From here, steep craggy rocks towered up to the Frauenalpe. Almost instinctively, I turned left and entered another Alpine forest. Here a narrow path led upward in small serpentines. A cowherd offered me some milk and asked me where my parents were. "They're coming. I always start out half an hour ahead of them." I walked outside the door of his hut as if to look for my parents. When the cheese-maker began to ask more questions, I ran off in the direction of the Kennerberg. There was no path, and I made my way up through dwarf pines and crags. Occasionally, I had to do real rock climbing. These were joyous, festive moments. I imitated the pictures I had seen

238

and was enraptured when I was able to come to grips with the cliffs themselves.

Before I knew it, I was standing on the summit of the Kennerberg. I could hardly believe it. The houses in the valley looked very tiny beneath the haze that lay over our valley. On the other side of the mountain, infinite precipices plunged abruptly down toward the Brandner Valley. I saw the Zwölfer with its vertical north wall. It was very close—only a stone's throw away. It was my goal. I was about to reach the object of many long days of yearning. The Zwölfer rises up out of a wild mountain valley and is silhouetted against a sky of such intense blueness as can be found only in mountains. A narrow ridge brought me directly over to the Zwölfer massif. There I found a narrow path that led along its walls. There was a groove in the wall, and I saw a small iron cross placed against the rocks. On it was inscribed the name of a climber who had fallen.

This monument to a dead climber standing in the solitude and loneliness of the rocks made a deep impression on me. I had to force myself to turn my thoughts back to climbing my Zwölfer. In my restless search, I finally found a possible route. The wall was about 60 meters (ca. 200 feet) high. Above this cliff, the path seemed easier. Decisively, I began to climb the wall. Cautiously, I tested every foothold, every handhold. It was possible. I was euphoric; my heart rejoiced. I began to sense the glorious feeling of self-abandonment; I was in another world. Joy and fear had reached a state of equilibrium. At first, I just wanted to test myself out and climb a few meters. Now that I had reached a significant height, I gave up all thoughts of turning back. I realized I had to stand on my Zwölfer. I had to get to the top of my mountain at last. The dangerous wall lay behind me. Galloping over a steep grass slope and across a narrow rock ridge, I reached the summit.

I was happy, incredibly happy. Even my hunger was forgotten. I heard the church bells from the valley. I felt in a holiday mood. Then I remembered it was Sunday. And, really, I could not have had a more beautiful Sunday. It was a day of joy, a day of fulfillment.

For the first time in my life I had gone up into the mountains to experience that ineffable something—and it was beautiful. I thought of my friends who were probably walking through town with their parents, dressed in their Sunday best, perhaps topping off the day with a soda in a cafe.

To the southeast, I saw a fantastically beautiful mountain. It looked like the Matterhorn, which I knew from my father's books. It was the Zimba—the Mat-terhorn of the Vorarlberg. It became the new mountain of my dreams. Even my teacher had told us about the Zimba. He said it was a difficult and dangerous mountain. I now saw it in all its grandeur and in the full perfection of its form.

By nightfall I was back in Bludenz with my mother, who had cried her eyes out over my disappearance. She held me tightly in her arms. I myself was radiant, for I had climbed my first mountain. A new life had begun for me, a life dedicated to mountains. Although I was overcome by the experience itself, I was also impressed by a few factual things: you must know more about your mountains in the future, I told myself. If your Zwölfer was that steep and dangerous, just imagine what the others will be like: you saw the cross on the Zwölfer.

Now, Father will take you along, I thought. But when my father returned home from the mountains several weeks later, he wasn't the least bit interested in my Zwölfer. World War II had broken out and he was called up. "When I come back from the war," he said, "I'll take you along." But the war didn't end for a long time.

The next summer my mother sent me to the Lech Valley as a goatherd. With the forty-seven goats entrusted to me, I got to know the mountains in a way that is otherwise impossible. I became acquainted with rocky crags, debris-strewn slopes, and steep grassy flanks covered with patches of old snow. I climbed them in the heat, in the rain, in snow, and in wind—every day for two whole months. I often contemplated the movements of the goats and chamois. They seemed to have perfect mastery of the mountains. They climbed quickly, surefootedly, with a sense of confident deliberation.

Today I know that the most important thing in mountain climbing is the way one walks and paces oneself. It is more difficult to acquire total security on every type of slope and in every kind of weather than it is to learn how to rock climb. Indeed, a bad rock climber is exposed to far fewer dangers than is a novice mountain climber on his harmless paths. For the rock climber usually has a friend nearby, and his rope will generally save him from the consequences of a mistake.

As a goatherd, I had the most marvelous time racing down grassy slopes and craggy flanks. I loved to leap into steep firn gulleys and slide down the mountain in the snow. The winter following my initiation as a goatherd, only one thought occupied me: the Zimba. I learned that one had to sleep over in the Sarotla hut, that one had to climb another four or five hours from there to reach the summit, and that the Zimba was a difficult mountain.

It was said that if one could climb the Hanging Stone—an 80-meter (263-foot) high rock needle near Nüziders, 6 kilometers (3.7 miles) from Bludenz—then one could also take on the Zimba. Needless to say, I hiked over to the Hanging Stone with the first good spring weather—barefoot and dressed only in short leather pants. It was a frighteningly narrow rock tower. I was relieved when I saw a weather vane on the summit; otherwise, I would have doubted that the tower could be climbed. There is only one route to the top of the Hanging Stone, and I found it. It was a breathlessly exciting climb. My knees and feet were scraped and bled—but I didn't feel any pain. If you want to climb the Zimba, I kept thinking, then . . .

When I reached the tiny area that forms the summit of the Hanging Stone, I yodeled a few times out of pure joy, but no one heard me. No one could hear my enthusiasm and enchantment. And—from the summit I could see the Zimba. George Leigh Mallory could not have felt greater yearning for Mount Everest when he first set eyes on it in 1921 than I felt for my Zimba as I gazed at it from the top of the Hanging Stone.

I now had to turn my thoughts to climbing down. The descent was harder than anything I had ever done. And I learned one of the most important things a mountain climber must know in order to survive: if the difficulty of the ascent pushes one to the limits of one's ability, then a descent by the same route will actually be life threatening. I arrived home with bloody feet and legs.

Never before and never since has my world appeared so entirely wrapped up in happiness as on the spring day when I conquered the Hanging Stone. I couldn't wait for the summer to come. I yearned for it as if for paradise.

When summer did arrive, it brought me the Zimba. And a human disappointment. I needed a partner for the climb, even if we only used a clothesline for a rope. My school friend Karl, who used to boast that he was the bravest and the best, agreed to come along but gave up on the Zimbajoch. He was overcome, literally robbed of his senses, by the mountain. Karl left me in the lurch.

I continued alone, following the west ridge, which was only very difficult at the entrance chimney. Even here, I only had trouble because my leather shorts and nailed boots were not the most appropriate clothing for mountain climbing. The Zimba was a landmark in my climbing career, for I learned here that mountains do not tolerate cheating—also, that one cannot conceal with big words one's lack of skill and one's fear. The relationship between man and mountain is quickly established, and the rules are clear. After my conquest of the Zimba, I felt big and

strong and considered myself to be the best mountain climber far and wide.

Even Felix, who maintained the hut and was normally very laconic, had a few words of praise for me. He had been a guide but was now too old and too tired for the mountains. Just then, however, there was a manufacturer from Radolfzell in the hut. He wanted to climb the Zimba the next day. Felix suggested that I "take" the man up. All he really knew about me was that my father had been a competent guide!

Herr Adolf and I took Felix's rope and headed for the Zimba the next day. Everything went according to plan. This time, even the chimney was a game, in spite of my nailed shoes and short lederhosen. The descent was also easy—until we reached the Zimbajoch. In early summer—it was Whitsuntide—a blanket of old snow always covers the northern flank of the Zimbajoch. Further below, this flank breaks off above a 70-meter (230-foot) high, nearly vertical rock step. When Herr Adolf got to the upper edge of the hard-packed snowy slope, I explained the procedure for getting down. I then leaped into the snow as I had done during my goatherd days and was off and away. Toward the end of the descent, I dug the edges of my shoes into the snow, slowed down, and came to a stop about 20 meters (65 feet) from the drop-off. I waited here for Herr Adolf. He too now leaped into the snow—but lost his balance after only a few meters. He landed on his bottom and began to slide down the slope at an ever-increasing and a horrifying speed. In his desperate attempt to brake the slide, he turned a somersault. He now began to roll diagonally down the slope. Fear began to engulf me, and a horrible image arose. Suddenly I remembered the drop-off.

Adolf lost total control of his movements. He slid down a path far to the side of my track and headed toward a little island of rock. He collided—and the impact brought his fatal ride to a halt. I reached him within a matter of seconds. He looked awful, because he too was wearing shorts. He had abrasions on his hands, legs, and face as well as many bruises. But Adolf was tough and had a strong spirit. Moreover, he didn't find out about the drop-off until several days later. And, so, the two happy climbers had a wonderful day in the mountains after all.

This second ascent of the Zimba taught me something very important: old snow represents one of the greatest of all possible dangers for the climber (not everyone can spend a summer playing in it as goatherd!). Today I know that most fatal accidents have occurred because a climber has slid on snow or slushy ice or has fallen on slippery rock.

I climbed the Zimba more than forty times, and with

each ascent I learned something new. After the first Zimba experiences, I spent nearly every free day in the mountains—soon, with my father's rope.

During the war years, then during the postwar years—I would go off into the mountains with a few potatoes and come back with a miracle. My father, who had been a prisoner of war, returned home, but I no longer needed him to teach me Alpinism. I went my own way. My climbing school was the mountains themselves, which I usually set out to experience alone—until a young woman named Poldi invited me to accompany her to the Wilder Kaiser. I was to be both rope leader and climbing comrade. I was eighteen years old and as poor as a church mouse.

With respect to its weather conditions, the Wilder Kaiser is quite similar to the Eiger. The massif is also a lonely northern barrier against the flatlands, and there are no other mountain chains in the vicinity. Thus, the bad weather and storm fronts coming in from the north are dammed up by the Wilder Kaiser. Within the shortest possible time, the most devastating storms can occur. Only, most climbers don't know this.

"Well, Toni, what'll it be tomorrow, the southeast?" Poldi asked after we had completed the first three tours.

"In this weather?" I answered. (When you say "the southeast" while standing on the Stripsenjoch, everyone knows you mean the 350-meter (1,148-foot) high, smoothly polished southeast wall of the Fleischbank.)

"My God," Poldi said. "The weather isn't that bad."

The next morning the weather really wasn't all that bad, so off we went. We had two 40-meter (130-foot) long ropes. They were new, very good hemp ropes. We also had ten carabiners, a few pitons, and a few slings. What we did not have were anoraks and bivouac sacks. Such things were not yet available in these early postwar years.

It was almost noon by the time we reached the top of the Steinerne Rinne ("stone gulley")—clouds, everywhere clouds. Poldi was no longer as enthusiastic about climbing the Fleischbank as she had been earlier in the day. After all—it was the notorious Fleischbank southwest wall, and neither of us was familiar with it.

"Look, Poldi!" I said, both excited and pleased. "Those climbers are about to start up the east wall. If all four of them can climb the east wall at this hour, the two of us will have time to do the southeast wall." One could see right away that they were not the best climbers.

"Hey," I called up to them, "if you don't get a move on, you'll never get there today."

"Thanks for your advice, but keep it to yourself," one of them shouted back.

They weren't very friendly, I thought, but you know how people from Vienna are . . .

"Poldi, come on, let's go."

"You must know what you're doing."

I should have known what I was doing! We climbed effortlessly over an easy spur without using the rope. Then the wall began. One doesn't say much as one begins the real climb up a difficult route, especially if one doesn't like the looks of it.

"It's pretty cool today, isn't it?"

"Pretty cool," answered Poldi.

"The first slab there—pretty nice, no?"

"It's steep, not nice!" said Poldi.

"I know it's steep, Poldi, but the pitons are holding."

"Yes, some of them."

"Well, good luck, Poldi," I said and prepared to begin.

"Look," Poldi said. Her face had darkened like the clouds above.

"What?"

"What if the weather doesn't hold?"

"It'll probably hold," I answered, already excited by the very feel of the rocks in my hands. My fingers were itching to really grab hold and begin.

"And if it doesn't?"

"Look, Poldi," I said. "In two or three rope lengths we'll get to a narrow band. Above the band is the Rossi Overhang. After the Rossi Overhang comes another band. From there we can get off the wall to the left. We'll do that if the weather doesn't improve. okay?"

"If you say so."

One hour later we stood beneath the Rossi Overhang. A wild storm started. It began to pour. Just above the overhang is an easy grass band that leads off the wall to the left. From there one can reach safe footing in less than an hour on the normal route, a fact we both knew. I finally reached the overhang itself. There were already pitons in the rock.

"Thank God, the rain has stopped—nothing bad can happen now," I shouted down cheerfully to Poldi.

"You must be dreaming. Keep your stupid jokes to yourself."

Poldi was in a bad mood. It was pouring buckets. I don't know how, but I quickly surmounted the overhang. There was lots of water. Streams of it. But also a place to stand.

"Come on up, quickly!"

"Pull in the rope!"

"Let it out!"

"They are both loose!" Poldi shouted.

It can't be, I thought. The ropes wouldn't budge. They were stiff as boards, and threading them through the carabiners had caused too much friction. The storm raged like an inferno—it was a good thing I had secured myself with a piton. The rain turned into hail. A few minutes later, the whole landscape was white. Just a few easy meters above me was the escape route off the wall. But Poldi was still standing below the overhang. She could not get up if I could not help her with the ropes.

That's it, I thought to myself. The cold began to penetrate through my clothing, and I began to experience a leaden feeling. Was it just the cold? We're in a trap, I thought. We can't survive a bivouac in this cold and wet. No human being could endure such exposure.

"He-e-l-pp!" What was that? I thought I heard something and strained to hear it through the storm. Yes—there it was again. Louder, longer, with fewer intervals. I clearly heard someone calling for help. The sound was coming from the east wall, just around the edge of the cliff on which I was standing.

It had to be the party from Vienna, I thought. The desperate cries for help, sounding through the fury of the storm, had an electrifying effect. Poldi heard it too. It was awful not to be able to help. Help? Our own lives were in danger if we didn't do something—soon!

We now had fog to contend with in addition to the hail and thunderstorms. "Get down," an insistent inner voice urged. I climbed a little way down the overhang and attached a carabiner. Then I pulled myself back to my standing place and again tried the ropes. I was able to draw one of them slowly toward me. I roped myself down with it.

All the carabiners were used on the overhang. Poldi pulled the second rope toward her. I soon reached her.

"We must rappel, Poldi," I said as calmly as I could.

"Where?"

"Down, straight down."

"Not over the slab we climbed up?"

"No, that's impossible. The slab is almost 40 meters (130 feet) high. Too high for these stiff ropes. We wouldn't be able to pull them in."

"And you think the direct route down from here is less high?"

"I hope so."

"And if it isn't?"

"I don't know what we'll do then, but we have to try it."

In the thick fog we couldn't see even 20 meters (65 feet) ahead of us. Already the ropes were hanging down into the void. I made a Dülfer seat and set off for the depths. Friction arose between my pants and the stiff hemp. My downward movement was spasmodic. It was like starting a car in fourth gear.

It was unbelievable—a gift from all the good angels of heaven! After a 30-meter (98-foot) descent, I reached a tiny spot to stand on. It was about the size of a bar stool. And there was a very secure ring piton in the rock. One sometimes believes his guardian angels are keeping watch.

"Help!" Again these imploring calls. Anxiety mounted. I secured myself to the ring piton with a chest sling. Our retreat was going well—it was as orderly as a practice exercise. Rope in, thread the carabiners; second rappel. The storm was still howling. Thirty meters (98 feet) of absolutely smooth rock. No place to stand. No pitons.

Just a few more meters, I thought. I'll surely find the next place to stand. It was clear that others had roped down here; therefore, I had cause to hope. Thirty-five meters (115 feet). Still nothing. No place to stand. No pitons. I began to feel peculiar. I trembled slightly. Thirty-eight meters (125 feet). A little further down, the two rope ends were knotted together. I couldn't go any further. There was no more rope. And no place to stand.

"Help!" The sound was more staccato, more piercing. Terror gripped me. "Swing, Toni, swing for your life," an inner voice insisted. Perhaps . . .

I swung like a pendulum, feverishly seeking footing in the fog. The swings got stronger; I oscillated ever further left and right. Even through the fog, I could see nothing but smooth rock to the left. It was hopeless. To the right was an edge.

I must have looked quite desperate—like a raving maniac. The edge! I hoped to find a place to stand behind it. "Swing, Toni, swing harder. You must reach that edge." I swung like one possessed—there, the edge! I grabbed for it and held fast. Could it be? Yes . . . there was actually a place to stand and a piton.

The maneuver was a little easier for Poldi. I was able to draw her toward me by the rope ends. But she looked terrible. Her eyes had an expression I will never forget: unreal, alien.

"One more rappel and we'll be down, Poldi." But Poldi did not respond. Nothing more can go wrong, I thought. Somewhere down there in the fog the rope ends have to make contact with the easy spur. Rappel—spasmodic as before—meter by meter. The fog below became grayer and darker. Yes, it was rock: the rock of the wall spur. We were saved. "My God, my God, puh—," I stammered.

"Help! Help! Help!"

Half an hour later I reached the Stripsenjoch house and reported the emergency. Toward midnight, a rescue team arrived from Kufstein. The next day, we were able to save only two of the four climbers from Vienna.

But one of them soon died—right before my eyes, right there at the foot of the wall—of exposure and exhaustion.

For Poldi and me, the Fleischbank southeast wall was a climb without a summit. A few days later we realized how lucky we had been.

Death on the mountain shattered me. I suddenly realized that mountain climbing is the most meaningless activity in the world if one does not survive, if one cannot bring the wonders home and incorporate the experience into one's earthly life.

Today, mountain climbing is much easier. There are fifty climbing schools in the Alps alone, and equipment is available the likes of which one could not have imagined forty years ago. Fabulous, tempting tours are offered to all the mountains of the world.

Young mountain enthusiasts can be envied. However, there is still no substitute for experience. Experience is everything in mountain climbing. Experience and survival.

By the way, my father finally did take me on a real climb—to the Zimba. By then, I was a father myself. My oldest son, eleven-year-old Mathias, came with us. It was another wonderful day in the mountains. ☐

Franz Berghold

Icy Summits beneath an African Sun

Africa—a place of deserts, primal forests, and drought. Africa—a gigantic continent with great rivers, diamonds, and famines, with countless, even thousands of tribes and ferocious wars. Africa—the second largest continent on earth. Africa—a land of high mountains, whose summits are ice-capped and whose sides are covered with glaciers even in the vicinity of the equator.

Africa was also the continent of great adventure at the time of its discovery and exploration. Important information was brought out of the interior of the continent by German and British missionaries such as the evangelical theologians Krapf and Rebmann, both from Swabia, and David Livingstone from England. In 1848, the two daring Swabians penetrated as far as Kilimanjaro, the highest mountain on the continent. They were looking for tribes whose languages they were investigating. Between 1869 and 1871, John Rowlands, who later became Sir Henry Morton Stanley, was sent by the *New York Herald* to find David Livingstone, who had headed north from South Africa. Two years later Stanley found Livingstone. In 1875 Stanley returned to Africa and discovered the Ruwenzori. Livingstone had investigated the Zambesi and discovered its Victoria Falls. He died in the vicinity of Lake Bangweolo, while searching for the sources of the Nile. Count von Götzen reached the Virunga volcano in 1893–94. Hans Meyer climbed the Nirangono in 1911.

Today, the high mountains of Africa that stretch from the bizarrely formed cliffs of the Sahara to the Drakensberg Mountains in southern Africa, whose spires and towers remind one of the Dolomites, have been climbed many times.

No part of the earth has exercised such fascination for the European mind as has Africa. Even today it remains full of enigmas and surprises and thus continues to attract travelers, adventurers, and researchers as it has since human thought began. Rugged mountains, immeasurably large desert areas, luxuriant forests, savannas filled with animals, native straw huts, paradisiacal palm beaches . . . who has not dreamed of these scenes?

Nevertheless, this second largest continent of the earth is filled with contradiction and remains as incomprehensible and mysterious to the European mind as ever. Africa is separated from Europe only by the relatively small Mediterranean Sea and the Straits of Gibraltar. Just the Red Sea and the Suez Canal separate Africa from Asia, the cradle of culture. And, yet, Africa was reconnoitered only very late and only by a slow and gradual process of exploration. The main reason why penetration into the interior was so slow is the Sahara Desert. The Sahara is the largest desert in the world; it is a huge band that stretches like a 5,000-kilometer (3,000-mile) long belt diagonally across Africa from the Atlantic coast to the Red Sea, forming a natural barrier. For thousands of years, it separated the Mediterranean area from the interior, so that Black Africa became ever more mysterious. Only incredible fables and legendary rumors seeped through with the slave trade and isolated caravans of merchants. The ocean coasts of Africa are also dangerous and relatively inaccessible. Moreover, the river currents are very strong, impenetrable jungles reach all the way to the coast, and the climate is murderous for European visitors.

For these reasons, light was thrown relatively late upon the darkness of the Dark Continent. The result of contact with the outside world, however, was tragic and fateful for Africa. From the sixteenth century on, at least ten million Africans were dragged to America as slaves. The New World ultimately owes its rise to the blood and sweat of these people who were unjustly and incorrectly regarded as black wild men—even though they possessed high cultures unparalleled at the time. Soon, explorers and researchers came. They were driven partly by curiosity and the search for scientific knowledge; they were also attracted by the legendary gold of Africa. The ancient reports of Herodotus, Ptolemy, and Sallustus were fantastic and fairy-tale like. The ancients wrote of unbelievable paradises, of fabulous animals, of enigmatic people, and of splendid riches. These writings were the only sources available to daring men, and they were not at all reliable. Thus, it was not unusual for these foreign explorers to suffer disappointment after years of unspeak-

able exertion. The experience of René Caillé and Heinrich Barth were typical. When they reached the legendary golden city of Timbuktu, they found a poor, filthy mud village in a desert scorched by the blistering heat of the sun. Others, however, saw things on their trips that they would not have considered possible and that no one at home would believe.

In 1876, the Africa explorer Henry M. Stanley wandered through the primeval forests between Uganda and the Belgian Congo in search of the sources of the Nile. One day he heard native stories about a cold white mountain. How could there be glacial mountains in Africa, which, after all, every European knew was a hot place? That had to be a fantasy. On May 24, 1888, Stanley learned the truth: from the shores of Lake Albert, near the equator, he saw the white summits of the Ruwenzori, covered with eternal snow. The spell was broken: in the middle of the Dark Continent there really was a mountain of cliffs, ice, and snow.

The summits of the Ruwenzori massif [(Margherita Peak, 5,119 meters (16,794 feet); Alexandra Peak, 5,098 meters (16,725 feet); Savoy Peak, 5,005 meters (16,420 feet)] were climbed not long after their discovery by an expedition led by the courageous Duke of Abruzzi. But they are not the highest mountains of Africa, as soon became apparent. The Kibo [5,895 meters (19,340 feet)] summit of the Kilimanjaro—the White Mountain—towers above all the other mountains on the African continent. Its brother Mawenzi [5,353 meters (17,562 feet)], which lies only about 10 kilometers away, is by contrast only a dark lump of rock that juts out of the earth's rubble. After an unusually dramatic first climb, during which the English missionary and scientist Charles New was murdered by natives, Hans Meyer and Ludwig Purtscheller finally stood on the summit of the highest peak in Africa. The date was October 6, 1889.

Today, only nine decades later, there hardly exists an enterprising tourist in Africa who does not by hook or crook want to stand on the crater edge of the Kibo. The route to the top presents no technical difficulties; by jet from Europe the climb is almost a weekend tour. The dangers of the 6,000-meter (19,685-foot) mountain lie elsewhere: its great height has already proved fatal to many who were not sufficiently acclimatized.

No less attractive and quite different in character is Mount Kenya [5,199 meters (17,056 feet)], lying about 300 kilometers (186 miles) to the north of Kilimanjaro. It is the goal of particularly demanding climbers, for its double summit can only be reached by rock-climbing techniques.

The summit of Batian [highest point 5,199 meters (17,056 feet)] was climbed in 1899, but it was not until 1929 that Eric Shipton climbed its twin peak, the 5,188-meter (17,020-foot) high Nelion. A year later, Shipton made the first traverse from one peak to the other. By now there are an impressive number of routes of varying degrees of difficulty in the area of Mount Kenya. Even the most difficult grades are represented. The history of first climbs is still not closed, even if routes of the Sixth Degree of difficulty have already been opened up.

Kilimanjaro and Mount Kenya, the most famous mountains of Africa, have still not lost their charm and magic. One need not slavishly follow a group or join one of the many organized 21-day, $2,000 tours. A tourist with initiative can chart his own route, using existing maps and descriptions as a basis, and can thus provide himself with one of the stimulating adventures an Africa trip can offer.

Nairobi—somewhere in the glittering capital city of Kenya, one can round up a rental that will take one through the magical Massai National Park to the borders of Tanzania. Beyond the border, the road continues past Arusha, the former capital of German East Africa, and Moshi, to the Safari Hotel in Marangu. This trip through the brush will already have provided one with impressions for a lifetime: the 5,100-meter (16,732-foot) high Kilimanjaro towers above the savannas that surround it. Little clouds play around its glittering, perpetually snow-covered crown—an incomparable volcano.

In the hospitable Marangu, which lies in the middle of the rain forest zone, one must say good-bye to the amenities of a safari. One must now march for five hours through subtropical forests and further up through the monotonous brush to Mandara [Bismarck hut, 2,780 meters (9,120 feet)]. One may not feel the height until the next day. Nevertheless, it is essential to give oneself sufficient time, even though the urge to continue on may be irresistible. Whoever reaches the Peters' hut [Horombo, 3,760 meters (12,335 feet)] and insists on immediately proceeding further in order to achieve the Kibo hut [4,740 meters (15,550 feet)] on the same day should not be surprised when he is attacked the following day by severe mountain sickness and must return to the lowlands to save his life. Even the best-trained climbers occasionally fall victim to their own irrationality and so have had to renounce the culmination of the venture, the unforgettably beautiful view into the 30-meter (98-foot) deep, frozen Kibo crater.

Already at two o'clock in the morning, some people are starting out from the little Kibo hut. The first steps out into the freezing cold night are awkward and difficult. Slowly, extremely slowly, but with even steps, the march ascends over the almost 1,000-meter (3,280-foot) high field of rubble to the edge of the crater. At the Hans Meyer Cave, the first people are already turning back. A little later, the morning light appears. And then, all at once, the sun rises in the east over the broad horizon, flooding the land with its golden morning light. Gilman's Point [5,681 meters (18,638 feet)] is reached. At the crater's edge, a bitter cold, gale-force wind blows, turning the next two hours of climbing into torture. Finally, the Uhuru Peak is reached. We have reached the top. There is no place further to go, however far one may look around in this wonderful world.

Between the blooming jacaranda trees, vast coffee plantations, and waving hemp fields, the bluish volcanic peak of Mount Kenya sometimes emerges in the distance. In the middle of the tropical vegetation and only a few miles south of the equator lies the idyllic town of Naro Moru. A short distance beyond the town, we come upon the camp, which consists of small, wooden bungalows. Everywhere there are fragrant exotic shrubs; in the trees strange birds are circling; and at the other end of the garden murmurs the Naro Moru River. A few hours before, one may have just left a cold and wintry Europe. One doesn't want to leave the Naro Moru lodge so quickly.

The next morning: At a height of about 3,000 meters (ca. 9,800 feet), the red mud road that goes through the tropical bamboo forest of the Mount Kenya National Park comes to an end. From here a slippery footpath leads uphill through a dense rain forest, choking with underbrush. About noon, one reaches the foggy moor where the Teleky Valley actually begins. After about six hours, one arrives at Mackinder's camp, which lies at 4,220 meters (13,845 feet) above sea level.

This tent camp reminds one of the adventurous story of Halford J. Mackinder: with six warriors and one hundred naked Kikuyus, he headed for the summit of Mount Kenya in September 1899. As one sits around the campfire in the company of one's native porters, one attempts to imagine how these men must have felt here in the heart of Africa on the way to a rugged summit that was entirely unknown.

Today everything is different. The path is plotted. Five solid shelters in the immediate vicinity of the defiant icy summit of Mount Kenya are available to the climber. Just 600 meters (1,968 feet) above Mackinder's camp lies the Austrian hut. From here, it is particularly rewarding to climb to Point Thompson [4,955 meters (16,256 feet)] or Point Lenana [4,985 meters (16,354 feet)]. From the Lenana, one has a magnificent view of the 300-meter (984-foot) high south face of the Nélion. This is reason enough to make this climb. The two main summits of Mount Kenya, Nelion [5,188 meters (17,020 feet)] and Batian [5,199 meters (17,056 feet)], lie only 150 meters (492 feet) from each other in a straight line. During the early months of the year, one generally climbs to the Nelion by way of the Mackinder route. This is a climb of the Fourth Degree of difficulty, exacerbated by the rarefied air of 5,000 meters (ca. 16,500 feet). There is one other thing that makes this climb a serious venture. With unvarying regularity, terrible storms occur every day between two and four o'clock. One must be absolutely sure to be off the wall by then. If one prefers to spare oneself such tension, however, one can wander around the summit massif from Mackinder's camp and return the same evening.

With the first light of morning, we crossed the Lewis Glacier to the starting point of the Mackinder route. The granitelike towers of the cliff jut vertically skyward, and, looking at this wild scenery, one cannot help but feel a little anxiety. After a few rope lengths, one reaches the first key position, a difficult chimney that one can circumvent by going to the right. Climbing at this height quickly makes one breathless. But one soon finds one's proper pace, and the next rope lengths proceed without difficulty along the famous route: Mackinder Gendarme; pause for breakfast in front of a little bivouac shelter; then across mostly ice-covered gulleys, and on to the cutoffs, steps, and ledges; next comes the airy south ridge, followed by a rappel into the amphitheater; and, finally, after five hours of climbing, one reaches the much-yearned-for summit.

One will probably have to take the same route back. We observe the gathering thunderclouds and remember the many rope lengths that have to be made! It is unfortunate that time presses one so in this bizarre garden paradise.

Can one really picture a surface of 30 million square kilometers (11,583,000 square miles), an area as large as the U.S.S.R. and China put together? For this is the size of Africa. It is an immeasurable continent with all sorts of mountains. While everyone knows the Ruwenzori, the Kilimanjaro, and Mount Kenya, there are other, less well-known, but equally extraordinary mountains to visit. These landscapes are quite unique in character, as one quickly discovers when one sets off and leaves the well-known tourist paths behind.

Several 4,000-meter (ca. 13,000-foot) volcanic massifs tower up in the barren highlands of Ethiopia. The highest summit in the southeast Goba massif is the Batu [4,307 meters (14,130 feet)]. The Semien Mountains lie in northern Ethiopia. Somewhere among these peaks stands the Ras Dashan [4,550 meters (14,927 feet)], the fourth highest mountain in Africa. This wild, almost inaccessible area was made a national park in 1969. Between boulder-strewn highlands, villages, and fields there soar wild and formidable rock towers. Between them lie steep abysses and deeply eroded gorges and valleys.

An eight-day tour passes through this area to the extravagant Ras Dashan. The point of departure is Debarek, on the road from Gondar to Aksum, situated 2,800 meters (ca. 9,200 feet) above the valley of Takkaze. In this corner of the earth, there is no tourism. For this reason, the people are friendly, cooperative, and, above all, honest. In fact, this is true everywhere in the North African deserts and steppes.

On the three-day march, one encounters ibex and foxes, as well as packs of screeching monkeys. Vultures and eagles often circle in the sky. The vegetation is decidedly high Alpine, that is, very scanty. The plants remind one of the Alps—except that here everything is wilder, more primeval, and more unique. Was it not here that the remains of our oldest human predecessors were found? Three passes with steep ascents and descents have to be crossed before one can break camp in Gäbriko [3,100 meters (10,170 feet)]. From this point, the climb to the summit of Ras Dashan is arduous and long. Worst of all, there is no water to refresh one as one climbs through the burning heat of Africa's merciless sun.

The sun . . . the Sahara! A few thousand years ago, a flourishing savanna and luxuriant forest lands occupied the area that is now covered by the world's largest desert. Today, the black-baked cyclopslike mountain massifs— Hoggar and Tibesti—form the backbone of the North African Sahara, surrounded by broad gravel planes and endless rocky plateaus. Around this almost lifeless stony wasteland lies a multiple ring of gigantic sand dunes, which, although constituting only one-eighth of the 9 million square kilometers (3,475,000 square miles) of the Sahara, have come to symbolize the very essence of a desert. The most uncanny and wildest mountain landscape of the Sahara is the Hoggar. Together with its branches, this mountain chain is almost twice as large as Austria. The mysterious Tuaregs call it "land of fear." From whatever direction one approaches this gigantic mountain, one must cross an area of never-ending rock debris almost entirely devoid of springs and oases.

Then somewhere on the gravelly horizon, scintillating in the heat, appear the first grey-black monoliths—lonely, gloomy, ghostly cliffs that jut up out of the earth and gradually join together to form bizarre massifs. Before one realizes it, one finds oneself in the middle of this gloomy volcanic landscape. One cannot rid oneself of the oppressive feeling that, in primeval times, the roaring, bubbling, churning elements cast up from the earth's interior were here condemned to silence, were suddenly petrified forever. One has the sense that, on a fateful day in primeval history, time itself once came to a halt. A colossal landscape was formed 3,000 meters (ca. 9,800 feet) above the Sahara bed.

The Hoggar massif, like the Tibesti, which lies further to the east between Libya and Chad, is surely one of the most extraordinary mountain landscapes of the earth. More than two million years ago, on the fracture points of tectonic moving masses, fluid material rose from the center of the earth. A volcanic garden arose here, as later in central Africa. Cones of rubble and ashes arose out of the millions of eruptions and endless lava streams that flowed through the prehistoric valleys. When the volcanoes became extinct, the lava in the craters hardened into basalt columns that were given their eventual shape by erosion over the years. Thus, a moonlike landscape arose, which probably nothing and no one can reawaken into life. One can reach the Atakor Mountains in the heart of the Hoggar by way of a hundred-kilometer-long caravan trail leading from the south Algerian oasis of Tamanrasset. The last bit of this stretch, the steep rise to the Assekrem Pass, demands the utmost from one's jeep. Once on the top, we take our rucksacks and send our driver back to Tamanrasset. We can now remain alone up here for a long time, for a very long time.

Tireggunin, Tamahagne, Taheleft, Imoran, Ilaman, Tenzuyeg, Tidjemaine . . . these Tuareg names for the surrounding summits sound like words from a magical language. On the horizon sits Tahat [3,003 meters (9,852 feet)], the highest peak in the Hoggar Mountains. During the colonial period, French and Italian expeditions conquered a number of these peaks and faces. Nevertheless, one will rarely meet another climber in the Hoggar, and often one will discover completely unexplored land.

The south face of the 2,650-meter (8,694-foot) high Sawinan, one among thousands of rock pinnacles, requires Third Degree ability. I finally reached the spur after hours of wandering through boulders and debris. This tower of rock rises vertically out of the rubble like a warning finger. Soon the sun will be standing high in the midday sky; therefore, I must hurry in order to escape the worst of the heat. From a cliff terrace, perpendicular chimneys lead to a small rocky ledge. Exposed traverses take me back into the chimney system: firm, warm basalt. Before long, I am standing on a tiny, dizzying summit platform; I feel absolutely lost among the stony giants of this science fiction world. I recall St. Exupéry and can find no more intense form of experience than these mountains and desert wastelands.

For most people, the Sahara is the archetypal desert; it is the largest and most fascinating desert on earth. Most Europeans picture only endless sand dunes. It is a world of absolute lifelessness, a zone of death that from time immemorial has stretched between Black Africa and the Mediterranean. From time immemorial?

In the 1950s, a sensational story spread round the world: in the inaccessible labyrinthine stone garden of Tassili n'Ajjer—a bizarre mountainous country in the middle of the Sahara between Hoggar and Tibesti—a French archaeologist, Henri Lhote, discovered ten thousand incredible cliff paintings lying barely concealed beneath the countless overhangs of this region. Many of them were more than ten thousand years old. They were of a brilliance and expressive power that left the viewer breathless. Here, in the heart of this merciless desert, giant herds are seen crossing lush landscapes; cattle graze by the hundreds of thousands in luscious grasses; hunters armed with bows and arrows chase antelope herds; warriors fight each other with clubs; hippopotamuses roll in the mud; men in canoes chase crocodiles and hippopotamuses; elephant herds stamp through flourishing savannas; giraffes and ostriches move with elegance across the plains. Here is suddenly revealed the largest, most beautiful, and most impressive museum of prehistoric art; it is evidence from a world that was completely unknown to us. These artistic documents will doubtless give rise to new conclusions regarding the origin of man. They also have much to tell us about the amazing history of the great Sahara Desert.

Ten thousand years ago, the Sahara was a flourishing garden with rivers, lakes, sumptuous vegetation, and dense settlements unlike anywhere else in the world at that time. The early pictures in the rocky niches of the Tassili massif show us negroid hunters. The predominantly magical and religious motives, which are painted on a large scale and are somewhat stiff, served to enhance the magic of the hunt, which is a primal form of many later religions.

(The Swiss scholar Däniken erroneously concluded that the tribesmen were followers of Mars, that is to say, preeminently warriors.) These people possibly came from the area around Lake Chad, which is said to be the Ur-homeland of the Black race. As these round-headed hunters settled the Tassili and created their cultic sites, the last ice age was coming to an end about 10,000 to 6000 B.C.

Around 5000 B.C. immense members of new tribes must have wandered into the Tassili Mountains. Tassili was probably then the turntable or midpoint of the world. The style of the frescoes changed completely. Mediterranean people now begin to appear, and they are no longer solely engaged in hunting. Rather, they are beginning to domesticate animals and keep herds of cattle. Here and there they begin to form permanent settlements. Events of everyday life are depicted with great dynamic and dramatic force. The magical symbolism of early times retreats entirely into the background.

A new and decisive change began to occur about 1200 B.C. During this period, the first signs of the drying up of the Sahara become evident. Pictures of cattle and hunting scenes become ever rarer, and wild animal motifs, which were once so abundant, disappear totally from the pictures; horses and warriors take their place. During the final period, just before the birth of Christ, camels also appear. These, too, must eventually yield to the desert sands. The striking picture book of Tassili n'Ajjer comes to an end and is eventually forgotten.

The long path that mirrors human history and that leads from the prehistoric times of the oldest frescoes in Tassili—the primal language of man on rock—to the written language of the Tuareg nomads, who were the last inhabitants of the Sahara and who eternalized their love poetry and epigrammatic truths on the naked sandstone pillars of their homeland, has now run dry like the desert springs.

Anyone who wants to get to know the mountains of Africa must pass through the deserts of this continent. Knowledge about their past expectedly opens doors to an understanding of Africa's past. The key to this understanding is to be found in the remote interior of the desert, in the enigmatic Tassili n'Ajjer.

Whoever has once succumbed to the magic of the desert will never escape its spell. One can also say the same about mountains. In the deserts, normal dimensions are incredibly distorted. A unique volcano exists in the interior of the Libyan Desert. It is only 538 meters (1,765 feet) high but is nevertheless one of the most extraordinary mountain formations in all of Africa. To get there, one must undertake an adventurous 4,000-kilometer (2,485-mile) journey through the desert to Wau-en-Namus, the "crater of flies." One needs almost three weeks just for the trip through Libya, a country that is twenty-two times larger than Austria. Only then does one reach the oasis Wau-el-Kebir, about 300 kilometers (186 miles) from the Chad border. From here to the volcano there still remains a 116-kilometer (72-mile) cross-country trip over rock debris, sand, and dunes. About 30 kilometers (18 miles) from the crater wall, the sand suddenly becomes pitch-black.

In the middle of this gloomy desert plain sits the crater itself, 12 kilometers (7.5 miles) in diameter; its depths contain the volcanic cone—nothing special in and of itself. But what one sees around the inner cone when one looks down from the outermost edge of the crater takes one's breath away: there sparkle many small lakes in every shade of green and blue, surrounded by tender green reeds and clusters of palm trees. It is so beautiful that one thinks one must be dreaming. And it is all so infinitely peaceful.

In the year 1922, something happened that astonished the world: the 4,060-meter (13,320-foot) high Mongoma Loba ("mountain of the gods"), only 20 kilometers from the coast, came to life again; hissing and roaring, it sent a glowing stream of lava through the rain forests and plantations and into the waters of the Gulf of Guinea.

An attractive volcanic chain runs from this point northward and ends in the 2,600-meter (8,530-foot) high Bambouto massif, which today lies mostly in a national park. This area has hardly been touched by European climbers. Making one's way through the tropical jungles and past rubber and cocoa plantations, one begins to ascend into a savannalike grassland from which arises the Cameroon massif. The snow, which coats the summits like a sprinkling of sugar, is the result of frequent monsoonlike precipitation. One also comes upon much snow in the 4,000-meter (ca. 13,000-foot) peaks of the Atlas Mountains in North Africa. This interconnected chain of folded mountain formations, which stretches over a distance of 700 kilometers (435 miles) is similar in character to the mountains of Europe. And in the valleys of the Atlas Mountains dwell decidedly Mediterranean cultures.

There is so much more that one could say about the various mountains of the African continent. They are extraordinarily interesting, even though most of the summits are not high enough to be capped with snow. There are the high plateaus of South Africa, the mountains of the Cape as well as the Drakesberg massif; there are the sandstone sculptures of the Tassili n'Ajjer, which have been modeled over the millennia by the desert winds; there is the 4,500-meter (14,763-foot) high Virunga volcano, which serves as a watershed between the Nile and the Congo. And these are just a few. This Africa, this yet mysterious and largely unexplored part of the globe, cannot be cataloged. It does not fit into any scheme. In order to and largely unexplored part of the globe, cannot be cataloged. It does not fit into any scheme. In order to experience the magic of the mountain world of Africa, one must go there oneself. One must set out upon one's own quest for the wonderful mountains of the Dark Continent.

□

Herbert Tichy

In his old age, Sven Hedin, the great researcher and explorer, expressed regret that the large white areas on geographical maps had been reduced to tiny dots. From this point of view, it may be regrettable that the highest summits in the Himalayas and Karakorams were all climbed in such quick succession within a single decade. It is perhaps also regrettable that "civilized" people have begun to descend upon the mountains in ever-increasing swarms—to experience them, to gaze in wonder, or, perhaps, to climb a high, distant peak in order to win admiration and honors at home.

As a young student, Herbert Tichy set out on an adventurous motorcycle trip from Vienna to India, where he first saw the Himalayas. Since then he has returned many times. On his countless travels to Alaska, Africa, China, Indonesia, Japan, Tibet, and, of course, Nepal, he has gotten to know many mountains and various landscapes; most important, he has become acquainted with the people who inhabit these regions. He has watched the development of small, so-called "primitive" peoples as they came increasingly into contact with highly touted "civilization." He has observed the progress of their becoming "civilized." He has also taken note of how mountain landscapes have been changed by people. And, as long as man cannot set limits to his own activities, adverse changes are likely to continue.

On the basis of Alpine history, one cannot be too optimistic about possible future developments in mountain climbing and the effect such developments will have on the mountains of the world: the human being tends to modify his environment without pausing to consider that the world he inhabits can only be created once.

There Are Still Thousands of Summits and Ridges To Climb

251

Futurologists predict with astonishing pedantry how life will be in the year 2000 or 2080. The progress of technology will soon make it unnecessary for man to exert himself physically at all. New political systems will create global units that will guarantee prosperity and a more equal redistribution of wealth. Many diseases will disappear; others will arise and become rampant as a result of stress and boredom. Futurologists rely on statistics, on past developments in human history, on modern trends, on new discoveries in physics, biology, and medicine, and, primarily, on optimism. They believe that Homo sapiens will be wise enough to be careful with atomic power.

Any predictions regarding the future of mountain climbing in the next decades, which is one tiny aspect of man's future as a whole, are limited by the number of available peaks. This statement is comforting, however superfluous it may seem. In other spheres of human endeavor, so much can be discovered and constructed that completely new relationships are possible; not so in mountain climbing. We must rest content with the mountains that exist today. We can build roads, trails, cable cars, and even artificial walls for rock climbing. We cannot build new mountains. However, we will continue to have better equipment—better nylon, better radio transmission, and better oxygen systems. We will also be able to set off for the mountains with new feelings and for new reasons.

Francesco Petrarch, the poet laureate of the Middle Ages, is regarded as the first real mountain climber, because he climbed Monte Ventoso (Mont Ventoux) for pure joy. Shepherds had climbed mountains so that their animals could graze; soldiers climbed for strategic military advantage. Petrarch, however, climbed the Windy Mountain "because it was there." This was the classical answer given by George Leigh Mallory when he was asked why he wanted to climb Mount Everest. Petrarch's favorite reading was the confessions of Saint Augustine. He read the following: "Men admire mountaintops . . . and lose themselves in the process."

The old question remains: Why do people climb mountains? There are as many answers as there are different types of people: to enjoy nature, to discover new territory, to find oneself, to confirm oneself, to reach the limits of one's own abilities, to feel the presence of death—these are just some of the reasons. Those who wander from hut to hut will respond differently from climbers who aspire to the Sixth Degree. But both are driven by a single wish: to escape from the treadmill of everyday life.

People in future years will probably seek refuge in the mountains for similar reasons, but they will undoubtedly find different conditions waiting for them. Mass tourism has destroyed the experience of solitude. Even now, one must often stand in line beneath several of the more popular summits if one wants to reach the top. In Europe, all the Alpine problems have been solved and all the stages of historical development have been completed: first ascent, direttissima, traverse, and conquest of the most difficult routes. Every possible winter climb or solo ascent has been done. One can only set records for speed or be the first woman to climb this or that mountain alone. This is mere detail, small facets of eccentric individualism. The great epoch of the exploration of the Alps ended with the first conquests of the 4,000-meter (13,000-foot) peaks. Acrobatic Alpinism (Dyhrenfurth) took its place.

We are at this very turning point in the Himalayas (for simplicity's sake, I will not distinguish here between the Himalayas and the Karakorams). All fourteen of the 8,000-meter (ca. 26,000-foot) peaks have been conquered—many, more than once. Climbers can still select a goal from among four hundred peaks in the 7,000-meter (ca. 23,000-foot) range. Of these, one hundred are giants of more than 7,300 meters (ca. 24,000 feet); three hundred are somewhat smaller. Many of these mountains have been climbed already, but in comparison with the 8,000-meter peaks they have little attraction. One reason for this may be that even modest expeditions to the Himalayas are very expensive. Therefore, in order to finance a trip, its organizer must pick out a famous name. If one measures these mountains in terms of feet rather than meters, the arbitrary and artificial barrier that separates the 7,000 and 8,000-meter peaks disappears. Nevertheless, the fourteen 8,000-meter peaks (even if measured in feet!) have retained their charm. The "Third Pole"—as Marcel Kurz first called Mount Everest, a term that Günter Oskar Dyhrenfurth popularized and that today stands for all of the eight-thousanders—still radiates magic. On these peaks, the history of the Alps is being reenacted: first conquests, walls, edges, direttissimas, traverses, female climbers. This eternal recurrence would be tiresome and boring—if the walls were not so forbidding, if the heights were not, quite literally, so breathtaking, if previous achievements were not so nearly superhuman, and if the number of dead climbers had not reached such tragic proportions.

There are many reasons for the recent explosion of successes: first of all, Nepal reopened its borders and thus made the mighty summits accessible: Alpine equipment

252

96

The snows do not melt even under the equatorial sun: the glaciers, snow fields, and steep rock columns of Mount Kenya [5,199 meters (17,056 feet)] remind one of the Alps. More and more climbers are beginning to visit the high mountains of Africa. Many a difficult, tempting route has been discovered. Hikers are led up in large groups.

97/98
Stretched out like a colossal
prehistoric animal: Africa's
highest mountain,
Kilimanjaro, with its
highest peak, the Kibo
[5,895 meters (19,340 feet)].
The upper reaches of this
extinct volcano are covered
by eternal snows (98)
sculpted by the tropical sun.

98

99
Ceaselessly, the desert
winds whip up the sand,
whirling it, swirling it,
forming dunes and troughs.
The mountains of the Sahara
are also wind formations to
some extent. Hills, towers,
ramparts stand out against
the sky, like remnants of
some ruined castle. Here

and there a few windblown,
lonely, but defiant trees
have taken root.
Somewhere they have
managed to find a little
moisture, a drop of water.
An unreal landscape, full of
mysteries, in the whispering
breeze, in the howling wind.

100

The mountains of Ethiopia: rugged land of the Queen of Sheba, land of the wise Solomon. Steep, barren rock formations, pushed up by subterranean pressures, hurled out from the core of the earth! Impoverished high plateaus cultivated now as in ancient times. Dense forests and narrow gorges—hiding places for those who were persecuted. High up in these mountains may well lie hidden the legendary Valley of Dreams which mountain people have whispered in awed tones since time began. They do not dare to look for it, however, because gods and spirits are said to dwell there. Although these gods rule the mountains, every now and then a man does dare to climb the heights. Gazing into the yearned-for valley he discovers it is none other than his own land from which he had set out. The great King was born on one of these mountains in order to bring salvation to man. The hope that he will descend is born anew each day, just as each morning the sun rises after a cool refreshing night to let a new day dawn. But then the sun sets and night falls once more!

102/103

Black tribes in the south of Africa, such as the Basuto, speak in hushed tones of giant dragons which inhabit the high plateaus and slopes of the Dragon Range. These mountains, over 3,000 meters (9,800 feet) high, are barren. What gnarled underbrush does exist leaves no room for animal life. The people live in round huts, farm as best they can, and breed world-famous Merino sheep. When the clouds release their waters over the Machane Mountains, small rivulets become torrential streams. Although the floods are absorbed within a matter of hours, the moisture nourishes whatever green plant life exists. The water is a blessing from the gods which the dragons had concealed. The two rock needles in the Dragon massif are called Thabana li'Mele (103).

103

104

Golden light from an unknown source streams down upon the bay: in the haze which lies upon the water, crystalline ice fragments glitter. Reeds grow along the banks. Umanak: Greenland. A barren mountain chain rises abruptly from the sea and swings toward the interior of this large island in the North Atlantic. Covered by a thick layer of ice, this world is impenetrable, eternal, mysterious. In ancient times Eskimo hunters paddled through these coastal waters in kayaks, hunting with spears and harpoons. Today noisy motorboats shatter the silence. Steamships enter the bays bringing people from all over the world who have come to see nature's icy wonders. And yet, peaceful, lonely places still exist whose mysteries reveal themselves to those with eyes to see them.

The Antarctic: a land of ice ear the South Pole. A olossal mountain andscape, immeasurable, overed by ice and snow; ough for centuries, found y daring men who suffered nspeakable physical orment to get there. Now nhabited by scientists and partitioned by the great powers of the world, the Antarctic is a land of hope for mankind. It is believed that inexhaustible wealth lies beneath this rock and stone: oil, metal ores, coal. It is hoped, too, that one day icebergs will be dragged from here across the seas to provide water for arid, distant lands. Scientists measure the wind, the cold, the ice. They listen to sounds from the interior of the earth. The mountains are no longer guardians of a new continent. The glaciers are no longer its lifeless, petrified streams.

There are not enough people on earth to ascend every summit, traverse every ridge, climb every face. The expanse, the variety is nfinite. A tiny human being, pausing to rest upon the summit, gazes in amazement at the sight of ever new miracles, wonderful new formations below and beyond. Armchair travelers tell us that the world has grown small, that there are no more uncharted places left on earth. And yet, how countless are the mountain tops, the ridges, the walls. How many climbers will yet be able to toil up new walls, discover new ridges, reach new summits, to gaze from there into the distance, meditatively, in quiet contemplation. To gaze perhaps to dream, of finding yet another summit, of climbing yet another precipitous flank of some unknown, yet untouched mountain. To find a mountain, to taste to the full the experiences it offers: physical effort, heat, cold, anxiety, joy. The great happiness that overwhelms one when one has reached the top.

improved immeasurably, particularly the heavy and unwieldy oxygen tanks; aerial pictures have made it easier to plan routes; radio contact can now warn of the coming monsoons. In addition to these merely factual reasons, I believe there is also a psychological determinant: the conquest of Annapurna destroyed the myth of the unapproachable 8,000-meter peak; a mystical sound barrier was broken. Until this time, many people believed that human beings would never stand upon any of these high summits. The cold alone was fatal, they thought. The notion of a "zone of death" [altitudes above 7,500 meters (24,600 feet)] was imprinted on the general consciousness, and those who first intruded into this borderland returned to earth confused and radiant as if from another realm, a distant world. The zone of death has lost none of its dangers, but many climbers have now experienced it without the aid of supplementary oxygen—not only for hours, but for whole days and nights. During the traverse of Mount Everest (1963, from the west ridge to the south saddle), four Americans bivouacked at 8,530 meters (27,985 feet)—the highest open-air campsite ever. They came down alive, though, admittedly, two suffered from severe frostbite. Nevertheless, the terrors of the zone of death grew less.

A new style of Himalayan climbing was born: Alpine methods were applied to the Himalayas. Reinhold Messner and Peter Habeler climbed the northwest face of Hidden Peak in 1975 in the style of a West Alpine tour. They brought the "new method" to its extreme fulfillment. At the same time, this climb marked the end of the Golden Age. The age of acrobatics is now at hand. Already in 1970, the Japanese climber Yuichiro Miura skied down the south flank of Mount Everest, starting out at a point 7,700 meters (25,262 feet) above sea level. He reached the speed of 150 kilometers per hour (93 miles per hour) and needed parachutes to brake the descent. He survived unharmed,

and Japanese television was greatly pleased with this sensation.

Women have also set out to climb the highest summits. In the premonsoon period of 1975, a Japanese wife and mother, Junko Tabei, was the first woman to stand on the summit of the highest mountain in the world. Eleven days later she was followed by Phanthog, a woman from Tibet, who reached the summit of Everest from the north together with eight other members of a Chinese expedition.

In the postmonsoon weeks of that same year, a British expedition led by Christian Bonington finally conquered the south face of Mount Everest. In the premonsoon period of 1978, new attempts were made to reach the summit without supplementary oxygen.

There is much coming and going in the Himalayas, as well as in the other great mountain chains of the world. Every year, fifty expeditions are busy in the Himalayas alone—not including the many trekkers (high-mountain wanderers), who are supposed to remain below 20,000 feet (ca. 6,100 meters). Today's activities may provide an answer to the future of mountain climbing. In the Himalayas, the Karakorams, and the other Asian chains as well as those of South America and Alaska, there are still many attractive goals—still thousands of summits and ridges to climb. There are enough mountaintops to occupy generations of climbers.

The future of mountains and mountain climbing lies in our own hands. Will mountains become a backdrop for sensations? Will climbing become a mere performance for the mass media? Or—will mountains remain a refuge, a place where we can compensate for the supremacy of technology in our lives? A better quality of life is something we are all increasingly seeking. Mountains can provide this quality, perhaps the highest quality. If we do not ruin them . . . ☐

Editor's Postscript

In his letter from the Diamir Valley, Reinhold Messner wrote that he was eager to know how this book would turn out. Those of us who participated in its making are also eager to know how it will be received.

Mountain, mountains, mountain chains—a largely unresolved phenomenon in the history of the earth as well as in the lives of many men. All attempts to represent mountains, to portray the relationship that exists between mountains and man, to express man's curiosity and his yearning to discover what might lie on a mountaintop, to put into words the ineffable motives that have always driven men to scale the heights—all this can only be part of a whole.

"You climb to the top. As you look around, you breathlessly tell yourself what a terrific fellow you are to have reached such heights, you alone! Then you discover other footprints in the snow. Someone else was here before you!" It was not a climber who wrote these words; it was Kurt Tucholsky. To scale the heights, to climb a mountain, to reach one's goal—fulfillment and disappointment all at once?

Reflecting still upon Tucholsky's words, the editor would like to express his heartfelt thanks to all those who made this book possible: the authors; the climbing personalities; the experts and observers who have written on the manifold phenomena connected with the mountain world; the friends who have shared his experience of the mountains; the photographers, who were always ready to make the greatest efforts to take pictures; the designer Hans Schwarz, who was able to select the most representative examples from the mountain of photographs of mountains; the publisher and its chief nonfiction reader Hans-Helmut Röhring, who, like a rope leader and with the able assistance of Regine Stützner, reduced the mountain of problems and tasks to a small hill. Finally, I would like to express my thanks to Reinhard Gross, who, with great sensitivity, was ultimately responsible for the appearance of this book.

Now that "the strains and stresses of the mountain" are behind us, there are only "the strains and stresses of the flatlands" (Brecht). As to how this book will fare—the answer lies with the readers.

Bruno Moravetz

Appendix

Glossary

Alpine clubs: Associations of mountain climbers; local, regional, national. The oldest Alpine Club was founded in London in 1857. CAF = Club Alpin Français, founded in 1874. CAI = Club Alpino Italiano, founded in 1863. DAV = Deutscher (German) Alpen-Verein, founded in 1869. ÖAV = Öesterreichischer (Austrian) Alpen-Verein, founded in 1862; SAC = Schweizer (Swiss) Alpenclub, founded in 1863. Alpine clubs maintain huts and trails and publish Alpine literature, guidebooks, and maps.

Alpine schools: climbing schools, particularly abundant in Alpine countries. Locally organized; directed by state-licensed mountain guides. Basic courses in rock and ice climbing; week-long tours; special courses for children and senior citizens. Climbing schools are also conducted by Alpine clubs, which offer, among other programs, excursions to distant mountain ranges.

Alpinism: General term for undertakings in the Alps and other high mountains of the world. It covers mountain climbing, scientific research in the mountains, sport climbing, and artistic activities (mountain painting, etc.). Alpinism began with the first ascent of Mont Blanc in 1786. Alpinism in South America is called Andinism.

Artificial climbing: See Pitons.

Ascent: Mountain climbing by way of routes, paths, or trails. Sometimes up walls.

Ascent route: Paths, routes, or trails selected for the climb.

Band: Found on steep cliffs, snow, or ice. Usually a horizontal or slightly inclining ledge or step which provides a landing where one can secure oneself, as well as rest or bivouac.

Bivouac: Sleeping in the open air, usually during more ambitious Alpine enterprises. Also, emergency bivouacs—for example, while ascending big walls. Modern equipment: bivouac sack, sleeping bag, hanging nets with foam rubber mattresses. On many high mountains, such as the Matterhorn, one finds tiny huts for bivouacking. Used on expeditions, bivouac tents are very light and suitable for one or two people.

By fair means: English concept that was circulated by British Alpinists. Now generally covers ethical principles that demand restraint in the use of technical climbing aids that destroy rock. Expanded use of the term encompasses environmental protection in general.

Carabiners: Snap rings of light metal or steel; various shapes. Carabiners connect the climbing rope to the piton and provide a smooth sliding surface for the rope. The rope is threaded through the carabiners, which hang from the eye of the piton.

Chimney: Cleft in the rock, usually wide enough for the climber to make his way up by the technique of stemming.

Cirque glacier: (cwms): A deep rounded hollow at the head or side of a valley.

Clean climbing: English term. Restraint in the use of pitons and technical aids. Free climbing. Securing proceeds with cramp-wedges. No equipment may be left in the rocks along the climbing route.

Climbing (ascent): Ascents over cliffs, ice ridges, faces, pillars; the conquest of rock walls; first climbs, for example, alone, in the winter, or by women.

Climbing (conquest): More specific than ascent or traverse. Means reaching the highest point on a mountain, needle, or rock tower. The successful climb can take place on rock-climbing routes or on so-called normal paths.

Climbing (mountain): All human activities in the mountains; hiking, rock climbing, combination ski and mountain climbing in winter; *see also* Alpinism.

Cornice: Overhanging snow structure formed by the wind and lacking a solid foundation. Usually found on summits and ridges. Very dangerous for climbers because it can easily break off.

Couloir: French term. Steep gully, generally in icy mountain regions.

Crampons: Climbing aid for ice-covered slopes. Usually twelve-tooth irons, which are clamped to the sole of the boot to provide secure footing on firn or ice. Two of the twelve teeth, called frontal prongs, jut out horizontally from the tip of the boot. This helps the climber ascend steep ice with the aid of his ice axe or ice pick. The frontal-prong technique requires great physical strength.

Cramp-wedge: See Pitons.

Cutoff: Groove or notch in the cliffs, where very steep segments of rock faces meet one another.

Dangers in the mountains: All the possible ways of suffering injury in the mountains. Objective dangers are those caused by nature, particularly weather conditions: rapid changes in weather, thunderstorms, fog, rain, avalanches, ice slides, rock slides, landslides. Subjective dangers are those resulting from human error: overestimation of one's abilities, lack of training, exhaustion, freezing, falls, poor equipment, lack of attention to weather conditions.

Descent: Return route. After a rock climb, climbers usually take the normal or easiest route down. Sometimes, they return down rock faces or rope themselves down (rappel).

Direttissima: Line of the falling drop; direct route, usually to the summit. Regarded as the most difficult form of rock and ice climbing.

Double-rope technique: Two ropes or half-ropes used together with pitons on difficult technical routes. Leader has two independent lines of connection to the mountain; protected by one line while transferring to the other. The two-rope maneuver provides additional safety, because the leader can be belayed by two companions (one is also possible). Ropes are usually 40 to 50 meters (130 to 165 feet) long. Bicolored (red and blue).

Dülfer-Sitz: Rappel technique perfected by Hans Dülfer. The double rope is wrapped around the thigh from inside to outside, then draped diagonally across the chest to the opposite shoulder, and held firmly behind the back with one hand. The other hand grasps the rope that hangs down from above. By holding onto the rope in this fashion with the uphill hand, the climber is able to control the speed of his descent. He generally tries to support his body by stemming his feet against the cliff edges.

Equipment: All objects absolutely required for a stay in the mountains, whether for hiking or for advanced climbing: climbing boots, proper clothing, underwear, rucksack, bad-weather clothing, hat, sunglasses, climbing tools such as rope, pitons, and hammer, as well as a helmet to protect the head from falling rock. Equipment should be of good quality and as lightweight as possible. Expert advice in the selection of climbing equipment is desirable. Improper equipment is often the cause of accidents.

Exit: End of a very difficult ascent or part of an ascent (such as a chimney). "Leaving the wall" to reach the summit.

Expansion bolts: See Pitons.

Expedition style: Alpine enterprises in the high mountains, also in the Western Alps. Large outlays in men and material are necessary. Usual procedure is to have several small groups deployed alternatively on the climb, in the camps, or in bivouacs. Sometimes an advance party lays out fixed ropes to secure the team during the ascent and descent.

Extreme climbing: Alpine activities of the highest degrees of difficulty. Now regarded as a sport. Records are sought and training is required. Extreme climbers are called "extremists" or "sestogradists."

First climb: See Climbing (ascent).

Fixed rope: Firmly anchored rope for securing the climbers. Mostly on expeditions to the highest mountains. Necessary for safe ascents and descents between the camps. Used by both Alpinists and porters.

Flank: Steep slopes of rock or ice with grades of up to 45°. Sometimes used as a general term for large areas on the highest mountains, e.g., the south flank of Dhaulagiri.

Free climbing: Method of climbing in which only natural holds and anchor points are used. Developed in the USA. *See* Clean climbing.

Glissading: Fast descent in a standing or sitting position down steep snowfields, névé, or debris.

Grades or degrees of difficulty: Method of evaluating a climb, according to a scale introduced in the 1920s. Subdivided in 1973 into free climbing and artificial climbing (so-called UIAA scale):

I: easy	IV: very difficult
II: moderately difficult	V: particularly difficult
III: difficult	VI: extremely difficult

All grades beginning with III are further subdivided into three grades, e.g., III − equals the lower level of class III difficulty; III equals difficult; III + equals the upper reaches of class III difficulty.

Three grades exist for the evaluation of artificial climbing (A = *artificiel* — French term for *artificial*):

A0 = few pitons used as a foothold or step in relatively unobstructed passages.

A1 = pitons and other aids are relatively easy to use. The passage requires relatively little physical stamina.

A2 and A3 = pitons more difficult to insert; more physical strength is required to surmount the difficulties of the climb. Two ètriers (stirrups) are necessary. The French system substitutes letters for numbers:

F = facile (easy)
PD = peu difficile (not too difficult)
AD = assez difficile (moderately difficult)
D = difficile (difficult)
TD = très difficile (very difficult)
ED = extrèmement difficile (extremely difficult)

In addition to the so-called UIAA scale, which has been expanded to include Grades VII, VIII, and IX (each of which is further subdivided into three classes), there are also special grades for free climbing in the Elbsandstein cliffs (Saxony) and Yosemite (USA). In the Elbsandstein mountains, there are now 12 classes: I through VI and VII a–f.

The Yosemite scale is described in Arabic numbers: 1–4 corresponds to UIAA I–III; 5.1–5.9 corresponds to UIAA IV–VI+ (5.9 = VI+); 5.10, 5.11, and 5.12 are each further subdivided into classes a, b, c, and d. The highest UIAA ranges, VII+ to IX+ as well as the Yosemite 5.12c and 5.12d have not yet been achieved. The introduction of UIAA VII is controversial and has been much discussed.

Gumpe: Bavarian term for small mountain lake or for widened areas of a stream.

Hardware: Equipment for technical climbing; includes all available types of pitons, carabiners, hammers, etc. In a general sense, "hardware" refers to technical piton climbing. It is a method of "drilling oneself up."

Ice slide: Avalanche of ice masses down steep slopes, usually caused by the breaking off of a hanging glacier.

K2: Refers to Mount Ghogori.

Key position: Difficult section of a rock climb; decisive for ultimate success or failure.

Klettergarten: Practice walls for climbers; often located far from mountain landscapes, for example, in the Elbsandstein cliffs of Saxony, the Danube Valley, and the Maas cliffs of Belgium.

Kofel: Bavarian and Tyrolean term for an independent, dome-shaped mountain. In parts of the Tyrol, it is called *Kogel*.

Ledge: Flat place on slopes or walls, often found in horizontal or gently inclined cliffs. Used as a landing or for bivouacs.

Overhang: Rock jutting out above a vertical rock or ice wall.

Pillar: Steep abutment jutting out from a rock wall. Upper end is towerlike in shape. Pillars provide especially difficult routes. Depending on their height and the direction they face, pillars are covered with ice, e.g., the Walker Pillar of the Grandes Jorasses.

Pitons: Climbing aids; usually driven into the fine cracks (hairline cracks) of a rock face. Wide variety of pitons now available for different purposes, depending upon the type of stone to be climbed: hard steel or light metal such as titanium. Bore or screw pitons require advance preparation. Holes must first be made in the rock by means of a compression drill or a boring-chisel. Free climbing eschews the use of pitons. Instead, six-edged or square-shaped conical cramp-wedges made of aluminum are plugged into the cracks. Technical climbing makes use of such objects as clogs, stoppers, bongs, and rurps. The ascent is facilitated by pitons and wedges.

Profile piton: See Pitons.

Ramps: Steep cliff ledges; *see* Band. Usually very difficult rock-climbing passages.

Rappel: Roping-down technique, used on difficult descents; occasionally used as an intermediate maneuver during the ascent.

Ridge: Very narrow mountain crest falling off steeply to both sides. Generally partly covered with snow and ice. Connects summits or provides an ascent route to the summit. Ridges often serve as watersheds. Known as arretes.

Ring piton: See Pitons.

Roping up: Necessary for rock climbing, ice climbing, and glacier tours. Various methods for securing oneself available; chest or seat slings popular.

Route: See Trails, Ascent.

Serac: A pinnacle, sharp ridge, or block of ice among the crevasses of a glacier.

Solo climber, solo climb: Alpine tours without partners. The most famous Alpinists of the past and present generally have engaged in solo climbs.

Starting point: The place where the climb begins. One usually ropes up here. On routes that have not yet been climbed, a successful ascent depends on finding the correct starting point.

Trail: Known paths or routes.

Trekking: Tours, generally in large groups, in non-Alpine regions. Trekking tours are now organized by travel agencies. Ordinarily, hikers live under the most primitive conditions and carry the necessary equipment and provisions themselves in their own rucksacks. Booked agency tours, however, provide guides, porters, cooks, and tents.

UIAA: Union Internationale des Associations d'Alpinisme; international organization of mountain climbing clubs. *See* Grades of difficulty (UIAA scale).

The Highest Mountains of Each Continent

The following list contains the names of the world's highest mountains as well as a selection of other significant mountains on the various continents. It is obviously not complete. Data regarding the heights of these mountains is not uniform. One reason why differing figures appear in atlases and similar publications is that the numbers are not always rounded off when feet are converted into meters. The differences are more striking in the case of non-European mountains. The figures that have been selected for the Himalayan Mountains are based on those of Günter Oskar Dyhrenfurth (*The Third Pole*) and are identical to those published by the Swiss Institute for Alpine Research (*Mountains of the World*). Although new surveys are being made, the results are not yet conclusive. Therefore, new official figures have not yet been published.

Asia

8,848 Mount Everest, Chomo Longma, Sagarmatha; Himalaya, Nepal/Tibet
8,611 K2, Chogori; Karakoram, Pakistan
8,597 Kangchenjunga; Himalaya, Nepal/Sikkim
8,501 Lhotse; Himalaya, Nepal
8,481 Makalu; Himalaya, Nepal/Tibet
8,189 Cho Oyu; Himalaya, Nepal/Tibet
8,167 Dhaulagiri; Himalaya, Nepal
8,156 Manaslu; Himalaya, Nepal
8,125 Nanga Parbat, Diamir; Karakoram, Pakistan
8,078 Annapurna I; Himalaya, Nepal
8,068 Gasherbrum I, Hidden Peak; Karakoram, Pakistan
8,047 Broad Peak; Karakoram, Pakistan
8,035 Gasherbrum II; Karakoram, Pakistan
8,013 Shisha Pangma, Gosainthan; Himalaya, Tibet
7,952 Gasherbrum III; Karakoram, Pakistan
7,937 Annapurna II; Himalaya, Nepal
7,925 Gasherbrum IV; Karakoram, Pakistan
7,922 Gyachung Kang; Himalaya, Nepal/Tibet
7,902 Kangbachen Peak; Himalaya, Sikkim/Nepal
7,893 Himalchuli; Himalaya, Nepal
7,885 Disteghil Sar; Karakoram, Pakistan
7,879 Nuptse; Himalaya, Nepal
7,816 Nanda Devi; Himalaya, Nepal
7,785 Batura Mustagh I; Karakoram, Pakistan
7,756 Kamet; Himalaya, Garwhal
7,755 Namche Barwa; Himalaya, Bhutan/Tibet
7,751 Dhaulagiri II; Himalaya, Nepal
7,710 Jannu; Himalaya, Nepal
7,705 Tirich Mir; Hundu Kush, Afghanistan
7,656 Kangchungtse, Makalu II; Himalaya, Nepal/Tibet
7,654 Chogolisa; Karakoram, Pakistan
7,595 Kungur Tjube Tagh; Pamir, U.S.S.R./China
7,587 Minyag Gangkar; Szechwan, China
7,554 Künla Kari; Himalaya, Tibet/Bhutan
7,546 Mustagh Ata; Pamir, U.S.S.R./China
7,500 Ganker Punzum; Himalaya, Bhutan
7,492 Noshaq; Hindu Kush, Afghanistan
7,482 Pik Kommunismus; Transaltai, U.S.S.R.
7,454 Gangapurna; Himalaya, Nepal
7,439 Pik Pobeda; Tien Shan, U.S.S.R.
7,349 Talung Peak; Himalaya, Sikkim/Nepal
7,134 Pik Lenin; Transaltai, U.S.S.R.
5,654 Demawend; Iran
5,633 Elbrus; Caucasus, U.S.S.R.
5,165 Ararat; Turkey
4,101 Kinabalu; Borneo
3,970 Niitaka Yama; Taiwan
3,805 Gunung Kerentji; Sumatra
3,776 Fujiyama; Japan
2,637 Sinai

Europe

4,807 Mont Blanc; France
4,634 Monte Rosa, Dufour-Spitze; Switzerland
4,477 Matterhorn, Cervin, Cervino; Switzerland/Italy
4,158 Jungfrau; Switzerland
3,902 Ortler; Italy
3,798 Grossglockner; Austria
3,774 Wildspitze; Austria
3,478 Mulhacén; Sierra Nevada, Spain
3,355 Monte Perdido; Pyrenees, Spain
3,344 Marmolada, Punta di Penia; Dolomites, Italy
3,265 Etna; Italy
2,995 Dachstein; Austria
2,963 Zugspitze; Germany
2,925 Rila Dagh, Musala; Balkan, Bulgaria
2,918 Olympus; Greece
2,863 Triglav; Yugoslavia
2,714 Watzmann; Germany
2,663 Gerlsdorfer Spitze; High Tatras, Czechoslovakia
2,543 Moldoveanu; South Carpathians, Rumania
2,469 Galdhöppig; Norway
2,123 Kebnekaise; Sweden

North America

6,193 Mount McKinley; Alaska, USA
6,050 Mount Logan; Alaska/Canada
5,489 Mount Saint Elias; Alaska, USA
4,418 Mount Whitney; Sierra Nevada, USA

Central America

5,700 Pico de Orizaba; Mexico
5,452 Popocatepetl; Mexico

South America

6,959 Aconcagua; Argentina
6,880 Ojos de Salado; Argentina/Chile
6,768 Huascaran; Peru
6,723 Llullaillaco; Chile
6,550 Illampu; Bolivia
6,287 Chimborasso; Ecuador
5,775 Pico Cristobal Colon; Colombia
3,500 Cerro Moreno; Patagonia, Argentina
3,441 Cerro Fitz Roy; Patagonia, Argentina
2,820 Itatiaya; Brazil
2,810 Roraima; Guiana
2,350 Monte Italia; Tierra del Fuego

Africa

5,895 Kibo, Kilimanjaro; Kenya
5,119 Ruwenzori, Margheritaspitze; Central Africa
4,165 Ibel Toubgal; Morocco
3,718 Pico de Tejde; Tenerife
3,660 Cathkin Peak; Drakensberg massif, South Africa
3,003 Tahat; Hoggar/Sahara, Algeria
2,638 Tsiafajavona; Madagascar

Australia/Oceania

5,030 Carstensz; New Guinea
3,764 Mount Cook; New Zealand
2,234 Mount Kosciusko; Australia

Arctic

3,733 Gunnbjorn Fjeld; Greenland
3,383 Mount Forel; Greenland
1,717 Newtontopp; Spitzbergen

Antarctic

5,138 Mount Vinson
4,967 Mount Tyree
3,794 Mount Erebus
2,900 South Pole

Mountain-Climbing Records

based on Dyhrenfurth/Bolinder's *Mountains of the World* (Frankfurt/Vienna/Zurich, 1966/67)

6,723 Llullaillaco/Andes; before 1550, Atacama Indians
6,900 Zogputaran/Kun-Lun; 1865, W. J. Johnson
6,959 Aconcagua/Andes; 1897, M. Zurbriggen
7,120 Trisul/Himalaya; 1907, Longstaff, A. and E. Brocherel, Gurkha Karbir
7,128 Pauhunri/Himalaya; 1911, Kellas, Sherpa Sonam, 1 porter
7,134 Pik Lenin/Pamir; 1928, Schneider, Allwein, Wien
7,473 Jongsang Peak/Himalaya; 1930, Schneider, Hoerlin
7,756 Kamet/Himalaya; 1931, Smythe, Shipton, Holdsworth, Lewa
7,422 Sia Kangri/Karakoram; 1934, Hettie Dyhrenfurth, G. O. Dyhrenfurth, Ertl, Höcht (women's record)
7,816 Nanda Devi/Himalaya; 1936, Tilman, Odell
8,078 Annapurna I/Himalaya; 1950, Herzog, Lachenal
7,600 Cho Oyu/Himalaya (8189); 1954, Claude Kogan, R. Lambert (women's record)
8,848 Mount Everest/Himalaya; 1953, Hillary, Tenzing Norkay
8,156 Manaslu/Himalaya; 1974, Naoko Nagaseko (women's expedition, women's record)
8,848 Mount Everest/Himalaya; 1975, Junko Tabei, Ang Tsering (women's record)

Note: Mountain heights are designated in meters.

Contributors to This Book

Franz Berghold. Doctor of medicine. Born 1948. Head of the Institute for Alpine Medicine in Kaprun. Participated in several expeditions and travels around the world. Active extreme climber. Guide. Author of travel reports, publications on high-altitude medicine.

Heidede Carstensen. Since 1971, London-based free-lance journalist on German subjects. Since 1972, worked with German Language Section BBC-Radio, London. Main subjects since 1975: adventurers, explorers, expedition members.

Hoimar V. Ditfurth. Professor of psychiatry and neurology. Born 1921. Science journalist. Known to television audiences through his programs on natural science ("Cross Section"). Author of several books.

Joachim Hauff. Teacher. Born 1944. Studied biology and chemistry in Frankfurt/Main and Darmstadt. Has made numerous mountain climbs to pursue scientific questions. Has made attempts to clarify and explain problems in natural science to a general public.

Günter Hauser. Mechanical engineer. Born 1928. Royal Nepalese Consul in Bavaria. Participated in numerous large- and small-scale expeditions. Author of several books.

Anderl Heckmair. Guide. Born 1906. Attended College of Landscape Design. Alpine teacher. Active in youth hostel movement. Cofounder of the Association of German Mountain and Ski Guides. Author of several books.

Toni Hiebeler. Born 1930. From 1957 to 1973, editor of mountain and skiing publications. Member of Himalayan expeditions. Author of more than twenty books and picture books; author of the *Lexicon of the Alps.* Film scriptwriter. Popular lecturer.

Reinhart Hoffmeister. Born 1923. Since 1962, has worked in television. From 1969 to 1975, editor in chief of the cultural journal *Aspects.* Now ZDF editor for literature and cultural politics. Author of reportage books; award-winning writer of television scripts.

Martin Hörrmann. Protestant minister. Born 1929. Pastoral duties since 1956. From 1970 to 1975, chaplain to EKD athletes; chaplain at Olympic games in Grenoble, 1968, and Munich, 1972. Author of publications on the ethical problems of sports.

Hermann Huber. Born 1930. Head of Alpine section DAV, Munich. Member of DAV Safety Patrol. Concerned with the development of technical mountain sports equipment on an international level. Author of several books and magazine articles.

Nicolas Jaeger. Doctor of medicine. Born 1946. High mountain guide. Alpine sports specialist, Gold Medal recipient for youth activities and sports. Since the end of the 1960s, numerous extreme tours. Leader, expedition Peru 1977: Central Cordilleras.

Reinhard Karl. Born 1946. Currently student of geography, natural sciences, and chemistry. In 1975, most difficult free climbing, Yosemite Method. In 1977, participated in International Speed-Climbing Competition, U.S.S.R. Made many first Arctic tours.

Elmar Landes. Born 1936. Studied architecture. Builder. Since 1970, head of publications, German Alpine Club. Participated in the 1971 Soviet Speed-Climbing Championship.

Reinhold Messner. Born 1944. Studied at the University of Padua. Surveyor and Architect. First Alpinist to stand on the summits of five 8,000-meter (ca. 26,000 foot) peaks (among others, Nanga Parbat in 1970 and 1978). Author of numerous books.

Fritz Moravec. Professor, engineer. Born 1922. Expedition leader. Head of the Climbing School for Friends of Nature in Kaprun. Film producer. Author of many books. In 1961, received Austrian Prize for Literature for Young People.

Wolfgang Nairz. Glaciologist. Born 1944. Head of the High Alpine Section of the Austrian Alpine Club. Teacher in the Austrian program for mountain guides. Leader of several Himalayan expeditions. Kite flyer.

Hans Reiner. Doctor of philosophy. Born 1919. Studied geography and history. Teacher. Alpine Club: Youth Sections. Taught courses in ski patrolling and mountaineering to sports students at the University of Graz.

Christine Schemmann. Born 1925. From 1947, reporter in the Ruhr Valley. Since 1963, traveled through the Alpine foothills and Mont Blanc with rucksack and camera. Journalist on Alpinism and mountain hiking. Numerous books and magazine articles.

Herbert Tichy. Professor of natural sciences. Born 1912. Traveled to Alaska, China, the Himalayas. First white man to cross West Nepal. Other trips: Kenya, Hindu Kush, India, Taiwan, Indonesia, Borneo, Philippines. Numerous books and prizes.

Guido Tonella. Doctor of political science. Born 1903. Free-lance journalist. Worked for Italian newspapers first, in connection with the League of Nations; currently, United Nations correspondent. Still active participant in ski marathons.

Luis Trenker. Born 1892. Studied architecture in Vienna. Made numerous independent films since 1928. Novelist. Won many prizes at the Venice Film Festival. Gold Medal winner at the Mountain Film Festival of Trient, 1977. 1977, Distinguished Service Medal, State Government of Tyrol.

Helmuth Zebhauser. Doctor of philosophy. Born 1927. Advertising consultant to BDW. Runs own advertising agency in Munich. Teaches at the Academy for Market Research and Advertising in Munich. Author of many books and articles. Collaborator on numerous journals, among others, *Painting in the Mountains.*

Franz Berghold

Heidede Carstensen

Hoimar v. Ditfurth

Joachim Hauff

Günter Hauser

Anderl Heckmair

Toni Hiebeler

Reinhart Hoffmeister

Martin Hörrmann

Hermann Huber

Nicolas Jaeger

Reinhard Karl

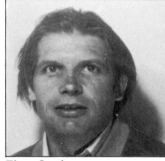

Elmar Landes

Reinhold Messner

Fritz Moravec

Wolfgang Nairz

Hans Reiner

Christine Schemmann

Herbert Tichy

Guido Tonella

Luis Trenker

Helmut Zebhauser

Index

Arabic numerals refer to page numbers in the text. Italic numerals refer to illustration numbers and captions.

Proper Names

Mountains

Credits

Photos

Cover picture:
Yoshikazu Shirakawa

1
Konrad Renzler

2, 17, 21
Klammet and Aberl

3
Emil Schulthess

4, 9, 26, 35, 46, 47, 48, 57, 80, 81, 83, 93, 96, 98
Jürgen Winkler

5, 6, 15, 49, 59, 60, 61, 62, 63, 64, 100, 101, 107
Herbert Karasek

7, 8, 28, 71, 72, 73, 74, 75, 76, 77, 78, 79, 82, 84, 86, 102, 103
Erich Reismüller

10, 16, 97
Paolo Koch

11
Georg Gerster

12, 70
Carlo Mauri

13
Günter Ziesler

14
Roland Michaud (Rapho)

18
Werner H. Müller

19, 22, 24, 25, 27, 31, 32
Toni Hiebeler Archives

20
Süddeutscher Verlag

23
Marka Archives

29
Kurt Diemberger

30
Eugenie Buhl

33
Heinz Lothar Stutte

34
Guido Tonella

36
Franz Berghold

37
Horst Schumann

38, 39, 40, 95
Chris Bonington

41
Albrecht Dürer, *Lament of Christ* (section)
Alte Pinakothek, Munich
Blauel Kunst-Dias

42
Albrecht Altdorfer, *The Battle of Alexander*
Alte Pinakothek, Munich
Blauel Kunst-Dias

43
Caspar David Friedrich, *Riesengebirge Landscape*
Neue Pinakothek, Munich
Blauel Kunst-Dias

44
Ferdinand Hodler, *Lake Geneva Facing the Savoy Alps*
Neue Pinakothek, Munich
Blauel Kunst-Dias

45
Siegfried Gimpel

50, 51, 52, 53, 108
Leo Dickinson

54, 55, 56
Reinhard Karl

58
Helmut Voelk

65
Rudolf Lindner

66
Anna Okopinska

67, 68
Nicholas Jaeger

69
Casimiro Ferrari

85
Josef Probst

87
Luis Trenker

88
Herbert Apelt

89, 90, 91, 92
Gerhard Baur

94
Royal Geographical Society, London

99
Thomas Höpker

104
Franz Herzog

105, 106
Franz Lazi

The cover photo by Yoshikazu Shirakawa served as a model for the suggested inclusions.

Sketches

Sketches were prepared by the Final Art Center, Hamburg, on the basis of Hans-Georg Wunderlich's book *A New Picture of the Earth*, Hamburg 1974 (p. 274 and p. 275, above) as well as of sketches by the author Wolfgang Nairz.

Production

Project leader:
Hans-Helmut Röhring

Text editor:
Bruno Moravetz
Regine Stützner

Picture editor:
Hans Schwarz

Captions:
Bruno Moravetz

Associate editors:
Marita Ellert
Doris Leuthold

Graphic design:
Reinhard Gross
Michael Lenek
Hans Schwarz